—Searching—
For A Heart
OF
Gold

JBI: Jacob Bergen Insight is not a version or translation—just what the original Version (KJV) suggests in a particular passage. Would you please use the author's thoughts only in a paraphrased manner?

JBI will often include the words of the original (KJV). Many thoughts of The Bible I refer to are—

(A Jacob Bergen Insight Version)
—The Powerhouse (JBI)—
—I Have Not Used "The Powerhouse" yet! —

I often use big words, and to some folks, they're not as understandable as the to-the-point words I could use. I don't wish to show off my word skills—only to open doors of encouragement for folks who like the depth of reading to dig a little deeper from where they've been and encourage those who want more of a shallow read; to go deeper as well.

However, I usually try to include a defining word in brackets (or other comments about the big word), so those who like a shallower read are better able to do so without a dictionary and or Thesaurus in hand. Defining terms opens doors to other synonyms that take the thoughts and themes into an even greater understanding of what I mean.

—SEARCHING—

FOR A HEART

OF

GOLD

[NOT A POT OF GOLD]

Jacob Bergen

TTOTH PUBLISHING

TABLE OF CONTENTS

DEDICATION

I Appreciate Life And Its Giver.

"To Him Who can keep us from falling, Be Glory, Honor, and Praise Now and Forever." (Jude 1:24)

DETERMINING TRUTH—is worth committing our time to follow—God's Word, The Bible, and the path suggested therein needs to be our principal aim in life.

My prayer is to write kindly words relevant to readers worldwide. The work that God placed in my heart and the blessed hope in this heart can be a forever thing in the eyes of God.

My wife, Mary Ann, is my soul mate and friend, and she deserves and has my appreciation. She allows me the needed time and space to carry out the necessity to share my heart, whether reading, writing notes, articles, or writing books. (Jacob Bergen)

Four sons, their wives, twenty grandchildren, two great-grandsons, [a great-grandchild on the way], friends, and strangers are all part of the potion (mixture), strengthening my writing niche. The thoughts of our yesterdays that are ready to surface today are taxing. The unseen tomorrows each of us encounter came alive in Everybody: Everybody Is A Somebody and does so in Searching For A Heart of Gold; Not A Pot of Gold. Life is the most significant reason why I write—that's if Jesus is The Headliner!

WRITING—WHAT A JOY!

"A great cloud of witnesses surrounds us, so we need to rid ourselves of the things which get in our way and keep us from following Christ whole-heartedly—the sin we so easily entangle ourselves in needs to go! We need to run (with perseverance) the race marked out for us, fixing our eyes on Jesus, The Pioneer and Perfecter of our Faith. There was the joy set in front of Jesus as He endured the cross, scorned its shame, and sat down at the right hand of the throne of God; 'Think Jesus' when opposed by sinners; don't get weary and lose heart." (Re. Hebrews 12: 1-3; JBI)

STEEPLECHASING

A STEEPLECHASE RACE is a horserace run on a grass track having ditches and fencing of one description or another—and obstacles that horse and rider need to conquer to enable any prospect of a successful run. A Steeplechase Race has a set-in-stone starting line and a finish line—it's a unique race.

In large part, A Steeplechase Race relates to horses; however, it's also associated with being a cross-country people-run foot race, where the runners will jump over ditches and hurdles. In both cases, the layout is similar—ditches and hurdles are part of the package. Though many countries engage in Steeplechase races, it originated in Ireland.

These defining words are much like plain old living—on the drawing board. It seems we cannot manage our way through a day without jumping through a few hoops and over the many obstacles along our way, which attempt to deter us from a smooth run from the time we wake up to when we lay back to sleep after a day of ups and downs—leastwise, so they tell us. Many days are like this; many days are a pure joy from start to finish. Hope is also one of life's attachments.

The Psalms of the Bible guide us with hope's directive—over the hurdles we fail to overcome with our resources. When I am having one of those steeplechase days, when I cannot figure out which way is up, I tend to find my way to one Psalm or the other to stay the course. There will always be days when we don't want to go another mile, not even another step. Quitting the race comes to mind when I have one of these days.

I'm not writing anything new—I only refer to ancient words! As time progressed, those Old Testament Commandments, which we rarely understood but treated as the obscurity of unseen truth, became a lively new entrance of The Everlasting Truth—a powerful beacon of light displaying our path. We became aware of Jesus, The Light of The World. He came to help us see more clearly—the way spread out before us, framing the reality of life.

THE EVERLASTING GOD LEADS MY WAY!

Most people know all about the just of doing life. We all need a nudge towards completing the things we once began with gusto—things we may have let slide from our day-to-day. Here's The Thing; I hope to write to remind us of the promises we made to God and other people; prompting us as we read and or me as I write to remember those things which aren't as fresh as they once were and letting them grow to bear fruit again. Growing produce properly can be a challenge. Growing children will be more challenging yet! Please don't let me deter you from this joy! If we ever needed Joy In The Journey Of Life—We Need It Today [2022].

The Bible is my guideline (plumbline). I wish to demonstrate challenging examples of what life once was in us individually; to see if the past models will allow us a glimpse of how things can grow effectively towards the tomorrow we want to experience someday—To Be With Jesus; To See Him As He Is!

<u>If this is where you are at, would you please read on?</u>

Life itself offers us the theme of being Set In Stone at some intersection along the way. Please look at some Set In Stone definitions: Implacable, inescapable, ruthless, relentless, unrelenting, adamant, adamantine, bound, bound and determined, compulsory, dead set on, dogged, rigid, harsh, hell-bent on, immobile, immovable, ineluctable, inflexible, ironclad, like death and taxes, locked in, meaning business, necessary, no going back, stubborn, obstinate, remorseless, relentless, rigid, severe, single-minded, unappeasable, unbending, uncompromising, unmovable, unyielding.

The journey of life describes My Story; maybe it also displays yours. How does our trip 'fit with the idea' that if we had never faced adversity, we might have done worse than what we did? I recall family blessings I've experienced in the past. Where would I be if I'd not married into the family I did, experienced its hardships, and persevered because of God? I shudder to think where I would have ended up if God had not gotten my attention at precisely the right moment! Proper timing isn't always the easiest thing to facilitate or realize effectively. We are undecided on so many things concerning the decision-making approach in the significant events of our lives—we may miss the excellent timing point on other issues as well.

I'm thinking about some vehicles I've owned and the difficulties of keeping them running at an efficient level long enough so I could continue to make a living to support my family. I most often tried to maintain my vehicles by doing the work myself. No offence to mechanics, but I never quite knew which mechanics or service shops I could trust. We all have horror stories of being taken price-wise and quality of service-wise.

Until we build up a trust level, we will always second guess what to do. Some of us have the skills to do the work—others don't. Either way, we'll need to take a chance ("*Take A Chance On Me*"— ABBA) on someone else to do the work on our vehicles (and our lives); otherwise, we'll never learn to trust anyone.

When it comes to buying and installing new tires and doing the timing on my vehicle, I need assistance. Replacing the motor and or transmission; front-end work, and a host of other things, I need to take a chance on someone other than myself to get my vehicle back on the road—it's tough to say, but— 'no matter what the cost.'

Realization sets in as I think back to Steeplechasing. If we don't check and practice our timing, we will not win many races; we'll mess up our attempt at success. This race is all about obstacles. Steeplechasing is gruelling, as are Iron-Man Triathlons and Olympic Decathlons—. The faint of heart or unprepared should not consider making a name for themselves in these and other sports. I'm not saying we should not attempt great things—we need to Go For The Gold; we need an approach of preparedness for the long haul of the journey that these and other races present. If making a name for ourselves is the bottom-line purpose for enduring something, I wonder if we chose a proper course in life for ourselves!

As I write, it seems like an excess of information and ideas spin around in my head—this requires that I search through many resources on the Information Highway—The Internet. If my ideas were a penny per ten ideas, it would cost me plenty. However, the free resources [which aren't free because we need to pay someone for the services to get us out on the Information Highway] assist us in getting our stuff. In today's world, this includes nearly every communicator. The Ironman Triathlon is one of many mega challenges in long-distance and endurance races—there are many others to examine— (My initial thoughts came from "Wikipedia.")

Most of us could only dream of accomplishing feats of this magnitude, but dreams of this nature come true for some folks. I applaud those who have the tenacity to train and persevere until they accomplish their objective.

The Ironman consists of swimming 2.4 miles, riding a bike for 112 miles, and running The Marathon [26.22 miles]. Ironman's usually time-out at about sixteen to seventeen hours—for being a one-day meet, this is a significant challenge or accomplishment. When we relate this sequentially, it looks like the following—two and a-third hours of swimming, just over eight hours of biking, and about six and a half hours of running. All who finish within these constraints are "Ironman (Iron-People)" members.

Many other races present challenges that require nearly unspeakable resolve—The Race of Life; Reality—is one of the most challenging. The number of issues involved in The Race of Life is almost more than we can manage at times. However, my primary source informs me it's possible—God Is My Main Source!

Why would someone want to challenge the Course Of Life? Well, life is all about priorities and purpose. Each of these and the other sentiments on our list all have a Starting Line from which to begin. It comes down to making sure they pour a good foundation for a builder or a contractor to succeed. A good foundation is paramount; the story of the building process does not begin here. Any building process we intend to present as an entity of grandeur or just as a valuable part of humanity requires an arduous purpose.

God had a building plan before He created anything. He foreknew us, how we would choose, and how we would begin to prepare or not prepare for the road which lay ahead of us after we rejected His plan. I ask you—Did God have a plan or just 'helter-skelter' throw things together?

God's plans for us are not arbitrary (irresponsible)—. His plans are such that He has a Best Before Date in His will for us to experience the best possible entities in the span of our lives—from The Starting Line (Birth)—To The Finish Line (Death). Our existence extends from when God foreknew us before He created anything else—through an eternity beyond the death of the human body. In simple words, We Will Live Forever—in one fashion or another. God doesn't force us to go anywhere—we must choose today—Adam and Eve had to decide to go—with God or Alone!

Although God does not force us to do anything, He does give us many opportunities to respond to His loving invitation to have a personal relationship with Him throughout the earthly portion of our existence. The benefit of this is that we get to spend an unprecedented (unique) time beyond physical death in a relationship we may never fully understand until we get there after death! We require enrollment in a Faith Journey, believe in The LORD Jesus Christ, ask forgiveness for our sin of unbelief; repent or turn away from our sin, and live according to what the Bible gives us as a guideline.

"No Faith—No Pleasing God—." Those who come to God must first believe He exists and that He'll reward people who Search For Him first and foremost! God Is The First and The Last—before anything or anybody—eternal.
(Hebrews 11:6; JBI) KJV)

—[Scriptures In The Front Matter]—
—Hebrew 11:6
—Psalm 139:1-6/ 1-19/ 23-24
—Isaiah 55:11; Psalm 21:10-13; 1 Peter 5:7
—Psalm 139; Philippians 4:6-8; Genesis 1; John 1
—Genesis 1:9-13; Genesis 2:10-12
—Matthew 22:34-40.
—1 John 4:8; Matthew 19:17

THE SEARCH PROCESS

O LORD, YOU'VE SEARCHED ME and known me. You know when I sit down and when I get up. You understand my thoughts from a distance. You cover my path, protect me as I travel, and are familiar with all my ways. There are no words in my tongue, but, lo, O Lord, You know all I want to say. You have (surrounded me with Your love until I understood) my back and clear the way of what lies ahead, and You've laid Your hand upon me. (Psalm 139:1-6; JBI)

Such knowledge is too incredible for me; it's out of my reach on my own. Where can I go from Your Spirit? Where can I run from Your presence? If I ascend into Heaven, You are there. If I make my bed in hell, behold, You are there. If I take the wings of the morning and dwell in the farthest parts of the sea; even there (Faith in Action), You will lead me wherever I go, and Your right hand will keep me from falling.

I'll be wrong if I say I can hide in the dark; even the night will be like the light of day. The darkness doesn't hide me from You. The night shines as the day—the evening and the morning are the same to You. You manage my reins—You have covered me in my mother's womb (Eternal Protection). I will praise You because You fashioned me perfectly, without fear. Your works are marvellous; I recognize these things within the depth of my heart. My substance didn't hide from You at my secretive inception, and You shaped me curiously, somewhere in the depth of the earth.

Your eyes saw my substance when I wasn't yet perfected (Imperfect). In Your book, You recorded my history thoroughly— LORD. You built (predetermined) me when none of my parts were yet available (You spoke them into existence). How precious are Your thoughts of me, O God! How significant is the sum of them! If I count them, they are more in number than the sand—I'm still with You when I awake in the morning. (Psalms 139: 1-19)

Search me, O God, and know my heart—try me and know my thoughts—see if there's an evil way in me and lead me in the way everlasting. (Psalms 139: 23-24; KJV)

IT'S ALL ABOUT GOD!

JUST A MENTION

IT'S A GOOD THING to display self-assurance. The demeanour or pattern of our actions with others outside of ourselves can be such that people may crave to know what 'us' is inside. What keeps 'us' ticking? If our activities display us wrongly, people may want to keep their distance (as we're learning to do the COVID-19 experience). Our daily living needs to be serene (calm). If we manage life this way consistently, our presentation is not superficial. When this is the case, the resulting factor in the people nearest to us and the world beyond our immediate proximity can be a fantastic positive result.

An impervious (unyielding) serenity gives the appearance of being impenetrable. The harshest attack of outside forces cannot destroy this picture of life. This sort of peaceable outward reflection is just the review of a spirit of peace instilled within us when The Peace Giver Himself lives within our being. The examination of aplomb (poise), imperturbable calm assurance, is no such entity we can manufacture. Any attempt at building a demeanour opposite peaceful self-assurance to reflect enough on the outside in the most endearing and enduring manner or fashion—will allow the cracks to form and widen as the storm increases to hurricane proportions. Without an inner peace that doesn't remain unshaken when the storm winds howl—the temptation to manage the issues alone may deter us from the right path.

> "Go away—Go Away from now on from your lack of peace—get rid of things that hinder your progress and walk with God!" (Isaiah 55:11; JBI)
>
> "Those who get in your way to seek after God will be ineffective because they fight against Him with evil intentions—you will send them from your sight. You will sing the praises of God and acknowledge that God is enough for every situation you face!" (Psalm 21:10-13; JBI)

"When we're up against it in life—we're to remember God cares enough to bring us the victory!" (1 Peter 5:7; JBI)

THE INTIMACY OF THE SEARCH
REQUIRES THE SHEPHERD

THE SHEPHERD'S HEART

PSALMS 139 IS A BACKDROP in aiding our understanding of Genesis 1; and John 1;1. The Genesis God and The Gospel Of John God are the same—and are (Father, Son, and Holy Spirit—working as One Unit) essential, explorable passages for us to come to grips with the depth of Psalm 139.

We will be weaving In & Out of Psalm 139 throughout this book. If one set of verses out of all the Scriptures in this book stands out above the rest, it will be Psalm 139; (referred to often!)

Psalm 139 is a setting of sorts for me. Think about a video presentation by astronomers as they present the upper Constellations and other Wonders of The Universe—as opposed to my thoughts of The Lower Presence (not Lesser) as what we understand clearly to be God Within Us In Jesus in this earthly part of our lives.

As the presence of God displays the elements on a clear, otherwise starry night, God becomes especially real to us. When we see this kind of night, we may feel as though we could reach out our arms and grasp all of God from The Big Dipper; with our mini hands—and take a sip from the water of life that only a Perfect Designer could manage for us to even think of accessing.

I've seen many such nights, and they always speak to me of the grandeur of God. *The Indescribable God* by Louie Giglio comes into play for me here. I've watched a video from Mr. Giglio about these indescribable wonders that God put into the Universe for us. I've always been in awe when I take in these presentations.

Anxiety will get you nowhere, don't sweat it—just be thankful for all you have and are in Christ; tell God about the things that bother you. When we do these things, we will have a peace we may not always understand. Our heart [mind] can settle into this position, knowing Jesus is Enough!

Ultimately—think good reflective thoughts of truth, honesty, just ideas, pure thoughts, and think about lovely and well-reported entities. Please look for excellent, Biblical ways of treating God's Word and other people. We can share these easily when we think praiseworthy thoughts without wondering if we said the wrong things." (Philippians 4:6-8; JBI)

TELL ME A STORY

OKAY!

THE LAST GOLD NUGGET!

I NEVER DREAMT about billionaires—The Richest People on The Planet. There are many people we know well because they highlight the news often. Donald Trump had many mentions because he was the President of The USA; we could list many others.

There are mega amounts of people with more wealth than they will ever spend; however, this does not mean they will never lose those resources. Many more people on this planet are not anything close to being wealthy in the dollar figure worth sector. Know this; not only money defines riches (My Book, *Everybody: Everybody Is A Somebody*). If we are on or near the poverty line, we may think it's All About The Money!

'Forbes List People' have more money than many Third World Countries. More millionaires and billionaires are coming on the scene at an accelerating pace. According to Rose Leadem (a freelance writer for "Entrepreneur," March 24, 2017), it's no longer as huge a dream as it once seemed to be—valued in the millions and the billions in personal worth.

I remember when the TV Series *The Millionaire* was a popular Television Show. Each week one rich person gave away a cheque for a million dollars on The Millionaire Show. A million dollars was seemingly out of reach for many folks back in the day.

I've seen Rainbow's End more than once; my physical coffers never grew significantly. The treasures I've gleaned came in a far greater form than finding the hidden gem supposedly hidden there. Rainbows after rain have me thinking of Fulfilled Promises. I think of the loss of lives and futures left unrealized so long ago because of the Flood of Noah's Day (should we question its reason?) This story is more significant than what I could receive today because of any farfetched promise I may have received on Planet Earth—more dominant than any dream I've had about riches gained in this life.

Rainbows are magical—aren't they? The magic usually doesn't appear instantly. Because rainbows don't come often, we imagine many things about them. When we see a rainbow after a good rain, it is somewhat refreshing—I suppose. Even the shower is refreshing because everything seems so fresh and new again. Sometimes we fashion a make-believe story about what may lay in wait for us because some Higher Power picked us over someone else to be a beneficiary of some magnitude because We Saw Where The End of The Rainbow Settled Down.

The myth of the Pot of Gold is just that, a legend that will never die—so it seems. My search tells me this tale began in Ireland long ago—the treasure in the Pot of Gold was guarded by leprechauns—waiting for just the right person to claim the gold. So how many pots of gold have there been throughout the history of this fable? Was it only to be a one-time bounty, or was it to be a continuing stipend. I might say, "Dream On, Little Dreamer, Dream On!"

For a moment or two, three—look at a story I will fashion here before your eyes. As I look out from my patio, I see a Rainbow's End come to rest on My Windowsill (I am not presently seeing this; I'm just surmising this for story's sake). I rush outside and locate my shovel, and I begin to dig. I dig, I dig, and I explored some more until I had almost dug down to China when I heard a clank, clank, bang, chime, sound, or clink as my shovel hits what I reckon as Paydirt. There it is, That Last Gold Nugget. I Am So Excited!

It must be the last one; I worked so hard to find it. I'm so far down in this hole that I have no idea how I will ever get back to where I came from at the top of the hole. Somehow I manage to get back up by using the sidewalls of the hole to edge my way up. YES, I'm excited; you can only imagine how excited I am! Now I need to hurry off to an assayer's outlet to have this gem examined.

Well, I prepare to present my gem from 'my' Pot of Gold—I go to great lengths to tell my story about how I was so blessed to find The Last Gold Nugget. The Assayer listens to me with tremendous interest and says, I Got To See This Nugget. I pull it out of the POT; he sees it and says it's the same as the last person who brought their Last Gold Nugget—Fool's Gold! Expectations—how easily they disappoint us.

How will we best affect other people for the long haul? Will our wealth be the ticket to the BIG SHOW for the rest of the world? Can we best facilitate caring in the many ways open to us by using our hearts to show love, compassion, understanding, resourcefulness, or to take a bit of the load off of the burden other people carry?

We observe life with the eyes of REFLECTIVE FAITH by looking at The Past. We should see how we have rated in the past. Now, we can see if there are changes to be made by us, within us, in our hearts, today—so we'll equip ourselves to help the world around us be all that it can be for living out our unknown tomorrow. Hanging a guilt trip on people never helps much. Allowing someone to see the realities of life and how they affect us adversely is essential.

What will be the Gold Nugget for us when all is said and done in this life? As I look at my day-to-day, the challenge of finding answers looks me in the face, not so much about if I did enough things, but if I put God first in the things I did!

INTRODUCTION

THAR'S GOLD IN THEM THAR HILLS!

D R. MATTHEW FLEMING "M. F." Stephenson (1802–1882) was born in Virginia. He was a Georgian geologist and although there is no record of him receiving any formal education in geology. He collected lazulite, rutile, pyrophyllite, and other minerals.

We have various articles on his observations of minerals and mound excavations in Georgia. In the 1870s, several of his writings came through the Smithsonian Institutions, plus the Account of Ancient Mounds in Georgia and Mounds in Bartow County near Carterville, Georgia. These are some descriptive sites of his work and the artifacts found: such as mica mirrors, copper vessels, and quartz. He also published a significant thesis in 1871 called Geology and Mineralogy of Georgia, for which he is most. Diamonds and Precious Stones was a Georgian printed pamphlet done in 1878 and a historical sketch in 1866—a Lewis Mine Property Report on the White County, Georgia.

Stephenson was an assayer of the Dahlonega Mint in Dahlonega, Georgia, in the 1840s. When the gold rush in Georgia was over—many miners joined in on the gold rush in California. Stephenson proclaimed to over 200 men— "Why go to California? More gold than anyone ever dreamt possible lay in that ridge in Georgia—one could garner millions of dollars here." Mark Twain heard stories from the miners who moved to California from Georgia—Some of the things that might have inspired his character—Mulberry Sellers. Sellers was known for his lines, "There's gold in them thar hills" and "there may be millions of dollars involved there." (https://en.wikipedia.org/wiki/m._f._stephenson)

Amongst the vast array of poets, all of whom have something pertinent to say, I like Robert Service; his verse is some of the best, not to say there isn't a world of good poets. As he travelled about to so many places, he recorded his poetry. Part of The Cremation of Sam McGee fits well here: "Strange things surface under the midnight sun by the men who toil for gold—." (Mallory, Under the Spell of the Yukon, Second Edition).

Some everyday pictures of minerals are salt, Tums, Rolaids, Gaviscon, pencils, and paint products. We use many different minerals for cars, roads, buildings, the fertilizers. We use minerals to make foods and cell phones (one of the most used products of our day)—. Hundreds of thousands of people in the USA alone consume trillions of tons of mineral goods annually, averaging over ten tons of mineral resources per person yearly. No matter the product, someone is always searching for new stuff.

We should explore to understand better what I'm writing about in *Searching For A Heart Of Gold, Not A Pot of Gold*. We should do some prospecting (seeking, panning, mining—) for gold—begin a search process of understanding the value of gold and the value of searching for the gold we may not yet think of as gold—*"Searching For The Heart Of God!"* We search for many things in our lives—often, we don't give God a second thought in the process!

The Mineral Gold (https://www.minerals.net/)

Gold, one of the most popular—well-known minerals, suggests value to us Seekers for its unique properties since the earliest of time. People smelted most natural specimens of gold in earlier times for their production needs. Therefore, we highly regard excellent illustrations—many of these are worth much more than the standard gold value. More representatives are available to collectors—only recently as more miners have saved some of the larger pieces for the collectors' market. (Careful planning is a huge asset when we conceive Searching for Gold!)

In its natural mineral form, silver almost always traces through gold as a lesser by-product—traces of copper and iron also find a haven in gold. A gold nugget is generally 70 to 95 percent gold; silver and the other residents follow different percentages. Pure gold is a bright golden yellow degree of silver content that whitens gold's colour accordingly. Mined gold generally comes from gold ore, not gold specimens—possibly, brown, iron-stained rock or massive white quartz also contains minute traces of gold. We crush the ore to extract the gold, and then the ore is separated by various methods. Every trade or exploration demands hard work!

One form of gold that collectors like is gold nuggets that form when large pieces of gold separate from the mother rock—streams and the like carry the load farther along its course. When the flowing water tumbles, we see a distinct rounded shape in the nuggets' appearance. Eventually, the gold falls to the bottom of the water; due to its heaviness, it remains there. Some nuggets wind up in the same area as placer deposits.

One of the heaviest minerals is Gold. In its purest form, the specific gravity in gold is 19.3. Panned gold sinks to the bottom because of the weight it holds. Weight differences allow for separation from other substances in the process. Gold is also the most flexible and pliable substance known. It flattens to less than .00001 of an inch (less than .000065 cm) and a 1 oz. (28 gram) the mass can stretch to over 50 miles (75 kilometres). One of the most resistant metals is Gold. It won't tarnish, discolour, or crumble, and most solvents won't affect gold. There's a unique added allure to this mineral we call gold. Gold is exceptional.

We often associate gold with Pyrite and other sulphides and sometimes may go unnoticed because of the association with these resembling minerals. In certain localities, minerals that contain these sulphides are heated high enough for the sulphides to melt away, enabling the gold to remain intact on the matrix. Such gold is known as "Roasted Gold." Occasionally, collectors buy this gold. (There's additional information at Minerals.net)

Gold—what a perfect gem; even God thought so. Early in The Bible, in Genesis 2:10 & 12, we have the first mention of gold.

"The Garden of Eden included a river branching into four heads. The first name is Pison—it covers the whole land of Havilah, where there is gold, and the gold of that land is good—it also has the bdellium and onyx stones."

The first mineral God made was dirt. Dirt is a lesser item, as we think of it, compared to gold. We ought to consider that farmers place a considerable value on dirt. If the dirt on their farmland is full of weeds and otherwise useless, we should do what we can to restore the land to a useable condition.

The words God spoke here are, "Let the waters under the heaven be gathered together unto one place, and let the dry land appear—and that's what happened."

The gathering of the waters God called Seas—and He called the dry land Earth—God said—It's All Good!

God also said—Let the earth bring forth grass, the herb yielding seed, and the fruit tree yielding fruit after his kind, whose source is in itself, in the ground—and it did as God commanded.

The earth grew grass, the herb yielding seed after its kind, and the tree yielding fruit, whose source existed in itself, after its kind—and God saw it was good.

The third day housed evening and morning as one capsule of time. (Genesis 1: 9-13; KJV - JBI)

We often think that when God made dirt, He must have been unaware that we would disobey Him in the Garden of Eden. This thought is often confusing to us because we think, 'if God was aware of this, why did He even give us the concept of choice and put us in this vulnerable state of fleshly humanity—where we are prone to make mistakes over, and over, and over again!'

God's overall purpose is for things to grow—including us. The issue of soil is essential to God. God made minerals in the ground. He made gold important in the scheme of His plan in creation. God did not only want us to get excited about the beauty and glitter of gold. By looking down the line of the existence of people, He knew we would have dependencies. One of those dependencies is money. Bartering was one of the means of handling financial matters and the survival aspect of living. But, moving along, people wanted to get wealth—personal worth beyond just the soil beneath their feet.

From The Beginning, God had a plan for and around the mineral we call gold. The value of gold in this world has always been immense. Oil is almost the lifeblood of our planet; it's almost as if it's in our veins instead of the blood of life God created within us. What will we ever do when we run out of the oil mineral God also created, and why did He make oil? In The Beginning, every part of God's creation smacks of preparation—before our arrival via the soil—which He created after He thought intently about 'US!'

Blood is more than an element for our physical survival. Regarding The Words of The Bible—"without the shedding of blood" (Hebrews 9:22) Jesus's blood, there isn't a pathway or means for us to get to the eternity we didn't deserve when we rejected God's input into our lives for our benefit, in The Garden of Eden. *Where are the most significant oil reserves in history found? Some folks think it's in Iraq. I don't have sufficient knowledge of this; however, the Middle East is the place we think of like the crux or heart of the area we depend upon for this mineral—Black Gold!*

So, in our search for gold, do we remember God made us from the dirt to become more than just soil, for His purpose on earth to come about. We are the vessels in the Potter's hand, not the Potter; we are the creation, not the Creator; we didn't initiate life; God did! As we think of the commodity we call gold, we ought to consider it more than a physical reality. Pure gold comes from the fire of purification!

We've become accustomed to physical reality so much so that we often forget God throughout our lives. We've grown accustomed to living as though it's 'All About Us!' Before the underpinnings of the world, God had us in mind. Everything He created apart from us was because of us and for us. However, before we get too proud, let's remember it was not for us individually as much as it was for us corporately; yes, it was for us to be something for someone else. Wow! If this doesn't take the lead (the mineral) out of our pencil—What can I say!

The English language can be complicated. We can misinterpret communications if we don't consider the context when using certain words. In my opinion, LEAD (the mineral) should spell out as LED. But, used in its other form, L E A D, to LEAD someone down the Garden Path, is another context entirely.

Mathew 22:34-40 puts much of the 'us' thing into perspective—the proper context. If we want life to be all it can be, God says we need to put Him first in everything we do. We need to put all our strength, energy, and other resources into loving Him first. In one respect, this is a tall order because we cannot see God physically. People say we must believe in Him, do what He has scoped out as the best-case scenario—then life will be all it can be! A pure search 'predicated' (built) within our Hearts will accomplish wonders beyond our imagination!

Second to this, much the same in context, God says we need to love our neighbour in the same way. So what remains as the 'subject' matter of the context? —GOD IS! The 'complement' is that God is enough to get through life in the most desirable way. Please look at the kicker!

"If we don't love—we don't know God—because God is love!" (1 John 4:8; JBI)

Do we have time? Every one of us is so busy! Can we afford to waste our time? I don't think so. Hendrik Willem van Loon's theory about our journey "From Here To Eternity" is 'near-endless.' In God's Eyes, Eternity is Endless!

"In the High North in Svithjod, there's a mountain. It's a hundred miles long and a hundred miles high. Once every thousand years, a tiny bird comes to this mountain to hone its bill. Only one day of eternity passes before this mountain wears away—not much hope here of ridding ourselves of this Albatross." (Re. Thoughts on, The History of Mankind, published 1922)

God also gave us the promise of a Street of Gold—for the time down the pike! The Promise of a Street of Gold provides us with some hope of getting over our flaws and becoming more than we are today. By staying the course while searching to understand God's Promise of a Street of Gold, we'll be on the right track to some degree in our *Search For This Heart Of Gold*.

God is The Right Overall Perspective. We need this to be our proper perspective and keep it front and center; then, we and our wishes will fall into the appropriate context, and we'll be able to say, It's All Good Because God Is Good!

People asked Jesus, "What is Good?" "Why do you question Me about what is good? Don't you yet know there's no Good in humankind unless The Goodness of God leads us into Goodness? Only One is Good (God)—but if you want to enter into life effectively—Keep My Commandments." (Mathew 19:17; JBI)

◊◊◊

Part One
The Shepherd's Landing

THE FIELDS ARE DENSE WITH HAND CLAPPING TREES— "You shall be led joyfully—over the mountains of difficulty, with peace—the mountains and the hills sing as you go—all the trees in the fields will clap their hands to cheer you as you go!" (Isaiah 55:12; JBI)

Nehemiah told the people, go, don't be fearful, feast on the good things God has already provided. Share your surplus with less fortunate people—Today is a Holy Day Prepared for your God—don't be downhearted; because the Joy Of The LORD will continue to strengthen you! (Nehemiah 8:10; JBI)

Scriptures In Part One Opener
The Shepherd's Landing
Isaiah 55:12; Nehemiah 8:10
Galatians 5:22; Matthew 22:34-40
John 4:35
Heart Sense

◊ THE VISTA VIEW—THE OASIS ◊

◊

I take collective steps to be inclusive here, including *Bridging The Gap*. There, I used the words *Looking Over The Horizon* at the onset of each Chapter—I closed each Chapter with *A Quick Peek In Retrospect*. I always like to set a 'Pace' at the beginning of each Chapter—the ending of each Chapter has the potential (if presented rightly) to wrap itself around the Chapter in Context (Perspective), carefully summarizing the Chapter— throwing out a Lifeline to the Next Chapter.

In 'Book Number Six,' *Searching For A Heart of Gold*, I will Begin each Chapter with HEART SENSE and wrap up the Chapter with THE VISTA VIEW—THE OASIS. Please observe and use the tools to grasp a better understanding of what may often appear as being otherworldly—

Eternity—seems nonexistent at the moment;
It's A Reality—Whether We Understand It Or Not;
But Worth The Wait!

Think—Buck-Up Pilgrim!

◊

What's a pilgrim? A Pilgrim is simply a Traveller—Someone on the Journey of Life!

Life is a picture of Grand Design. We each receive the Gift Of Life through the birth process, allowing us to use those capabilities to form positive strategies or approaches toward life. Not everybody has usage skills equal to another person, although, with proper training and or preparation, many can learn to do almost anything. Even when we think we can't postulate or suggest the value of what we possess as things and ideas that come into our formative mental arena, we are as important as the next person!

Some folks cannot grasp this concept. Simplicity is their forte, gift, where they are at—what they become are variables, fluid, or uncertain qualities they were born with; these may outline or framework their position. Their inherent value does not determine them to be losers. Limitations—we all have some, but these are not other people's business for determining our value—The Equality of Birth Equates Value.

As we read through Searching For A Heart of Gold, it's imperative (exceptionally important) to remember everyone has inherent worth, a natural inbred value credited to the fact of their birth. What we become in the process of time as Pilgrims on Planet Earth is within our grasp because of our choices.

Because some folks are born with health issues, upbringing, and other reasons—life may be more challenging to manage within these seasons. I am not making excuses for why some individuals don't live their God decreed pattern of life.

God's allowances to circumvent or grade on the curve are within my observations, but judging or criticizing isn't mine to dish out. It's incumbent on us to continually point to what God said in The Bible (The Bible is The Bottom Line—as a go-to resource). I don't have all the answers to the apparent assertions in Galatians 5: 22-26; Matthew 22: 35-40; however, we need to love one another as we want to be loved—The answers are available in the Bible!

Past The Edge of The Field

PREPARE FOR THE ADVENTURE

Don't you say, 'The harvest isn't in the picture yet—there's still four months till that time—I don't need to panic.' I [Jesus] tell you, wake up early, listen up; look out into the fields—they are bursting in a readiness to be harvested! (John 4:35; JBI)

"The earth, sky, woods, fields, lakes, rivers, mountains, and the seas can teach us much—many of us will glean more from these than books can teach us." (Thoughts I read in John Lubbock's writings—these cheered me on).

"If you're joyful because of the blue skies, does a blade of grass springing up in the fields empower you to action? If nature sends a clear direction and encouragement to you; celebrate; you're still alive. Life offers more than you are absorbing to fill your bucket." (Thoughts Gleaned from Eleonora Duse's Writings)

Life is a hassle for some people—for some folks, life is a dream; whichever category fits best? Does life show on our shirt sleeves? How about this—we get to choose how we'll live the challenge of what lives in our hearts and the reality people see when they see us. Life regularly bargains or engages with us about how we deal with each Field Of Dreams or the lack of success we think is our lot in life.

As part of the human race, we each prepare for tomorrow differently. Some of us study our path to determine what steps we will follow while trying to force life to track a direct route to the best life can be according to our own rules—we embark on *The Pursuit Of Happiness*! Some of us think life will surreptitiously, secretly, or mysteriously look after the details; all we have to do is watch and wait and Que sera, sera (whatever will be, will be). Some of us think we don't need to prepare for the journey (pack any bags); we will pick up what we need along the way, and our life will be the best it can be for us!

HEART SENSE

Lord; Hear My Prayer

————————————◊————————————

CHANGE, CREATE, COMPOSE MY HEART and Recharge It; Oh God—so it's more like Yours every day. Help me to see the Miracle of You!

Change the way I look at life to see the permanence of Your love, LORD. LORD, the constancy of Your thoughts towards me from before anything You fashioned— 'this is my desire to know;' I want to know You More.

HERE'S MY HEART, LORD!

The Lay of The Land
[The Preparation]
Scriptures In Chapter One
Isaiah 52
Isaiah 55:11-12; Joshua 24:15
1 Peter 5:7
Psalm 139:1
Ecclesiastes 3:2-8
Exodus 9:16; Romans 9:17; Philippians 2:4-8
Galatians 6:2; Philippians 4:4-8; Psalm 139
Philippians 4:8; Matthew 22:34-40; John 3:3
Isaiah 54:17; Romans 8:1; John 3;
Isaiah 52:7; Psalms 23; Psalm 139
Isaiah 52: 1-15
John 14:26; Isaiah 52; Ecclesiastes 3:2-8; Psalm 23; Psalm 139
The Vista View—The Oasis
Genesis 3:1
Heart Sense
Joshua 18:8-9

Chapter One

The Lay Of The Land

――――――――――――――― ◊ ―――――――――――――――

LORD—IT'S WONDERFUL WHEN PEOPLE SHARE THE GOOD NEWS after *meeting* Y̱ou. They share Your heart—guiding us to *Prepare* with Purpose—for Progress' sake—for our Preservation! "How beautiful are these thoughts of peace—they bring good news to weary pilgrims who are oppressed daily by news broadcasts publishing everything but the saving Grace of God! God Still Rules." (Isaiah 52; JBI). [—The Preparation—]

Fear need not deter us because of like words 'at length' [wordily]—long-windedly. I know sometimes more is overkill. My Hope, My Heart—acknowledges The God Source as the only resource for strength enough to carry out anything of eternal value. My Creator—God The Father, God in The Person of Jesus Christ, and God The Holy Spirit, this is how my strength comes to 'get out of me' what I have inside of me—to share with the world.

Robin Mark sings the song *Be Unto Your Name*; he expresses his heart with words parallel to 'us being a moment;' "God is forever." Robin suggests God is forever in the eternal past; Mr. Mark acknowledges God with 'heart words' expressing themselves as Love—reigning for eternity. Robin declares God to be "Holy, Almighty, and Worthy." These are my sentiments as well!

Robin expresses God, Jesus, to be a freely given payment to allow us a chance at eternal salvation: No cost to us! We are broken containers; God is the Potter who repairs these vessels if we only ask Him to fix our sinful condition. Robin Mark places God on the throne of his heart. God is The Love Song allowing Jesus the position of being The Ultimate, The Potentate, and Worthy of our praise, enabling us to bow before Him willingly—to be with Him forever, on earth, and forever after our defeat in death.

The Lay of The Land stretches uniformly across each sector of life, mingling peoples of different cultures to live with kindness and love, as though being One People—in so far as equality pans out. God tells us we can have it all. It's there for the taking; we need to be thirsty enough to drink from His cup, God's Cup of Salvation. Someone said— "Choose You This Day Whom You Will Serve," this is challenging. Joshua stood before an audience who never knew which side of the fence they wanted. 'Sitting on the fence' always leaves us wondering what to do next!

"The thought of serving, as opposed to receiving, seems complicated as a route to take. We need not choose to serve; it's our choice to make. The folks who served God in Biblical history is one path we might follow—for some people, this is equivalent to choosing evil. If serving God is the way you choose, it will be like the path Joshua took" (as Robert Frost, in a sense, implies in *The Road Not Taken*). (Joshua 24:15; JBI) (Please also check your Bible Version)

Aplomb—Calm Assurance (poise) suggests reliance upon other people. Self-assurance offers a controlling factor we can muster up without the help of a higher authority. When we risk putting our hope in other people's hands, we risk experiencing emotional setbacks.

By placing our trust in an Unfailing Source (God), we have the strength to move on because the Anchor of all life keeps us in place. The grace of this source helps us over the rough spots. Faith in this Source gives us peace and inner strength. There's only One Source of power great enough to accomplish lasting peace for us.

You will be joyful and at peace on your journey—the hills and the mountains will liven up at your arrival—like they are singing vibrantly—even the trees of the field shall clap their hands when you come near: God Said So! (Isaiah 55: 11&12— JBI)

Some folks say, 'A Picture has The Value of A Thousand Words!' I try to imagine the world cheering me on at birth— implying successes with acclaim worthy of a King. Sure, my parents were delighted—I guess. I did not know them yet, but logic sees them filled with joy. Maybe they clapped their hands. I cannot ask them; they are no longer able to hear me in this earthly physicality; I think of my parents as sitting at the feet of Jesus and looking down on me; maybe they are clapping because of a victory I've just won!

Some time ago now, I wrote an article called *The Trees Are Walking*. One day I saw a large tree from the vantage point of my deck; it was waving furiously. The wind was blowing feverously or restlessly as if wanting to rush over and tell me a story. I don't remember if the answer to my problems was blowing in the gusts (Chapter Ten—*The Answer 'Is Blown' In The Wind*, in *Everybody; Everybody Is A Somebody*). I imagined a 'Word From Higher Up' was in the making for me! Although I have never heard an audible from God, He does, in His way, call me to attention at times.

It's not a hard job for God to make me aware of an event or speak to me in a manner possibly strange or openly through an occurrence of nature and or an array of other things. It's often difficult for me to understand—God is trying to 'capture' my attention with His presence for a specific purpose.

While I sat in my living room chair just this morning, I wondered if anything I wrote had any appreciable good attached. I was not down on myself—but I looked around me through the eyes of my memory and mused over these things, thinking I might be better suited to use my resources in another manner, one not costing so much time, energy, and yes, even money.

My wife and I share coffee every morning—it sees us chatting about many things in our Daily Devotional Time. I opened up *Our Daily Bread Devotional* and nearly toppled to the floor as I read the title of Today's Devotional: *The Reason For Writing*!

I told my wife about this, and we wondered together about moments when she also experienced situations like this—about how many people have had moments where God made Himself especially real to them. All we could do was acknowledge God again as the guiding hand of our lives—[*all in reminiscent fashion*]. While in repose (*the stillness of the moment*), we often say, "God Is Good!" The comeback reply is, "All The Time, God Is Good!"

Throughout my day, times are I don't hear so good! Sometimes I don't! When I've listened to Him, I get excited when I realize He is interested in Little Old Me! I know The Forever God of All-Time even cares about me in times like these! Often, He only wants me to give Him my fears (worries). The Scripture says,

> Give all your *stuff* to Him because He cares enough to want you to share everything with Him. (1 Peter 5:7; JBI)

I'm leading up to something—The theme of this book. Psalms 139 has long stood as a favourite of mine. The reasons will be clear as I break them apart throughout the book—God Cares About Us!

> LORD, You searched for me with intent—You know me well. (Ps. 139:1; JBI)

I get shivers when I recognize the intimacy of God. He wants to know about me this intently—not only because of the realization that He cares so deeply, although this is true, but also because He also knows when I'm not behaving so well! These thoughts caution me to watch my step, not to suggest it makes me perfect all the time, but it makes me want to be a better person today than yesterday.

The song *Be Unto Your Name* prompts me to grasp again Who God is! God is so Ultimately Majestic—AWESOME says it better in every context. Nothing draws me nearer to Him than when I hear the mention of His name. If I say God is at my beck and call, it may seem disrespectful to Him, but there is no intent for this to be the case.' However, in an instant, God will hear my call for help; He often makes this as Clear As Day.

Why do I even honour God? Why would I say, *Be Unto Your Name*, as if to say, YOU LORD are enough for all my needs? I knowingly say, LORD, You are more than enough! Without Purpose, I am nothing, nada, zilch—. To fulfill my purpose, I must prepare for many things. Life itself demands preparation. The reality of life requires many things which we ignore as unimportant!

Dallas Lore Sharp wrote *The Lay of The Land*. Not until I chose this Chapter to be *The Lay Of The Land* and ensued (began) writing it that I went exploring and discovered this neat book by Mr. Sharp. Chapter One of Dallas's book is *The Muskrats Are Building*; I'm 'Blown-Away' by the content and how its context agrees with what I set out to say in Chapter One.

In Chapter One of *The Lay Of The Land*, Lore Sharp said: "We've had a run of prolonged, intense rains, and rainwater is standing over the swampy meadow. It's a dreary stretch in the cold twilight, this wet, sedgy land. It's bleaker than any part of the woods or the upland pastures—empty, but the meadow is flat, wet, naked and lonely. A November evening is sinking into darkness." (I've changed some words in this paragraph to suit my thoughts.)

"Darkness is deepening, and a crude wind is emerging. At nine o'clock, the moon shifts around and moves to the crest of the ridge as it flows softly over. I button my heavy coat—go down to the river in my rubber boots, and follow the river out to the central point of the meadow—where it meets the main ditch at the sharp turn toward the swamp. At the bend in the river, I sit quietly, waiting behind a clump of black alders.

I'm not mad nor melancholy; nothing is the matter with me. I've come out to the bend to watch the muskrats building, for that small mound up the ditch isn't an old rounded haystack but a half-finished muskrat house.

The moon climbs higher—the pools in the meadow shimmer in the darkness. The wind cuts through my thick parka and tosses me back, but not until I have seen a few little shapes climb up the sides of the house with lots of mud-and-reed putties. I'm driven back by the chilly wind convincingly—the lonely meadow provides the lodge with a protective barrier against harshest winters. (I've also changed some words in this paragraph to suit my thoughts)

Near the end of November—My wood is in the cellar; I'm about ready to double insulate the windows and storm doors—the muskrats' home is almost finished. Winter's at hand—we're *prepared*, the muskrats also seem ready—maybe better than I am; their house is perfectly planned" [Sharp, Dallas Lore. The Lay of the Land (pp. 1-3). Kindle Edition. (Page 1 or Location 10—some alterations are mine)]

During the summer, the muskrat had no house. These Eager Beavers were busy night and day to fashion what would be their home when the time to occupy was just right. Preparations and Planning were no small matter. The Beaver is much like the ant when building its habitat.

Many are the seasons of life—I usually dig deep, past the Four Seasons of the year. Let's ask King Solomon to account for these many seasons, other than the Four Seasons.

"Everybody has their time of birth—there are no exceptions; each of us is unique in this way. Attached to these thoughts, we have the inevitability of death. Again, there are no acceptions in this matter as well."

"We can liken this process to the one we see in the plant world—if the plant gets planted, it will be plucked up or trimmed down in the fall. In certain seasons we die off, and then comes another season where healing comes instead of death. Life shows us times to weep, laugh, mourn, and dance; times to gather stones from a field and a time to use stones for building."

"Sometimes we embrace, and sometimes we don't. Sometimes we lose, and sometimes we keep. There are times to tear apart and times to sew together. Sometimes we should be silent, and sometimes we should speak. Loving—making war is part of life; in the end, we need peace." (Ecclesiastes 3:2-8; JBI)

I count twenty-eight seasons in this well-known passage of life and how it plays out over and above The Four Seasons of the calendar year. A complete portrait (subject matter) of this setting shows us more of the story than what we find in this passage. When I concoct or create **preparation** scenarios for each of these seasons, it looks like this; 'there's a time to be born;' I have no role in **preparing** for this time. Only God and my parents played a part in this extravaganza (play of life).

Preparation is assured; God had His part prepped and finished. My Parents may have had a plan in place, or they may have come upon this event inadvertently or in a state of **unpreparedness**— Only God knows.

The other twenty-seven parts of these seasons share elements revolving around people's enactment to play their role in the *Play of Life*. These parts are not written in stone by a scriptwriter, as in the Ten Commandments of God. However, God is not ignorant of the showcases we play in life. God may or may not (*I think of this God and Pharaoh picture in the Old Testament*) orchestrate them as purposes He alone will explain or not.

I cannot, nor do I want the responsibility to present the may or may not part I mention. This passage repulses many people who may respond like this: 'If this is God, who needs Him?' These other parts are also important; they are the Complements, the factors that complete the Subjects. Any job having begun must have an end; at this juncture, we often cringe because this tomorrow is forever! It's hard to imagine 'tomorrow being forever!' Many issues of life cause us trepidation—this is one such case!

We talk boldly about how God is there for us when the blessings are like the songwriter says—*There Shall Be Showers of Blessing, Oh That Today They Might Fall*. Is our sentiment the same when *The Lay Of The Land* is not so bright? When the outlook for the day looks to be panning out adversely—'Does Jesus Care Then?' To sort this out, we need to trust that God is always in control— whether we see it physically or not.

Sometimes, God has us set in place to walk through some hard times—maybe, just maybe, we're there to walk alongside someone else as they face the rough road in *The Lay Of The Land* in their lives—alongside them! These seasons can be as hard to maneuver as walking the hard road in our own lives. Please listen to God with me—.

God says, 'I created you to be an example to show the world My Power.' I'm always in the process of showing the world—My name is above any other. (Exodus 9:16; Romans 9:17)

We all prepare differently for the many varied events or seasons of life; the definition of each setup demands different preparation. Many of the results or consequences, pro or con, vary so much so that between the synonym and the antonym version of a scenario, we cannot **prepare** physically for the situations that may arise because the variables are out of our control—Only God knows! When we think of the synonyms and antonyms of Pros and Cons— 'For and Against' play an equal part.

When it comes to weighing out Pros and Cons, I'm sure we all lean towards loading up on THE PROS! Naturally, who in their right mind wouldn't? However, if we search out looking for the will of God in everything in our lives, should we not at least give the nod to the CONS—? Let's peek at what Paul says—

Look not every man on his things, but every man also on the things of others. May the same mind be in you as was in Jesus Christ. Who was in the form of God and didn't think of it as robbery to be equal with God—He didn't seek a mega reputation—but became a servant, showing Himself to have the same flesh as have all other people. Jesus appeared to us as a man; He humbled Himself—and obedience unto death, the end of the cross fulfilled His Mandate. (Philippians 2: 4-8; KJV & JBI).

Share other people's burdens—by so doing, we do as Jesus would do. (Galatians 6: 2; JBI)

Challenges come when we get involved in other people's lives—especially when it involves the distasteful parts of how life often outfits us. These things can be true both for ourselves and maybe even to a greater degree for how we address the issues where we may need to involve ourselves in the lives of other people who are facing adversities [cons]. I don't choose to begin my day in trouble—but you can bet your bottom dollar, it'll come!

Listen to what Paul feels about the issue—[I need to ask him, "Do You Know What You Are Saying—Paul]." His response is—

"Always celebrate in the Lord—I'll repeat it—Delight in The LORD." (Philippians 4:4-8; JBI)

"Let your moderation be 'evident' unto all men. The Lord is at hand. Be careful about nothing, but in everything by prayer and supplication with thanksgiving, let your requests be made known unto God. And the peace of God, which passeth all understanding, shall keep your hearts and minds through Christ Jesus.

Finally, folks, whatever is genuine—honest and just, things that are pure and lovely, reportedly good—if there's any suitable value in them—if they're praiseworthy, these should be your dwelling places." (Philippians 4:4-8)

Sometimes I wonder if Paul The Apostle had it all together? "Celebrate in the Lord—I'll repeat it—Delight in The LORD." Then he says what is equivalent to 'Jesus Is Coming Soon,' "The Lord is at hand." Then he tells us not to worry about anything—even the CONS of life. Paul shares the problem with God—doesn't God know all about all issues. [Psalm 139 says God knows everything.]

We can tell God our problems, be thankful for everything we have, and be grateful even for the part we play in helping someone else through a crisis. If this is the pattern we follow from a sincere heart, everything will work out fine from God's perspective. We'll have the unfathomable peace of God—even when we are in the bottomless part of our understanding. Paul finishes by telling us to keep our minds—truthful, honest, just, pure, lovely, with things of good report—if they're virtuous and praiseworthy, "Think About These Things!" [Careful—I've altered Paul's word to make a point].

"Finally: Think good reflective thoughts—truth, honesty, justice, purity, lovely things, and well-reported entities; if they are virtuous [right-minded, clean, moral, ethical], they fall in line with Biblical thinking. We can share these easily when we think praiseworthy thoughts without wondering if we said the wrong things." (Philippians 4: 8; JBI)

Is Paul A Mensch [person of integrity]—Or What?!

Paul wraps up this section of verses in verse eight [KJV]—when he says, 'Finally!' Now he's nailing the casket shut! Maybe He should've said these verses before the others and saved us a lot of jargon. But think again, though some of his words may be harsh or challenging, they are certainly not just jargon (nonsense). If we have our hearts set right, if we have searched God's own words through Jesus, the story of it all comes out the same, and The Prompter's Box suggests we follow these thoughts through

"The Sadducees (those who didn't believe in the resurrection of the dead, the existence of spirits, or the duty of verbal beliefs) heard that Jesus silenced the group of people who didn't believe in traditions credited to The Bible (Pharisees), they called a conference. One such person, a lawyer, asked Jesus about the Greatest Commandment in the Law. Jesus replied—You're to love God firstly with everything within you—Secondly, you're to love your neighbour as you would love yourself—this is the sum of the answer to your question." (Mathew 22: 34-40; JBI)

Paul and others are often just asking us to Get Our Head On Straight! It means to think clearly and stop making quick dumb decisions; slow down and think about what is going on, and get our priorities straight—all this is for our good, like a mom telling us to eat our peas and carrots; they'll help us see better!

Searching For A Heart of Gold is more than looking for the pleasantries of life. *Searching For A Heart of Gold* is undoubtedly appropriate, but the caveats or cautions for how we get there can be straightforward and or even harsh! As we talk about the *Lay of The Land*, we need to consider many aspects of Christ Followers! The words "Born Again" may confuse us, but they came from Jesus—they're relevant. (John 3: 3)! So, human writers spread the same message— "You must be Born Again to enter Heaven."

Suppose we prepare to live God's way one hundred percent. Can the guarantee of satisfaction be set to the truth mode correctly? We might just as well say, Not In This Life! The plan is in place for Satisfaction Guaranteed. As we are still human, God's grace and mercy are factors that can keep us from killing ourselves over a guilt factor—we beat ourselves up over things out of our control, and we let guilt tear us down—we don't need to.

No weapon formed against you shall prosper—every tongue rising against you in judgment you shall condemn. God's servants' legacy and righteousness are all of what God is—Father, Son and Holy Spirit. (Isaiah 54:17)

In relationship to the previous scripture, we hear Paul The Apostle say—"there's no judgment against those which claim to be Christ Followers if they follow the dictates of Christ. (Romans 8:1)

I look forward to a time we will no longer need to choose to 'keep on keeping on' in the trial and error deportment [department] on earth. Yes, it'll always be like this until Jesus returns to accept us into the Kingdom He's prepared for those who believe in Him while we're still living—thinking He'll do what He said He would do! Doors of understanding need to be unlocked to understand what someone says—this requires that we choose the right path.

Please read carefully, with an attitude of receptivity, trusting God with faith enough to understand He is in charge—even when everything does not seem to line up as we think it should. Firstly, we need to decide if we will believe The Bible is The Word of God! We need to decide if God is Who He says He is. Suppose we realize that God's in charge by faith—we can forge ahead to the next level.

What are we talking about? —The Next Level. When we observe John 3, the thought "Born Again To Get To Heaven" may unsettle us for a moment in what we are doing. Look at Nicodemus and how Jesus dealt with him. See how much God loves us and doesn't want to send anyone to hell. Believe these things, and we can be at peace for the rest of our pilgrimage on earth. Heaven will be our Eternal home—Forever! Every story has a beginning. Every stage has an end; there's stuff in-between these. Every journey I know of has more than getting from 'A—B' and back to 'A' again. In-Between is where the Differing Levels appear.

The Lay Of The Land is the title of Chapter One of My book—I fashioned the title before I heard of Mr. Sharp's book by the same name. Dallas's book is a great read! I can't reproduce it here because it would require me to have copyright permission—this permission is always only to produce portions of an author's work—with proper accreditation. I pray my intent or motive's always right in this sense.

The Heartbeat—The Muskrats Are Building

The main thing I glean from this piece by Dallas Sharp's Chapter One is the tenacity and purpose-driven incentive with which The Muskrat gets ready for winter. The *preparation package* changes as the seasons of their lives and the Four Seasons of the year change. It's not only the Muskrats Dallas mentions; he also includes many other animal life species; however, it's mainly the Muskrat's story. I often sit on our patio and observe many things: Summer to Fall; Fall to Winter—*Vigilance* is hard at work. Every species prepares for the 'Next Level [*Season*].'

> Lord, You searched for me with intent—You know me well. (Psalm 139; JBI)

Searching For A Heart Of Gold enlightens the first steps for our journey—glazing a clear path in the field of life we all amble through. Isaiah 52 sets apart an attractive thought, acknowledging people who give their time to share themselves with other people.

> The mountains share their beauty with folks who share good tidings—by offering peace to them and freely expressing that 'God reigns.' (Isaiah 52:7; JBI)

The First Steps of *Chapter One, The Lay of The Land,* lead us to 'settle in' on what God has in mind. Though I don't begin with Psalms 23, it becomes an essential jumping-off platform for us to see what Isaiah 52:7 points us to—The Ultimate Care God Has For Each Of Us!

> Wake up—strengthen yourselves, O Zion; don your stunning garments, O Jerusalem, the holy city—from now on, those who have no respect for Me (God) will not oppress you anymore. (Isaiah 52:1)

Shake yourself loose from the dust; arise—sit down, O Jerusalem—let loose the heavy burden off your shoulders, O captive daughter of Zion. I Am telling you this. You've sold yourselves for nothing—your deliverance will come to pass without any pressure on you.

Thus saith the Lord God—My people went down into Egypt in the past to dwell there, and the Assyrians oppressed them without cause.

I don't need to hear this cry for help—I've already taken care of the problem. These oppressors cause you grief—says the Lord, these enemies use My Name profanely every day. You, My people, are assured—you who know Me will know [In That Day] Who is on your side—I Am He, Your deliverer—this is My Guarantee— It Is Me, Your God!

The mountains share their beauty with folks who share good tidings—by offering peace to them and freely expressing that 'God reigns.'

Sentries, lift your voices, so we can sing together when The LORD brings release to Zion—and they shall again see eye-to-eye.

Jerusalem, be joyful and sing in unison; your wasted land is now good because the Lord has and is comforting His people. Jerusalem has been redeemed. In His way, The Lord shared Himself with strength in a fashion that everyone would notice. The whole earth shall see the saving grace of God! Never fear; no one can harm you!

Leave—depart from where you are, don't involve yourselves with evil, run from this evil and come and worship The LORD! You aren't alone, so don't fret—God is going before you to prepare a road of safety for you. Israel, I, your God, will always be your reward!

Behold, My servant shall deal prudently, and He shall be exalted and extolled and be very high.

Many astonied people saw Him; His countenance showed massive abuse, more than any person ever suffered; nobody else has ever seen the like of the suffering like unto His. Many will stand in awe of Jesus when they see Him—because He paid such a huge price—they'd be surprised and reconsider. (Isaiah 52: 1-15 KJV)—[Word changes by Jacob Bergen.]

Then, as if Isaiah 52 is not enough, Ecclesiastes 3:2-8 points to the seasons of our lives, which are confusing to us because we try to figure God out rather than just trusting He has our best interest at heart. "There's a Time for Everything and Everything in its Time."

As if these thoughts mentioned above are not enough, Psalm 23 and Psalms 139 assure us God is Complete—we are the subjects of His whole Plan; He is the Complementing factor of and for our existence: God Is The I AM, The Complement. So, Complement expresses itself to us like this,

> "It's a noun; it is someone or something that completes or makes perfect. Many folks like a good wine—for many folks, a good wine complements a good dinner meal. The quantity that completes anything: 'We now have a full complement of packers.' The complement is that either of two parts or things needed to complete the whole, the counterpart, is the finishing touch."

As a preacher, I'd walk us through the scriptures step-by-step—nudging us through The Bible, trying to effect change in the reader's life—. As The Teacher, I'd build thoughts into the passages we read or study—there's a difference between the two. The work of the Holy Spirit is at work in both scenarios.

> The Comforter, The Holy Ghost, it's He that the Father shall send in My name, He'll teach you all everything, and bring everything to your remembrance, everything I told you. (John 14:26; KJV—Jesus Speaking)

The vitality, energy, or joint action (cooperation of The Bible and my thoughts) in Chapter One of *Searching For A Heart of Gold* expresses my reliance or trust in Him, Who matters most. I wish to express wordily any success I may have in committing words to paper. Please don't let fear deter you because of the word wordily—long-windedly. My Hope—My Heart, is to acknowledge The God Source as the only resource for strength enough for carrying out anything of eternal value. My Creator, God The Father; God in The Person of Jesus Christ; through the avenue of The Holy Spirit, is how I look to expedite or further what I have in my heart to share.

Furthermore, the theme of this book, *Searching For A Heart Of Gold*, will become more impactful incrementally—inclusively (in stages in toto—across the board), into the scriptures, which may blow your mind as you gain a greater understanding of the Heart of God! As we progress toward whatever we have set as our Heart's Purpose, we all search for something in life. Is 'home' [as they say], "Where the Heart Is?" We often wander around home restlessly because things around The Old Homeplace are insufficient to carry the day for us.

"Have you ever watched the movie, *Where The Heart Is*? It is a romantic drama—based on a Best Selling Book by the same name. Novalee Nation is a 17-year-old girl in this movie—when her boyfriend abandons her in a Walmart Store in a small town in Oklahoma. She is pregnant and moves into the Walmart Store in secret, and in time she has her baby. Things become a household entity when the media gets hold of the story. Ultimately Novalee begins to build a new life in the small town."

Because "the bubble gum has lost its flavour on the bedpost overnight [*you can laugh here!*]," we are left wanting for *new stuff* all the time. We bankrupt ourselves by charging more than we ought to; we destroy our peace of mind [*our satisfaction level*] because something always seems to be missing from our day-to-day. HMMM! I don't think we are spoiled! —or are we? Have we got some Heart Issues? In the day-to-day—Where Is Our Heart in the big picture when it comes to other people.

When we don't know what to buy anymore to satisfy the missing link to success and pure happiness, we begin to think it is the fault of our mate. Remember Adam? He said his problem was Eve. In the beginning, Adam seemed to think Eve was what he wanted. So, Eve gave Adam some of her ideas for success, and Adam bought the idea. The Column of Desire got a hold of the Heart of Adam and Eve—they wanted more than what they had in what God already provided!

When Calls The Heart is a Canadian TV Series; it ran for eight seasons. Stories such as these—*Where The Heart Is* and *When Calls The Heart*, challenge us to Search Our Hearts!

Sometimes I feel like something is missing for the season before me. When the pleasures of this earth are not yet strangely dim, and I still live with too many worldly desires in my sights, and the Heaven I desire still seems so distant, my frailties often curtail my progress to that perspective which will leave me feeling complete. We all want everything to be Tickety Boo, you know, at least tolerable enough to get through the day and, for that matter, something to carry us through most of life. Yes, there are times for all of us when we don't think we'll get it done right.

If we don't see 'it' [whatever it is], it doesn't exist—I Guess—The next 'Pot of Gold' waiting at the end of the rainbow keeps slipping away from us. We have access to the aplomb, style, balance, and surety we can have—Life Is Good [LG]. The thing is, we'll need to trust in something we do not see! If I have said it once in all my writings, I have said it a thousand times: **Complete Faith in God** is the only satisfying entity to bring us everything we need.

As we travel the Long Road, our eyes get dimmer [we get older]; the time we have left is now the Short Road. We used to think all of life was the Short Road; live for the brevity of Today ['The Now'], tomorrow may never come—but it does. Tomorrow comes in one way or another—In Life or Death. The Long Road does continue—some of it is part of Life and Death.

People search out travel guides with their travelogue [travel program]. We can use these measures for today and the remaining tomorrows we have left to breathe in real life, but we may miss seeing the Travel Guide, which can take us home to where The Heart Wants To Be! I ask myself this question—Is this Where Our Heart Is Now?

The answer does not lie in the "Spirit Guides" presented on Planet Earth [The Temporal]. These guides lead us to another world, one outside of the reality of the Truth of What God says. The only Eternal Spirit of Truth is God's Holy Spirit—if this is where we are at, "*The Lay of The Land*" for each of us is on point. The Guide is The Bible—The Truth that the Bible leaves us with is something to hold onto passionately; it's the road to follow. Adam and Eve had this fact pointed out to them; they refused the offer—Will We?

God, I'm helpless—help me walk the 'Long Road!'

◊ THE VISTA VIEW—THE OASIS ◊

In essence, we are all God's Creation. The core of what makes us people—is Somebody, or for some folks, something unintelligent, which puts us in motion as Human Beings. Did some inanimate Inteligencia (evolution) fashion everything needed for humans, animals, and celestial survival? Did all plant life have an ingrained purpose for coming into existence? Yes, in this world, just as it has always been, Choice is the Culprit causing us the most grief! We have the God Side, and we have The No God Side.

> The clever serpent (devil), who was more brilliant than other animals that God made, spoke questioningly, asking Eve, 'did God say You shouldn't eat of every tree of the garden?' (Genesis 3: 1; JBI)

Why do we plan the holiday trips we take?—so we don't forget anything; then we'll have the time of respite and pleasantry we need to keep a good head on our shoulders. So we map out our roadmap; plan our accommodations—we need to know where we are going. We don't just say we are going on a holiday, get in our vehicle, back out of the driveway, and flip a coin to see which way we would drive—this would be ludicrous!

'This said,' I recall one year when our family went on our yearly vacation, I came home from work entirely worn out, frustrated—told my wife to get packing and get the kids ready—we were going on a month's holidays! We did make some plans, but they were sketchy—the ordeal was nerve-racking for my wife. She will never forget this Holiday Season—I'm Sorry, My Dear!

The quintessential [essential] reason for *The Vista View—The Oasis* is to know where we came from, our present state, and knowing our destination is a huge plus. The ideal or perfect plan for this book and its Chapters would be to triple its size, reflecting on every possible scenario for getting my message out there!

So, "God Created" [this book is my story; I can say this—God Created]. He had a plan—we did not listen; this initiated *consequences*; instead of One Path, life twinned into Two Highways going in opposite directions. In His forethought, before one entity came to be, or anyone built or sodded anything, God knew what *The Lay Of The Land* would be.

HEART SENSE

Lord; Hear My Prayer

———————————◇———————————

CHALLENGE MY HEART, OH GOD, to see the people of this world through Your eyes— knowing that as we commit ourselves to You, LORD, You will defeat the enemy who is bent on causing us to fall on our face. LORD, strengthen us with the courage which only You can instill in us as we prepare for the battles in the Journey 'we must travel.'

As you have explained to us in Your Word, LORD, You always give us certain words to accomplish particular tasks, lead people towards You, and empower us to win the victory over evil.

LORD, we know You use different people in other places, each having certain borders to work within. Some people live in specific quadrants of this world to observe, map out the path for others where they might be suited to work, and become leaders in helping others of Your people enable more people to achieve their best potential—And So On!

And the men (these people) got their plans in order and set out to do what Joshua charged them, which was—walk the breadth of 'the land,' and 'describe' it, and return, and I will begin to divide the land as the Lord has desired, before Him in Shiloh.

So they went and passed through 'the land' and 'described' it by cities into seven parts in a book and returned to Joshua, to the host at Shiloh. (Joshua 18: 8-9; KJV and JBI Additions)

As we the people of your Heart—LORD, Survey The Land You have laid out before each of us individually and corporately, 'I pray that we'll be found Faithful!'

<u>Surveying The Land</u>
[The Purpose]
Scriptures In Chapter Two
Psalm 23
Psalm 103:1-2
Psalm 23
Acts 2:39; Psalm 23
Philippians 2:5-8
Matthew 25:21
2 Timothy 2:15
2 Timothy 2:15
Psalm 23; Psalm 23:5
Psalm 23
The Vista View-The Oasis
Romans 1: 19-21; John 3:16; Psalm 23
Heart Sense
Psalm 73: 1-9; 73: 13-26

Chapter Two

Surveying The Land

———————————◊———————————

THE LORD IS MY SHEPHERD; I shall not want. He clears my way to the green pastures—to lie down and rest. The LORD leads me beside the still waters. He restores my soul: He leads me in the ways of justice for His name's sake. If I walk through the valley of the shadow of death, I fear no evil—You are with me; Your rod and staff comfort me. You prepare a table before me in the presence of my enemies, with a divine purpose in mind, as I seek progress along my path: You anoint my head with oil; my cup runs over. Goodness and mercy shall follow me everywhere I go—LORD, I'll dwell in Your House Forever! (Psalms 23—JBI) [—The Purpose—]

While reflecting on *The Lay Of The Land,* clarity surfaces—The LORD wants His best for us. The Green Pastures of Psalms 23 allow us to grasp a complete sense of God's love. It breaks down into bite-size pieces for us. We all know that our digestive system does not work so well if we gobble our food down.

Chapter Two, *Surveying The Land* is a Purposeful Layout after Chapter One. Chapter Three is *The LORD Is My Shepherd* is a foundation builder—we need to mark out the boundary lines and elevations to get to the next step in the building process—.

We need to find the best place to pour the Foundation and find The Source of supply for furthering the project. The Foundation we have before us in this book—Is God. Beforehand we had to observe the whole project to decide whether it was worth the effort and if it would be a value-added subject to pursue. When life throws us a *curve*, and we miss hitting the ball too many times, we need help to learn how to *slam* a Curveball! God is the One Who will support us. All of life is about learning to manage issues confronting us—the best way for this to happen is to look to God for help!

This Chapter begins with Psalm 23—setting out the portrait of a place. David found a resource for living that sustained him in the past. I sense he invites us to engage in his story—he makes the story personal by saying, "My Shepherd!" I anticipate David is looking forward; I surmise he observed *The Lay of The Land*—The Prep-Time [Chapter One]. We can see this while looking speculatively [on paper] or in principle for a Special place which we can also experience— "Surely Goodness and Mercy shall follow me all the days of my life." As we examine these thoughts, it seems to be a 'given' to expect God to show up for us in the personal sense— if our relationship with Him is unbroken. God loves everybody— however, we must all choose to accept His Love—or not.

The Psalmist David is relating his personal experience. After calculating the benefits he found within this context of sustainability for authentic living, he begins describing the source of all his help— 'The Subject' of what lay ahead—"The LORD—My SHEPHERD!"

"Hey you, [I'm talking to myself]—Honour God first with every part of your being—understand He is Holy. Don't forget that God only has your best interest at heart!" (Psalm 103:1&2; JBI)

Now we can define the 'Subject' of Psalm 23—I pray it causes us to look at *The Lay of The Land* of our own lives. Yes, the Subject is "The Lord—Shepherd" [actually established within the 'Subject Phrase "The LORD is my Shepherd"]. Briefly—we do the math (the proper etiquette for preaching—finding the Subject). The 'Subject' can be a 'Subject Question'—. Sorting out subject and complement items is not only about the 'who' issue. It will always be about an entity such as—who, what, when, where, why and how. We can look at the Subject as The Subject Matter.

Let's now look at the next step—understanding the 'Complement' [the answer to the 'Question' of the 'Subject'], which is the 'next step' in laying the groundwork for an effective sermon outline. What is the complement of Psalms 23? Please consider looking at the link to the subject in Psalms 23—suggesting the 'Compliment' directionally. Suppose we look at the 'complement' of Psalms 23 as a balancing act—for that matter, and we can look at the rest of the Bible this way—our understanding of portions of The Bible always builds better by looking for the perspective (context).

For the moment, let's consider the majority of the words of Psalms Twenty-Three. By doing so, it seems like every word broadcasts loudly, as if over a mega speaker system. I ask you to input thoughts to yourself here—think it through for a moment.

Do words such as 'I shall not want' suggest anything? What about, "He leads me beside still waters; He prepares (Chapter One prepares us) a place of protection for me when my enemies are coming down on me; my cup is running over (blessed down to my toenails—God blesses my socks off);" do these suggest 'anything at all?' Might I recommend—Provision—the subject matter of Psalm Twenty-three. (Note some of my own JBI input.)

The 'Initiator (God)' of my overall provisions affords me huge benefits—which I may not deserve when I consider the scenario of other folks against what I see I am. We often take too dim a view of the value each of us holds—thinking of ourselves as Poor Little Old Me! Who am I compared to the people we see on the World News Scene? It's like they live in our home!

My appetite to take blessings too casually is only a heartbeat away—much like my 'Appetite' for eating often. Do I need a wake-up call or not, rather than the grace and mercy I want? Yes, but if we look for the source of the 'proviso' laid out before us when we break it down to the lowest possible denominator in Psalms 23, we need only look at the first five words to find the complement [supplement].

"The LORD Is My Shepherd!" Though it's the 'Subject,' it's a Subject like none other I've ever known! We could separate the subject phrase, "The LORD is my Shepherd," to isolate 'The LORD' to be the 'Subject,' and the "is my Shepherd" to be the 'Compliment;' but God is so complete, He's everything, He's Enough for everyone and every situation! The LORD, The SHEPHERD, is the ultimate reliance factor.

If we're talking about earthly things (entities) and the characteristics 'earthly shepherds sheep have,' no matter where they may be, this shepherd cannot be ALL IN ALL [we herd cows; we lead sheep!]. What does the Shepherd of a flock [not a herd] of sheep do? In the case of Psalm 23, we have an Eternal picture, and we have a temporal [earthly] picture. We want to look for the Complement—the companion and supplement of the provisions we read throughout The Psalms.

<u>You may wish to open your Bible</u> to see that God provides everything for life as we know it—The LORD shows us how to understand and live life to the fullest. If we want to live life without wants—with Only Physical Satisfaction and Spiritual Results guaranteed for eternity, "Good Luck With That!" We need to find a resource that accommodates these desires. David says God is the answer! As David sat in God's presence, he realized The LORD would supply his diverse physical and 'hopeful' spiritual needs. David says God laid out a table of goodies to prepare him for living successfully. The Shepherd Boy, now a writer, felt an Eternal Blessing and Home was waiting for his arrival! God will Shepherd us—Our acceptance of His offer is vital to the cause! (Psalm 23)

All but the five opening words of this, One Small Chapter of The Bible in Psalms 23, describe the Complement part of the scenario we are looking at as if it were a Preacher giving us *The Lay of The Land* or the outline of his sermon. There arc 'one-hundred and twelve' words here, giving us a brief overview of What God Is All About!

How does a casual look at *The Lay of The Land* play out? There are differences between it and *Surveying The Land* in the developmental stages of preparing any theme or project. We often look at life casually with a Que Sera Sera mindset—not necessarily trying to find the 'Ultimate Purpose' for our place on Planet Earth. What a difference it makes for each of us in our own lives to know the feeling and or the fact of the life enrichment we will experience if we look at the bigger picture. All life comes into 'better focus' in the 'bigger focus.'

Frequently I reference the Johnny Nash song; *I Can See Clearly Now*. The story is vast, What A Difference A Day Makes, as we look farther down the pike for the pattern of life needed to be read carefully—like an architectural blueprint. One might even say, 'if we observe well' *The Lay of The Land*, we may find and understand The God of The Universe 'to be as if' built within each of us as a pattern of what we are in the physical sphere—the life we live may even be a part of our 'Directional DNA.'

We Observe Life—We Look At Life From Both Sides, then we pull out our 'transit level' and our 'theodolite—' Our THEO— What??? I thought you might ask; I didn't know either, so I checked with Mrs. And Or Mr. Google. Here's what they say—

"The two pieces of survey equipment that surveyors use most are a transit level and a theodolite. The surveyor uses them to measure both horizontal and vertical angles. In comparison, the purpose of the two surveyor tools is similar. Generally, a theodolite is more accurate than a transit level. How do surveyors measure distance? (In my words—JBI)."

As we work through *Searching For A Heart Of Gold*, we need to realize I'm using The Physical Tools of Life [they come in many forms] to represent the Ethereal or Non-Earthly picture of our purpose; to understand better; to see more clearly now, after we have read this book.

If we think about candescent (glowing) lighting and incandescent lighting (radiant or brilliant), we have a starting point about how much we can see in the detail of an entity. However, this is just a very weak illustration when comparing The Earthly Elements of Life with The Spiritual Elements of Life. For this, we need "The Holy Spirit of God!"

My God And I, We Walk This Road Together—is a song that takes the lead when I try to make sure I'm on track. If we wish to go it alone or think Eternity In Heaven is a given because it's a Birthright, some disappointment may be waiting at the End of This Road.

The guidance of The Holy Spirit comes because God's presence is in place everywhere; for those folks who wish to understand God better, The Holy Spirit of God is at The Ready twenty-four-seven—no matter Where We Are!

"God's promises are open to everyone who forms a relationship with Him—believing Jesus died to pay for our sin. Salvation is colossal—provided because of God's love, through mercy—Salvation is eternal because of God's Grace!" (Acts 2:39; JBI)

The Road Not Taken
[Robert Frost—Public Domain]

Two roads diverged in a *yellow* (Fall) wood,
And sorry I could not travel both
And be one traveller, long I stood
And looked down one as far as I could
To where it bent in the undergrowth.

Then took the other, just as fair,
And having perhaps the better claim,
Because it was grassy and wanted wear.
Though as for that, the passing there
Had worn them really about the same,

And both that morning equally lay
In leaves, no step had trodden black.
Oh, I kept the first for another day!
Yet knowing how way leads on to way,
I doubted if I should ever come back.

I shall be telling this with a sigh
Somewhere ages and ages hence:
Two roads diverged in a wood, and I—
I took the one less travelled by,
And that has made all the difference.

M Scott Peck gives us *The Road Less Travelled*—In Summary, it looks like this— "We try to avoid our problems—our spiritual growth depends on confronting our concerns and working through the suffering they cause. In The Road Less Traveled, psychotherapist M. Scott Peck teaches us how to face the inevitable challenges in our lives, grow through hardship, and ultimately attain deeper awareness. Mr. Peck recommends a path to spiritual enlightenment that includes four key elements: discipline, love, personal religion, and grace. We risk spiritual stagnation and mental health problems accompanying inactivity without these four qualities. Adopting these four qualities leads to better health, better relationships, and flourishing lives".

Both Robert Frost's *The Road Not Taken* and M. Scott Peck's work are great contributors to the theme we are looking at, *Searching For A Heart Of Gold; Not A Pot Of Gold*. Psalm 23 gives us subject matter and directive insights to put into our sights to find our target. Sometimes I get lost in my work to where I don't want any disturbances—at other times, I get lost because of a lack of the driving force I need; Psalm 23 helps me refocus. Nothing ever comes into existence without someone having prepared for a task— purposed to commit to it—and finished the job!

I'll try to fashion this book effectively to change minds and lives. In this case, it's essential to realize the make-up of God. We should position ourselves to appreciate *The Lay of The Land* He scales out for each of us in the personal sphere; we need to know also how God's plan works on the corporate level—with our immediate neighbour and the whole world.

By first surveying the Subject of a passage, we realize there is more to search for than this. Subject and or Substance have a source; this is where we must go next. Finding the depth of a topic also asks us to look for the Complement (balance). It's essential to realize that the 'subject' is like a servant (subservient), [needing to fulfill a promise] to the Complement (another participant) in the story.

Jesus was and is God; He became a man, as The Son of Man, while He remained God The Son; as The Son of Man, Jesus became a servant to show us *The Lay Of The Land*!

We talk about living like Jesus did—having the mind of Christ. As far as a value level goes, Jesus was in every respect on the same plane as God The Father and God The Holy Spirit. However, Jesus lived in the rankings of servitude—putting Himself aside and giving up everything He was entitled to for the benefit of the whole of humanity's crime of sin. Jesus knew His Purpose—fulfilled it to The Death! (Philippians 2: 5-8; JBI)

Finding out what the author, David, in Psalm 23 suggests and discovering the sum of what is on his mind is not optional. When David spreads ideas on the sorting table to flesh out the process begun in this passage, I want to have an open mind.

Firstly, let's nail down what the author presents—the subject [The LORD]. While seeing a full-scale presentation, like a video, clarity in decision-making is paramount or vital. Information is often a key element in working out the details to understand and best process the issue; however, too much information can muddy the waters.

Secondly—because there is a First Cause and or Purpose, The Subject—The Complement would never have become a reality, and we cannot have one without the other. Should we think of this as something we can't overlook? David lets us know there is more to the passage than what might first meet the eye.

God is the Source, He has the advantage over all; life depends on His rule. We need to acknowledge Him. As previously stated, The LORD is the Subject. The second part plays out like this; The Complement—Is My Shepherd; this part suggests 'what' we're explaining. There's a preservation factor infused in God's promises—as we study Psalm 23, our understanding skyrockets.

Psalms 23 challenges me in ways outside of most of my wants. My Wannabe [Wannabee] Is—I want to be a Great Writer who garners the attention it requires for readers to enjoy what I write. I Wannabe respectful of people for their value sense as human beings. I Wannabe Somebody too— somebody from whom people can learn. If I succeed, I'll 'feel' (suggesting subjectivity) blessed— I Know The LORD's incredibly near!

I wannabe all these and much more, as far as the principle, rule, system, tenets, or position of life allows any one of us to be this complete. Am I so distinct from others who feel they have somewhat to offer? The Wannabees top a never-ending list of things that thrive on pulling us into what might often be a web of deceit—it may not be anything this dreadful. We have the opportunity to select from a vast list of desirable elements—be a good neighbour, live life in a positive light and love our families sacrificially—.

Many are the credible basics of life to which we could say GOD would be proud to call us Christ Followers. As I survey what lies before me, I need to look for the tools, if you would, which will do more than get me from point A to Point B! If getting from A to B is the only purpose of life, I see no purpose in the effort taken.

When I know the end is near for me, let me clarify that I don't want anyone to dwell on the things I did My Way for selfie reasons. When all is said and done for me, I pray folks will say Jacob committed to being a Christ Follower, albeit however imperfect he may have been.

When they draw down the final curtain on me, I wish my prayer to be, "Lord, here I am; I have run my race; I have gotten 'kinda' tired from time to time; I am looking forward to what you planned for me all along. I'm not looking behind me. LORD, when I face the Final Curtain, ready to see what's on the other side; when I close my eyes in death and open my eyes with a different perspective than I've had on this earth, in this life of fleshly Wannabees—I want to hear You say following words—.

"Well done—good and faithful servant!"

A while ago, we saw how Jesus became a servant to all—in this role, He demonstrated faithfulness. Jesus commended others for their commitment—faithfulness engages the privilege of promotion. Jesus illustrated how a servant who respected his master's goods was worthy of higher placements in life. (Mathew 25:21)

"The LORD is my Shepherd;" "I shall not want!"

Remember—we talked a while ago about the Subject [Part One] of the scripture we read and the Complement [Part Two] of the same passage or story. We know well enough what the word Subject means—It's a noun; it forms a fundamental matter of thought, discussion, and investigation—on a subject of conversation, an area of understanding as a course of study.

The second part of a two-part dissertation, study, or critique is the Complement—as we look at it, we seek to find out what balances out all the descriptive words which the Subject supplies us. Who or what can we credit in a value sense [not in a flattering complementary] for the benefit we receive in the Subject Part—the provision we can rightly accredit for our newfound bounty?

While looking for the Complementary or Harmonizing factor, we can seal up the discussion in Psalms 23—Sounding like this, "The LORD is my SHEPHERD; I shall not want!" Can we live in faith and trust in this way? We can—though it may not be easy. The Subject cannot play the part of being a loner (hermit). We all know what a hermit looks like in a 'word sense' and a 'visual sense.'

Yes, it's good in the realization sector to look thankfully at the subject matter—we can do it with many words. However, we can sum it up in a few words; "I was in dire need, and The LORD fixed the issue for me!" If we always summarized everything in a book, as in this fashion, the book we have before us would not be large enough to publish!

If we did this with The Bible, and we could, we would need to be careful not to summarize God out of His rightful place. God says in Deuteronomy 4:2—and in at least eight other passages we are not to take away or make less of what He says, saying that "this is God saying what we summarized it as." He says things to input The Full Impact of the story of life.

God predestined or preordained we *should have* life—I say, 'should have' because none of us has ever lived life to God's Exact Expectations. So, we do face The Full Impact of the reality of both sides; if we do or if we don't, consequences and or results will apply in the 'reality sector.'

Complement expresses itself to us like this—

It's a noun; it's someone or something completing or making perfect: Some say, "a good wine complements a delicious meal—" "We now have a full complement of packers." The complement is that we need two parts or things to complete the whole; the counterpart is the finishing touch [working front to back and back to front].

I still feel I need help at times for the season before me. When the things of this earth are not yet strangely dim, I still live with the world before me, and the Heaven I desire still seems so distant—my frailties often curtail my progress towards the perspective which 'will leave me feeling complete.' We want everything to be "Tickety Boo," you know, tolerable enough to get through the day—for that matter, most of life. Yes, there are times when we don't think we'll make it to the end of the road ahead.

Though I can take the shortcut, saying, "The LORD is my SHEPHERD, I shall not want;" I don't want to miss anything God has designed for me, so I go for the 'big cut' rather than a summarized slice of the pie. Why stop with a summary at the gate; when a wealth of luxuries lies beyond the gate.

He makes me lie down in green pastures: He leads me beside the still waters. (Psalm 23; 2; KJV)

'Aplomb (poise)' was a trailblazing word awakening me this morning. It isn't like I never knew this word; I just never used it before. I never sought to find the needed balance the word 'aplomb' suggests. The variant (something derived from something else, which has roots in something else—like a COVID-19 Variant) or different modicum's this word makes gives us a complete picture of changes in tone as it divvies up between assurance and self-assurance. The opposite of 'assurance' is 'self-doubt;' the opposite of self-assurance is reluctance [hesitancy] or helplessness.

Aplomb—Equanimity, nonchalance, tact, balance, confidence, coolness, nerve, poise, self-possession, surety—.

In their most straightforward sense, words call for action on our part when we hear them. They insist we take the bull by the horns and turn the 'bull' [our stubborn spirit] around half-circle [like in a traffic circle] from going the wrong direction in which we 'think we need to go—' to get to where we 'need to go in the right direction—the opposite route.'

"Compatibility (when two entities exist or occur sensibly without complications or struggles) and reliability (being trustworthy or performing consistently well) are crucial elements to observe and live with accordingly. The Bible lays out our faith walk. Disharmony and disloyalty are antonyms of 'compatibility and reliability.' When we manage life from these constants. 'compatibility and reliabilities,' we avoid the errors of defeat. From the error, we certainly need to take the bull by the horns and 'turn it around."

It's no secret [we don't need to be a Rocket Scientist to get the message here] that the opposite of error is truth; from such, we shouldn't steer a different course; but let the 'Spirit of Truth guide the ride we're taking. I don't recommend lacking confidence in our God-mandated abilities to search out—being fully prepared to do what we can do within God's Governing Authority. When we consider this matter seriously—getting past the Starting Gate and into the winner's circle is a given: A Gift of God!

Research feverishly to prove yourself worthy of God's trust in you, like a worker who doesn't need to be ashamed— because you are sending God's Word out to the world— truthfully! (2 Timothy 2:15; JBI)

Aplomb—calm assurance suggests dependence, faith, confidence—not need in the sense of addiction. Self-Assurance suggests a controlling factor that we can muster up without the help of a higher authority. Dependability [our efforts and those which require our dependence on someone or something else?] derives from an intersection of thought, such as The Road Not Taken by Robert Frost, where we can take one road or the other—but taking the right road "makes all the difference."

Grace offers us hope when we mess up. Faith in Someone—sometimes faith in something non-spiritual in one sense helps us believe there are possibilities in one way or the other. Peace, Inner Strength and Balance also come from Assurance. We can receive 'assurances' from other people—God begins the Assurance process! [Somewhat different than Assurance (Insurance) Companies].

The most outstanding leaders of known history, the Pharaohs, Kings, Queens, Monarchs, Presidents, Dictators, Autocratic [despotic, depressive, repressive, authoritarian, oppressive] Leaders, Democratic (elected) Leaders, Strategic Leaders, and Transformational Leaders—were and always will be dependent on something or Someone [someone] for their success and or demise—Here lay The Facts of Life—*The Lay Of The Land*!

We can't do anything unless Someone helps us Somehow [think it over—]. We can Survey all the variables and still miss hitting the target goal of a project—if we have faulty toolsets. Without a "Transit Level or a Theodolite," trying to Survey The Land [Our Project in Chapter Two] without a Transit Level or a Theodolite will leave us short on the Accuracy Level.

The word 'Theodolite' interests me. Split the word like this [theo-dolite], drop [dolite] ['substance'—my definition only JBI], and I think of "Theo" as Theos. The Greek word for God is "Theos." Many names beginning with the root 'Theo-,' are derived from the Ancient Greek word Theos (Θεός), which means God. In a play on words scenario, I think of us being unable to do anything without God—if God had not created—we would be non-existent— There You Go! Is Theodolite an essential tool for surveying, or what?

Suppose I carry this train of thought just a little further for my imaginative or creative thinking. In that case, I suggest we observe Theodolite as it breaks into two syllables commonly—having a prefix and a suffix (postfix). *Theodo* is the prefix, and *lite* is the suffix (*postfix*).

Let's look at the meaning of *theodo* according to Wikipedia:

"Theodore is a masculine given name. It comes from the Ancient Greek name Θεόδωρος (Theódoros), meaning 'gift of God' (from the Ancient Greek words θεός, (theós) 'God' and δῶρον (dóron) 'gift').[1] The name was borne by several figures in ancient Greece, such as Theodorus of Samos and Theodorus of Byzantium, but gained popularity due to the rise of Christendom."

In any form, it means God-Given or Gift of God, as do the given names Jonathan, Nathaniel, Matthew, Attaullah, Devadatta, Dosetai, Bogdan, and Adeodatus. The feminine form of Theodore is Theodora—The names Dorothy and Godiva also mean Gift of God—Theodore is the feminine form in German and Theodor's masculine form.

Now, because I am daring (gutsy), I will invent the Word Theodolight. For my purpose only, I see Theodo as relating to Jesus, The Gift of God, The Word, The 'Light' of The World. So, in my JBI [Jacob Bergen Insight] Style, thinking format, TheodoLight, says Jesus is God—Jesus is Enough to get us by at all times—Jesus is Immanuel, God Is With Us. So, as we observe the history lesson of the past, we realize that Theodo means Theodore (Theodorus)— Gift of God.

> Study to *show* yourself approved unto God, a workman who need not be ashamed, rightly dividing the word of truth. (2 Timothy 2: 15; KJV)

We can't do anything unless Someone helps us Somehow [think it over—]. We can Survey all the variables and still miss hitting the target goal of a project—if we have faulty toolsets. Without a "Transit Level or a Theodolite," trying to Survey The Land [Our Project in Chapter Two] without a Transit Level or a Theodolite will leave us short on the Accuracy Level. (IBID)

Let's quickly do an Acronym for Theodo—

T—is for The Time you give to friends.
H—is for The Heart; warm and loving.
E—is for elegant; born within you.
O—is for organized; you always know where things are
D—is for desire; your thoughts do aspire.
O—is for optimism; look at the bright side!

Is it possible to have a calm, peaceable assurance—An Aplomb—Is it feasible to have an assured faith for the outcome, The Final Answer? Is certainty an Absolute, backed by an authority in our uncertain world? Can a life without a Designer Oriented System offer sufficiency? I'll Answer NO—when God isn't in The Picture! Yes, With God! With God—Possibilities Abound!

Is it best for me if GOD gives me the nod to lie down in green pastures? Is it best if I avail myself of these pleasures—greener pastures? Should I circumvent or outflank someone else to get that quiet fishing hole? You know, the serene peace sending lake where I can get my Respite Moment, my Selah Moment beside those still waters, where I can come to grips with the All Sufficiency of God and His desire to share His Stuff with me!

He restores my soul: He leads me in the paths of righteousness for His name's sake. [with a Pure Purpose, for His Name's sake]. (Psalm 23: 3; KJV & JBI)

It's Great if Someone goes ahead of us on the journey we prepared for ourselves and our families—making sure we've ironed out the creases and there are no 'chinks in the armour' [a narrow opening. We use the phrase chink in (one's) armour, which refers to a weakness that supplies a space for an attack to begin]. How about a front person [re the term— 'front man'] checking out to see if the whole journey will be safe—if we will get back home in one piece! I Wannabee there, in the paths of righteousness!

"You prepare a table before me in the presence of my enemies: You anoint my head with oil; my cup runs over." (Psalm 23:5)

Anytime we head out on the Long Road, it simply means it may be tough sledding for a time—like The Goodtimes Quit Rolling Forever! However, the Journey is better when we have a purpose, making it worthwhile. One-night stands present many enemies on the road—challenging bus rides, quick trip plane flights, sleepless nights, wake-up pills—. Sometimes, from where we sit in the Emotive Concert Hall, we think it's Glory Road on this life trip, and it'll be this way forever!

Look at the money—entertainers and others of their ilk haul in; it seems to be an exciting life—or so we think! Where does the story end? Where should the story end when we give all we got to entertain and or minister to other people who think they need what we got. If Someone doesn't prepare a table in this 'so it seems wilderness,' we'll never make it on The Journey Of The Long Road:

—we wish for so long to get out there and get at it—Our Dream Come True!

    —all the prized flashes of Now I Have It Made; these only hold a gaze for a moment of truth.

    —if the wings don't break off the plane, or the wheels don't come off the bus, I will be in Great Shape!

    —In the midst of it all, there are still some 'not so little unknowns' pulling at our insides.

    —we believe life will treat us fairly; we believe our faith will carry us through the hard times on the journey of The Long Road, but sometimes there is still something missing.

    —most of us run the gambit [cover or extend across a wide and varied range]; some exceptions arise from the unknown circumstances life offers. However, The Long Road does include more than what we experience on this side of the curtain. Memories can keep hope alive for some folks; memories may aggravate The Journey of The Long Road for other people. When we set up our Spiritual Transit Level and Theodolite, we can better evaluate Life!

    What's our impetus or motivation to get the job of first finding our purpose in life—then, after surveying all the variables, put together a package with the help of the right source to get the job done?

HOPE COMES FROM HIM—GOD!
WHO MEASURES AND MANAGES ETERNITY.

Oh, for a drink from the Big Dipper stationed on the Backdrop of Him Who controls the Indescribable Universe: The Indescribable God! Louie Giglio's *The Indescribable God* is so unique and extraordinary—one might feel as though they are with Louie in the presence of God Himself. When I watch this video, I feel as if God were saying, "I did all of this and more; I did all this and more, Just For You!" While watching this presentation, one may think, "How Much More Is There?" Before we finish Chapter Two, let's do a 'sneak a peek.'

More, Yes, Much More: It is not always about what we see. Someone said, "It's What Is In Your Heart That Counts." Yes, Jesus, God in the flesh, created all the fantastic colour schemes, flashing lights, and the sounds of the universe in so many ways, as it speaks to us in every language: Known and Unknown. When someone talks to us, we need to Take Note—it may be important!

What's more, you ask? This amazing God came to this earth to feel 'the full misery humankind brought on themselves by not taking God's Word for it in The Garden of Eden.' "This you may do, and this you may not do." Oh yeah, we could do it our way, and we did! What did we get? "Another Day Older and Deeper in Debt*!*"

Jesus came and paid that debt on a wooden cross—slated to be enough to take care of the whole wad of debt—Once again, the alternative of choice surfaces.

> Surely goodness and mercy shall follow me all the days of my life: and I will dwell in the house of the Lord forever. (Psalms 23; KJV)

The whole of Psalm 23 requires Major Faith & Trust on our part, as it did for The Shepherd Boy David—. Many thought that David wrote Psalm 23 later in life, not when he was a Shepherd Boy. So, as I see it, in retrospect, David thought back to when he was the young lad out in his father's pastures, looking out for the Ewes, Rams, and the Lambs. He began most of the maturing process that would carry him through the many hard times to follow him to the grave—At The Oasis of Psalm Twenty-Three!

◊ THE VISTA VIEW—THE OASIS ◊

My title for Chapter Endings is *The Vista View—The Oasis.* When I check the thesaurus, I find Vista and View mean very much the same in the larger perspective—however, both *Vista* and *View* have individuality—as do People. People have an identity in colour, race, and character—but the bottom line is, we're constantly All' Still People.

People must all adhere to the same rules of life. There are no exceptions. It often appears as if this is an oxymoron, bathos, or simply a 'letdown' because we see some groupings of people who never seem to be adversely affected by the rules of life that are such a hardship to other folks. Life seems so unfair at times in such cases. But 'they' [whoever 'they' are] say, "Every Dog Has It's Day!"

The picture of life looks to be unfair for some folks. I don't understand everything, and some folks are never living on top of the world in this life, but I Know Who Holds The Future, and I am sure He will get it right. In some way, the part they play may even be more significant in the Big Picture than the role played by others who never seem to take the hit.

Synonyms show us the difference between Vista and View in a simple, synonymic, or equal way.

Vista—a glimpse, panorama, outline, perspective, landscape, look, scene, scenery, seascape, sight, vision, a field of vision—.

View—aspect, *glimpse*, *look*, outlook, *perspective*, picture, prospect, *scene*, *sight*, *vision*, way, appearance, composition, contour, design, illustration, *landscape*, opening, *outline*, *panorama*, representation, *seascape*, spectacle, stretch, show, tableau, vista, a *field of vision*, range of vision—.

Vista and View are separated into descriptive synonyms by the underlined words in 'View.' If we removed these words, we could save a lot of time and energy and say there are no distinguishing differences between Vista and View. When we check our Thesaurus, many words fall into the same category. The folks who write the Thesauruses' go to great lengths to help us understand every angle with the clarity of thought we may otherwise miss. I'd be nearly lost insofar a writing goes without the Thesaurus.

However, this would remove the individuality [differing ways] factor, which is essential in saying, "We Are All People, So What's The Big Deal." The Big Deal Is, 'if there weren't' defining character and other differences, we'd all be robotic, along with every other entity in the universe.

Another way to look at it is if we look at how Transformers function. Please look at the description of Transformers.

"Transformers toys are robots in disguise. They resemble your average [or not-so-average] car, motorcycle, or jet one minute—the next, they transform into supercharged robots that shoot missiles or grappling hooks from their arms."
(Bing Search)

Let's look at the Leopard—they [again, whoever they are] say a Leopard Changes its Spots. When we observe the Chameleon, we see a similar trait. The changeability factor is such that it is like someone trying to hide their identity—in the hypocritical view, we can bring the whole picture full circle. Life would be one big flip-flop adventure twenty-four seven if people and other entities had no individuality.

They say there should be a separation between state and religion. In one respect, this is so because not all people under the state's rule are religious or Christian. However, in another sense, I ask, and I do so from the side of my bias or choice to be on the "Religious or Christian side," 'If God Created Everything, Then, Should He Not Rule Everything?' Should State and Religion rule as one?

I know Individuality can be confusing—if only God would have made it simple in Creation Week—not allowing us to choose how life should be. Yes, His Best Case Scenario would've been to have all Creation governed in this perfect way so life would always be One Big Heaven. However, God must've seen some value in allowing individuality. Might that have been because of Love—on this earth as we know it has never operated very well under the rule of Arbitration? Love is outside of negotiation!

"God so loved the world that He gave—"

He gave us a choice to choose Individuality, so we, by choice, would LOVE Him in return just for Who He Was and Is!

Vista and View Come Together in God's Love!

In Chapter One, we covered *The Lay Of The Land*—I'm referring to the Physical Lay of The Land because this is the actuality (reality) we see with our physical eyes. This physicality requires no Faith; it is Objective (factual) evidence that doesn't deceive or lie; it is what it is—. A tree will always be a tree; a cloud is a cloud; the sky is the sky; the dirt (earth) is always dirt.

As I refer to *The Lay Of The Land* in *Searching For A Heart Of Gold; Not A Pot Of Gold*, I'm reaching beyond earthly things. In Chapter Two, *Surveying The Land*, I'm doing the same as I've done in everything I write. My purpose is always to help people see the Spiritual Things through the eyes of the things that are understandable [material things]—it requires FAITH: Faith requires us to believe something even though we don't see it. It's an outrageous idea for many people—the idea of believing in something if they can't see it with their natural eyes.

By The Holy Spirit of God, God Himself comes to us somehow because of the witness of people. Unless the Bible points us to what Jesus has done to provide for us the forgiveness of our sins, we have NO HOPE! Please hear what Paul The Apostle says in Romans 1—Paul clearly shows us that God doesn't leave us in the dark. If God requires us to have FAITH, and He says He does (Hebrews 11:6), He also gives us a Helper to know for sure about Faith!

> Because what we can know of God is manifest in them, for God has shown it to them. For we see the invisible things of Him from the creation of the world—we understand even His eternal power and Godhead; because of the created things, so that they are without excuse: Because that, when they knew God, they glorified Him not as God, neither were thankful; but became vain in their imaginations, and their foolish heart became darkened. (Romans 1:19-21; KJV)

The big problem is that God Planted Two Special Trees in the Garden of Eden [among others]. He gave clear direction even then as to which was the right way to live without sin forever—God said, "The Tree Of Life" IS "The Right Tree To Choose." "The Tree of The Knowledge of Good and Evil" IS The Wrong Tree." Everything took a turn for the worse in a perfect setting!

We chose the "Tree of The Worst-Case Scenario!" We decided to say, "We Are Smart Enough To Figure It Out For Ourselves—We Do Not Need Any Help From You, God!" We left the Garden of Eden because of our sin of disobedience. Later on in the story of Life and of God—God began "The Story Of Bringing Us Back—" in a sense, "Bringing Us Full Circle" back to The Garden of Eden [In A Sense] to choose again to follow Him and have Eternal Life. But now, we'd need to select this path through Jesus and what Jesus did on The Cross.

In the Person of Jesus The Christ, God made Himself to be 'The Sin' for which we needed forgiveness. God said, "Believe This, Trust in Me by Faith." All God ever said is true—He said, you will have what you would've had if you'd believed Me in The first place in The Garden of Eden! The whole story is so much bigger than these few words I write here; the simplicity of it is, "Believe On The Lord Jesus Christ—and you will glean Salvation from Eternal Damnation!" (John 3: 16—)

When I talk about *Searching For A Heart Of Gold; Not A Pot Of Gold; The Lay Of The Land; Surveying The Land;* I'm looking through the eyes of Spiritual things. God talks about these things in The Bible through the senses of the things we can see [without faith], so we can understand what we need to see through The Eyes of Faith [The Things We Cannot See].

Next, we find *The LORD Is My Shepherd* in Chapter Three.

My Prayer Is That These "Vista Views" will carry us through *Searching For A Heart of Gold, Not A Pot of Gold.*

ENJOY–As We Continue In Chapter Three.

HEART SENSE

God Is Good!

◊

TRULY GOD IS GOOD TO ISRAEL, even to such a clean heart. But my feet were almost gone; my steps had well nigh slipped, for I was envious at the foolish when I saw the prosperity of the wicked; for there are no bands in their death: but their strength is firm. (Psalm 73:1-4 KJV)

They are not in trouble as other men; neither are they plagued like other men. Therefore pride compasseth them about as a chain; violence covereth them as a garment. Their eyes stand out with fatness: they have more than a heart could wish. They are corrupt and speak wickedly concerning oppression: they speak loftily. They set their mouth against the heavens, and their tongue walketh through the earth.

Verily I have cleansed my heart in vain and washed my hands in innocency. For all the day long have I been plagued and chastened every morning. If I say, I will speak thus; behold, I should offend against the generation of thy children. When I thought about knowing this, it was too painful for me; Until I went into the sanctuary of God, then I understood their end. Indeed You didst set them in slippery places: You cast them down into destruction. How are they brought into desolation, as in a moment! They are— consumed with terrors. As a dream when one awaketh; so, O Lord, when You awoke, You despised their image.

Thus my heart was grieved—pricked in my reins. So foolish was I, and ignorant: I was as a beast before thee. Nevertheless, I'm with You continually— You have held me by my right hand. You will guide me with Your counsel and afterward receive me to glory. Whom have I in heaven but You? There is none on earth that I desire besides YOU.

My flesh and my heart faileth: but God is the strength of my heart, and my portion forever. (Psalms 73: 1-9; 13-26; KJV)

The LORD Is My Shepherd
[The Progress]
Scriptures In Chapter Three
Psalm 23
Ecclesiastes 3:2
Psalm 23
Psalm 70: 1-5; Psalm 109
Psalm 23
Psalm 23:2
Psalm 23
Take A Breather—Psalm 23
Psalm 23; Galatians 2:20
Galatians 2:20; Psalm 23
Hebrews 12; Psalm 23
Psalm 139:1; Psalm 23; Psalm 1; 3 John 2:2
The Vista View—The Oasis
Philippians 2:4; Matthew 22:35-40; John 10:11
Heart Sense
Isaiah 40:1-11

Chapter Three

The Lord Is My Shepherd

———————————— ◊ ————————————

AS WE REFLECT on The Shepherd care so far, God shows Himself as Someone who wants His best for us. Ahead of us are the Green Pastures which Psalms 23 allows us to grasp in a profound sense—as Preparation sets the course for us to seek out. Preparation demands Purpose—Purpose calls for Progress, and Progress necessitates our need for Your hand of Preservation to be readily available to the nth degree!

LORD, You are my Shepherd; I shall not want. I'll lie down in green pastures by calm waters. My soul gets refreshing as I traverse paths of virtue for Your name's sake. As I stroll the depths of the valley of the shadow of death, no evil will overcome me—You'll see to that. Your rod and staff comfort me. With Purpose in mind, Preparation on the table, Progress a given and Your guarantee of Preservation in my hand, my enemies don't have any hope of derailing Your Plans! You anoint my head with oil; my cup runs over. Goodness and mercy will Always follow me: and in Your Presence, I'll remain forever. (Psalms 23; JBI)—The Progress—

Without Faith, it's impossible! What more can I say to explain the context? The predetermined plan (not parameters that suggest limits or walls that do not allow us to connect to the rest of the content of The Bible or portion thereof) of Psalms 23 needs no explanation. The LORD Is My Shepherd! The Information Highway is an endless journey of resources to search out! One subject leads to another, and The Short Road soon becomes The Long Road!

As I begin to survey [as in *Surveying The Land*] the list of books and other info, I see the presentations are multi-inclusive of many aspects of thought. Some titles are for children—it seems they include every genre of study. Even skeptics and former skeptics have opinions about the validity of Psalms 23 and what the whole Bible has to say about God's identity and purpose.

The folks we meet have mega questions about the possibility of God. People struggle with God's value in the world of uncertain capacities, feeling 'the God they perceive (imagine) of, should quantify, measure out or supply.' It becomes increasingly difficult to press on [make progress] to another set of thoughts about the topic in Chapter Three, The LORD Is My Shepherd (Looking For Green Pastures), without duplicating previous studies from Psalms 23. My extension of these thoughts will fit into what I choose to call this book, *Searching For A Heart Of Gold; Not A Pot Of Gold*.

I'm often in a quandary when I hear songs from singers who are great artists in their own right because of the gifts of communication they have. I love to listen to songs like, *Imagine All the People* by John Lennon and *I Can Only Imagine* by Bart Millard. The song which sent me on a search for a book theme that has captured me for many years, *Heart Of Gold* by Neil Young, is another inclusive (wide-ranging) reason why I named this book we are working through—as I did. I appreciate Neil's heart-felt words.

My difficulty is evaluating what I hear the singers saying; the lyrics are so impacting; they seem to be crying out with what appears to be the only means they have of telling the world of that need for more than what they have in the present. John Lennon asks us to 'Imagine all the people living for today.' At the same time, he says, 'Imagine if there were no heaven,' [but somehow, on the crest of his heart, his mind, he must be thinking heaven exists]. Then he tells us how easy it is to imagine there being no heaven. Imagine— what a problem or difficulty we get fitted into when we hear these songs—I enjoy them for the moment because they speak to me about the magnitude of God. I look at the flip side of the words people express in their reach for more than what they are experiencing; I think they are looking for God, but they don't seem to realize the magnitude of the Search!

Lennon and McCartney wrote *Help*, which cries for someone's help in their dire situation. [the context here seems to be someone other than God]. I try to 'Imagine' the obstacles people place in front of themselves when the resource they might be looking for isn't God as the Helper. As I look at *Help* and *Imagine All The People*, I think of the song *Desperado* by The Eagles, and I literally 'feel the feeling' of someone so desperate for help! I know my thoughts present a different context than the one they represent.

Amongst these songs of desperation by some very talented and famous singers, I cannot resist mentioning another gifted and admired singer, who has his perspective of 'Imagination.' Bart Millard wrote and sang *I Can Only Imagine*. The difference spirals into another avenue of Heart Stuff—gripping me with the love of a differing kind than what we all experience while doing life every day. Bart sings these words; *I Can Only Imagine* the feeling of walking with Jesus (The Answer Man), [and what my heart will feel]. I wonder about many things I don't fully understand. Many folks have their questions about the difficulties The Bible asks us to accept by faith. Heaven is the 'Vista' and or reality of God—not the 'imagination' of what 'a heaven' will be.

In his song, *Heart of Gold*, Neil Young expresses feelings as if he were a 'Miner,' who mines for gold, looking for the value of life. Neil says, 'I Want To Live; I Want To Give;' he searched the world over—I sometimes feel he didn't find what was out there for him; while getting older, the difficulty (mystery) still seems to grip his heart—. Where and what is the gold worth looking for anyway? However, Neil Young doesn't give up; he says, 'these expressions he never had, keep him searching' for this Heart Of Gold.

Age has us accentuating or emphasizing our sense of how we use our time. The writer of Ecclesiastes [within the 'context' of Ecclesiastes] gets right in our face to say,

> God planned a time of birth and death for each of us who lived. During the Seasons of Time, there's always been a planting season and a harvest time. (Ecclesiastes 3:2; JBI)

All the singers and songwriters mentioned express thoughts that present seasons of time in which they seem to be looking for a solution. The answer they search for is to get themselves into some Nirvana—some paradise, or heaven where they'll find their Final Answer—the ultimate accomplishment of life for which most folks are searching.

Psalms 23 offers us Green Pastures, or a perspective of the heart of singers, poets, writers, and communicators—the rest of us are all looking for more of life than seems to be in our grasp! The sadness encompassing the expressions of thought many people try to imagine, without ever seeming to come to the place of the 'Satisfaction' they desire—never seems to dissipate.

What more can I say about Psalms 23 to explain the context? There are numerous contexts in every book, setting or agenda. I'm not speaking of parameters that suggest limits or walls that don't allow us to connect the rest of the content of The Bible or portion thereof relating to Psalm Twenty-Three.

THE LORD IS MY SHEPHERD—

I shall not want—The LORD 'allows me' to lie down in the pure grassy green fields: He walks along with me beside peaceful waters. He refreshes me in body, mind and spirit. God leads me along the Right Path. Even when I'm wandering through deathly places, I can still trust God because I know He is at my side. God gets a little thorough with me during my wayward times to bring me comfort rather than being hurt by my wanderings. You *prepare* sustenance when evil ones try taking me out. You refresh me when I need it, with Your goodness and mercy. While I live, I can depend on You—after that, I will dwell in the house of the Lord forever. (Psalms 23; JBI)

David was about thirty years old within the structure of Psalm 23—It's tough to narrow down his age breakdown in today's world. Everyone is so conscious about being tagged as 'this, that or the other.' However, I think of thirty as nearing middle age. Thirty seemed to be like this back in the day [in what we think of as Bible Timeline Days]. I'll let you figure out what the age of thirty signifies—how we fit into our society in comparison.

Psalm 23 suggests hope, care, the requirement of faith, confidence and much more. Throughout the study of this passage, we find a troubled king, one who, while in his mess, remained convinced of the competence of God to take him through his difficulties. The setting of this Psalm seems to be a place in life where David was hiding in the wilderness. He was on the run from his son—who usurped his throne.

The first value I see encircling this passage is when the writer says, 'The Lord is my shepherd; I shall not want—' this transpired after a time when David may not have fully understood this statement he made here. David arrived at this conclusion through a few seasons of plain old living. Here, he insinuated—or firmly stated by his cries for help—"God Is Good!"

David came to this conclusion because of the many answered prayers he sent heavenward. David likely shed a few tears before he got to this season of confidence (God is always Who and What He says He is). If you've read the Psalms to any degree, you'll come across The 'Poor Me Factor of David's Life.' Psalms 70 and Psalms 109 are two of many where I see David feeling as if saying, 'LORD, You are my Shepherd,' but I'm 'wanting' a little bit more here because of my circumstances. I'll only include the words of Psalms 70 here:

Hurry LORD my God—deliver me. LORD, please help me quickly! Cause my enemies to be ashamed and mystify those who seek to destroy me. Let them be pushed back—put to confusion. Trigger those that desire my hurt to pay dearly.

Let them be pushed back, quashed—put to confusion—those who mock You as a reward for their evil ways. Let all those that seek You rejoice and be glad in You—let those that want Your salvation always say, God, I magnify You!

I'm poor and needy—please rush to my assistance, O God—You're my help and my deliverer; O LORD, make no tarrying. (Psalms 70: 1-5; JBI)

Before writing Chapter 23 of Psalms, I believe David had questions about how God would get him out of the issues on his path of living. He experienced things because he yielded to temptations from time to time [The Bathsheba incident seems yet to be on the horizon, in his fifties]. Life often hits us square in the face as it did to David. It's hard to avoid being "Caught In A Trap" from time to time in one way or the other.

Please don't miss my 'Elvis' Sidebar—[A short tabloid or journal clip, usually boxed or set beside the compelling story; covers extra or descriptive stuff] *Suspicious Minds*! I think of Elvis Presley's song as talking to me directly because of my own life experiences, which look much like those of David The Shepherd. The song's opening words pan out like this, *Caught In A Trap*. Preceding these four words, he says—"We're." Elvis is speaking to a girl in the song. My take is that he's pointing at the rest of us to take a look—and take note. Let me pick up a few words and place them into a scenario looking as if Elvis suggests The Story of Life takes on much the same design.

Let's take an extension of thought as if to see Elvis saying, "Take a look—can't you see what you're laying on me?" Taken to the next level—Spiritually, we say, LORD, can't You see what's happening to me? Nobody seems to be on my side! Life only offers suspicion and confusion—I should've taken the other road when I chose my present road.

A few keywords for me are, Here We Go Again! I see the Poor Me Psalms in the story of *Suspicious Minds*. Though Psalm 23 lays out Green Pastures—Eternal Supplies, David didn't always live in this secure place. We get *Caught In A Trap* while simply doing Life! God always has better days in-store. (Psalm 23:2&3; JBI)

> "God allows me to lie comfortably in green pastures. He guides me gently to rest on the banks of calm waters. He rebuilds my spirit—He shows me the vividly marked paths of righteousness—the way of truth; for my benefit and His glory!"

'How Green Is My Valley?' No, I am not confused about the Title of the Book and or the Movie *How Green Was My Valley*. If we begin to see the relevance of the Present Tense manner in saying, 'How Green Is My Valley,' the message becomes more precise.

Comparing the Past Tense setting in *How Green Was My Valley* to when David was The Shepherd Boy to the time he had an affair with Bathsheba—the contrasting effects are like the reality of life even today. At this time, David was a King—Did he feel he had an entitlement or right to a guilt-free relationship with another man's wife? Many people in [2021-22] represent folks who felt and or still feel they have the freedom to explore extracurricular relationships—by so doing, destroy many relationships and physical lives that were once intact—there's no need to elaborate; the media has told their stories.

It's reasonably safe to say David was about Fifty-Five or so when he saw *Bath*sheba 'Bathing' [Re The Name 'Bath' Sheba (My Play on words)], and then proceeded to yield to temptation and take her to bed. These events happened many years after David *was* 'The Innocent Young Shepherd Boy.' Much of the story we have before us deals with what's happened to us in the past. These things always leave us with questions concerning The Hope Factor the future presents—or doesn't present, because we cannot seem to get past our current dire situation—which hinders necessary progress.

While observing the Context of these two seasons of David's life, it's relatively easy to see the perspective as two different pictures. When David was the Shepherd Boy sitting on a 'Knoll' (a grassy mound or small hill) overlooking The Green Valley around him, while he watched his Father's Sheep—I have no difficulty imagining him thinking, "How Green 'IS' My Valley." Furthermore, if I stretch my imagination somewhat, he may not yet be able to see far enough into the future to surmise that life may not always be this good!

It's quite a different story when David commits adultery with Bathsheba. But in retrospect, the difference in thinking was about the same. DA! When David was a young lad, he had an untested vision. Yes, he was tested for his 'Strength Of Resolve To Do The Job To The Best Of His Ability.' It was within the best of the ability of his youth that he could only see to a distance within this Season of Youth—maybe, it was to his benefit that he didn't have aspirations of Greater Grandeur at this time. Still, he had no way of knowing 'The Future' he would explore at 'Freedom Fifty-Five.' Added to the Freedoms he may have thought he had—were the consequences life would present then and the gap between the two. In the Season of being Young, David faced up to a lion, bear, and a giant—Goliath!

The difference in thinking was that he couldn't possibly see far enough down the pike to see the rest of his life. When David was in bed with Bathsheba, he didn't take the time to look at the life of being young and innocent and how "Green his Valley <u>Was</u> Then!" Had his perspective changed? 'I'd say so.' David's responsibility factor then was less than when he was King—fifty-five years old. In each 'Season of Life,' we live within specific parameters—that specific Season! We don't know what lies ahead.

When David was an adolescent (immature), he lived within the Season of Youth—just being a young man was more than enough. When David was Fifty-five, he'd moved past Youth—Through to the next season [whatever it may have been thought of then] to what was nearer to being considered old age then than it is now. Now David had a 'Jaded Vision' [World-Weary Vision].

Let's look into what '*How Green <u>Was</u> My Valley*' presents as a Book, Film, and TV Series. Richard Llewellyn, Author of the Novel—.

How Green Was My Valley is a nineteen thirty-nine fictional production by Richard Llewellyn—was circulated as the book version and recounted by Huw Morgan for the film version. His primary personality was his Welsh family and the digging district in which they lived. Llewellyn declared the book to be about his practices; people realized this to be incorrect after his death. Llewellyn was English-born and didn't spend much time in Wales, though he was of Welsh origin. Llewellyn garnered material for the novel from talks with district mining groups in Gilfach Goch.

Wikipedia helped me illustrate the perspective of 'Reflection' we often have about the past— "How Good Things Were In The Olden Days [The Golden Days]." We may have a better chance to form a mental visual about this scenario of 'How Green IS My Valley' in the context of where we are at in life in the present—this is what we know for today.

The opposite picture we may grasp with a genuine sense of reality is when we have messed up, and we may look back and say 'How Green <u>Was</u> My Valley—' in a retrospective look of regret because we may not have followed Victory Road. Depending on whom we serve—God or a host of people of 'so many' ilk's (*varieties*), it's hard to agree on what is right or wrong—What's Good and What isn't So Good Anymore.

When David thought back to The Green Valley—Greener Pastures, "What was he thinking?" Yes, I believe David did look back with regret! I feel he may have been thinking—If Only I Had Heard And Listened To The Voice Of GOD!

"When I'm in *The Valley of Doubt*, very close to 'The Shadow of Death' betimes, God opens my eyes to those Green Pastures—they're oh so inviting. My spirit refreshes by quiet waters—I rest there and then walk the truth trails. Everything is to my advantage and for me to praise God!" (Psalm 23:2)

We observe this verse while living life in 'The Now,' with these promises in hand from a person called a "Man after God's Own Heart." Even after sinning so grievously, "What Are We Thinking Today" about God's decision to hold David out as an example? One way is to learn that we can overcome a 'Bad Lifestyle' and become helpful in the eyes of God by repenting and turning away from this sinful life. It's never time to give up as long as God has the door open for us to come to Him!

The second thing we can learn is that God loves us all and never gives up on the chance we might yet believe His promises and accept Him in The Person of Jesus Christ! There are many more things to learn from God. If we are interested in learning more every day—God will accommodate us: Our part, "Pray and Listen." Praying incorporates speaking to God and waiting to hear what He will say as we are still before Him in His presence.

I ask, "When and How did David come to this confidence that 'The LORD is (was) my (his) Shepherd; I shall not want?'" We often question the validity of the *subject* the writer portrays and the *complement or connection* to the BIG answer—.

From a readers' point of view, the 'subject' may be subjective because we do not acknowledge every situation—"God's Part." David was not perfect; he had his questions about why God didn't answer more clearly at times, rather than letting him face the "Through It All" Seasons of life too!

I'm talking about the substantial impact these six verses of Psalms 23 can have when we connect to God relationally. *The LORD is my Shepherd*; this is the actual 'Subject' of the passage. The 'Complement' and or balance of the words, *I shall not want [or need]* 'completes' the subject by answering the question. What am I saying?

Here it is—David is trying to help us understand by balancing and connecting to the subject by giving it the final touch. The 'Complement,' which I'm attempting to explain for my reader's understanding, is that God is Faithful. The 'Complement' throughout the passage—the list, acknowledges God for His faithfulness without ever saying the words, "Lord, You are Faithful!" In a summarized fashion, the explicit declaration 'IS,' "*The Lord is my shepherd; I shall not want.*" The "Proof Is In The Pudding." The journey of life can express positive results for me throughout my life.

A subject with no complement (answer or balance) is like a falling star—the 'star' is the 'subject.' If there were a 'compliment,' it would be that the 'star' fell on earth and smashed into a thousand pieces. However, if the falling 'star' fell endlessly into a bottomless pit, there would be no 'complement' to form a conversation.

Complements without subjects resemble automobile parts not attached to a car. An idea only merges when the 'complement' joins a definite 'subject.' I read in *Biblical Preaching* by Haddon Robinson that Napoleon had three commands for his messengers that apply to any communicator: "Be clear! Be clear! Be clear!" I pray that I'm in this bailiwick!

Let's survey an example of a 'subject' without a 'compliment.' If while talking to someone in a particular context; *Sports,* for instance, an 'awkward' moment of silence comes about, I say in an out of 'The Blue Moment,' "SKY," what would the response of my listener be— 'DA?'

Then, if we got back to talking 'sports,' would the 'SKY' mentioned moment pass as if never said, or would it remain in the mind of the 'listener?' Would that moment cause the 'Listener' to always look at me somewhat confused about my mental state?

In the above-said scenario, the 'subject' was 'sports,' and the 'Complement' should have come in the rest of the conversation—. In that awkward moment, if I said, 'Sky Sports' can tell us much about what is happening in the Sports World—here is where you can check it out: https://www.skysports.com/roi— I would have kept the scenario of the 'Subject Matter' intact.

In whichever way the subject here follows another 'subject,' a 'complement' needs to be involved in the context of the whole conversation. With a *'previously unexplained context* [the DA Moment]' which now became an issue that needed explaining, the conclusion that we'd had a pleasantly chatted 'moment—' still leaves us with a 'NADA' [Nothing] Moment.

After the subject of 'sports' was mentioned, we would still only have two 'subjects' in a row if I said football. Without some descriptive conversation following the word 'football,' we would still only have a scenario like the falling star into a bottomless pit! "Be Clear! Be Clear! Be Clear!" We always need to finish what we start to accomplish!

Take A Breather

In and of themselves, Green Pastures allow for a worthy cause to break from the pressures of life—Not Life Itself! When we are in holiday mode, and it comes time to take a break from driving, a respite at a cozy Green Fielded Picnic Sight isn't always possible. However, we can either imagine [or not], as if in a Virtual Reality Moment, that the sight is a Green Pasture and make the best of the time we stop. Furthermore, we can acquire the same benefits of Taking A Breather as it would be at A Green Pasture in Reality!

Looking For Greener Pastures—Taking A Break From Life Itself may not always be The Crackerjack (Proficient) Answer to solving our problems. If this is the intent, it's profitable to "Take A Break" from the rush of life to handle our situation to get back to doing life with renewed strength.

THE LORD IS MY SHEPHERD.

When this is the case, we certainly have a Great Resource from which to draw strength—like we are at an Oasis.

I shall not want—The LORD leads me to the Green Pastures so I can rest for a while. When I'm beside the still waters, I realize God brought me there—it's here God refurbishes my soul. Paths of righteousness seem to come my way at just the correct times—I understand that it's for the Glory of God that I'm at these places. When it appears I'm entering The Valley of The Shadow of Death, I can send fear packing! LORD, Your corrective measures are suitable for me because they lead me to the paths of righteousness—on top of this, I'm comforted. Just when I feel You've deserted me, You spread a table of sustenance, You refresh me from head to toe, and I'm overflowing with Your blessings. I know goodness and mercy will follow me all the days of my life—LORD, I will dwell in Your house forever. (Psalms 23; JBI)

[Continued from before our Breather Break—]

The world we live in doesn't always leave clarity on the table. Writing the Complement [Re Subject and Complement status] isn't an option. Transparency is often out of reach because there are so many voices on every issue—often, we send *context* on the run! At the moment, I'm thinking of politics, Covid-19, religion, and living in general—in our world. While studying the life of David and any other person in whatever season of life they've lived, [my question is] was the context any different for them than it is today in the context we live? From what I see of both perspectives, I'd say we could well enough surmise they are the same—Ditto!

David often fell into disarray, chaos, shambles, confusion, and panic—ultimately, the mess he was so often in got him off track. Amongst the diversity [no matter what the degree of it was] of his complaint (the subject), he most often credited the sovereignty of God and His right to *work things according to His plans—this is the 'compliment;' God working out David's complaint.* According to God's will here, David 'simply' said, God—I see how You're always giving me what I need (complement)—maybe not everything I want, but what I most need at the moment. We are prone to paint our needs and wants with the same brush; this is a Colossal Error—the difference between the two is humungous.

As communicators, *we set out to* dissect subject matter—in the end, we should've connected the 'subject matter' to the 'complement.' The Finishing Touch or the Credit for any positive results belong to God. God designed our *purpose* [allowing for *progress*] in the Universe we live in—ours is to follow His Design Pattern as outlined in The Bible. Life's problems always go awry when 'We The People' go off the God-prescribed course.

"The whole dialogue should lay out where we came from (our context—our story) and reveal where we are going. At the end of the day, if it doesn't portray *positive* results, it's not so pretty. The communicator (in this instance—me) should be able to present practical tools whereby the story can change throughout the process. If what happened called for the hurt or death of someone, the method may seem to have ended. However, if the communicator examines and presents the results thoroughly, where the future will have produced a better life for those in the rest of the story—trust the fact that 'clouds may have silver linings.'"

The significant subject matter in *Searching For A Heart Of Gold*, here in Chapter Three, is finding out if we can live in the promise of The Green Pastures of Psalm 23, 'Today,' and for the 'Tomorrow' we cannot yet see! *The life we now live in the flesh—* (Galatians 2:20), as I understand it, speaks to us of an extension of ONE SEASON [The Long-Haul] in one sense. God always has our *preservation* in mind! God's care for us and about us came before we were born—before The Foundations of The Earth. The Four Seasons of Earth Time physically; The Four Seasons of Life as we look at it in an Ethereal Sense [The Spiritual World], are encased in God's timeline. The end of it all is 'endless' [like The Bottomless Pit Scenario—in our sense of it—not God's]; this is the time after our present on earth experience—God's thoughts and ours differ!

The *Long Haul Scenario* is often somewhat hard to understand for us Mere Mortals—if we try to figure out every last detail of the Theory of Everything! In the *Short Haul,* the incremental stages of all the seasons I mentioned (some of them are the making of my crazy thoughts), we can better grasp *things* and *life* as best as we can understand them.

Steven Hawking had his "*Theory Of Everything.*" In "*Brief History,*" he stated, "if we ever discovered a 'theory of everything,' it would be 'the ultimate triumph of human reason—for then, we should know the mind of God.'" "Before we understand science, it is natural to believe God created the universe. But now, science offers a more convincing explanation. By 'we would know God's mind,' I meant that we'd know everything that God would know; if there were a God—there isn't—I'm an atheist.'"

The Long and The Short of it all is that none of us were where the 'Beginning Of Everything began—' none of us has a clue! We think we're smart enough to put together a Great Creation or Evolution Package; however, when push comes to shove—at the end of it all as we know it—Someone other than us will tell the story.

When life throws us a curveball, it's not always so easy to hit it out of the park. Where did David get the fortitude to hit Psalm 23 out of the park? Did he get it back when he was a Shepherd Boy looking after Daddies Sheep? Did David write it after living a season or two? 'I think' he wrote Psalm 23 while in a "Through It All Mode or Moment" in his life. Methinks most of life incorporates these times more often than we realize.

When David stepped back from the plate to plan how he would address the next pitch, I think he did a quick memory check of the last time he was at the plate. With the same pitcher on the mound this time, he determined what pitch he would get, then stepped up, 'took the pitch,' and hit it out of the park. The last time he faced the same situation—it might have had him *unprepared*; he failed to hit the pitch out of the park but struck out miserably—"But This Time, It Was A Different Story!"

We don't always get a second chance to address the catalogue of past failures. However, we can learn from our mistakes. When the next temptation or major challenge requires us to perform better, we beat the odds; we can win if we've been in a *building process* (*preparation*) or on an exercise program that strengthened us to face those significant challenges.

David was a man after God's own heart; it didn't make him any better than the rest of us. However, for the sake of history and God's plan to express certain things to us, I accept the insertion into scripture that "David was a man after God's own heart."

God's *provision* is always enough; it is always intact enough to carry His plans for eternity. God never forgets what He's promised—we are all a part of the package where *He wills* to use us equally as enormously as he did David. David expresses the heart of God in the 23rd. Psalm. In the opening few words, He says, "GOD, LORD, You are enough no matter what I am facing and or going to face throughout my journey." David lived merrily for a time, methinks—in The Green Pastures of Psalm 23.

It's the same for us today as it was for Adam, David, and The Apostle Paul. Thoughts like, "I'm crucified with Christ— nevertheless, I live; yet it isn't about me and my accomplishments; but Christ lives in me—the life I live presently, I live by the 'faith of the Son of God;' it's He that loved me and gave it up for me." Everyone, past, present or future, must have relied on Faith as our source and resource. (Re. Galatians 2:20; KJV& JBI.)

Tucked away almost in obscurity in this passage, as far as our usage of the action of faith lives out in us, is a word we don't like to rely on—FAITH! Paul isn't speaking of our 'Faith' in this passage, but the 'Faith of The Son of God—' It's an incumbent [inescapable] Season of The Seasons of our lives which will carry us through when 'Life Gets Tough,' and when 'Life Is Good!'

You ask—what's the Heart of God?' Glad you asked. God's love is for His creation, like the Shepherd's love for His Sheep. God's love always was for 'His Creation;' when we messed up in the Garden of Eden, God showed us the rest of His plan by pointing us forward (as in the *Forward Focus* article I wrote) to Jesus, Who would show us 'this love' in such a complete way; we couldn't make a mistake of understanding. God Himself sacrificed Himself for us on a 'miserable cross' [not His words but mine]. As we grasp the entire perspective of the plan of God as He formed it, we may get a glimpse of what pans out in the days yet ahead of us.

The cross was a cruel, miserable picture if we look at the shame of God having to do it this way to get our attention. In Hebrews 12, we see Jesus experiencing the chagrin of the cross because He saw the joy that would be the outcome of it all. Psalm 23 paints such a graphic picture of *provision*. If we can capture the full extent or scope of the thoughts of the scene sketched out in this Psalm as if in a video presentation, we'll be overwhelmed. Part of what I talked about a bit ago plays out in the following:

> "The whole dialogue should lay out where we came from (our context—our story) and reveal where we are going. At the end of the day, if it doesn't portray *positive* results, it's not so pretty. The communicator (in this instance—me) should be able to present practical tools whereby the story can change throughout the process. If what happened called for the hurt or death of someone, the method may seem to have ended. However, if the communicator examines and presents the results thoroughly, where the future will have produced a better life for those in the rest of the story—trust the fact that 'clouds may have silver linings.'" (*IBID*)

"Where Are You From?" 'This is a good question for getting to know someone.' If we keep stepping back to 'scene after scene' of history; all the experiences endured over time while believing we would never survive the day; we'll be in the same picture David was in before he wrote Psalm 23. David did not wake up one morning and notice 'Someone' was looking at Him with eyes of love, just because he was so handsome or pretty. David came out of the same history that the rest of us did—only he faced it before us. Might we keep our eyes open to the "Before and After" of living.

The Garden of Eden is the primary life placement we received at our entry point into what could've been a Garden of Perfect Peace for eternity for us all and for all time. We've all had the same heritage—Adam and Eve. By taking a step back from the plate, into the placement of wherever God has continuously resided—we should realize He was not just sucking His thumb, wondering—HMMM, what should I do. In the Heart of God, somewhere so long ago, God already fashioned us before we showed up in the family He began in the Garden of Eden.

By looking at the 23rd Psalm, we see so much in what David wrote—which God told Jacob way back in Genesis; He would watch over him on his many journeys; many of which were not always free of the curveball. Many are other weary pilgrims who knew the hand of God at work when they were facing the tough pitches of life. Life has a way of delivering brutal fastballs to the plate, hoping to strike us out.

As you'll know, if you read The Bible intentionally, David did not run a trouble-free course. He was often in the scenario of being a long-distance runner, where endurance gets more efficiently put to the test—as opposed to a relay race where there's more than just one person racing to get the prize. Each runner has a leg to run; in the proper order, they pass off the baton for the next runner to do their part—freeing each participant in the race from the stress of needing the endurance to run a mega race alone!

It is easier running alone in shorter races. David shows us pictures of himself in the mode of the Victories he accomplished—showing us pictures of when he was running for his life. David displays images of himself playing the "POOR ME CARD!" Like Jacob—David was as human as we are today!

I discovered the creativity of thought within me for reasoning through some Psalms. Most of the time, those of a particular value come as my first thrust from Psalm 139—where I see God already knew about me from before He created anything concrete [not as literal concrete].

As I look at the opening verse of Psalm 139, I'm somewhat perplexed—until I realize people made of mud are the authors of the words written here. I wonder why the first verse presents the perspective of the thoughts David wrote about God in what I see as a reverse order from what the scriptures do in other places.

I don't question these words— "all scripture is given by the inspiration of God." I accept the scriptures as the writers wrote them at God's will. While penning the words of the 139th Psalm, verse one, David was praying to God. God understands our frailty. I believe God Himself straightens out what seems to us as if it were a winding path as we express our thoughts as the imperfect humans we are. A straight 'pathway' is much easier to maneuver. Many of life's meanderings pan out as if as *'crooked as all get out!'*

God comes back at us with His Heart to say He understands us better than we do ourselves. The more I come to understand this full relational character of God, the more intimacy I feel as I 'Search for Him.' Psalms 23; 139; 51—and many more passages come alive in the world of life—I often miss them when I don't crave the presence of God for every part of my life and what I need!

"O LORD, You've searched for me, found me, and You're infatuated with me." (Psalms 139:1; slightly rephrased; JBI)

When I consider how David expresses himself as he talks to God, just like he would to his audience (us); just letting out what was in his heart; I understand things better. When David wrote whatever he did write, I wonder if he even knew we would call what he wrote 'a book.' Like me or any other writer, I think David just needed to vent what was 'penned' up (written on his heart) within his spirit. These things can become lengthy and taxing at times.

The thoughts we [writers] have seem so big when they are in our 'hearts of hearts,' so we look for as many expressions as possible to put on paper. We do so to be sure our audience will get the message we feel is imperative to the eternal health of humanity: We need to get the picture—RIGHT?

My motivation might differ somewhat in focus or scope from my thoughts in this dialogue if they were in the setting of an author who has no spiritual or religious inclinations. It may or may not be related to how much money or recognition they may get; this may or may not be the motive for their endeavours—Who am I to judge.

However, I still believe every author has something possibly buried deep within their being, which they need to express. God gave us each a unique character, or somehow, as if magical, we just received and or developed a uniqueness which can impede us— puzzle us betimes (on occasion)—[Something to think about].

Imagining such intricacies without fitting a designer into the picture isn't an easy matter to understand. We write so many words in many books and other means of expression to *clarify* the magnitude of what All Of Creation offers us finite beings. Should we try to grasp the scale of Psalm Twenty-Three's author's demands because 'they' [whoever they are] say it is part of The Bible; everyone knows the Bible is God speaking to us feeble-minded folk at times—finite (limited) humans—Right?

I'm heading towards dissecting Psalms 139, laying out every possible piece of the body of thought on a massive table in this passage. While I allow everyone to pull up a chair to join me in the process (I look for Progress), I face the mega challenge of bringing as much clarity to the table as is 'humanly thinkable.' As if there is not enough on the table to digest, I pull out another table and add more food for thought for us to consume. I'll try to initiate connective references to many other portions of The Bible in this manner. Would you please look for 'Subject (object) and Complement (explaining)' ideas!

Psalms 139 should not feel left out of what God intended to bring to His Banqueting Table for the *entirety* of eternity. Let's not miss the whole point of why God even bothers with us, whom He made from dirt. We may miss the point of why God didn't end it all concerning us as far back as The Garden of Eden if we don't give God the time of day. God loved us before He made anything.

The way I see it, GOD could've had David write the words, I LOVE YOU PEOPLE; up and down over the whole Chapter of Psalm 139—we'd still not understand ALL of Who and What God Is! Am I biting off more than I can chew? Believe it or not, I have a plan—[Martin Luther King said, "I have a dream!"]

On my *motivational trek* [as if on a route to run a race], I wish to pace myself by including part of Psalm 1 as a 'bite-sized' morsel, treating it as 'one serving' on God's spread-out Banqueting Table.

Blessed are those who don't walk as though counselled by those who don't care about God and His Counsel—by standing in league with them and their evil desires—but they delight in the law of the Lord—they meditate on His law day and night.

These folks shall be like a tree planted by the rivers of water that bring forth fruit in their season of fruitfulness; these folks shall not faint—and they will prosper in the context of what God considers prospering.

The immoral people aren't like this—they're like the chaff which the wind driveth away. So, the ungodly shall not stand in the judgment, nor sinners in the righteous congregation. The Lord knows the way of the righteous; the course of the wicked shall perish. (Psalm 1:1-6; JBI)

> Dearly beloved, I wish above everything that you would prosper and be healthy to the extent that your soul prospers. (3 John 2:2; somewhat revised; JBI)

Please don't get the idea that I'm trying to rewrite the whole Bible or the whole Book of Psalms. I never intend to do this; I wish to present things as if God invited us to a 'Taste Testing' event. The taste testing example isn't to see which food groups of the world of The Bible are better than the other. We are not trying to say that if you like Psalms better than Leviticus or Numbers or any other book of The Bible, only read or study those.

As I see it, "all Scripture is God-breathed," through faithful servants who came to understand God as being the Ultimate Source of Creation. What He made will suffice for us; this is what we need to understand. The Taste Test, as I use it here, sets out as an example to see what the offerings are and come to realize how we can use said same, so we can become the best we can become for God's *purpose* on this earth—not to determine how we can bend and fit God's Word to suit our SELFIE desires. As we begin to see *Progress* on our Walk With God, we'll also see God's hand of Preservation at work!

I understand that David wrote about half of the one-hundred and fifty Psalms. We credit some Psalms to other writers; this is the case in Psalm One. 'Anonymous' gets the nod or accreditation for this Psalm. Here's me, 'Just Thinking Again;' I'm wondering 'IF,' because God called David "a man after His own heart," the importance of what David says in the Psalms he wrote is necessary, and as a result of this, suggesting the other Psalms are not. Just remember, 'I'm Just Surmising.' In some places, I'm just putting it out there for you to decide how you'll deal with life yourself!

However, what I'm feeling [*and I strongly mark these thoughts as only my subjective thoughts*] is that God set out a course of events, which David lays out as somewhat of what a Relay Race runner does. In a 'Relay Race,' runners are taking part in a middle-distance race—the distances vary for different events of this sort. The Relay Race does challenge our beliefs about the endurance factor people can manage in the race.

The runners pace themselves for shorter distances in the Relay Race, running faster than a long-distance runner. In long-distance races, the runners start slower than they will 'press towards' as they get nearer the end of the race; they're conserving their energy to FINISH THE RACE.

Throughout Chapter Three—I think of how God always *preserved us who believed in Him*—trusting that He's always enough for every situation.

"With this thought in mind, please remember that God loved and still loves the Whole of Humankind as well—it's our choice as to whether or not we want to be a part of the package God offered and still makes available to everyone!"

Throughout the First Three Chapters, I've been stressing—not stressing out, Three Themes, inclusive of all the rest of what I've laid out.

Preparation
Purpose
Progress
—NOW—
Chapter Four will house my Fourth Theme—

PRESERVATION

Would you please think back to T*he Beginning* of This Book—
STEEPLECHASING!
[Re-Read It If Necessary!]

◊ THE VISTA VIEW—THE OASIS ◊

We don't often enough recognize other people for their contribution to life. In the broader sense—the World Scene, it's understandable because few people position themselves to know what we did unless we do something out of the ordinary in the public exposure sense. Few people can even realize how life-changing it was for someone else when we did 'That Little Something' for a neighbour, a friend, a casual acquaintance, or a host of other folks— kindness is a tremendous tool.

It's easy for us to load up recognition on Singers, Actors, Politicians (maybe), Preachers of Renown, Orators of many sorts, Book Writers (not all, but many)—the list is massive. We certainly know about it when there is a Mass Murder, a Major Criminal Act, and those trying to deal with the Pandemic (Covid-19)—again, the list is too long to detail for every available situation.

However, where it matters in the 'Big Picture,' in the Eternal Sense, it's the 'One-On-One' stories that few people know about apart from those closely involved. Isn't this where we have the best chance to make a difference in someone else's life?

The Bible tells us to 'Love God with all we have within us.' In Second Place, we are supposed to love our neighbour as much as we love ourselves. As we look out over The Green Pastures of Life, each of us needs to put ourselves in Third Place in the Order of Things; this way, we can know we are on track with God's will and *Purpose* for Planet Earth and its people. These are not my words; The Bible bears this out. When investing in someone else's life, we shouldn't broadcast it for all to see and hear, how Great A Thing We Did! (Philippians 2:4; Matthew 22: 35-40)

I get it; we need to spend some time in The Green Valley. When The Holy Spirit coaxes us to walk with God and sit by the still waters, He'll refresh us in our walk with God. When we yield to the leading of The Spirit of God and follow the *Paths of Righteousness, for His Name Sake*, God keeps the Shadow of Death *at bay*. Our enemies cannot get 'In Our Face' to destroy any chance we have of Hope and Victory over the Hard Parts of living life day-to-day!

THE LORD IS MY SHEPHERD!

What do we realize when we take a good look at the makeup of a Shepherd? Shepherds concerns themselves more in detail for the safety of their sheep—in most cases, the picture of a Shepherd suggests they would give their lives to protect their flock—this is the kind of Shepherd Jesus is!

At least a hundred or more Scriptures tell us about the Shepherds of The Bible—and they tell us about shepherds who'll be with us even today in the World of The Church Era. John Chapter 10 is one of the best representations of what a true Shepherd portrays. The most significant passage in John 10, as far as I'm concerned, is verse eleven—

"I Am the Good Shepherd: the Good Shepherd gives His life for the sheep." (John 10:11; KJV)

Unless we *progress* along life's journey—we might say the word shouldn't exist—we'd all remain as we were born. If this were the case, Me-thinks God might not exist—and this is a harsh thought for me because I believe that God Does Indeed Exist. We know that we never remain as we were when the mother's womb freed us to have an authentic look at life; after so carefully looking out for life inside the womb. The mother, the caregiver, gave herself to do what comes naturally because The Life-Giver, The Great Shepherd, began *Preserving* life even then, so it would continue making progress after the birth.

Life Is All About Moving Forward—!

Shall We Do The Same As We Look To Chapter Four!

HEART SENSE

Comfort Ye, Comfort Ye My People, Saith Your God.

———————————————◊———————————————

SPEAK YE COMFORTABLY TO JERUSALEM, and cry unto her, that *she accomplished her warfare*, that *she got a pardon for her iniquity*: for she hath received of the Lord's hand double for all her sins. The voice of him that crieth in the wilderness, *Prepare* ye the way of the LORD, make straight in the desert a highway for our God.

Every valley shall be exalted, and every mountain and hill shall be made low: and the crooked shall be made straight, and the rough places plain: And the glory of the LORD shall be revealed, and all flesh shall see it together: for the mouth of the LORD has spoken it. The voice said, Cry. And He said, What shall I cry? All flesh is grass, and all the goodliness 'thereof' is as the flower of the field: The grass withereth, the flower fades: because the spirit of the LORD blows on it: *indeed* the people are grass. The grass withereth, the flower fades—but the Word of our God shall stand forever.

O Zion, that brings good tidings, get up into the high mountain; O Jerusalem, that brings good tidings, 'lift' your voice with strength; lift it 'up' be not afraid; say unto the cities of Judah, Behold your God! Behold, the Lord God will come with a strong hand, and His arm shall rule for Him: behold, His reward is with Him, and His work before Him. He shall feed His flock like a shepherd: He shall gather the lambs with His arm, carry them in His bosom, and gently lead those with young.

(Isaiah 40: 1-11; KJV)

<u>Led By The Shepherd</u>
<u>[The Preservation]</u>
Scriptures In Chapter Four
Psalm 78; Psalm 23
Psalm 78:1-52
Psalm 78:65-72
Psalm 1: 1-6; Psalm 1
Psalm 1:1-3; Psalm 51; Psalm 139:1-18
Psalm 139:19-22; Psalm 23;
Psalm 139:19-22
John 10:27; Hebrews 5:12-13
Matthew 22:34-40; Matthew 7; Luke 5
Job 38
Psalm 139: 23-24; Psalm 139; Job 38-40; Psalm 23
The Vista View—The Oasis
Psalm 139:1-3

Chapter Four

Led By The Shepherd

WE'VE LOOKED AT SOME OF PSALM 23—
taking some of it apart piece by piece, but the
end has not yet become 'Total Insight' as we begin Chapter
Four, *Led By The Shepherd*. We've 'sighted' many particulars
of this passage—yet the end is not 'In Sight—' The depth of
'Knowledge' and 'Insightful' helps often remains
undiscovered. We've weaved through *Preparation, Purpose,
Progress,* and now, [—The Preservation—].

Would you please look at Psalm 78 (JBI—Jacob Bergen Insight
Version)? The Scriptures to follow are in my words and thoughts as I
glean from the King James Version—don't take them to be the
actual KJV by the author of Psalm 78. As we read scripture, we all
think about what the Scripture means for us in the day we live now,
keeping the *context* of Scripture intact—This Is My Prayer!

However, to stay true to the *context*—we shouldn't think
God said something He Did Not Say. Many thoughts flood my mind
as I write—this is the challenge of most writers. We try to bring in
a Bird's Eye View like that of an Eagle, who has one of the keenest
eyesight of all birds—this is the vantage point I hope to use as best
I can to transfer thoughts of scripture; that I tag as "JBI."

Listen-Up Folks—We need to Perk up our ears. We need to
notice what's going on in the life around us, with an eye open to
what may lay ahead of us as is needful to live life successfully!

I'll be speaking in and about tones, mental hues, varieties of
characters, and pictures so we can get the most up-to-date
information available. If we Listen Up, the past will become the
present for us in so far as giving us sufficient INSIGHT to be able
to confront and or manage whatever jumps out of the bush to halt
our *Progress*. Adversity often strikes in a moment while we move
about nonchalantly—.

We shouldn't hide all God has done, is doing, and yet is planning to do in our day. The things we learn from our children, grandchildren, and great-grandchildren are rewarding. God's strength and beautiful words stand out plainly; for this, we will Praise God All The Days of Our Lives in the hope that the generations following us will also continue remembering God and never cease to Praise Him Always as *they* walk in His ways.

God established His presence in the People of The Past—Abraham, Isaac, Jacob—He expected they would pass the torch to those who would live after them. God has done all this and more, so all people everywhere would not forget Him and how He made way for them in places they would otherwise have feared beyond the measure of being fit to travel. He made His will and Laws clear, so the responsibility is ours.

God noticed when many of the past generations were a little stubborn, and in fact, they were often obstinate and inflexible—so He used desperate measures to change their minds. Their hearts of unbelief often deterred them from following God's ways—this was to their detriment, loss, and injury.

Ephraim, armed and so-called ready, turned and ran away on the day of conflict—they broke their bond with God and balked at walking with God. They quickly forgot the wonders God performed with and for them—down the line, down through the land of Egypt.

When Israel came up against their enemy at the Red Sea, with Pharoah hot on their heels, God opened up the Sea. God dried up the ocean floor so they could manage their steps without dragging their feet through mud—allowing them safe passage to the other side, even though they sometimes thought the wall of water would come crashing down upon them!

As they looked behind them, this same water came down on Pharaoh's hordes [army], which for a time gave the people a heart of thanksgiving. God provided a cloud to lead them during the day—at nighttime, He lit the way for them with a pillar of fire, as if led by a tour guide. How much more intense could life have been in favour of God's way! God held nothing back while He showed His love for them.

While these folks were in the wilderness, God split the rocks so the people could draw water from deep down, as well; He caused water to run like a river for them to be satisfied—not leaving them dehydrated. Then, as if God would have killed them off by hunger, they bent God's wishes and will out of context; they continually complained and went against God's laws. They taunted God, doubting He could supply their wants and needs—the thirst for their needs should have exceeded the lust of their heart.

God was angry, but He still supplied food and water—but the people's taste buds remained unsatiated by God's gift of sustenance according to His dietary plan. When He gave them bread, they wanted meat— 'The Story Never Ends'—so it seems. The folks never reasonably believed God had their best interest at heart, so they didn't trust He would save them from their enemy and might I add, keep them from themselves.

God taught them a lesson from time to time for the good of the whole. He killed off the "Fat Cats" (pardon the possible intolerance, no offence intended); even this didn't deter the people from distrusting God; they continued their diatribe of sinful lusts for forty years in the wilderness. (Psalm 78 1-52; JBI)

In their own hands, 'Trouble Followed Them Like A Plague.' After many got killed, they returned for a time, so to speak [as if this was true repentance, it doesn't look like it to me]. Because it seemed like they said the proper thing's tongue in cheek, they flattered God with their mouths, but their heart was not right—they were a bunch of Flip-Floppers. They openly acknowledged God as the "Rock of Their Defense," their Saviour, when they were in 'Big Trouble!'

Even amid all the STUFF these folks pulled—here's God, reaching out His arm of 'Strength and Compassion' when the next wave hit them square in the face. He, being the loving God He is, forgave them. He didn't eradicate them—though they deserved payback. God remembered they were only human; they needed reminding from time to time—nothing has changed; we are in the same boat. When the disciples were on the Raging Sea, their Faith was also weak. Let's not point the finger at these folks; we are no different! Dottie Rambo wrote *Remind Me, Dear LORD*! Let me remind you of a few things she said in her lyrics.

In effect, Dottie says she considers as precious—the things she loves as only on loan—she does not claim ownership. God (Jesus) only let her use them to refresh her days. Dottie tells the LORD to remind her from time to time. [God does Remind us!]

As per Dottie's request, The LORD reminded her to remember from time to time how He sustained her. We all need to remember whence we came from and look forward to where we'll finish. The LORD reminded Dottie she is only still human; humans still forget to be thankful at times.

Dottie acknowledges she has done nothing of merit to be worthy of the grace and mercy of God—Jesus's scars which He chose as a part of the *Via Dolorosa: The Way of The Cross*! Jesus died here in our place, leaving us with the hard-to-understand challenge of, "Why Did He Consider Us So Valuable?"

Once again, Dottie sounds out from her sounding board, "LORD, I'm just human, I'll forget you unintentionally from time to time—So when you remind me, LORD, I'll try to take it to heart—even when it hurts.

So God led these folks [Israel] of the past, safely along 'Life's Road,' on the journey of a Lifetime Through The Wilderness, as they continually asked Him to "Forget Them Not—" and, God Didn't Forget Them! He repeatedly defeated their enemies—and DITTO, 'Same Old, Same Old' raised its ugly face more often than it should have, just like those who had travelled that road before them—their ancestors. (JBI)

"After the people (sometimes I'm tempted to use this term loosely—because 'The People of God' didn't demonstrate their alliance or allegiance with God very well) angered God, through disobedience, He took action to bring them back to Himself. God always forgave them—providing hope. People are inconsistent; this wasn't the last time they fled God's presence for what their enemies offered!

God's leadership decisions brought an excellent view of being a 'God Follower.' He focused on the tribe of Judah—chose David, His servant from the 'sheepfolds—he'd proven to be a 'Good Shepherd.' God fed 'His People' because of the integrity of His heart. Throughout the term of these times, God guided them skilfully through the rough." (Psalm 78 65-72; JBI)

BOOK ONE (Psalms 1: 1—41; 13). In Book One of the Psalms, the authors worship God for His fairness. They convey their trust in God's empathy, report the immorality of civilization, appeal to God for acquittal, ask God to save them from their foes, voice the purity of the absolved offender, and describe God as a shepherd. We should reverence God with the same common sense of adulation learned in these Psalms. We'll find a running Theme of Life's Two Roads as we offset the life cycle of the devoted individual with the life of the unfaithful beings. Anonymous is the Author of Psalms 1, and it looks like this—

Blessed are those who don't walk as though counselled by those who don't care about God and His Counsel—by standing in league with them and their evil desires—but they delight in the law of the Lord—they meditate on His law twenty-four seven. These folks are like a tree planted at the water's edge—bearing fruit in the appropriate season; they don't faint—they'll prosper in what God considers prospering.

The morally wrong people aren't like this—they're like chaff taken in the gusts of the wind. So, the depraved won't survive God's judgment, nor will wrongdoers (sinners) in the righteous flock. The LORD knows those in the 'upright path;' the wicked person's way will pass away. (Psalm 1:1-6; JBI)

As I'm *Searching For A Heart of Gold*, I won't elaborate or concentrate too much on Psalm 1. However, I want to leave behind a pointer to connect with Psalm 139. I have so much to share throughout The Bible—it's hard to capsulize any one Scripture.

"People who don't associate wrongfully with people who have no use for God—experience the blessings of God. If we don't sit with ridiculers, our lives will also know God's blessings. The other side of the coin sounds like this: Ungodly folks are like chaff wafted in the wind. So, the wicked shall not survive punishment at God's judgment seat, neither will sinners endure in the crowd of the blameless." (Psalm 1; JBI)

I see a separation factor as an invisible insertion—our world houses people who believe in God and those who don't. Some folks believe in the fact of God but don't acknowledge Him in the day-to-day—including The Person of Jesus Christ.

The day-to-day operation calls for a "Relationship With God;" this ties us together with Psalms like—Psalms 1:1-3, Psalms 51, Psalms 139—and a host of other scriptures which say there are benefits we can all have. However, the Garden of Eden shows us we each have a choice as to whether or not we want to be bothered with what it requires to have a personal, moment-by-moment relationship with the God of all creation. The Jesus factor separates the "Relationship Factor" we call becoming a Christ Follower and the other side of the coin. We cannot cash into the benefits promised to Christ Followers when we aren't Christ Followers.

"LORD, You've examined me and understood me. You reach beyond my path and where I lay down and are acquainted with all my ways. There's nothing I can think to say that You don't already know. You've gathered all around me with the whole force of Who You are—and laid Your hand upon me. Such knowledge is too incredible for me; it's beyond my understanding.

Where can I go that Your Spirit isn't abundantly present? If I fly upwards to the sky, I've not escaped Your Presence. If I seek to sleep in hell—*Wonder of Wonders*, You're waiting for me. If I leave in the morning to disappear seaward, You're already there, and You lead me back to where I was already safe in Your Arms. I'm held safely in Your hands wherever I am.

If I think I can hide in the darkness of the night—a miracle comes to save the day—You turn on the Light! Don't I know it? I can't even have a time-out anymore—or so it seems. "Why would I even want to hide from You, LORD!" Darkness and Light are equal in Your Orbit. You got the reins—You had it covered in my mother's belly!" (Psalm 139:1-13 JBI)

"I'll praise You—You created me with outstanding loving care; Your works are Wonderful—I know well how You are. My substance didn't hide from You when You fashioned me in a secret place and shaped me curiously where no one else could see. Your eyes saw my essence (real meaning) while I was still lacking. You recorded all of me in Your Book. You made me precisely according to Your best-case scenario.

How priceless are Your thoughts towards me, how significant are Your reflections about me, LORD! I cannot count high enough to count Your Blessings on me. After a sound sleep, I'm still with YOU." (Psalm 139: 14-18; JBI)

I wonder why The Psalmist changes pace here after the first eighteen verses in Psalm 139—at verses 19-22! Why? Why? Why? For eighteen verses David, who was The Shepherd Boy in his early years—now a grown man—is the leader of a nation of people (as best I understand the chronology, [history] of his life). It's tough to determine precisely when David wrote Psalm 23. I believe (this is just my thought) that David wrote this Psalm later in life while he reminisced during some tough-sledding Seasons of his Life! Maybe it was during this time when he prayed Psalm 139.

In these eighteen verses, David acknowledges God's supremacy—realizing the AWESOMENESS of God! In Psalm 23: 1-3, he seems to make an open, public acknowledgement of the power of God to be what he talks about in Psalm 139. Then in Psalm 23: 4-5, he speaks directly TO God; David always seems to express a 'Reliance' or 'Trust' factor in Psalm 23 and Psalm 139 and many other places.

In Psalm 139: 19-22, as per my observation, there's a picture of David 'Thinking He Has To Help God Out' by saying, "God, I Feel Sorry For You!" In this short moment, it's like David doesn't understand the 'Ultimate Supremacy of God—' that All By Himself, God Can Deal With The Issues The Wicked Present!

These passages remind me of Peter in the Garden Of Gethsemane. Here, I sense Jesus experiencing the 'Darkest' moments of His life on earth [When Jesus didn't turn on the Light of Deliverance], as He feels the absolute depth of what it means to take on All EARTHLY SIN—For All Earthly Time. Here Peter feels He can help Jesus through this challenging time by taking up the fight—beginning by cutting off the ear of one of Jesus's oppressors.

Jesus, 'God—' Knowing what He had to do to secure a place for fallen humanity to experience redemption (saving them from themselves), was capable of handling whatever it took to battle the evil forces of humankind, no matter how intense they were. A while later, not too long after the Garden Of Gethsemane moment, Peter also denied even knowing Jesus—The Big Flip Flop; we, only being humans, do this too!

By deciphering these Psalms for myself and grasping the enormity of—Who God is, I can logically express what's in my heart. The thoughts I write or say are enormous resources for understanding David's heartfelt expression as he sits before God!

BEING LED BY THE SHEPHERD

There's no better place for developing the SEARCH FOR A HEART OF GOLD than in the Psalms of David. With these Vista Views of information, I almost understand how David could insert the following words into what is such a Beautiful Passage in Psalm 139—As 'The Shepherd' was leading him!

LORD, I know You'll kill off the enemy!—Won't You? [I sense a glimpse of doubt!]. LORD, You do know there are Evil Folks out there! They hate You! Yes, David—I realize some folks are hard to deal with in our world. David's reply may be—"These folks get under my skin—!" LORD—I believe I'm justified to have these thoughts. (Psalm 139: 19-22; JBI)

Let's try to get a clear perspective of these words. If we are Christ Followers, we don't like it when people tear down what Christianity represents in its truest sense. When other people talk about what we consider as 'evil,' these people, who don't know God as we do, 'like David' does in the verses above, they, in my opinion, are not looking at the Whole Picture. God created all humankind— and yes, with the intent that all people everywhere should be 'Christ Followers,' but something got in the way.

Sin—in The Garden of Eden changed the course of this intent by God. Does this lessen the Supremacy of God? Does this suggest God made a mistake? We all have so many other questions about the WHYS of what God did and did not do in Creation. If He is God, could He not have done a better job? I don't question the fact of God; many people do. However, the question does surface in the mind of many people—even many God-fearing people.

Even Christians often tear down the Christ Followers who are not like them. We should know better because God tells us in His Word, The Bible, how we should treat all peoples. We do so because of how the people we don't understand—live life. These folks may do things that are against Christian principles. I ask, "Why Would They Not Do Things Other Than What We Believe, Right?" Their fascination with the world [physical or Spiritual] doesn't align with the God they don't know. "Case in point—if I'm a die-hard fan of only one sport—and someone 'Chats Up' another sport with me—I may listen politely, but my heart is not in the chat at hand!"

Being *Led By The Shepherd* is an excellent *possibility* on our part. Frankly, it's not just a possibility—it's a necessity if we call ourselves Christ Followers! The dividing line between being a Christ Follower and not being one—is like dividing light and dark!

> My sheep hear My voice, and I know them, and they follow Me: (John 10: 27; KJV)

There's no more straightforward way to paint this picture! It may sound harsh—and it's not always an immediate action, one as easily embedded into our lives. For instance, if we come from an atheist background (worst case scenario), this New Believer may take some time to grasp what it is all about to be a 'Christ Follower.' The full picture story encompasses the Whole Bible—with illustrations, commands, and examples for us to practice life today.

There are other exceptions to the rule of John 10:27. The Bible also speaks of people who come to believe—become Christ Followers, as being 'Babes.'

> All people don't learn at the same pace; this might be for the good of the whole story—leaving others to be teachers. The plan of God is varied and unique for each season of life we all traverse. Not everyone understands God's Word directly, needing extra help with 'Good and Evil.'(Hebrews 5: 12-13; JBI)

Scripture points a clear path to come to the place of being *Led By The Shepherd.* Those who have been in the Fold for some time have the greater responsibility to understand the process New Believers face and be examples and teachers to those in the first stages of Christianity. (Herein lies the importance of Church and Home Bible Studies).

Not everyone born into the world will become Christ Followers—It's unimaginable to think they will. Often, maybe most often, the concern of non-believers is on what feels right in the context of Tolerance (Acceptance of anything and everything)—no matter if it follows the Christian Principles we are so adamant about living out. We, the 'Christ Followers,' are often as guilty as Sin Too!

I do not mean to be harsh, but the big question is, does 'The Golden Rule' apply to one and all or just to those who care about Godly Values. Matthew 22 34-40 sets out clear principles for 'Life As It Ought To Be.'

"The Sadducees (those who didn't believe in the resurrection of the dead, the existence of spirits, or the duty of verbal beliefs) heard that Jesus silenced the group of people who didn't believe in traditions credited to The Bible (Pharisees), they called a conference. One such person, a lawyer, asked Jesus about the Greatest Commandment in the Law. Jesus replied—You're to love God firstly with everything within you—Secondly, you're to love your neighbour as you would love yourself—this is the sum of the answer to your question." (Mathew 22: 34-40) (IBID)

I realize God also has harsh words for those who don't acknowledge Him for Who He is and what He came and showed us we needed to do to have Eternal Life with Jesus at the end of it all. We have a responsibility to live life as God encourages us to do—as per Matthew 22. But do we have 'A God-Given Right To Tear Down People Who Do Not Believe In Jesus, The message of The Cross—?' I don't think Jesus gives us this right—This Is God's Job! Always! Always! Always! I'm 'Guilty As Sin' more often than I admit. But for the Grace and Mercy of God, I would end up without Eternal Life in The End! They did not build Rome in a day, so how can we expect to Change A World that chose its course selfishly—to now follow God's Route?

In Matthew 7, Jesus said, "Judge not lest you yourselves fall into judgement." Though this is enough to satisfy me, it's not enough for everybody! There is much more in The Bible which lends credence (weight) to this message. Jesus said He did not come to call the righteous, [those who believed], but 'Sinners,' [those who 'do not believe;' Luke 5].

The Bottomline is, no matter what this world looks like to us, in the case of their wrongdoing, the world has got to come to disorder before Jesus comes to bring us into that New Kingdom He promises to believers—according to prophecy. If it doesn't, might we be justified in throwing out The Bible? God is a BIG BOY!—He handled all the detractors of yesteryear (history). In many passages, the Bible assures us that God had every situation in hand, no matter what it looked like to us!

Let's take a peek at what God said to Job when the world he was living in got tough!'

Then the Lord answered Job out of the whirlwind and said, who is this darkened counsel by words without knowledge? Gird up now thy loins like a man; for I will demand of you—I require an answer from you. When God says He needs an answer, I believe He'll get The Answer! As I study The Bible, I see more and more that God's Always in charge!

Where were you when I laid the foundations of the earth? Declare if you have understanding—who was it that measured these foundations—do you even know? Who stretched out their tape measure over the land?

Where is the foundation of the earth fastened? Who placed the cornerstone—when 'the stars of the morning' sang, and the sons of God shouted for joy? Who shut up the sea with doors when it broke forth as if it had issued out of the womb?

When I made the garment's cloud and thick darkness a swaddling band for it— I provided a place for these things and said, 'you must stay within these parameters' you can't venture any further—your relentless waves must stay put!

Have you managed the mornings in your life—as if you could? Did you cause the dawn to know its place; that it might take hold of the ends of the earth, that the wicked might fall out of the land? The land is as clay when one presses it as if making a seal; the earth's imprint now shows itself boldly like when the morning dawns and the light makes everything clear (clear as day!) The wicked don't seem to function because they are still in the dark, and their violent actions are now as if crushed.

Have you entered into the springs of the sea? Have you walked in search of death? Can you see death while you are still alive? Have you even got an inkling of what death is since you are not yet there? Have you perceived the breadth of the earth? Pray, tell Me if you know it all.

Where is the way where light dwells? Job, can you tell Me where the darkness originated? Lead Me to the farthest limits—on the path to the house of the night—if you can?

Job, do you know because you were born then? Or because the number of thy days is significant? Have you entered into the treasures of the snow? The treasures of the hail, are these in your sights? I've reserved these things against the time of trouble, against the day of battle and war.

By what way is the light parted, which scattered the east wind upon the earth? Who divided a watercourse for the overflowing of waters, or a way for the lightning of thunder; to cause it to rain on the planet, where no one exists; or in the wilderness, wherein there are no people, to satisfy the desolate and waste ground, causing the bud of the tender herb to spring forth?

Does the rain have a father? Who has begotten the drops of dew? Out of whose womb came the ice? And the hoary frost of heaven, who made it gender-specific? The waters hide like a stone, and the "face of the deep" is in a deep freeze. Can you bind the sweet influences of Pleiades or unfasten the bands of Orion? Can you bring forth Mazzaroth in his season? or can you guide Arcturus with his sons?

Do you know the ordinances of heaven? Can you set the dominion thereof in the earth? Can you lift your voice to the clouds, that abundance of waters may cover thee? Can you send flashes of lightning that they may go and say to you, here we are?

Who's put wisdom in the inward parts? Or who has given understanding to the heart? Who can number the clouds in wisdom or stay the bottles of heaven when the dust grows into hardness, and the clods cleave fast together?

Will you hunt the prey for the lion or fill the appetite of the young lions when they huddle in their dens and abide in the covert to lie in wait? Who provided for the raven his food—? When his young ones cry unto God, they wander for lack of meat. (Job 38) [I've changed many words to be words I better understand—paraphrased words].

These words from God Almighty to Job in Chapter 38, when he got messed up by all the stuff his friends told him was wrong with him (Job), drew to a close in Chapter 40, with these words from God in Verse 1—"Moreover the Lord answered Job, and said, 'Shall he that contendeth with the Almighty instruct him? He that reproveth God, let him answer it.'"

As I write—as I look to the most reliable source I know of, 'The Bible,' I come away SATISFIED that I can find the ANSWERS to life's most important questions!

So, here I am, right alongside David The Shepherd Boy, David The King, and simply, David, "The Man After God's Own Heart!" Here I am ready to say with David these words as he wraps up Psalm 139, with all the reflections of Psalm 139; possibly Psalm 23; perhaps Job 38-40—and probably many more words at his disposal:

"Search me, O God, and know my heart: try me, and know my thoughts—see if there be any wicked way in me and lead me in the way everlasting." (Psalm 139: 23-24; KJV)

Chapter Three of *Searching For A Heart of Gold* is *"The Lord Is My Shepherd,"* and I lead with Psalms 23: Why?

Psalms 139 is the theme of this book, but it leads us beside the still waters of life, where we begin to understand God in the stillness of those Selah moments which fill the whole of the book of Psalms. I will be in and out of many Psalms, and I will go to Psalms 1 and others to grasp the whole meaning of Psalms 139. *Chapter One* and *Chapter Two* take me to Psalms 23 to begin to walk through the meadows, beside the still waters—and through the rest of God's Creation! I consider Psalm 23 an OASIS, a place we can do a 'Stopover' in the parts of the Journey of Our Lives, which often leaves us wondering 'If God Cares.'

Exegetical, illustrative, or thoroughly instructive studies clarify messages like those of a preacher. They sermonize in churches on Sunday mornings to bring the narrative across to parishioners within *the context* of an hour.

'Because of how I grew up,' I seriously believe God tries to get our attention to duty through The Bible. I believe Jesus is the living, expressed WORD of God for us to look back on to find a reason for living and answer the ultimate questions of time and eternity. The problem lies in the initiation or opening line of all we know as created or fashioned in some format for the possibility of life to become complete.

The other problem questions out like this, "what is the trustable basis we can count on to get us through this life and the next life that most people everywhere believe exists:" In one fashion or another. Yes, many folks believe we live and then die and "That's All She Wrote!" If that's all she wrote, we don't have much to hope for in The Future!

◊ THE VISTA VIEW—THE OASIS ◊

Leadership was always a vital issue throughout HISTORY. Never, since time as we know it, has any generation existed without somebody leading The Pack! Be it humankind or the animal species; some entity always headed a group of people, a herd, a gaggle, a tribe, a Pride of lions, a Coalition of Lions, a School of Fish—some person or animal species always led those who are 'The Followers.' Die-Hard Evolutionists believe we all began as The Animal Species; I Do Not. You Know my take on origins—God created everything! If we learn this early in life, 'Life' will be the best of the best.

In Life, as we know it, we see pictures of being 'Led' in many directions—as we observe the Media Sources of The Day. There are ever only 'Two Sides' to every scenario—one would think Life is either 'Right or Wrong;' 'Black or White;' 'Existent or Non-Existent.' A hundred, seventy-five, fifty, and maybe only twenty-five years ago, who would've thought we would be in a mess of every genre's multi 'rights and wrongs.'

It seems to me that the Melting-Pot of Humanity is a confusing mix of entities, leaving us to believe and choose whether we are human, animal, or spirit versions of some form of being. Children can now Choose to be Female or Male [if there is even such a differentiation of the two anymore] before they are old enough to make rational life-affecting decisions.

Where is the Leadership we need today to get us relevant for Today, Tomorrow, or Eternity? Elections for the Leadership of Countries usually come at defined or designated times on the calendar. Some folks even want sixteen-year-olds to be able to vote.

Being incompetent does not negate a leader's mandate to lead a party or country. Unless they're unable to pass the bills, those they wish to legislate while only having a minority Governing Position, thereby forcing an election. Elections usually occur every four years.

At the best of times—leadership is precarious. It matters not whether the topic of conversation is political, religious, casual [whatever this means], or one of a host of other issues; someone always seems to be LEADING the way; be it along rational lines or down the lines of "Conspiracy Theories" [Whatever they are?].

In the book "*A Tale of Two Cities*," Charles Dickens says,

"It was the best of times; it was the worst of times, it was the age of wisdom, it was the age of foolishness, it was the epoch of belief, it was the epoch of incredulity, it was the season of light, it was the season of darkness, it was the spring of hope, it was the winter of despair." (Charles Dickens, A Tale of Two Cities)

It seems History has survived these fluctuations of Divisions. Have we stayed with these variations of belief, direction, insanity, and rationalization—? I suppose we have a picture of "The Survival of The Fittest!" Are we surmising (assuming) this to be The Survival of The Fittest Leaders to get us from Point A to Point B, but through 'Life' in a fashion of what we may think of as 'Real Living?'

What does REAL LIVING look like anyway? Honest Living is when we honour our Creator; Love our Neighbor as we would have them love us—then look at ourselves as a little less important than we do in what often comes out as The Selfie Mode.

I realize that if we don't look after ourselves physically and articulately in the day-today, we have no hope of assisting life for others. If we lead others 'Down The Garden Path' [mislead them], life for everyone is headed 'Downhill At An Accelerating Speed; For Destruction as The Bottomline!'

One Exception is God! We cannot Lead God Down The Garden Path! God Is God! Always.

O LORD, You have searched me and known me. When I sit down and get up, I know you're always watching over me. You understandest my thought afar off. (Psalm 139: 1-3)

Through The Four Chapters of Part One—We've Hit Four Targets—The Preparation; The Purpose; The Progress, and The Preservation.—These are Key Elements for the entirety of this book! If this is all we realize throughout—Let These Carry The Day!

When we come to this realization; if we come to this realization; we may wish more than anything else to be,

LED BY THE SHEPHERD!

We need to be Led By The Shepherd!

Part Two

Our Heartbeat—God's Heartbeat

"—O MY MOUNTAIN IN THE FIELD—" What you see as a mountain of beauty, and a place of refuge will just be as if it were an empty byway—where you no longer own anything! In this place, you'll feel that you have to pay and keep paying without any benefit for your labours.

If you thought you had an inheritance coming from Me while you had no heart for me—you'd lose that idea soon enough—. You'll serve your enemies—they'll not bow down to you! Why? Because you have sought to be "God" yourselves, I Am angry, and you will forever suffer the consequences! Diatribe.

If you think you have the wherewithal [*resources*] to trust other people instead of Me, *Do It*—and you will fall flat on your face in the end. Instead of prospering, your Booty Bag will be empty, and you'll be as if parched in the desert without an Oasis—A Watering Hole!

Blessed are the folks that trust in Me [The LORD] and whose hope is in Me Alone. These people shall be as a tree planted by the waters, spreading out its roots by the river, and shall not feel the desert heat when it comes. The leaves of this tree shall remain green—it won't be bereft or wanting of water when the drought comes; it'll continue bearing fruit. "If The Tree Is Alive, It Will Bear Fruit."

"The heart is deceitful above all things and desperately wicked: who can know it."

"I Am The Lord! I search everybody's Heart. I try the reins, even giving everyone their dues tailored to their practices, fitting to the fruit of their doings." (Jeremiah 17: 3-10; JBI)

—THIS IS MY HEARTBEAT! *GOD*—

Our HeartBeat—God's HeartBeat?
Scriptures In Part Two Opener
Jeremiah 17:3-10
Heart Sense
Psalm 51: 10-13

HEART SENSE

Lord; Hear My Prayer

———————————◊———————————

CREATE A CLEAN HEART, O GOD, to be a copy of Yours within me. The 'Wonder of You,' created in me, would indeed be A Miracle of completion from my vantage point!

Transform the way I look at life so I'll recognize the durability of Your love, LORD. LORD, the devotion of Your thoughts towards me from before anything You shaped—I long to know this; I want to know You More.

Here's My Heart LORD!

CREATE IN ME A CLEAN HEART, O God, and renew a right spirit within me. Cast me not away from Thy presence and take not Thy Holy Spirit from me. Restore the joy of Thy salvation to me and uphold me with Thy free spirit. Then will I teach transgressors Thy ways, and sinners *will come to know You!* (Psalm 51: 10-13; KJV)

Searching For The Heart
[Take Heart]
Scriptures In Chapter Five
Jeremiah 17:9
Psalm 4: 1-8
Psalm 119
Isaiah 49: 16
Ephesians 1: 4-10
2 Corinthians 12:2
Jeremiah 17:9
Isaiah 6: 5-8
Romans 7: 14-15
Psalm 51: 10-13; Psalm 23; Psalm 1
Psalm 1: 1-6
Psalm 8: 1-9
Psalm 139; Psalm 23; Psalm 1; Psalm 19; Psalm 119;
Psalm 121: 2-4
The Vista View—The Oasis
Isaiah 40:29-31
Heart Sense
Psalm 51: 1-13

Chapter Five

Searching For 'The Heart!'

————————————◊————————————

IN PART ONE, WE LOOKED AT—*The Lay Of The Land*; *Surveying The Land*; *The Lord Is My Shepherd*, and *Led By The Shepherd*.

Now, let's plunge a little farther into 'The Matter Of The Heart!' The King James Bible records "HEART" '884' times. The book of Psalms records the word "HEART" '130' times—this is 14.7058823529% (1 out of nearly seven times. 'Heart' is mentioned in The Bible; it's in The Psalms) of all '884' references in The Bible. They say there are 783137 words in the KJV. So this tells us HEART is mentioned 0.0165999053% of the time out of all the words in the KJV. So, if and when we are interested in studying THE HEART, not only or necessarily the blood-pumping organ in the physical body, but the HEART which Jeremiah talks about— *Take Heart!*

"The heart and soul is dishonest beyond all ideas, and frantically sinful: who can know it?" (Jeremiah 17:9; JBI)

The above reference to the Heart isn't necessarily naturally positioned—just as evident to me is that not all the mentions of the Heart in The Bible say the Heart is always in disrepair as it seems the LORD presents as a rant in Jeremiah Seventeen.

If we miss the context of what someone is talking about in whatever dialogue they are addressing any subject, whatever it is— in this case, 'It's The Heart,' we often tend to end up with troublesome conversations or negotiations about Right and Wrong!

Please—Let's look at a few references to the 'Heart' in The Psalms. Many of them will overlap in context anyway, but I want to look at some of them; I often present Scriptures as JBI—*Jacob Bergen Insight*, not the actual KJV words. I'm not trying to lessen the impact of the original—'Please read them for yourselves in the version you read.' My thoughts are just that— "My Thoughts!"

"Please listen to me LORD when I talk to You—O God (sounds to me like a plea of despair because David in Psalm 3 was running away from his sin because his son didn't have pleasant thoughts about his dad). You're 'just' (fair-minded). You've always been there for me when I was in trouble—come alongside me again NOW; I especially need for You to LISTEN-UP and hear what is in my HEART." (Psalm 4:1; KJV)

In a moment of reflection, David seems to be hearing God say—I look around at the people you're worried about, and I see they're only interested in themselves; all they do is speak harshly against ME! Many are vain—useless, pointless, and hopeless; many are liars. I Am on your side David because you're a man after MY HEART. (Psalm 4: 2-3) (Selah—a pause—*Take Heart when you feel down*)

"David, come to grips in your own 'Heart,' with WHO I AM—Live Right, don't take up with those living against My will or purpose, and the things 'I Say.' Make the right decisions in your *spirit*, not only because of what other people say you should do. When you're awake in the wee hours of the night, meditate (think about) on ME, and you'll be at PEACE about what seems to be coming apart all around you." (Psalm 4: 4-6; KJV)

As David ambled mentally and emotionally on The Presence of The LORD, he grasped the awesomeness of WHO GOD IS! He said God made him *glad* he was a 'God Follower!' 'He understood that his HEART was so full of God, more so than when the prosperity of the whole country enriched him! (Psalm 4:7)

Peace and sleep will both come as I lay down at night after a day of labouring because *YOU, LORD Alone, make* me dwell in safety. (Psalm 4: 8; JBI)

Do the words in Psalm 4 suggest David is on the verge of a Heart Attack amid life's difficulties? The challenges of life are something everybody needs to live through at one time or another. We only realize how to get *through* [by going through] the hard times; by exercising Hope, Faith, and Trust in God! If our "Heart Attack" is such, it changes our inner person to be the *person* God created us to be—in His Image— "LG!" Life Is Good!

One of The Psalms, which is very important when we wish to see what a HEART in the right relationship with God looks like— is Psalm 119. This chapter introduces us to 22 sections of eight verses each, totalling 176 verses—giving us a colossal insight into the process of fashioning 'Our Heart' to be more like the 'Heart of God!' I'll not continue itemizing some of the Psalms that target words surrounding the 'Heart.' However, I intend to get into more of these moments David spent with his LORD. The Psalms are full of resources for encouraging us to persist in Faith.

Firstly—let's consider [in a devil's advocate scenario, which is a reality to many folks] "God does not exist; He never did." If this were the case, and God didn't ever live—nor does He exist today, we need to frame a different pattern of events, giving us an absolute platform explaining our source—"'Nothing' isn't a great explanation!" For now, let's say we always existed.

The Laws of Thermodynamics are three, and the first suggests 'the amount of matter never changes within a closed system.' It may mean there are many such systems, but within each one, what we got at the beginning of that beginning began, is what it will remain to be for as long as that system exists [WYSIWYG].

The energy within the closed system can't rise, drop, restore itself to double the amount, or be destroyed—the amount always remains stationary. The entity (thing) we know as energy can change its shape, character, and form from solid to liquid and gas, but the volume remains the same. We can all agree on this Law whether or not we believe in God. The First Law of Thermodynamics is The Law of Conservation.

The Second Law of Thermodynamics states, 'the entropy (randomness, unsteady state, information) of any isolated system always increases.' What is 'entropy?' "A lack of order or predictability; gradual decline into disorder." The amount or value doesn't change within a closed system [looking at the system as being like a sealed clear globe]—self-sustaining; laws for this were always there, or 'Someone' or something made it that way: It Is Just The Way It Is! If everything resided in this system, the solar system, earth, vegetation, water, animals, people—entropy in its own right, over time, would change everything from being what it was into being another form of energy: Gas—but could never revert to 'nothing.'

The Third Law of Thermodynamics shows us a picture of what happens when the temperature is at absolute zero—the entropy or disorder in a closed system is held intact.

I think of the First Law as being—God created the whole thing; He made the whole lot run in a clockwork fashion so we could handle living life effectively—in an orderly manner. What God made was 'all' contained within a set circumference, or a border controlled by gravity to keep the whole shebang in its proper place—to keep us active in the right perspective: The Universe— 'a closed system.'

The universe consists of the heavens and all they contain: Sun, Moon, Star, Galaxies, Planets, Land, Vegetation, Animals, People—Everything! Try placing the universe on or in a measuring device to imagine proportion. Imagine it to be one only 'A God' could bring into order and melt it down to a gaseous or liquid form, even to an invisible energy form. This energy would weigh in the same as if everything in the universe were in the created format—The First Law of Thermodynamics. The First Law is a Law of Conservation. What God made He'll look after throughout *earth time* and eternity. Believe It Or Not! To believe anything anyone tells us is challenging in 'Today's World!' "Doubt First; prove it to me, and I may believe what you say!—This Is Our World!"

God made the rules within an order—to be obeyed by everyone. He did it in the 'Garden of Conservation—' 'The Garden of Eden—' A picture of the First Law of Thermodynamics. God didn't call it this; he said, "Here's Everything You'll Ever Need." It'll be good if you don't break 'My Law.' *Question For You*— Would 'Entropy—(a move to disorder)' exist if we hadn't sinned? Personally—I Don't Think So!

Breaking The Law of God here in this Garden broke the Law of Order intended by God; it didn't break The Law of Conservation [Preservation]; God controls this. People suffered the consequences of violating this law, known as The Second Law of Thermodynamics; God never called it this. He explained it more simply—He just said, "The moment you disobey 'My Law,' you will SURELY DIE!" So what we know as 'Entropy,' 'Disorder,' came to be: God did not call it Entropy; God called it the death of the order and consistency we would rather have had. God Called What He Intended— Very Good! [Take Heart when life's tough!]

I'm no 'Scientist,' *this is clear*. God's The Scientist; this is not clear to most of us. If and when we get to the place of understanding Who God is, IT WILL BE VERY GOOD!

The Third Law of Thermodynamics was God's idea, not ours; it describes 'ETERNITY' and everything else. When this time as we know it comes, after the whole shebang we've depended on comes to a halt, God will remain in ABSOLUTE control over what He gave us to manage—Earth and Everything Else! Call me crazy, but as I see it, The Third Law of Thermodynamics suggests that at Absolute Zero, Entropy will be in order—not disorder. God didn't call The Laws of Thermodynamics what we call them; God had no problem managing the Universe He created; we shaped the issues ourselves, but God will fix all that one day. We think we need to figure everything out—God knows all about 'Everything!'

When God does bring back the world He intended, one of ABSOLUTE ORDER, there will be two ABSOLUTES—'Closed Systems:' Heaven and Hell. One—Heaven is the one we'll *wish* we had sought after, and we can still do so—The other, well, it will be Hell. It will be ABSOLUTE as well—Absolutely sealed off from Heaven. There will be no avenue leading from one to the other to allow us 'A Change of Heart—'at that juncture or place in eternity, we'll realize 'Reality.'

Within the 'God does not exist' setting, we fail to effectively establish a beginning we can pin down as 'this is how everything began.' Possibly, we can agree on the Laws of Thermodynamics: *Methinks* because both non-believers in God and believers in God seem to come to terms on these matters. Is God within this system or outside of it? He cannot change. If it came from nothing, could it return to nothing? I think God is outside and inside our closed system—controlling The System.

I've chosen to discuss all this HEART stuff in Chapter Five, *Searching For The Heart*—of *Searching For A Heart Of Gold; Not A Pot Of Gold*—might it be something outside of the 'Closed System—Our Uni-verse?' If there are what some folks call Multi-verses—each such 'One-Verse' (uni-verse) would have a governing 'System.' In a 'Spiritual' sense, what would this mean? If there were such a thing as God (for me, this is not even a question), each such 'Unit,' 'Closed System,' having a different God—would the present God which Christ Followers believe in be enough for everyone?

The God of Heaven and Earth as we know it, Ruler of All, would He be enough to satisfy all the questions we have about life in a 'Multi-Universal World?' Could He possibly answer all our 'Why's,' our 'Why Nots,' affirmatively, 'No One Else Seems Able To Do So?' If there were different Gods for each Universe, we would have a continual 'War of The Gods—' A War of The Worlds?

According to Traditional Christianity [that of being a 'Christ Follower'], God created 'Everything—' He even forethought the whole story before He created it. The Story doesn't stop there; God foreknew how everything would work out even after we were allowed to make our own choices. It makes sense that God is outside the Universe we call our home. He holds the whole of 'This Our Universe, in The Palm of His hand.' There's such a 'Mega' conglomeration of information on Planet Earth, let alone the stuff floating around in the space above our heads. Are we in La-La-Land because we don't Check It Out? Is it a *mental fog*, a lack of tutoring?

"I've inscribed You upon the palms of My hands; Your walls are continually before Me!" (Isaiah 49: 16; JBI)

Accordingly, as He hath chosen us in Him before the foundation of the world, that we should be holy and without blame before Him in love:

He predestinated us unto the adoption of children by Jesus Christ to Himself, according to the good pleasure of His will, to the praise of the glory of His grace, wherein He accepted us in the beloved.

Jesus, through whom the shedding of His blood redeemed us, we experience the forgiveness of sins. Affording us the riches of His grace, He reached out toward us in all wisdom and prudence; He made known unto us the mystery of His will. Jesus did all this and more according to His good pleasure. All things hold a purpose within His will: In the release of the fulness of times, God would gather together in one all things in Christ, both which are in heaven, and which are on earth; even in Him: (Thoughts on Ephesians 1: 4-10; JBI)

I knew a man (person) in Christ who went into the third heaven fourteen years ago. I don't know whether it was in the body or out of it. (2 Cor. 12: 2; KJV)

Scripture balances out nicely. If God is Who He says He is, then whatever He made— 'One Universe' or 'Multiverses' was all in His 'Heart' before any of it existed. I see no evidence for 'Multiverses—' It seems to be an idea concocted by people who cannot accept reality. Some folks need to shape ideas to present more than we'll ever need to sustain the lives we now live and ever hereafter. Even Mars is within our 'Uni-Verse—' we haven't yet conquered Mars or other planets.

The Moon, Stars, and a long list of other planets are now and forever will be whatever we see them as at present. These places need not dominate our lives or be out of reach for 'Day-To-Day living! We may observe them from a distance, but will God, or whatever other entity one might have as their 'First Source,' ever bring them into our reality for life as we have it on Planet Earth?

Does God have a Heartbeat? Good Question! The Bible tells us God is A Spirit—we who worship Him must do so in Spirit and Truth. Does a Spirit have a Heart? The Bible says Jesus is "The Way, The Truth, and The Life!" Jesus is God! If Jesus is God, and Jesus in His physical body had a 'Heart,' and He did, then 'God Had A Heartbeat!' Genesis says God created us in the "Image and The Likeness of Himself—" 'with God's Nature. We have a 'Heartbeat' and so must God—because something birthed inside of Who and What He is and ever was, made us be like Him, without us becoming Him—God—We Can Only Imagine!

THE HEARTBEAT

"Heartbeats," we cannot live without them. I've heard people say, "'*Women and or Men*,' you can't live with them, and you can't live without them." Some folks apply an addendum to this phrase, "But I'd Sure Like To Try!" (many people live in this mindset). The Bible tells us the "Heart is deceitful and desperately wicked,"

Life's not all bad—When your days seem to run together as One Bad Day After Another—"Take Heart!"

As I let my mind wander, I think through what I referred to about "Heartbeats:" 'you can't live without them.' I don't recommend experimenting with things of this nature. Some folks have trialled (tested) life—in a frozen state—they are still frozen!

How to check your pulse:

"Place your second and third finger over your carotid artery located underneath your jaw, on your neck. You will then count each beat for one minute (or 15 seconds and multiply it by four). Be sure that your fingers are resting gently on the neck and are not pressing down. Another location to check your heart rate is over your radial artery at your wrist. With your palm facing up, you can find your pulse by placing your second and third finger in the space located on the thumb side of your wrist, just above the base of your thumb."

Firstly, I am relieved when I find the area to check my pulse. Sometimes I think I don't have one because I often have to 'Search' for the spot. It's not always as easy as "X Marks The Spot." It's not always easy to find the right place to find my pulse.

Secondly, I check the clock or timer, and I proceed. My pulse reads out at about 60-65 beats a minute most of the time. Then I thank The LORD I am still alive. I may not say this, but if I appeared not to be breathing—someone else took my pulse, and *none* [no pulse] existed, the annals of 'History' would record me as 'Dead.' I may be speaking about this somewhat lightly, but in reality, it's no laughing matter. Some of our physical stats differ on the scale of numbers but may still register as predictable. Life's course may not be predictable, but, predictably, we'll all die someday. I don't think I want to know when my number is up—I just want to be ready!

Is this relevant to the second half of this Chapter—working towards the conclusion of *Searching For The Heart*? The reason I have an 'End Comment' for each Chapter is so we can look back for a few moments in the 'Rear-View Mirror' to gather a few thoughts to chew on before we move forward—we *prepare*, with *purpose*, to make *progress, and preservation keeps us ticking!*. Can we live without these thoughts? Probably. Can we live with them? Probably. We read from scripture,

> The mind is more untrustworthy than all things and badly depraved: who can know it? (Jeremiah 17:9; JBI)

I, for one, would love to live without the *desperately deceitful things* I do at times, but it seems I will have to live with them for as long as I'm in this 'Skin.' Before you think I'm such an awful person because I still have some human frailties, I know I'm in good company. The Apostle Paul in the Bible had thoughts like these—so did Isaiah.

Then I said, Woe is me, destruction has consumed me because I'm a person with impurities on my lips—I reside among a *people* of poisoned lips: for mine eyes have seen the King, the Lord of Hosts. (Isaiah 6:5-8)

We know that the law is spiritual: but I am carnal, sold under sin. For that which I do I allow not: for what I would, that do I not; but what I hate, that do I.
(Romans 7: 14-15; KJV)

All thoughts begin in The Heart! As we live life daily, adversity often jumps into the mix with deliberate intentions, or so it seems. Sometimes it's because of the company we keep. Sometimes we're living in the fast lane when we ought to be pulling back far enough, so we don't get overtaken and overwhelmed because we try 'Keeping company with the Jones's [no reflection good or bad intended here on anyone named Jones].'

If we treat our 'Spiritual Heart' to the 'Good Things of God, Who is Goodness Incorporated,' we may better understand how to deal with life effectively enough to have "The Peace of God which passes all understanding." However, let's remember, "We Are Just Human, And Humans Forget—." What do humans forget? We forget there is a natural pace to living life, which means we're not always 'On Our Game!'

Often, our desires overtake our needs. Sometimes our 'Hearts' aren't satiated enough by living by standards that don't produce heavily on the prosperity side. I don't necessarily call this greed. However, it can be—but when we are always reaching for the 'Green' (not Green Pastures per se) because everyone else is wanting and seemingly getting more than a look at 'The Pot Of Gold At Rainbows End,' we may be reaching for the carrot at the end of the moving stick. These traits and or tendencies can drain our Spiritual Hearts to where we have nothing left to offer our LORD.

I wrote an article called, *The Heart Attack*. It wasn't about having a Physical Heart Attack. In such a case, we face hindrances; we are less effective in managing the day-to-day; or, in the worst-case scenario, 'DEAD!' These physical detriments or losses are severe enough to curtail us in many obvious ways. They can also lead us to not being spiritually orientated or even able to be what the LORD had in mind for us to be in the 'Best-Case Scenario!'

The Heart Attack I wrote about was comparing physical entities and letting them be our *teachers* regarding how we might better live in the Spiritual Kingdom. Finding comparisons like these helps us be all we can be to produce Spiritually. To be all that our LORD had in mind for us to be is GREAT—not to say we should be on the go twenty-four-seven—working night and day to make points by burning ourselves out—then, in many cases having an actual "Heart Attack." Both Physical and Spiritual Heart Attacks can be terminal; a 'Spiritual Heart Attack' that sets us on a better course of Christian Living is Our Goal! Without goals or visions, we are limp or just limping along life's path.

I've been doing a series of articles called, The Oasis. The first on the list was The LORD Is My Shepherd. We must take Selah Moments—they help us remain *'lucid, unblurred, and clear' about our calling. They help us stay on track in 'Full Strength!'* We live life in the fast lane—not regarding the physical or spiritual effects—residing in the thinking mode of—"Whatever Will Be Will Be!"

When I read a book or most other material, I often get certain things out of them the first time I read. I do need heads-up reminders of what I just read. In not so many words, please hear some "Heartbeat" thoughts.

—God cares more about me than I often realize.

—God, though in the 'Spirit Sense,' doesn't have a 'physical heart' as we do—this is not what we are talking about for the most part. Yes, it is essential for us to 'Have a Heart' physically; otherwise, we could not have a shot at ever having a "Spiritual Heart." We need to be physically born before being "Spiritually" born. Jesus, God in the flesh, had both a physical heart and a Spiritual Heart. Jesus had and has a Heart Of Gold in the Spiritual Sense—Its 'Beat' and 'Bleed' are always for us.

—Psalms like Psalm Twenty-Three give us an in-depth look at just how much God cares for His Sheep: This is what we are; sheep needing a Shepherd.

—Psalm 51:10-13 gives us a picture of having our needs met, more than our wants satisfied.

—Psalm 1 points us to a little more of "The Heart of God [The Heart of Gold]; it doesn't leave much unsaid as far as our benefits package is concerned when it says,

"Happy and fortunate are people who don't seek pleasure or advice from wrong sources—to make sensible and decisive decisions about the delicate matters of reality—if these people turn in this direction, they stand a good chance of becoming mockers themselves. The best-case scenario for all people is to take pleasure in the things God directs us to follow—then we have an opportunity to flourish in this world where there are too many options to being a Christ Follower. It's vital [paramount] for us to seek God's will for our lives, no matter how our circumstances pan out.

We are the better person for it if we concentrate on God's measures. People like this will be like a tree planted by the water's edge [at the proper place], where they are fruitful at their appropriate season. These folks may not necessarily have mega financial success, but they'll be at the center of God's plan. I can't think of a place I'd rather be than in the center of God's will.

Immoral people—evil-minded and mocking folks have a different mindset than Christ Followers—these folks are wind-driven and won't pass the test at God's judgement seat—where the righteous people will be in a class different from the ungodly! For the LORD knows the moral path folks take: but the course of the ungodly shall perish." (Psalm 1: 1-6; JBI).

"The heart is deceitful above all things and desperately wicked: who can know it?" God always guides us through our issues with His great love if we give ourselves over to His undying care.

"LORD—there's no one like You! We exalt Your name forever—I revere You above the Heavens. From the tongue of the young ones [babies], You appointed strength for us to face the day against the onslaught of Your enemies—You frustrated those who are against You. The heavens, the moon and the stars You made are a testimony of the work of Your hands—in contrast, what are we the people you fashioned—and our sons and daughters? LORD, You always take notice of us no matter where we are.

You created us somewhat less than the angels and honoured us greatly—and empowered us to be higher in value than anything else. You placed everything under *people's* control—sheep, oxen, the beasts of the field, the fowl of the air, the fish of the sea, and whatsoever passes through the channels of the waters. LORD our Lord, You are more excellent than anything on earth! We exalt Your name!" (Psalm 8 1-9; JBI)

—Psalm 139: what can we say about the intimacy of this Psalm. I'll only share three verses from Psalm 139: [1, 23, & 24] here:

"O LORD, You have searched me and known me."

"Search me, O God, and know my heart: try me, and know my thoughts:"

"And see if there be any wicked way in me and lead me in the way everlasting."

I hear David saying, "LORD, You've checked me out thoroughly and 'You Still Care For Me;' WOW!" The more I read Psalm 139, Psalm 23, Psalm 1, Psalm 8, Psalm 19, and Psalm 119— the quicker I know how my strength to *carry the day* comes into reality.

All our help comes from the LORD, which made heaven and earth. He will not leave our feet on shaky ground—He that keeps us will not go to sleep in the process of our care. Behold, He that looks after Israel will not doze off in the process. (Psalm 121: 2-4; JBI)

Sometimes I wonder about what was going on in the head of 'David, as The Shepherd Boy!' Was he just in the 'Dream World' of a young lad—? Or was he, even unknowingly, *prepping* or *building* his life into the future he didn't yet know?

"O LORD, thou hast searched me and known me."

"Search me, O God, and know my heart: try me, and know my thoughts, "and see if there be any wicked way in me and lead me in the way everlasting." (Psalm 139: 23-24)

"Do It Again, LORD!"

"The LORD is my Shepherd; I shall not want."

IF YOU'RE STILL BREATHING—TAKE HEART—

Hope's Just Around The Corner

—WAIT FOR IT!—

Think this one through, seeing yourself as being like this. When we see we are not in calm waters—It is high time for an "Oasis Moment."

◊ THE VISTA VIEW—THE OASIS ◊

Searching for 'Gold' is not simply taking a trip to the mountains where there's a lot of rock. We cannot simply go down 'Easy Street—'a rockslide in the Rocky Mountains or any other mountain range and begin our search for 'Real Gold!' We cannot simply go down to a clear river and intently search until we see some 'Sparkle' in the water and when we pick it up, expect it to be the 'Real Thing!' It will likely be 'Fool's Gold [Pyrite].' Many folks who have searched for gold have likely first found Fool's Gold!

We find gold amongst rocks, in water, in the human body, and in many other places worldwide. We can discover gold throughout the earth and the sea. There are natural spots on the planet that contain more amounts of gold. Commonly, we find gold within rock and granite. We can Pan for gold— we can employ lode mining, placer mining, or any other gold mining process by enduring hard work—most of the time, we cannot just trek out to the boonies and expect to get rich quick—without a lot of effort to make it happen.

Searching For A Heart of Gold; Not A Pot of Gold, presents challenges, possibly even harder than mining for Pure Natural Gold in the physical sense. Life's difficulties are many; they are becoming increasingly harder to overcome. Not only do we face the challenges of the changes in the hearts of humanity, but the right and wrongs of life are also more changeable today than they ever were at any other point in history. While I could search out the practical resources *for you* on how to mine for natural gold, getting you on the path to riches—in any case, I can only point you in the right direction; I can't do the work for you!

Chapter Five is called *Searching For The 'Heart,'* not 'Searching For The Gold.' The 'Heart of Gold' I'm referring to is one of the conditions of the 'Spiritual Heart—' this also does not just lay on the ground or a shelf somewhere for us to latch onto it. We can find the information on the bookshelves in stores—but the primary source of this information is Bible-based.

The Search For The Heart—though Biblically based, still requires us to *mine hard* to put The Heart of Gold into action to where it can have any effect in our own lives and in the lives of others who may need it more.

When God concocts or blends a mix of life's ingredients—issues and events, and says—This IS You, we may or may not always appreciate the mixture. In the Melting Pot of the Past, The Present, and The Future [the tomorrows we will yet face], He is well aware of our ills, skills, gifts, failings, and possibilities—from this soup or stew, He can make something beautiful of our lives. God needs willing participants—That Could Be Us!

In blending everything to be one entity again—like soup, God alone can once again separate the items as if it were an "As You Were Soldier Scenario—" When soldiers are in front of a Commanding Officer, a Salute is in Order. The rigid position of Standing At Attention is in play until the Commander says—"As You Were!" Every Soldier is more relaxed when The Commander says, "At Ease, Soldier!"

Sometimes we are in a better place when we are in The Mix of things in life that may cause us some grief, frustration, and confusion—sometimes, we may not be in a better place in this scenario. It may be because we created The Soup or Stew that got us into 'The Melting Pot.' We may not have chosen to go it God's Way!

We cannot ever separate the stew—as if it was never concocted; before we ground up and boiled all the ingredients. David often got into these situations—his only help to separate himself from his mess was to call on God—This made him "a man after God's Own Heart." God, being Who He was [and still is], caring about The Promises He made, came to the rescue more than once—and God will do the said same for us if we will trust in His Promises—and Obey, allowing God To Create The Stew in The Melting Pot of our lives!

MANY OF THE ANSWERS TO OUR PROBLEMS STARE US IN THE FACE IN PSALM 139—

How could we not *"Take Heart"* when The God of All Creation is Always Waiting to spend time with us! If you are Spiritually faint, find strength in God's power. Even the young are not always "Young At Heart." If we wait for strength, we sit in God's presence; we'll take on the strength of the Eagle—we'll not be weary or fainthearted. (Isaiah 40:29-31; JBI)

HEART SENSE

Search My Heart

◊

HAVE MERCY UPON ME, O God, according to Your lovingkindness: [and] according to the multitude of Your tender mercies blot out my transgressions.

Wash me thoroughly from mine iniquity and cleanse me from my sin. For I acknowledge my transgressions: and my sin is ever before me. Against You, You only, have I sinned and done this evil in Your sight—that You might be justified when You speak and be clear when You judge.

Behold LORD, You shaped me in iniquity; and in sin, my mother conceived me. Behold, You desired truth in the inward parts: and in the hidden part, You will make me know wisdom. Purge me with hyssop, and I shall be clean—wash me, and I shall be whiter than snow. Make me hear joy and gladness so that the bones You have broken may rejoice. Hide Your face from my sins and blot out all mine iniquities.

O God, create a clean heart inside my being and renew a right spirit within me—Cast me not away from Your presence, and take not Your Holy Spirit from me. Restore the joy of Your salvation, and uphold me with Your free spirit.

Then will I teach transgressors Your ways, and sinners will learn Your ways. (Psalms 51: 1-13; KJV)

I was born guilty (Re Adam's guilt); yet, I was born innocent, not yet having committed any physical sins [needing saving from Adam's sin]; God offered me a means to be saved; I needed to respond to God the right time. Then, after some time, I yielded my life to God— at times, a few adjustments to my character were in order. Through these periods of God working on my personality (and there have been and are), I hope to become more like the end product He wants me to become.

Scriptures In Chapter Six
Finding The Heart—Then What?
[Seek & Find—Not Hide & Seek]
Genesis 1: 24-25; John 3:6; Jeremiah 29:13
Genesis 1: 26-28; Genesis 2
John 9:25; John 3:16
Matthew 7:12; Galatians 5:22-23
1 Corinthians 2: 9-14—
Psalm 19; Hebrews 1; Psalm 8
Matthew 5: 14-16
Mark 4: 10-13
John 15:15; Mark 4: 4-13
1 & 2 Timothy
The Vista View—The Oasis
Hebrews 4:12
Heart Sense
Jeremiah 12: 5

Chapter Six

Finding The Heart—Then What?

———————————————— ◊ ————————————————

DOES ANYONE REMEMBER the bumper sticker—"I found it?"

Have people ever really lived Through Life Completely while they lived and breathed? I'm not just asking, 'will we ever have lived through life just because we were born into it' and or died at birth—Will We Ever Have Lived Through Life!' To have lived 'Through Life' means we have gone 'Through' numerous seasons of time where the present Season of Life 'Today' is diametrically (entirely) different than what we experienced yesterday. By 'Yesterday,' I don't necessarily mean the day just passed— 'like only hours behind us!'

"I Found It" Bumper Stickers were a product of the 60s. When a person became a Christ Follower, they wanted to tell the world around them of their Newfound Faith. So it seems one of these folks started the "I Found It" craze or trend by making up Bumper Stickers to announce to the world that they were on a New Track of Life, meaning something was wrong on the inside of their life—this was true then and is true now as well. Then, as each day began, this SPIRITUAL 'HEART' became enriched. These folks didn't quit 'living a natural' life—they just added the Spiritual Life.

To Seek & Find—Not Hide & Seek is apropos (right)! When someone experiences the "I Found It" encounter, it only means their Old Heart of not believing God in the person of Jesus Christ is working on an about-face scenario. Now Jesus, who personally died, took the guilt and shame associated with that Old Life and its Heart of Unbelief and said, "I Will Take The Punishment For The Harm This Old Life Created." The Biblical term for this experience is being "Born Again," thereby creating a NEW HEART! Being Born Again is not a Physical thing—it's a Spiritual Thing.

Even though I believe all mentions of the I Found It Bumper Sticker and its history are as stated, I trust there's more to it than this. I don't lessen the first thoughts about what people suggest about the theme (Bumper Sticker and Reference to Salvation); I like to take a deeper look at the complete perspective.

Can we rightly say 'we' FOUND Life? Maybe Not—We *received* the Gift of Life! Life came about either by some process of development, such as Scientists and Evolutionary Researchers say happened over billions of years, 'or' acknowledge authority to God; Who in a moment as we know it, said, "Let There Be!" However, God paved the way for these words by declaring, AND GOD SAID!

> And God said, Let the earth bring forth the living creature after *its* kind, cattle, creeping things, and beast of the earth after his kind, and it was so—. God made the beast of the earth after *its nature*, cattle after their *sort*, and everything that creepeth upon the earth after *their nature*—God saw that it was good. (Genesis 1: 24-25; KJV)

The first Six Days were the essential *preparation aspect* of creation, but God didn't stop here! Nothing so far was like the Hard Labour of an inmate entity in a Prison Camp. These two verses were only part of Six Days Labor we call A LABOUR OF LOVE. It was essential to *prepare* the earth for human occupation. Non-human things were not everything on this Road Trip (Journey). The Final Step of Creation saw God create the image of Himself in human form. Throughout history, past, present and future—God was and will forever be in complete control!

In the Garden of God—The Garden of Eden—God was growing LIFE! God didn't form a single cell 'Processing Gene' to bring about all creation—A Machine of sorts (Evolution); He took a personal interest in all design, so much so that He spoke individuality into all creation except human life. Now God got even more unique [individual]—He, like a potter, shaped or sculpted us!

Yes, in Six Days Labour, God created everything except people. Within this Creation, He placed a Garden from which all life was to Grow Along Forever In Harmony without interference from an enemy (Satan). It seems human choice was the downfall. Satan's ways were no surprise to God. The process of Eternal Life, Past or Present, Is Not Now, nor Ever Has Been Out Of GOD'S Control!

The long and the short of it is—God Created The Universe [not a Multiverse, as some think]. He created the sun, moon, stars, planets, light, vegetation, animals—everything which was His plan to use as 'sustenance' for our existence. God made 'people' His most prized possession. From, and or in the extended process of His plan, He, God Himself, came to earth in human form, not only to show us the 'best case scenario' for living Life on earth—but above all, to teach us His Love, and how to love each other!

Through the Love He had for people, He would be born like us through much the same process [apart from the Immaculate Conception, not human conception]. The result—The Son Of Man, The Son Of God, God, Jesus, birthed as the living and breathing person that The Bible shows us that Jesus was. He not only showed us 'a way'—He was and is "The Way, The Truth, and The Life;" not only Life in the present—but Eternal Life! Much of these things are generally hard to understand until we, by faith, accept Jesus unconditionally! (That which is born of the flesh is flesh, and that which is born of the Spirit is spirit. John 3:6).

"If you're sincerely interested in Me with all that's in your heart —you'll find Me!" (Jeremiah 29:13; JBI)

Seek & Find—Not Hide & Seek

Jesus died on The Cross, declaring, It Is Finished; came back to life; thereby telling us Everything Can Now Be Good Again—if we accept being BORN AGAIN! Nicodemus didn't understand these things in The Gospel of John (The Bible).

God carefully laid out the recipe (process) for creating all 'things.' "The long and the short of it is—God Created The Universe, [not a Multiverse, as some think]. He created the sun, moon, stars, planets, light, vegetation, animals—everything was made for our 'sustenance—' our existence. God made 'people;' His most prized possession. From, and or in the extended process of His plan, He, God Himself, came to earth in human form, not only to show us the 'best case scenario' for living Life on earth—but above all, to teach us His Love—and how to love each other!" (*IBID*)

Creating 'things' was one thing God always had in His bailiwick. Another thing, and even 'more than just simplistic matter,' was when it came to the 'people' thing—once again, we hear the words "AND GOD SAID—." It Goes Like This—.

"And God said, Let Us make man (people) in Our image, after Our likeness: and let them have dominion over the fish of the sea, over the fowl of the air, over the cattle, over all the earth, and over every creeping thing that creeps upon the earth. So God created humanity (people) in his image, in the image of God created 'He' them—male and female. And God blessed them, and God said unto them, Be fruitful, and multiply, and replenish the earth, and subdue it: and have dominion over the fish of the sea, and over the fowl of the air, and over every living thing that moves upon the earth." (Genesis 1: 26-28; KJV)

God took Personal Charge! He didn't 'just give an Order' to declare His intent. He used His hands to make it personal. God made a 'Person—(with equality as a matter of importance)' 'Adam (A Man, as God, Not Me, declared him to be);' then God made a Soul Mate for Adam—Eve (A Woman, as God, Not Me, declared her to be). [Genesis 2 is the record]. (I have no intention to discuss these and other gender issues further— 'Just Saying.')

Where and or how can we come to say, I FOUND IT! [Or 'We Found It!']? The songwriter says, "Once I Was Lost, 'But Now I Am Found!'" John Newton was a slave trader and a person enslaved to sin, and he wrote Amazing Grace as a verse prayer called *Faith's Review and Expectation*, written by an English priest John Newton in 1773. In the 1830s, it captured the interest of American composer William Walker.

> AMAZING grace! (how sweet the sound!)
> That 'saved a wretch like me!
> I once was lost, but now am found;
> I was blind, but now I see.
>
> 'Twas grace that taught my heart to fear,
> And grace my fears relieved;
> How precious did that grace appear,
> The hour I first believed!
>
> Thro' many dangers, toils, and snares,
> I have already come;
> 'Tis grace has brought me safe thus far,
> And grace will lead me home.

The Lord has promised good to me,
His word my hope secures;
He will my shield and portion be,
As long as life endures.

Yes, when this flesh and heart shall fail,
And mortal life shall cease;
I shall possess, within the veil,
A life of joy and peace.

This earth shall soon dissolve like snow,
The sun forbear to shine;
But God, who called me here below,
'Will be forever mine.'

"Is he a sinner or not (speaking of Jesus)? I don't know, though, "I was blind—now I see." (John 9: 25; JBI)

Yes, the reality is that John Newton was Spiritually Blind. Yes, he gained Spiritual Sight because The Holy Spirit of God opened John's eyes enough to see he needed more than he could ever salvage for himself. I'd say John Newton was only ever able to say, "I Found It," because God first made Himself known to John Newton—God Found John Newton! God makes Himself known to us; we cannot ever come to Him—unless He invites us. (John 3:16)

God made us—we defaulted, left Dodge [dodged Him]—He Found Us—Not that He ever Lost Sight of Us—. God completed the deal in the Garden of God—The Garden of Eden—concerning humankind's destiny. There was No Hope In Sight unless God made the first move toward The Redemption of The Human Race. We, the people, were bent on Making It On Our Own; we still are. The difference-maker in the whole scenario is JESUS. We are still choosing human knowledge and human resources—(HR) to fix a World That Does Not Have Hope On Its Own! Jesus Is The Only Hope Any Of Us Have!

For instance, let's say we Find The Heart of Gold—The Heart of God—Then What? The expected response to this FIND should likely be to produce an action plan to facilitate or enable its usage for *purposes* that lend themselves to the fruits of THE GOLDEN RULE!

"We should already be doing everything we want others to do to make our lives better before we have expectations of said same for ourselves. If God is first (The Gold Medal Winner) on our priority list, the proper course to follow is to make other folks second (Silver Medal Winners)—the Bronze Medal naturally goes to ourselves. The natural flow of The Bible presents the pattern in like fashions." (Matthew 7: 12; JBI)

The "Fruits of The Spirit" don't take a back seat to The Golden Rule.

But the fruit of the Spirit is love, joy, peace, longsuffering, gentleness, goodness, faith, temperance: There's no law against this example. (Galatians 5: 22-23; KJV-JBI)

The "Fruit of The Spirit" collection here 'postdates [comes after]' The "Works of The Flesh" list of "Do's and Don'ts"— adultery, fornication, uncleanness, lasciviousness, idolatry, witchcraft, hatred, variance, emulations, wrath, strife, seditions, heresies, envying's, murders, drunkenness, revelling's—.

"In Part One, we looked at The Lay Of The Land, Surveying The Land, The LORD Is My Shepherd and Led By The Shepherd."

Now let's delve a little farther into Heart Matters! The KJV Bible records the word "HEART" '884' times. The book of Psalms records the word "HEART" '130' times—this is 14.7058823529% (The Book of Psalms records 1 of nearly seven times The Heart gets mentioned in The Bible). 783137 words are in play in the KJV Bible—leaving the heart said percentage at 0.0165999053%. So, if and when we are interested in studying "THE HEART," not the blood-pumping organ in the physical body, but the "HEART" which Jeremiah talks about—intensity can rise."

With the mentions of the 'HEART' in 'ex post facto' (backdated) format, I saw the context as those concerning our relationship with God—not our physical heart. Can we sustain life? Though we play a part in maintaining our physical lives, it has always been, and will always be, God who sustains us with the breath of life! It's ludicrous for me to entertain any suggestion that God doesn't know the score.

Here in Chapter Six, *Finding The Heart—Then What?* — we've determined what was predetermined before this book physically stated we're "AT THE POST" (At The Starting Gate)— what my intent was when I titled this book, *Searching For A Heart of Gold—Not A Pot of Gold!* Life is much more complex than we often think. We aren't just born, and then everything falls into place as if magically or logistically placed before us to have the Best of The Best all the time—It's Not All About Us! We may wish and sometimes even pray that God would look more favourably at 'our desires,' the Golden Rule of The Bible speaks contrary to this line of thinking.

The Bible speaks much about the word HEART. We need never be startled by these mentions. God spoke audibly to some folks—to others, He communicated through other people. For reasons of His own—for *purposes* falling under His Authority Alone—God does what is best for all. I have no issue with God being at the *front of the pack*, giving me the best possible advice.

It's often difficult for us mere humans (although God does not think of us as peons or any such lesser being) to fathom, grasp, or figure out the means God uses to get our attention. When it comes to God, many things in life seem to be a Mystery. However, God, through The Apostle Paul, says in 1 Corinthians 2: 9-14—

> "Eye hasn't seen, nor ear heard, neither have entered into the heart of people, the things which God hath prepared for those that love Him. 'But God has uncovered them for us by His Spirit;'—for the Spirit 'searches' everything, yes, the deep things of God. Who knows best what's in a person's heart— naturally, it's the person. Even so, the things God knows, only The Spirit of God knows ('But God has uncovered them for us by His Spirit;'). We now have the Spirit of God, not the spirit of the world, so we are well able to know the things God's given us freely. We also don't 'know,' in the words which the wisdom of people teaches, but which the Holy Ghost teaches; comparing spiritual things with spiritual. But the unsaved person does not understand these things of the Spirit of God—they are foolishness to them: they cannot understand fully because the two are worlds apart; one physical and one Spiritual." (written as Jacob Bergen Insight Paraphrase).

It's a considerable danger to use gender-specific pronouns in 2022. I consider all people equally valuable in the vital birth sector (I wrote about this in my previous book *Everybody; Everybody Is A Somebody*). God determined our gender before we even showed up in 'birth.' I'm not about to argue with God!

God speaks again from the heart of David—"The heavens declare God's glory; the sky shows us His handiwork. God speaks to us day after day—God helps us realize His 'Awesomeness' through what He created in the night skies. There's no language where 'their' (the heavens) voice—the message of every part of God's creation ever fails to ring out loud and clear." (David's Heart as I see it—JBI Re Psalm 19)

Please hear me—God has merit. I wish to make God known to the world as best as possible. The Undeniable Worth He Alone Holds is predominant within me.

Most people throughout history think Paul wrote The Book of Hebrews—these are my feelings. However, whoever wrote the opening chapter of Hebrews also recognized the magnitude of God as displayed in life and the heavens—as did David—especially in Psalms 19. The writer of Hebrews says—"At different times God talked to our ancestors through prophets, in many ways and certain seasons of each their individual lives. At the time of the writing of Hebrews, including the time since the birth of Jesus, as He grew to adulthood, God spoke clearly through Jesus as well."

"The words of this writer continue to express the majestic or breathtaking presence of Jesus in the completeness of Who He is, as The Son of God, Creator God, and much more. The humanity of God [in the picture of Jesus as The Son of Man] comes clear as we see the story of the cross, where Jesus became sin—even though He was innocent of ever sinning. But, to show us how much He cares for us, this is the path He chose to take." (Hebrews 1)

I'm often awestruck when I think of how uniquely many New Testament passages tie in so clearly to The Scriptures of Psalms. I realize the New Testament writers had written works of Old Testament writers for forage to present their hearts for God—Who and What God has always been. As the NT Authors wrote from their Heart, I feel as though they'd met guys like David personally. I know this is not the case, but when we see the Heart to Heart insertions, I sense a camaraderie only The Holy Spirit could arrange.

Scriptures like Psalm 19, Hebrews 1, Psalm 8—are only a modest portion of the Word of God spoken by so many different people in The Bible. I grasp more of the magnitude of God and how much He wants for us to know Him intimately (intensely) through the study of the Scriptures. We often think of *Intimacy* in the sexual sense. According to God's Best Case Scenario for our lives, this *Intimacy* has its proper place within marriage. Breaking the laws of God in the sexual sense, and breaking the marriage laws of God, have natural consequences—those which we understand in the physical sense. It's not my intent to fully disclose the effects—I'll leave it up to God; He made the rules, not me.

When I say, "He wants for us to know Him intimately (deeply)," I like to use Thesaurus Synonyms as a guideline to achieve a fuller understanding: Informally (casually), personally (individually), well (appropriately, due to His Sovereignty; respectfully; thoroughly), confidentially (in secret, behind closed doors—having quiet times with The God of All Creation—Intimately—Yet, in another sense, which sounds like a puzzle, (problem, or mystery, like an antonym—some of which are, open, public, and reserved), familiarly (closely, informally, casually), and lovingly.

Searching For A Heart of Gold—"Searching For The Heart of God" intimately has a specific context (God); not to confuse the tenets (principles) of the Spiritual Heart with the control (rules) of the operation of the Physical Heart.

A 'Biblical Principle,' or the art of effective preaching, is to lay out an example, story, or event—to add to the story of the Bible being preached or taught—. The Bible helps us use a passage when someone walks us through it to help us understand The Heart of God accurately or more clearly. Now, we are more adept or skilled at living in a proper relationship with the God Who Created us—God The Father, Jesus The Son, and The Holy Spirit of God! We call this Exegetic (explanatory) Preaching. Although I don't consider myself preaching while writing this book, I may sometimes sound a little PREACHY. (For this, I offer no apology).

The 'Heart' of Gold suggested in *Searching For A Heart of Gold* represents 'The Heart of God, The Spiritual Heart.' *Not A Pot of Gold* means what we talk about when discussing The Human Heart—Physical Things.

So, let's shift to the other side 'if you would,' just for a while, from the book's central theme—The Spiritual Heart, and delve into 'The Physical Heart.' Jesus taught the people in His circle, Christ Followers, by telling stories—Parables.

> Example: "You are the light of the world. A city set on a hill cannot *hide from view. People* don't light a candle *to hide it* and put it under a bushel, but on a candlestick; it giveth light unto all in the house. Let your light shine before others, so they can see your good works and glorify your Father in heaven." (Matthew 5: 14-16; KJV-JBI)

In effect, we may read into it that we are not a 'Secret Society.' The Parables of Jesus shouldn't muddy the waters for His followers; He shared the Parables to express 'Clarity' in handling life. Jesus expected His disciples to come to the place in their Spiritual lives where they could discern Spiritual things when they experienced the Physical things troubling them. God always wanted them to consider Him as their contact person when troubled times swarmed like a mess of wasps.

If you're anything like me, you know what a mess of wasps can do if they are left to do what wasps quite naturally do. We think of their attack as one with a personal vendetta against us because we are not like them–wasps. "It's not *personal*" for them. We are human, we don't like their attitude, so it's us who goes on the attack—whose the Bad Guy here? Wasps always do what comes naturally!

> And when He was alone, they that were about Him with the twelve asked of Him the parable. *Jesus told* them, Unto you it's a given to know 'the mystery of the kingdom of God,' but unto them that are without, all these things are done in parables.
> *So* that, seeing they may see, and not perceive: and hearing they may hear, and not understand*; in case they would convert, and find forgiveness for their sins.* 'Jesus said,' Don't you know this story? [No?] [Then] how will you know 'all stories?'" (Mark 4:10-13; KJV-JBI)

I often struggle with this passage of Scripture. It needs an in-depth study to understand this passage. The Bible, as per JBI, says it like this—

"Jesus spoke many things to a mixed crowd first—then He gathered alone with His disciples in a quiet place, where they inquired of Him about the stories He shared. God has already revealed the answers in stories—there's no secret about this. Some hear and listen with their hearts—others hear but never 'Get It,' and miss out on Salvation! Jesus gave Himself on the cross for everybody—but not everybody will ever accept His offer. Some people have eyes to see—but don't see anything. Other people have ears to hear—but don't hear anything. It's good to have 'eyes and ears—' but what good are they if they don't see God and listen to what He says about life now—so we are ready for Eternity! Jesus tells us stories so that we will learn! It's sad to see the Light of The World and choose to live in darkness." (RE. Mark 4: 9-13; JBI)

After looking at the KJV and The Message by Eugene H Peterson, I wrote the above. We see Jesus' Words in the actual Bible version, and that's what we should read and observe as the Final Word on The Subject of this passage. The process of trust is often a complicated matter for us to grasp. Jesus said,

From now on—I won't call you servants; because the servant doesn't know what his lord is doing—but I've called you friends—everything I've heard of my Father I've made known to you. (John 15: 15; KJV-JBI)

Jesus calls me His friend! I'm overwhelmed because of the vast degree of difference there is between God and me! Wow!

"The 'Heart' of Gold suggested in, *Searching For A Heart of Gold* represents 'The Heart of God, The Spiritual Heart.' *Not A Pot of Gold* represents what we talk about when discussing The Human Heart—Physical Things." (*IBID*)

How hard is it to find our Physical Heart? We put our hand to the left side of our Chest, and there it is, a few inches deep under some skin and bones. Asking ourselves if our Heart is at work is a foolish question—finding out if it is even pumping is simple. If we're still breathing, our heart is at least working enough to keep us alive!" To find out if our heart is completely healthy or failing is another matter. We may need professional help to ascertain this info.

Now, we take our pulse to find out if there are some deficiencies because we have concerns because of symptoms we are experiencing. Please look at a few tests listed below. The internet can help us, but it may not be the most reliable source.

"A standard resting heart rate for adults ranges from 60 to 100 beats per minute. Generally, a lower heart rate at rest implies more efficient heart function and better cardiovascular fitness. For example, a well-trained athlete might have an average resting heart rate closer to 40 beats per minute.

To measure your heart rate, simply check your pulse. Place your index and third fingers on your neck to the side of your windpipe. To analyze our pulse at our wrist, we place two fingers between the bone and the tendon over your radial artery located on the thumb side of your wrist. When we feel the thumps, we count the number of beats in 15 seconds. Multiply this number by four to calculate your beats per minute." (*https://www.mayoclinic.org/healthy-lifestyle/fitness/expert-answers/heart-rate/faq-20057979*)

So, sixty to one-hundred beats is a safe zone in most cases. Another thing to keep an eye on might be our blood pressure— mostly, we'll need a tester of some sort or visit the doctor. If we feel we have physical 'Heart' issues, it's a good time to check with the doctor; self-diagnoses are just a simple way to allay (calm) our fears. If we've lost our physical heart, we should've already settled the issues of our 'Spiritual Heart' with Doctor God!

For starters, give a doctor (Heart Surgeon) a scalpel, and they will soon dig out the heart and put it on a platter for replacement or donation to someone upon our death. The matter of the Spiritual Heart comes by each our own choice—we cannot donate The Spiritual Heart on a transfer basis. There is a vast difference between The Physical Heart and The Spiritual Heart—this is something we need to settle before we have any expectations about the destination of our Eternity in the Life After We Leave Our Present Earthly Existence.

There are many other Physical Instruments that the Medical Profession uses to work on the Physically functioning parts of our physique. For starters, let's look at a few and their Physical Functions—

1-*Scalpel*—A small knife with a sharp blade.

2-*Surgical Staples*—We use these in closing a surgical wound.

3-*Surgical Sutures*—Are stitches— thread, staples—.

4-*Hemostat*—This is an instrument for preventing blood flow from an open blood vessel by compression of the 'vessel.'

5-*Dilator*—An instrument to enlarge a tube or cavity in the body.

6-*Scissors*—We use these for snipping or cutting during surgery.

7-*Curette*—Is a surgical scrapper or cleaning instrument.

8-*Forceps* are instruments for grasping, holding firmly, or exerting traction upon objects for particularly delicate operations.

9-*Retractors*—These are tools for holding open the edges of a wound.

10-*Surgical Elevator*—We use these for scraping, elevating, or dissecting bones or tissues.

11-*Probe*—A slender, flexible surgical instrument used to explore a wound or body cavity.

12-*Needle Holder*—A needle holder, also called a needle driver, is a surgical instrument similar to a hemostat used by doctors and surgeons to hold a suturing needle for closing wounds during suturing and surgical procedures.

13-*Saws*—Are tools for cutting bones ETC.—.

14-*Drills*—Are tools for drilling into bones to attach screws.

15-*Hammers*—These are tools used in a fashion with a chisel—.

     Some of these tools leave us with the impression that the Physician is building houses—seemingly, there are no limits due to the increase of knowledge. Physical Surgery can be crude at best because when we see blood flowing from our body—we cringe! Basic Surgical Instruments and their usages are an interesting lot. Back In The Day, Doctors were unable to address Physical Body Issues as efficiently as we do now—as to the future, the possibilities which were more mind-boggling 'back in the day' are almost entirely understandable because of The Increase in Knowledge.

     The Apostle Paul mentored Timothy—a young pastor who had yet to learn a few things about leading sheep (people) in safety and the productivity to produce the best fruit. Like a Doctor tries to observe the symptoms we have, intending to help us get through the dire issue in our Body, Paul is instructing Timothy on how to get the best results for the people he is serving as their Pastor. It's no easy task to teach people to show them how to teach others.

We could look at the surgical instruments used in Physical Surgery, place them alongside ourselves as Christ Followers, and make some observations. The Bible shows us the different circumstances we face in life and how they may require the gentler means of just 'taking a pill' or administering a few sutures or stitches to heal a minor infraction such as not taking care of our body as we should. Disciplining our lives, so we don't fall into the more severe issues requiring surgery requires more detailed attention. The stricter life events we face are sometimes just because the environment affects our body, some of which are devastating, needing us to manage in a more serious tone: Skin Cancer and the like.

Life has many ways of altering the proper functioning of our body parts; many of them may only mean we need to make some adjustments to how we live. Many other things that we face, which bring in situations where surgery is necessary to remove or repair something in our body, are caused by what we do to harm our body.

For example, would you please look at a few known things we do that cause us harm, things we might avoid by lifestyle changes? Life freely offers us all things—had we abstained from certain things in our lifestyle, we may have survived better.

Smoking can facilitate lung diseases, diabetes, blindness, erectile dysfunction, reproductive problems complications, hip fractures, colorectal cancer, rheumatoid arthritis, fertility issues, gum disease, etc.

Addiction Issues: may contribute to liver-related diseases, Cardiovascular disease, Stroke, Cancer, HIV/AIDS, Hepatitis B and C, Lung disease, Mental disorders—and a list of other issues.

Eating disorders—can cause a massive list of problems; maybe we cause more issues by our eating disorders than all the rest of the things I mentioned—I do not know for sure, but let's look at some of them:

Anorexia and the Heart

Bradycardia: Slow/irregular heartbeat.

Dysrhythmia: Heart out of rhythm; an acute eating disorder complication; can cause sudden death.

Decreased cardiac muscle, mass chamber size, and output: Often leading to cardiac arrest.

Anorexia and the Blood.

Anemia—Insufficient iron in the blood; causes fatigue and frequent bruising. Acidosis: Blood becomes too acidic, which can cause internal damage. Hypocalcemia—Low blood glucose levels from low weight and malnutrition; can cause seizures. Hypokalemia: Deficiency of potassium; can result in diminished reflexes, fatigue, and cardiac arrhythmias.

Anorexia and Digestion

It can be dental erosion—from calcium depletion. Delayed gastric emptying (gastroparesis)—The 'stomach' takes too long to empty its contents due to weakened stomach and intestine muscles; it can cause bacterial overgrowth or obstruction.' Diarrhea—from delayed gastric emptying or laxative abuse. Dehydration. Ulcers. Urinary tract infections—bladder infections; caused by decreased fluid intake.

Anorexia and the Body as a Whole

Thermoregulatory problems—due to the decrease in body fat or electrolyte imbalance. Decreased eye movement. Insomnia—primarily due to electrolytic and hormonal imbalances. Osteoporosis—Bones weaken due to lack of calcium, making them susceptible to damage. Edema—water retention imbalance causing feet and hands to swell. Amenorrhea—Menstruation stops or does not start. Lanugo—Soft downy hair/fur, mostly found on the chest and arms, produced by the body to trap heat; due to lack of body fat. Dry skin. Brittle nails. Hair that is weak or falls out.

Bulimia and Digestion

Dental erosion: Intestinal acid that digests our food is vomited up with stomach contents and wears away the teeth causing cavities and decay.

Parotid swelling: Glands in the throat and mouth become irritated and swell. Esophageal tears: Vomiting thins and weakens stomach lining, eventually resulting in tears; can cause hemorrhaging or rupturing of the esophagus. Delayed gastric emptying (gastroparesis):

The stomach takes too long to empty its contents due to weakened stomach and intestine muscles; this can cause bacterial overgrowth or obstruction in the gut. Chronic diarrhea or constipation can be permanent; in severe cases, we may lose all control over the bowels: ulcers, chronic sore throat, and Dehydration. Hypocalcemia: Low blood glucose levels from low weight and malnutrition; can cause seizures, urinary tract infections: Also bladder infections; caused by decreased fluid intake.

Bulimia and the Blood

Anemia: Insufficient iron in the blood; causes fatigue and frequent bruising. Ruptured blood vessels in the eyes. Amenorrhea: Menstruation stops or does not start. Hypokalemia: Deficiency of potassium; can result in diminished reflexes, fatigue, and cardiac arrhythmias.

Bulimia and the Body as a Whole

Thermoregulatory problems: Due to electrolytic imbalances. Insomnia: Mostly due to electrolytic and hormonal imbalances. Acidosis: Blood becomes too acidic, which can cause internal damage. Osteoporosis: Bones weakened due to lack of calcium; makes bones susceptible to damage Bradycardia: slow/irregular heartbeat. Edema: Water retention imbalance causing feet and hands to swell. Dry skin. Brittle nails. Dysrhythmia: Heart out of rhythm; serious eating disorder complication; can cause sudden death.

Everyday living presents us with so many health-related issues and much more. We often encounter these problems through everyday entertainment exploration and desire issues we think will not harm us. However, many good things are alright for us to involve ourselves in; some of them can lead us wrong because they are more selfie-related than bent on the benefit of other folks.

Searching out life is something we all do. 'Searching' for anything can be a challenge at the best times. Sometimes we look around our tiny apartment for our car keys, glasses, and other necessary items—without immediate success. I've even searched for my car keys in the refrigerator freezer—Go Figure!

It is easier to find these particular items as we search for material things. The trick is to look in logical places—. Like, why would my keys be in the freezer? "DA!" When we venture out for a 'Search For What Life Itself Will Present For Us,' we need to look at life through different eyes—possibly, 'The Eyes of The Heart.'

Many things in and about life's everyday issues amount to Physical Issues; however, life is not only about 'Physicality. Physicality is one of 'Two Columns.' Though there are some connections between Physical Life (Column One) and Spiritual Life (Column Two), there are definitive differences. In the final count of Eternal Security, we'll know whether we made the right choice for Eternity while living our 'Physical Lives.'

Spiritual issues regarding our quality of life now and what we can expect on the Eternal side of things require somewhat of a 'Crossover Entity.' Many are Physical Heart Issues—many are Spiritual Heart Issues. We may cause physical heart issues by our physical habits of living Life—Our Spiritual practices of living Life cause spiritual Heart Issues! Physical and Spiritual issues are usually solvable—If Caught Early!

We are the 'Masters of Our Fate' in the many avenues of life. These affect (involve) Physical Things on Planet Earth. When this 'Column' fills up—is finished for all earthly good—we access the results of how we managed the 'Spiritual Column' while on planet Earth. God is The Master of Our Fate once we die. Yes, 'Physicality' is no longer part of the equation.

◊ THE VISTA VIEW—THE OASIS ◊

In the Physical Sense, Heart Surgery is 'No Laughing Matter—' it's a 'Significant' [Momentous, Serious, Important—] enough issue for us to be 'Seriously Attentive' (Watchful). If our existence were only about our inborn, natural, fleshly motives and life exercises to seek and maintain, it would be 'no less' essential to have a successful tenure on Planet Earth.

If the initial event of our 'Birth' were the only event to get us through to some 'Eternity' (and some folks believe we live and die, and that's 'all she wrote'), we should do the 'Best We Can' to look after ourselves. The Heart is the most paramount (vital) organ of our body—that is, 'Our Flesh and Bone' body.

However, throughout the history of 'Humankind,' people have believed in an 'Afterlife' of one sort or another—[We don't just live and die, and that's 'all she wrote']. If this is the case, we need to give 'due diligence' to live by proper standards to make the 'Afterlife' the possibility or expectation of our belief complete. It's hard to describe to everyone's satisfaction—the necessary 'Due Diligence' (Thoughtfulness, Caution) to 'Religious' issues; yet, it's an issue for the Spiritual Heart to manage!

We have a mittful or more choices of belief systems—each of them seems to have a varied range of views as to what each of their 'Afterlife' involves. I'll not go far into discussing the choices except to say there are two sides to every coin. Many of these belief systems are only about a god of sorts—one without the Personality or Person of Jesus Christ, The Holy Spirit of God, and God The Father, as Three Persons of equal value and power. Then there are many variations of this as well. Belief Systems are a 'Melting Pot' or a concoction of many ideas about The Spirit World.

The Hearts I speak of in *Searching For The Heart of Gold' Not A Pot of Gold*—presents 'Two Columns:' The Physical Heart and The Spiritual Heart. I believe my 'Search' foray or venture is quite clear—if it isn't yet clear to you, here it is again. I believe in God The Father, God The Son, Jesus Christ, and God The Holy Spirit, as written in the Holy Scriptures as per the original writings of Scripture—I usually quote from The Kings James Version (This Speaks Volumes To Me!)

To wrap it up here in Chapter Six and Help Us move into a Greater Degree of *What Then—? Steeplechasing*; in Chapter Seven and Onward, let's take a quick look at a few thoughts.

Life without Physical and or Spiritual Issues is impossible. What about Heaven—Not Heaven on Earth as we would like it to be? It's not—'Continue Doing As We Are Doing—Thinking, We'll Be Okay,' because that's the way it always was—or because, 'Why would a Good God not let us have our cake and eat it TOO?'

Let's look at a few tools in the easiest way we can—what we can understand with our natural 'Five Senses.' Seeing, hearing, tasting, smelling, and feeling—bring life to us in a realistic fashion, one we readily understand. Please follow me for a while as we look at some medical tools which I want to apply both Physically and Spiritually:

Scalpel— When is a Spiritual Operation necessary?

When we are only living in our bodies of 'flesh, blood and bones—' without regard for The Creator—we need a 'Spiritual Operation!' I realize that someone reading right now may be saying, "Jacob, you are crazy—'God Does Not Exist.' All we have is a one-celled spec that came miraculously—from some form of gravity or nothingness (hundreds of billions of years ago). This entity began a process out of nothing for us to realize everything we have today!"

Scalpel— What is a Scalpel, and what does it do Spiritually? We know what it does in the natural sense, 'It Cuts.' It's a 'Surgical Tool, and 'crafty (Not cunning or devious) people also use a scalpel to cut things in doing their crafty creations. In this case, it's called a 'Hobby Knife.' Let's not confuse the issue of The Spiritual Heart and the Operation of the Heart, which is necessary for us to get 'Totally On Track' with God's will and purpose for our journey on Planet Earth! In The Spiritual Sense, cutting, such as it is, will likely also be painful—not the same as when we cut our flesh or suffer another painful malady.

There is much more involved while performing an operation where we use the 'Scalpel.' When we cut open the flesh to complete a healing process—Two things follow:

#1-Organs are repaired or removed by the Doctor—Artificial or Human-made Organs take their place if removed. I'd rather have the original organ—but sometimes we need replacements—[I've got two knee replacements].

#2- If we cut the body open, we need to close it up again; in the physical sense, we use Surgical Sutures—in the other 'sense,' where we need Spiritual Stitches To Close The Surgical Cut. The Bible gives us The Guidelines—a thorough study of The Bible is a lifelong trend for living a successful life as a Christ Follower. If we look at the Life of Jesus, we have a Great Beginning for staying on track in this regard.

Many more things occur when the body needs a repair job—the following tools are some of the items used by the Surgical Mechanic or Surgical Carpenter. I say 'Mechanic or Carpenter' because the tools are saws, drills, and screwdrivers in some cases. We all need helpers to keep life intact while surgery—Physical or Spiritual—is under the knife; please observe the following:

Haemostats—Are clamps to control bleeding—A Spiritual Hemostat could be another person who comes alongside us in our time of struggling while Spiritual Surgery is taking place.

Dilators—Are expansion [widening tools to enlarge an opening or passage] tools to make it easier for the surgeon to operate—A Spiritual Dilator could be someone who expands our horizon to see past the difficulties.

Curettes—These are simply cleaning tools for scraping tissue [as n a biopsy—].

Many are the other Surgical Tools: Scissors [no secret here], Forceps [tongs], Retractors [Similar to Dilators], Surgical Elevators [A surgical elevator device used in the reduction of bone fractures, particularly facial bone fractures, and even more particularly zygomatic arch fractures], probe [an examination, investigating tool], needle holders [A needle holder, also called a needle driver, and is made from stainless steel and is used to hold a suturing needle during surgical procedures.] We could assign a 'Spiritual Sense' for helping our Spiritual Growth and The Spiritual Growth of other people—to these tools and many more.

When we "Find The Spiritual Heart" for ourselves, we are in good stead to be a part of The Solution in The Plan of God, Rather than a Problem. Much of the above takes place in the Church. The Workplace, Universities—are also places we get these education helpers. Hey, plain old living out on the Playing Field of Life will bring us all we need to know.

We often get waylaid when we take lousy advice—and there's much of that out there get hooked on, mainly because we think everything on The World Wide Web is The Gospel Truth! Sometimes the Church is the problem because they have the maligned misconception that It's Party Time Now! —According to some Preachers I've heard. Is This What the Bible Says—???

At The End of The Book—It's Not "Party Time"— Now— "Work For The Night Is Coming when no man shall work—" (The Bible!)

A complete Plan of Salvation—RSVP— Everything Needed to Make Everything About Salvation Perfectly Clear

"I Can See 'Clearly' Now!"
COME—For All Things are now Ready!!!

God's Word is quick and powerful, sharper than any two-edged sword, piercing even the dividing asunder of soul and spirit and the joints and marrow. The Word of God separates the thoughts and intents of the heart. (Hebrews 4: 12; KJV)

As we move along, let's often think about Medical Tools to walk us through the use of Spiritual Tools for completing Life's Purpose—To love God and keep His Commandments!

We've Prepped, Found Purpose, Made Progress, Been Preserved, Taken Heart, and now in Chapter Six, we've Sought and Found—Not Hidden and Just Hoped To Be in Search Mode.

Finding The Heart—Then What?

ISN'T THIS A GREAT CHALLENGE TO BEGIN OUR DAY?

HEART SENSE

Lord; Hear My Prayer

———————————◊———————————

RUNNING THE RACE

LORD—I'VE BEEN RUNNING A RACE IN THIS BOOK, trying to win what often seems like an unwinnable task. The challenge I face nearly every time I sit at my computer and place my fingers on the keyboard is to say what I think You are speaking into my spirit. LORD—it's a tough race.

I ask myself two questions—who am I running against, and for Whom am I running? LORD, I know that if I think too hard on 'who am I running against,' without first asking the central question—For Whom Am I Running to win This Race, I face an early setback. I may be 'Running In Last Place.'

"LORD, I remember when Jeremiah had some questions about his race. In Jeremiah Chapter Twelve, verses One to Four, he said his piece, and You LORD listened. However, You did not just listen and tell the man—you're on your own on this one; as usual, LORD, Your reply is fitting for us to notice and hear what You have to say!"

Jeremiah 12:4 poses a question to God. In effect, he asked God to look at the horrendous situation in Israel; then Jeremiah said, LORD, they say I will never finish my race! Jeremiah seemed to be asking, LORD, who am I running against anyway? God, as always, has a pertinent or relevant reply—. "How will you ever compete with horses if you have run with the footmen, and they've exhausted you? And if in the land of peace, wherein you trusted someone, and they undermined your resolve, how do you ever expect to manage when the floods come—to be sure, Jordon will overflow its banks, and you will either need to sink or swim?" (Jeremiah 12:5;)

I want to be more careful about addressing God. Often God kind of turns the tables on me; this is not a bad thing—It makes me think! Reflection can be good for the soul.

Whom are you running for, Jacob?—"You Lord!"

Scriptures In Chapter Seven
—What Then?—Steeplechasing—
[My Focus]
Hebrews 12:2; Hebrews 12:1; John 3: 1-3
Jeremiah 12:5
Psalm 139
Hebrews 11: 1-3; Hebrews 11:4
Hebrews 11:7; Hebrews 11:5-6; Hebrews 11:3; Ezekiel 14:13-14
Genesis 22: 16-18; Hebrews 11: 32-39
Psalm 139:1-4
The Vista View—The Oasis
Ecclesiastes 9:11
Ecclesiastes 9
Heart Sense
James 4: 13-17

Chapter Seven

What Then—? Steeplechasing—.

———————————◊———————————

FASTENING OUR GAZE ON JESUS, The One Who authored our shot at Faith; The One Who not only began for us this journey, He perfected it so we can Run The Race 'Set Before Us,' as given to us long before our birth. God knew each of us before He ever created anything else! If we never achieved any importance or recognition for anything else, the fact that God knew us before we were born is enough of an "Importance Factor" for me! (Re Hebrews 12:2; JBI) [My Focus] [Fixation Can Chart My Course To Success or Failure!]

Jesus braved the cross because of what He saw as laying ahead, as a possibility for us—'To Become Something!' This thought seemed to bring Jesus a huge Joy Factor. When Jesus finished His course of life as The Son of Man, His humanity completed, He took His rightful position as God, in all this represents, in the Throne Room of God. (Re Hebrews 12: 2; JBI)

"Behold, what manner of love the Father has bestowed upon us, that we should be called the sons of God—so, the world doesn't know us—because it didn't know Him. Beloved, now are we the sons of God, and it doesn't yet appear what we shall be—but we know that, when He shall appear, we shall be like Him; because we'll see Him Who is God for real. And every man (person) that has this hope in Him purifies themselves [himself], even as He is pure." (1 John 3: 1-3; KJV)

Let's flip to Hebrews 12: 2 to verse one—to help us see the background of the setting. So, as we are in The Race of Our Lives, we need to shed any hindrances [such as obstinate objectors to truth]. We must Run With Enduring Resolve to win against our greatest foe (the devil), not against each other—us honest living folks. God set The Rules for The Race (Re Hebrews 12:1).

I wish to mark as a reflector beam (reflecting light—or in this case, The Word of God in Jeremiah 12:5) a thought God gave Jeremiah to mull over when he had some difficulty *focusing* on The Race Set Before Him. I've read Eugene Petersen's book, *Run With The Horses*—A worthy read which extends many thoughts about the following passage.

"If thou hast run with the footmen, and they have wearied thee, then how canst thou contend with horses? And if in the land of peace, wherein thou trustedst, they wearied thee, how wilt thou do in the swelling of Jordan?" (Jeremiah 12:5; KJV)

As I began My Search—My Focus was to establish an entry point for *Searching For A Heart of Gold—Not A Pot of Gold*—in My Mind, I heard the term Steeplechase. Steeplechase will incorporate more than just My Over-repetition of the words of Psalms 139. Sometimes I'm '*just thinking*'—praying for insight into how to get this book on the rails to journey into the world—to make a difference for someone. A momentary flash of inspiration found me hooked on the word 'Steeplechase.' "*In Moments Like These*," [*I Sing Out A Love Song To Jesus*] my 'Reflector beam' works overtime!

Ordinary living naturally arouses captivating thoughts to help me *focus* on *specific themes* of life that became and still become part of my day to help me make decisions [embarking on what were and are often minor issues or events]. At other times these moments of insightful input are majorly eventful in creating a Starting Line for life-changing sessions—turning points. Missing out on 'Times Like These' could've been a disaster or at least damaging.

When I've claimed 'Inspiration' for these inserts into my psyche, some divine entity may have guided my thoughts. As I think like this, I evaluate the input rationally and spiritually to find the yardstick which will set a mark I can depend upon to be clear and concise—'To The Point.'

There are dangers when we say we had an "Inspiration or Directive from God—" these directives [if you would] may lead us down 'The Garden Path.' Our mind tricks us as if what we heard is the 'Pot Of Gold' at the rainbow's end. Temptation says there's no logic to ignore it—it sounds authentic. Every voice we hear may not, in Reality, be The Gospel Truth.

The Scriptures keep my eyes open for parallels to affirm that my reading points me to the needed path to follow for effectiveness in managing life.

I had ridden over hurdles up the country once or twice, by the side of Snowy River with a horse they called "The Ace." And we brought him down to Sydney, and our rider, Jimmy Rice, got a fall and broke his shoulder, so they "nabbed" me in a trice—me that never wore the colours for the open *Steeplechase*.

"Make the running," said the trainer, "it's your only chance whatever. Make it hot from start to finish, for the old black horse can stay, and think of how they'll take it when they hear on Snowy River that the country boy was "plucky," and the country horse was clever. You must ride for old Monaro and the mountain boys today."

"Are you ready? Said the starter as we held the horses back. All were blazing with impatience, with excitement all aglow; before us, like a ribbon, stretched the *Steeplechasing* track, and the sun-rays glistened brightly on the chestnut and the black as the starter's words came slowly, "Are—you—ready? Go!"

I scarcely knew we'd started; I was stupid-like with wonder, the field closed up beside me, and a jump appeared ahead. And we flew it like a hurdle, not a balk and not a blunder, as we charged it all together, and it fairly whistled under, and then some were pulled behind me, and a few shot out and led.

So we ran for half the distance. I'm making no pretences when I tell you I was feeling very nervous-like and *queer* (I'm not sure if the word 'queer' is an offensive term.) The jockeys rode like demons; you'd think they'd lost their senses if you saw them rush their horses at those rasping five-foot fences—and in place of making running, I was falling to the rear.

Till a chap came racing past me on a horse they called The Quiver and said he, My country joker, are you going to give it best? Do the fences frighten you? Does the stoutness they present shiver within you? Have they come to breeding cowards by the side of Snowy River? Are there riders in Monaro? But I never heard the rest.

I drove The Ace and sent him just as fast as he could pace it at the 'big' black line of timber stretching fair across the track, and he shot beside The Quiver. "Now," said I, "my boy, we'll race it. You can come with Snowy River if you're only game to face it; let us mend the pace a little, and we'll see who cries a crack."

So we raced away together, and we left the others standing, and the people cheered and shouted as we settled down to ride, and we clung beside The Quiver. At his taking off and landing, I could see his scarlet nostril and mighty ribs expanding, and The Ace stretched out in earnest, and we held him stride for stride.

But the pace was so terrific that they soon ran out their 'tether.' they rolled in their gallop—somewhat blown and beat—but they both were game as pebbles; neither would show the feather. And we rushed them at the fences, and they cleared them both together; nearly every time, they clouted, but they somehow kept their feet.

Then the last jump rose before us, and they faced it 'game' as ever—we were both at spur and whipcord, fetching blood at every bound—and above the people's cheering and the cries of "Ace" and "Quiver," I could hear the trainer shouting, "One more run for Snowy River." Then we struck the jump together and came smashing to the ground.

The Quiver ran to blazes, but The Ace stood still and waited, stood, and waited like a statue while I scrambled on its back. There was no one near me, for the field was 'fairly' slated, so I cantered home a winner with my shoulder dislocated while the man who rode The Quiver followed, limping down the track.

And he shook my hand and told me that he never met a man who rode more gamely in all his days, and our last set-to was prime. Then we wired them on Monaro how we chanced to beat The Quiver, and they sent us back an answer, "Good old sort from Snowy River: Send us 'word' each race you start in, and we'll back you every time." (The Open Steeplechase - Wikisource, the free online library)

[The Open Steeplechase by Banjo Paterson (1891)] This enactment of Banjo—gripped my Heart for what I'm writing here in this Chapter.

I aim to use much forage (food for exploration) as we ease through Psalms 139—The material will encompass the whole Bible in a position of connectedness with Psalms 139—relating to any and every part of The Scriptures. Every Scripture has value-added nutrition to elongate (extend) to present more than what we think of as the Word's Worth. The word might be 'and, if, for'—but each has much more to say.

Conjunctions fit firstly into four categories. One such conjunction—coordinating conjunctions, is like dressing for a formal function. Usually, we don't just don (throw on) our jeans or other grubbies to attend ceremonial gatherings; we typically wear clothing that doesn't look as if it were out of context—so wild we wouldn't fit in at the event we plan to attend. When we coordinate our attire, we'll be just like everybody else in terms of being considered of equal value when we get to the function.

'And, but, or, nor:' These are coordinating Conjunctions. 'And' tells us that 'this' and 'that' [certain entities] are involved. 'But' offers us the possibility of a choice that suggests 'one way' may be better than the other. 'But' sort of narrows things down. 'Or' also offers us a choice or an alternative of something: 'this or that;' but suggests more of a picture of opposing thoughts in one sense— in another manner, it gives us a choice of many options for moving forward. 'Not' presents more of a picture of negativity, like saying no to a possibility of sorts. 'Nor' is also a picture of 'choice.'

Again, we involve the dress code if we consider *prepping* for a formal occasion. We'll need to have an eye open for matching (*coordinating*) each of the visible items of clothing we wear—we can get a general picture of the use of coordinating conjunctions. I said we need to be careful of how we match our outerwear; our underwear does not need to be a match—some of our attire fits better in the hidden compartment of the dress code. (In the life we communicate in, some things are better left unsaid).

The story of 'conjunctions' (connections, unions—) is vast. The intent here isn't *to present* a complete academic discourse on English Grammar. However, I want to offer enough info to help us understand the value of the most seemingly uninteresting words we read as we read any document or book. If we don't, we may miss information vital to our success at living—possibly even affecting our afterlife destiny.

I'll step back a few paces—looking at the poem of Banjo Peterson, *The Open Steeplechase*. I chose to look at any relationship to the word "Steeplechase:" how it will help us in our observations of Psalms 139—for that matter, how it will help us as we use all of The Scriptures (The Bible), as The Guidebook on how to do life—these are stimulating thoughts—Why? We'll See!

A Steeplechase is a race run by horses and people; it presents obstacles such as water, hedges, and walls—it's not a race for the *unprepared* or untrained. The Steeplechase presents us with the challenge of endurance—somewhat like The Triathlon in make-up, it involves people. Endurance is the key to competing in and for life. No one ever born lived or lives without a measure of endurance—even a baby who dies at birth endured a race for life within a mother's womb for whatever time this was.

Words reveal a complete picture of a theme or context. Whether it's a blurb, an article or a book, expanding those words helps us grasp a clearer image of the context and meaning. Synonyms and Antonyms are a Godsend for me, the writer—I pray they are also for my readers. I may often apply more synonyms than are necessary to get the point.

Life can be so much better for us as we pass through our time if we observe the whole story of the journey. Can we know the Entire story? Will we ever know the Whole Story? Where will we be when we know the Whole Story? As we study Psalms 139 in relationship to the Whole Bible, will we better understand how to access the tools for living life in the most realistic possible way?

The Bible, historical books, and books of every genre are narratives of 'storied life' steeplechase winners. '*Everyday people*' still present their storyline. We face obstacles in life; we try to beat the odds, but some deterrents get thrown into life—not by God necessarily, but by another unseen adversary.

The steeplechase scenario is akin to what I was trying to achieve in *Bridging The Gap* [*published in 2018 on CreateSpace, Re Now Replaced by Amazon KDP*]. Following *Bridging The Gap*, I published *Everybody: Everybody Is A Somebody*, in 2020, on KDP (*Amazon*). This book is also hugely people-focused, as are the readers of *Twin Towers Of The Heart, The Mandate,* and *It's Jacob! My Name Is Jacob! What's Yours?* Now, I am concentrating on *Searching For A Heart of Gold—Not A Pot Of Gold*.

I daren't miss the mark here for the gift of my calling. Though I'm of equal value to the famous writers, I'm not a household word—they're in the public eye; all that matters is, if we are in God's vision in our endeavours, then 'all is well.' Again, I'm referencing here what our Heart [the soul of our being, not the heart that pumps blood through our body] is about and how we can best carry out the tasks our Maker personally selected us for—in His Best Case Scenario. The Bible tells us that God foreknew us before He created anything else. Knowing God thinks of me as 'important' gives me a good feeling—You and I are necessary for this Life!

Relationships—are they 'Important?' I'd say we can't live without them. 'Steeplechase Stories' of every conceivable creation rely on our connections with other people during our trek through life. I hope I've shared enough people links for us to agree that without the life stories of other folks, none of us would survive—I place The Good LORD atop my list!

I often pray that I'm connecting with you by introducing the Steeplechase scenarios of The Bible. If I don't present who I am, as included in 'Life Stories,' if I never consider you and your story as part of the whole scenario, I may be missing the key ingredients of this book. If I never form a relationship, how will I ever connect with you or any other person (those who will never read my stuff)?

I just came home from walking the streets of downtown Invermere. While doing so, I began thinking—this always puts me in a precarious position because now I need to find a way of introducing what is coursing through my mind; this is dangerous—if I don't get it right, I get it wrong; then I may mislead you!

I thought of myself as being on a platform with 'you, the audience' seated before me and ready to judge my presentation and performance—Scary Stuff. I thought of a setting where the host of the address I was about to give simply said, "I now present 'Someone' to you." That's it! No Name, No Title, No Accreditation—NADDA! I've not experienced this, so I have difficulty knowing how exactly I would feel—it may not be Great! I expect you'd also have trouble in this Arena. For openers, when I come onto the stage, I might well have stage fright because of the odd or awkward introduction someone gave me. Or, if I was a more experienced speaker, I may find a way to cut through this awkward moment, allowing us to get properly acquainted.

The following came to mind as I was walking the streets of *My Town*. I could simply say, *It's Jacob! My Name Is Jacob! What's Yours?* In reply to my introduction, you folks in the audience could all yell out your names in response to the questioning part of my introduction—MY NAME IS—! This way, we would all be acquainted with each other—Or Not?

Yes, this is one way of forming Connectedness. We'd be starting A Relationship. 'But' (another conjunction), even if I were lucky enough to catch a few of your names because you may have been in the front row, it wouldn't mean anything to me relationally. The same goes for telling you upfront that "My Name Is Jacob Bergen!" Unless you had prior knowledge of me, we'd have a considerable distance to cover to get to where we could be relational with each other on a personal level.

'Distancing' (we have considerable experience on this because of Covid) can be a brutal entity. It's challenging to have 'Enough Heart' to touch the 'often distant' hurting world. We can never recall the distance we've travelled. What we did on this journey is a done deal; this is why we need to *prepare* well for the next mile of our trip through life.

I'll include the *About The Author* part later; I do so in all my books. However, this only presents an overview of who I am. I spoke about each person voicing a blurb about themselves, saying 'I'm 'So and So.' Each person in the hall would be on a Starting Line positionally in this setting. We could then become relational with someone else in the room—'but' The Finish Line wouldn't arrive for any of us about the other person this easily—Possibly Never! Often, we don't have time for relationships outside of the family.

While I'm writing, I open myself up to you, my readership—you also have an excellent opportunity to begin seeing the placement of 'My Heart.' I'm still no closer to getting to know you by saying this. All I have is the knowledge that if you are reading this book, *Searching For A Heart of Gold—Not A Pot Of Gold*, you may have the same heart as I have for reaching out and touching someone else; someone you know, maybe, and or someone you have not 'yet' (another conjunction) met. All I can have about you are assumptions, hoping you will find something of value in your life; perchance, we'll meet someday somewhere on this planet or in the next world!

The Steeplechase Race has obstacles—runners usually *prepare* for the race by learning the barriers and practicing beforehand—perfecting their strength to overcome the challenges. Life is a race, whether it's a Steeplechase, Triathlon, Marathon or a Three-legged Race. The 'Three-Legged Race' is somewhat different than many other races in that it requires two people to work in tandem to accomplish anything close to winning the race. Some other races are done as a team event, even when they compete as separate entities. Yes, 'Life Is A Journey—'a 'Race' to The Finish Line—Every Race has a 'Finish Line!'

Pink Panther surprise attacks—these also present a race to be a winner—the way I see things, it appears as if someone was out to Search and Gain for themselves *The Pot Of Gold*, as opposed to *Searching For A Heart of Gold*. There's nothing wrong with working to achieve, supplying the needs of our families—even putting aside a little something for a rainy day; however, the 'Big Prize' comes when we "Seek First God's Kingdom—."

In *The Pink Panther*—the race is to find the 'Pink Panther Diamond.' Two actors associated with playing Inspector Clouseau in *The Pink Panther* at different times are Peter Sellers and Steve Martin—. In the original film's storyline, The Pink Panther was the name of a valuable 'Pink Diamond' named for a flaw that showed a figure of a Springing Panther when held up to the light; in the credits, this translated to being an animated pink panther.

Please take note of the panther being a 'springing' panther. Inspector Clouseau was always on the alert for a surprise attack. Cato Fong is Cousteau's Chinese manservant, trained to attack him regularly to keep him alert and skilled in martial arts. Cato and Clouseau have a love-hate relationship. Their fights are long and vicious and destructive to the furniture and constantly interrupted by the telephone ringing, at which point they will become civil again. These actors were a curious sort. Cato always *focused* on Clouseau.

I mention this because, for every race, the runners need to *prepare* well for what lay ahead—The Steeplechase, The Triathlon—and there are many more races with participants being human beings. As human beings ourselves, we can count on a few tough races of our own in processing our *Search For The Heart Of Gold* we wish to achieve before our earthly race ends—and it will someday end for us all; this is a given! "Dust to dust, ashes to ashes."

The race I'm talking about in this Chapter is a Spiritual one—we can fashion it somewhat in the likeness of how we run Physical races. Without a doubt, there are critical differences between a Physical race and a Spiritual race. One significant difference pans out in the matter of where our FOCUS lies. Are we in the race for an Earthly Crown or a Heavenly Crown—are we in the race of life to run an 'either-or race' between a Physical Race, The Journey of Life on earth—or a Spiritual Race—this being the FOCUS of importance.

Well, we would not be in any position to run either race without first being poised at a Starting Line. Before we can embark on The Spiritual Journey—this race we face requires a beginning—we call this Our Birth Moment. It amounts to running the Race of Life in a 'Tandem' fashion concurrently (in parallel with another entity)—The Physical Run comes first. The Spiritual Race is attached to the demands of life as we know it, somewhat like we would run The Three-Legged Race.

It's not easy to find the proper pace with 'One' other person to get any 'One' job done in life as we know it. When we elongate or stretch out this thought over the landscape of this world, for any of us to agree on any 'One Thing,' it's tough enough. Then, when we bring God into the picture, morality—and or entering a 'Search of The Heart' for the best means to be tolerant without bending the Truth of God to fit these tolerance demands we face—we see the need for massive and or more significant disciplines.

We know doing 'Life' isn't easy, ever since we decided to go it on our own in The Garden of God—The Garden of Eden. Life could have been so much easier if we let 'God be God' in the beginning—letting Him take the reins of our lives from 'Day One.' Oh, I know God could have arbitrarily 'Mandated' (a term we know much about because of COVID-19 vaccinations) 'The Tree of Life' as being our choice—but 'we chose' the Tree Of The Knowledge Of Good And Evil—in effect saying, "LORD, We Got This; Don't Fret About Us!" Right! We can see where that got us, alright!

We don't get far into Hebrews 11 before entering The Hall of Fame of Faith. The first three verses lay out the Game Plan! Might I rework the words 'Game Plan' to read in association with what I write in this Chapter—THE RULES OF THE RACE. We all know or ought to know 'Life Has Rules!'—If we are alive—!

"Now faith is the substance of things hoped for, the evidence of things not seen. By it, the elders obtained a good report—through faith, we understand that the worlds were framed by the word of God so that the created things we see don't appear from nothing." (Hebrew 11: 1-3; KJV)

Let's begin with the words "so that the created things we see don't appear from nothing." The big challenge here is that it takes us right back to The Beginning before anything made was already on a list that required a RULE—the Rule of Obedience. We are 'Right Smack Dab' back in the middle of The Garden of God—The Garden of Eden.

Janice McClain recorded the track *Smack Dab In The Middle* (*at about age fifteen*) and co-written and co-produced by Tennant and Thom Page. The release date of "*Smack Dab In The Middle*" was October 1979 and is registered in the Top Ten most-played tracks in discothèques around America for the first five weeks of 1980.

"Smack Dab In The Middle"
—so I can rock and roll to satisfy my soul—.
So let's run through some of the heroes of The Hall Of Fame Of Faith—

By faith, Abel offered unto God a more excellent sacrifice than Cain, by which he obtained witness that he was righteous, God testifying of his gifts: realizing that those who are dead still speaks volumes! (Hebrews 11:4; KJV)

Early in our record of Life (Physicality), Abel chose to honour God's wishes, and though his journey was pretty short compared to many others in The Hall of Fame of faith, Abel ran his leg of the race well. Abel won his portion of the Relay Race. He passed on the baton to the rest of us—for how to run our leg of the race. Most, or at least the majority of Christ Followers of any length, will know this story.

God knew all about Abel; He knew all about the rest who would follow Abel's obedience. God's foresight exceeds anything we could do in any foreknowledge about anything. We must remember to think back to before The Beginning of Earth.

By faith, Enoch—translated, kept from death, was not found because God had translated him—before his translation, he had this testimony that he pleased God. *But without faith,* it is impossible to please Him: for he that cometh to God must believe that He is and that He is a rewarder of them that diligently seek Him. (Hebrews 11: 5-6; KJV)

Jared, the father of Enoch, lived to be 962 years old, as the Bible records age back then. Enoch lived to be 65 years old, again, a relatively short life compared to his father (Jared) and Enoch's son Methuselah, who lived to be the oldest person in The Bible—969 years old. Enoch ran his race in TANDEM with God, not unlike what we know about the 'Three-Legged Race'— "he had this testimony, that he pleased God. *But without faith,* it is impossible to please Him." Was Enoch's life any less important because it was so short? No, no, no—. The quality of his race is what mattered. Again, reasonably early in life, as per history, which God gives us through the writers of the time, Enoch searched and found out what 'God Liked,' and this is how he ordered his life so that he would win out in the short journey in which he also ran 'The Race of *His Lifetime*!'

By faith Noah, being warned of God of things not seen as yet, moved with fear, prepared an ark to save his house, by which he condemned the world and became heir of the *righteousness which is by faith*. (Hebrews 11: 7; KJV)

Noah—Hardly a living soul is unaware of Noah—this 'person of Faith.' Let's come near to echoing a phrase we read in Hebrews 11: 3, with these words—*being warned of God of things not seen as 'yet.'* Again, reasonably early in the timespan of the years we have lived to in the present, Noah ran well his 'predetermined leg of the race of life.'

At times, God used harsh measures to get us onto the right track in life. Please look with me at what Ezekiel wrote about this— "Son of man, when the land sinneth against Me by trespassing grievously, then will I stretch out My hand upon it, and will break the staff of the bread thereof, and will send famine upon it, and will cut off man and beast from it: *Though these three men, Noah, Daniel, and Job*, were in it, they should deliver but their 'own' souls by their righteousness, saith the Lord God." (Ezekiel 14: 13-14; KJV)

By looking at the record of the life of Noah, we can see how highly God looked at how Noah ran his race. Noah lived to 950 years old. Why did Noah outlive someone like Enoch (65) by 885 years? God saw something in Enoch which caused Him [God] to pick Enoch up in His Carriage and take him [Enoch] to Heaven early in his life. God saw Noah's faithfulness in building The Ark and testifying about the Greatness of God throughout all this time. The only visible fruit born from Noah's witness was that Noah took only his immediate family onboard—at God's command. No one else seriously bought the 'God Thing' (God's warning about The Flood). Yes, Noah ran an 'Excellent Race.'

Right living garners or begets Faith. The list is long, containing the Heroes of Faith. Faith is the key to all the successes along this Journey of Life. I will look at a few more—there's too much history concerning all the Race participants to include all the runners.

The story of Abraham is lengthy—it includes Isaac, Jacob, Sarah—and all the extended family beyond this, enough so that God said of Abraham—,

> "And said, by Myself, I've sworn, saith the Lord, for because you have done this thing, and have not withheld your son, your only son: That in blessing I will bless you, and in multiplying I will multiply your seed as the stars of the heaven, and as the sand which is upon the seashore; and your seed shall possess the gate of his enemies; and in your seed shall all the nations of the earth be blessed; because you have obeyed My voice." (Genesis 22: 16-18; KJV)

Others in The Hall of Fame of Faith are Joseph, Moses, Rahab—

> "And what shall I more say? For the time would fail me to tell of Gedeon, and of Barak, and Samson, and of Jephthae (Jephthah); of David also, and Samuel, and of the prophets: who through subdued faith kingdoms, wrought righteousness, obtained promises, stopped the mouths of lions, quenched the violence of fire, escaped the edge of the sword, out of weakness were made strong, waxed valiant in fight, turned to flight the armies of the aliens."

Women received their dead raised to life again—tortures affected others, not accepting deliverance; that they might obtain a better resurrection: and others had trial of cruel mocking's and scourging's, yea, moreover of bonds and imprisonment—they stoned some, sawed others in half, and the killed off many others by the sword. They wandered about in sheepskins and goatskins; being destitute, afflicted, tormented; (of whom the world was not worthy:) they wandered in deserts, mountains, and dens and caves of the earth. And these all, having obtained a good report through faith, received not the promise: God having provided some better thing for us, that they without us should not be made perfect. (Hebrews 11: 32-39; KJV)

What does all this have to do with *Searching For A Heart Of Gold—Not A Pot Of Gold*? I'll begin to tell you that I will continue paving the pathway to the ANSWER. From the cover to here, I've set a course to follow through to the end of this book. As we pave the way to the conclusion, the Journey of Life will present many challenges—Centering on *preparation, purpose, progress, and preservation*.

Someone said, "The Journey of A Thousand Miles Begins With A Single Step!" This scenario is the pattern for any writer—I'm no exception. In Chapter Seven, I began with a mention which leads us to believe we'll be delving into Psalm 139. 'Delve' is a deep-rooted word, and I plan to do this as I go along. I will delve deep into God's Word, and as I do, I will also try hard to present life as we know it so we can have a backdrop that will be foundational for us to stand firm.

"Delve—Burrow, Inquire, Dig, Dredge, Examine—."

As I searched to begin at an entry point for *Searching For A Heart of Gold—Not A Pot of Gold*, which will incorporate more than just Psalms 139—"Steeplechase" sprang into my mind. While using some of my time just thinking, praying for insight into how to get this book on the rails to journey into the world to make a difference for someone [myself included], through a moment of inspiration, I found I couldn't unhook my mind off of the word "Steeplechase."

So as for Psalm 139 to at least have an Imprint, a 'Baby Step' movement in this Chapter, let's look at The opening verses of Psalm 139—. While we do this, please note how the first four verses begin telling the story. Take note of two of the three tenses—. 'Past, Present, and Future.' When I check the Internet for the 'Three Tenses,' it relays them as 'Simple Present Tense, Simple Past Tense, and Simple Future Tense.'

In one sense, I agree—I think, 'We cannot have a present if we did not have a past, and henceforth there would then be no future.' I realize that if we don't have a Present, we'll never have had a Past—or a projected Future. So, like life itself, it can get a little confusing at times.

I like to refer to the 'Tenses' as 'Past, Present and Future' because Psalm 139 opens with a realization that God is 'Eternal,' Sovereign! We always need to see God as Past (always has been), Present Now, and as there for our Future.

So, as we read Psalm 139: 1-4, please notice 'The Past Tense and The Present Tense—' we will get to the 'Future' tense at the end of Psalm 139.

> O Lord, _You have_ searched me and known me. _You know_ my downsitting and uprising; You understand my thoughts from afar. You reach out to me when I'm on the road and when I lie down and are acquainted with all my ways. There's not a word in my tongue, but, lo, O Lord, You know about it altogether. (Psalm 139: 1-4; KJV)

In 'The Vista View—The Oasis' between Chapters, I will connect 'The Dots—' so we can move on from Chapter Seven—_What Then? —Steeplechasing—_.

◊ THE VISTA VIEW—THE OASIS ◊

The Race Is Not Always To The Swift. "I glance at the world around me. When I took a quick look at how life emerges out of the crowd of folks wandering about here and there, I noticed the actions of many of the people under the sun; I became aware that "The Race Is Not To The Swift," the strong-ones do not usually win the battles. The wise people are not the most satisfied—the learned are not always the most gracious when it comes to an understanding of other people's issues—the skilled may make a name for themselves, but they are not the 'workhorses—' Time and Chance fit in the glove the same way for one and all! (Ecclesiastes 9:11; JBI)

I wondered if I should declare all this, that the righteous, and the wise, and their works, are in the hand of God—no man knoweth either love or hatred by all that is before them.

All things come similar to all: there is one event to the righteous, and to the wicked; to the good and the clean, and the unclean; to him that sacrificeth, and to him that sacrificeth not—as are the good, so are the sinners; and he that sweareth, as he that feareth an oath.

Evil lurks in everything that happens on earth. There is one event unto all—Yes, the heart of the sons of men is full of sin, and madness is in their heart while they live, and after that, they go to the dead.

Where there is life, there's still hope. A living dog is better than a dead lion.

The living know that they shall die, but the dead know not anything, neither have they any more a reward; for their memory is forgotten.

People's love, hatred, and envy have perished; neither have they a portion forever in anything done under the sun.

Go thy way, eat thy bread with joy, and drink thy wine with a merry heart; for God now accepteth thy works. Let your garments always be white, and let your head lack no ointment [Look after yourself].

Live joyfully with the wife whom thou lovest all the days of the life of thy vanity, which He hath given thee under the sun, all the days of thy vanity: for that is thy portion in this life, and in thy labour which thou takest under the sun.

Whatever thy hand findeth to do, do it with thy might; for there is no work, device, knowledge, knowledge, wisdom, in the grave, whither thou goest.

I realized that the race of life isn't only for the speedy, strong, wise, or rich in knowledge and understanding—the experienced don't simply win out over everybody else. Time and chance happen to everybody equally.

Like the fish in the water not knowing their fate or the birds not knowing their demise, people don't know the time of their death. Our end may come without warning—as suddenly as it does to all life.

This wisdom is also in play on the earth with live on, and it seemed great unto me. There was a little city, and few men within it, and there came a great king against it, and besieged it, and built great bulwarks against it—there was found a poor wise man in it, and he by his wisdom delivered the city; yet no man remembered that same poor man.

I said wisdom is better than strength; nevertheless, other people don't recognize or appreciate the poor man's understanding; no one seems to hear the words of knowledge displayed by supposed no-name folks. We hear the advice of the perceived wise people but despise those who go quietly about doing right. Wisdom is better than weapons of war: but one sinner destroyeth much good. (Ecclesiastes 9; KJV)

The Bible makes many references to 'Running The Race of Life!' The Steeplechase Race is a Great Example for us all—we have to jump over water and hurdles. Going The Distance and Clearing Hurdles presents a considerable challenge. Life is such a journey of challenges—as a *Steeplechase* suggests.

We've *focused* on many things in Chapter Seven—
God is the Center of that FOCUS.

HEART SENSE
Tomorrow Is Only A Day Away

◊

TOMORROW: How many songs, movies, books, poems, articles, and thoughts have through history shared expression about 'Tomorrow?' As I begin exploring—the list lengthens quickly—I can't give a number attributed to entities about 'Tomorrow,' even if I could, this would only change in a nanosecond because as I write, someone else is fashioning another entity concerning 'Tomorrow!'

Along with the above recollections of 'Tomorrow,' I know of at least one hundred scriptures in The Bible that express sentiments and facts about 'Tomorrow!'

Those of you who say, Today or Tomorrow, we'll travel here and there; consume some time there, do business, and make a lot of money—but you're unaware of the tomorrow ahead of you.

What's life anyway? You just get started, and it's over. If you were on the right track in life, you might say, "If it's God's will, we'll be alive and carry out some of our desires, but above all, we'll do what's on The LORD's Heart!"

It seems you are too proud of your accomplishments as if you did things in your strength and smarts; this is pretty rotten. Those who know the right things to do as per God's will, and don't do them, are guilty of being on opposing sides of The God you claim to know! (James 4:13-17; JBI)

I understand Ira Stanphill wrote, "*I Know Who Holds Tomorrow!*" As we proceed, I intend to appreciate some of his thoughts in my own words.

Scriptures In Chapter Eight
Tomorrow Is Only A Day Away
[Reflective Faith]
Psalm 139: 1-4
Ecclesiastes 1
Psalm 139: 1-4; Hebrews 11:5-6
Hebrews 11:1
Matthew 15: 19-20; Matthew 12: 34-37
Psalm 139: 1-4; 1 John 3:1-3
1 John 3: 1-3; Job 1:7-8; Job 1: 9-10
Ezekiel 22:30; 1 Corinthians 15: 51-53; Colossians 1:26
Ephesians 1:9; Isaiah 55; 8-11
Hebrews 11:5; Hebrews 11
Hebrews 11:1; James 5:7-8
The Vista View–The Oasis; Ecclesiastes 1
Galatians 2:20; Titus 2:13; Hebrews 3:15
Isaiah 30: 1921

Chapter Eight

Tomorrow Is Only A Day Away

———————————————◊———————————————

O LORD, YOU'VE SEARCHED ME—YOU KNOW ME. You understand my thoughts 'while I'm down or up' [I'm thinking emotively]—surrounding the road I'm travelling—when I'm resting, You know I need a time out! Not a word in my tongue escapes You—LORD; You realize everything! (Psalm 139: 1-4; JBI)

There are huge differences between Yesterday and Today. Though they are only hours apart—they present mega entities. It is imperative to deal with each new day differently than yesterday! We can never reclaim Yesterday, though it's just One Day Behind Us On The Calendar—it's gone! The overall Agenda we had Yesterday may be the same as Today. Let's look at the weather patterns; they are not the same; it may just be that Yesterday was sunny and today is cloudy; it may be that Today is a degree or two different than Yesterday, up or down one way or another.

My mood this morning isn't precisely the same today as yesterday at this exact time. As I'm writing these words and thinking about my mood, it's different today than yesterday at the same hour of the day. Yesterday was Easter Sunday—Yesterday, as I was trying to be in the right MOOD for Easter Sunday, 'Resurrection Day,' I was allowing the Yesterday of Yesterday to impact the Mood I was trying to create for Easter Sunday.

As Good Friday ended, I began to think about The Disciples of Jesus and the Saturday they were now having. It saddened me when I put myself [as much as is possible] in their shoes for a while—because they'd just lost the dearest friend they ever had in this life. The disciples and others felt the world had ended. Jesus told them what would happen, but somehow they hadn't looked past the present! ["Reflective Faith" can help us *through* tough times]. Can we move forward if we don't reflect on where we are in life?

On Saturday, between Good Friday and Easter Sunday, 'Resurrection Day' (filled with all the promises of Tomorrow), I allowed myself to fall into the same Pit of Despair as the Disciples of Jesus did in their Yesterday (Yesteryear) of so long ago now! When we think about it (a friend of mine in the 'Past' used to say to me, "Think About It!"), life is the same today as it was then. Solomon talks about this in Ecclesiastes—.

The person called The Preacher, the King of Jerusalem, the son of David (the Shepherd Boy at one time), said—

> Vanity, everything is vain (useless)—he stressed it by using repetition. (Ecclesiastes 1)

What does it profit as we work hard to get ahead day after day, whether it is sunny or cloudy—every day is the same, or so it seems. Solomon realized that the Earth as he knew it would be here for a long time ['forever,' as he understood forever to be, I guess].

> "Generation after generation, we live out life—everything seems hopeless and unfulfilling—but the earth faithfully fulfills itself at God's command. The sun comes up—it goes down and hurries back again to where it came up. The wind goes Southward, then it turns around and goes Northward. It whirls busily—continually, returning on the path from which it came. All the rivers go into the ocean, yet it's not full; like the wind, they go back to where they began." (Ecclesiastes 1; JBI)

Everything we do is laborious (exacting and searchingly painstaking)—It's tough to understand it all. As we look at life and hear about all the 'stuff' happening around us and beyond what we can see—we're not now satisfied, and it seems we're never going to be satisfied! It seems we cannot get any Satisfaction—As The Rolling Stones sang about not getting any Satisfaction, they made this clear from their viewpoint or framework of Life! It seems like "Satisfaction" is Number One on our Bucket List!

> "Whatever was, will be again. That which we did in the past, we'll do over again in some manner. There's nothing much new over the horizon. Is there anything we can credit for being new? As we think of the past, nothing much has changed in the pattern of people's lives." (Ecclesiastes 1; JBI)

In reality, no one knows what it was like Back In The Day—they, in turn, didn't know what it was going to be like in the TOMORROW they anticipated—when they looked back on their YESTERDAYS, it was the same as it is for us when we do the said same.

"I the Preacher was king over Israel in Jerusalem. I gave my heart to seek wisdom concerning all things done under heaven. This sore travail hath God given to the sons of man (people) to be (this is the way God said it would be) exercised in addition to what I saw in all the works done under the sun; behold all is vanity and vexation of spirit. That which is crooked cannot be made straight, and we cannot number our wants."

"I conversed with my heart (I mulled it over within my mind), saying, I've become wealthy. I've gotten more wisdom than those before my time in Jerusalem. Yes, my heart had great experience of wisdom and knowledge—and I gave my heart to know wisdom, and to know madness and folly: I perceived that this also vexes the spirit. In much wisdom is grief; those that increase knowledge-wise increase with sorrow." (Ecclesiastes 1; KJV and JBI thoughts, Jacob Bergen Insights Intermingled)

As I was grinding it out—trudging through the Saturday between Good Friday and Easter Sunday—thinking about the things which challenged my Peace of Mind on that Saturday and through the Catch-Up Time early Sunday, I tried to set my sights on what was The True Reality! "Jesus Did Rise From The Dead!" If this was true, and I believe it was and is, then my Mood should at some point begin to *reflect* this Reality—And it did! It's often A Three Day Journey for me to Catch Up With The Reality That God Is Always In Control. "Reflective Faith" can help us *through* life when tough times surface.

I won't go into any more detail to describe my dealings with 'mood' issues here—Sunday Evening nailed it down for me as I watched a Celebration from First Baptist Church in Jacksonville, Florida. I heard testimonies of how God met people's needs and how for them, Trusting In God's Word made The Difference! As a Christ Follower, the crux of the matter always stems back—To What God Said and What Still Echoes From His Word Today! "Are We The People Listening?"

157

"There are huge differences between 'Yesterday and Today.' Though they are only hours apart (up to twenty-four hours each day)—they present mega entities which we need to deal with differently." (*IBID*)

I mentioned things such as 'weather and moods' as examples of how yesterday's stuff is not always the same the following day. The people we meet in the Tomorrow of Yesterday most often differ. The jobs we work on vary significantly in many respects. The feelings we have about things happening to us now after Yesterday—A New Day we now call Today—differs. The many things that are diametrically or utterly different from day-to-day are almost 'impossible' to duplicate day after day—unless we live somewhat in a world of a "*Ground Hog Day*" movie situation. I got into this theme more in-depth in my previous book, *Everybody: Everybody Is A Somebody* (*EEIAS*)—here below are a few lines from page sixty-eight (and the theme extends here somewhat).

"Please observe some synonyms for 'ditto'—repetition, duplication, replication, rerun (and we all know what reruns are on TV), duplicate, replica (as in a redo of an old ship)—. A 'replica' of Noah's Ark would be attractive. No one seems to have made a replica of Moses's Ark. Moses Ark was a basket in the water amongst the bulrushes.

Ditto indicates what someone already stated when applied a second time— 'ditto mark.' If one person folds their arms or legs, everyone in view does the same; this is the picture we can define as ditto. We may all have a few memory-filled situations we'd like to 'ditto,' like some rich person we would like them to share their wealth with us—their bank account transferred to ours—Ditto.

In *Groundhog Day*—though every day was the same in the movie concept with the same time on the alarm clock ringing early in the morning—it offered something 'different!' Then, each day opened up new people and new opportunities to make a difference. As it seems he always had, Bill Murray has a way of lightening the moment by making a 'difficult moment' for someone else in the movement from a problem to a solution come out not so bad. Along with *Groundhog Day,* I'm thinking about the movie *What About Bob.*

What if every morning at 6 AM, my alarm clock (one which I have not used for many years because I've had an alarm clock in my head) lambasted me with *I got You Babe*, and the announcer chirped *Rise and Shine*—it would most certainly bring memories of repetition to mind?

I've detailed enough on this theme of how Each Day Is Different Than The Other—. Because of this, we need to have something we can hang onto to give us the strength we need to persevere as life changes before our very eyes. Do most folks like changes? I Don't Necessarily always take well to Change!"

Again, let's get into a part of Psalm 139 to see how it 'fits well' as a good glove does for us—furthering or broadening our thoughts of 'Tomorrows' we will yet encounter. Let's hear the first four verses again—

"O LORD, You have searched me and known me. You know my downsitting and uprising; You understand my thoughts afar off. Thou compassest my path and 'my' lying down, and art acquainted with all my ways. There is no word in my tongue, but, lo, O Lord, You know it altogether." (Psalm 139: 1-4; KJV)

We have an 'imprint' of a Baby Step entrance into Chapter Eight. Psalm 139 'begins' to tell the story. *Reflective Faith can help us sort things out.* The three tenses mentioned previously, 'Past, Present, and Future—' these are similar to how a 'relay race' manages the baton—each one comes more easily for us if we hear them like this, "Simple Present Tense; Simple Past Tense; and Simple Future Tense." 'Simplifying our speech helps people get the message we thrust out to 'their senses.' While dealing with the acceptance factor of other people regarding what we wish to enhance their lives with, one phrase says it well, KISS (Keep It Simple Stu—id! I am trying to be kind!)

Can we have a 'Present without a Past?' Adam—Eve had a 'Present,' without having had a natural 'Past' (except in the heart and forethought of God). The scenario of Adam and Eve is unique—being the very beginning of human reality. If we don't have a 'Present' (today), will we ever have had a 'Yesterday' (Past)?' All Of Life gets confusing at times!

Referring to these Tenses as Past, Present and Future, Psalm 139 says so clearly, and early, God is Eternal, Sovereign—He is Supreme! The passage helps us know we need to understand God as Past, Present Now, and ready ourselves to be there for our Future. While looking at Psalm 139: 1-4, please notice The Past Tense and The Present Tense—. The Future tense will follow as we continue to explore more of God.

Let's soul-search (examine) ourselves and check God's source or beginning (God has no beginning—if He did have a Genesis, He wouldn't be God). Please look at 'this' theme 'firstly' the only way we can, from a human understanding—last I looked, we are still human. 'Secondly,' let's try to look at it from Our New Birth Sense of Understanding—Spiritually.

From our Inborn understanding, we might think, 'How Can Any Entity Be Ever-Existent?' We can't come close in this matter from a Human Standpoint. Hebrews 11: 5-6 reveals the following—

"By faith, Enoch took flight at the workings of God— he didn't see death; and was not found, because God translated him: for before his translation he had this testimony, that he pleased God. But without faith, it is impossible to please Him: for he that cometh to God must believe He is and that He is a rewarder of them that diligently seek Him."
(RE. Hebrews 11:5-6; KJV-JBI)

Let's look at verse five for a moment—from a Human Angle and a Spiritual Image (we can only Imagine). As we see the word 'Translated' and check it out in the thesaurus, we see these words: 'adapted, rendered, reworded, rewritten, transliterated;' these words 'ask' me to think about Enoch—was he just 'Refaced or Resurfaced?' Did he have an 'Extreme Makeover?' From a mortal lookout point, I understand this to be the case. From this Human Point of View, I fashion thoughts like edited, reworked, recast, redrafted, rephrased, reworded—like the story of his Earthly Life was just retold after some significant changes took place.

In one sense, this is true; Enoch was a person who fashioned his daily life in such a way to be 'Everything' God created him to be. Enoch was different; he was somewhat 'Edited' to be more distinct than the rest of the crowd; to him, God 'was' and 'is' more than just another created being—God is DIFFERENT TOO!

I just read a Daily Devotional for April 16 (April 16/2021) as I write these words in *Searching For A Heart Of Gold; Not A Pot Of Gold*. The Devotional is *Sanctuary*, by David Jeremiah. David wrapped his thoughts in and around *Sanctuary* for today in Hebrews 11:1—he hit the target—BULLSEYE! There's relevancy here because I am dealing with the Faith aspect of *SFAHOG* in Chapter Eight. I attempt to understand how living Real Life is possible—unless we have FAITH. (This is the Mantra I cling to!).

> "Faith is the substance of things hoped for, the evidence of things not seen." (Hebrews 11: 1; KJV)

What Dr. Jeremiah brought to mind for me is that we live with what seems to be a notion that success comes through accumulating dough (wealth). The achievements we enrich ourselves with, and anything else we can fashion as the Ultimate Measure of Importance, 'leaves us lacking' Heroes. However—'On The Long Road (Life's Journey),' many of these quote-unquote heroes disappointed us—many more will yet do so!

As we SEARCH through the many avenues of Life in our Quest for success—are we Ever-On (Forever) farther afield (Astray) of the Success of Finding The Heart of Gold Within Our Being? In my recollection—today was the first time I *ever* heard the song *Ever On*, and for that matter, singer and songwriter Dan Fogelberg (1951-2007—56 years old). 'Absorbed' as I am in the importance of presenting another attempt at Discovering A Heart of Gold, my search continues *Ever On*. As I listen closely to the lyrics, I hear songs, watch movies, read books, or hear another communicator showing us their lives. How do we 'listen to someone's life?—' We observe their HEART.

As I heard *Ever On*, by Dan Fogelberg, it reminded me of another singer I have listened to often—Neil Young. As Neil sings *Heart of Gold*, he opens channels of expressive words. While *Searching For A Heart of Gold*, Neil says, "I wanna live (I want to live)—I wanna give (I want to give); I've seen it written on song sheets both ways. I set out on a seemingly uncharted course as I listened. When I listen to The Lives of Anyone, my Course is but one—Do The Words Match The Heart? While listening to what I observe—I'm tempted to evaluate The True Value of this person's life—this is not my job: "This Is God's Job!" Please forgive me!

Listening to *Ever On*, I feel Dan Fogelberg talking about us merely being like a solo stone whirling about as if on an earth-sized spindle. Seemingly, endlessly separated or isolated, *Ever-On* has us spinning our wheels in what we consider a Search for what life offers. We find ourselves moving forward in an open world of nothingness, posing as a motion picture of hopelessness—because the world we know best provides many of the fruits of the Fleshy Heart of desire.

Dan goes on, pointing us to an answer of an image of Nothingness. As I listen to *Ever On*, his thoughts come alive within me as he uses the word YOUR—I see him *reflecting* on God. Mr. Fogelberg doesn't ask for God's love (not in these actual words) to guide us, be vital for us—that we may have the courage and tenacity to follow in God's footsteps as He leads us *Ever On*.

David Jeremiah's Hero thing leaves us with only one option for HEROHOOD! JESUS can be our only Hero because only God can judge rightly and or fairly when it comes to knowing if one specific person's Search for a Pure Heart is right or wrong. God looks at the Heart.

"Out of the heart proceed evil thoughts, murders, adulteries, fornications, thefts, false witness, blasphemies: These are the things that defile a man (person): but eating with unwashed hands doesn't violate a person." (Matt. 15: 19-20; KJV).

"O generation of vipers, how can you, who are evil, speak good things?—for out of the abundance of the heart, the mouth speaks. A good man (person) out of the good treasure of the heart brings forth good things: and an evil man (person) out of the evil treasure bringeth forth 'evil' things. But I say unto you, that every idle word that men (people) shall speak, they shall give account thereof in the day of judgment. For by your words, you'll be justified, and by your words, condemnation will come your way." (Matt. 12: 34-37; KJV)

Neil Young also admirably expresses things related to our *Search For A Heart of Gold*. Neil Says, *Yes*, he wants to live—I hear in my spirit that he wants to live life in such a way as to be beneficial to humankind. He says, "I Want To Give!" Neil doesn't say he "Wants To Give 'EM Hell.'" Neil says I Want To Live; I Want To Give—I hear that he wants to give back to People!

I Was Here (written by Diane Warren) sung by Beyonce is a song talking about giving back for some of what life gave her—the *Search For A Heart of Gold* resonates (rings) within me here as I write. Words like *having left footprints on the shores of life* and *living and leaving with a no-regrets policy in hand*— "I was here, I lived, I loved, I was here, I did, I've done, everything that I wanted," "I wanna say I lived each day until I died."

"What a legacy for life to leave behind." After we've lived life, it'll be fantastic to search our earthly and spiritual terrain so that we can come to our end having done our best in both worlds. Thoughts come to mind as I've searched out people who have expressed a desire to have a *Heart of Gold*, and they encourage me to move ever onward. For me, to have had a 'Want To' which cannot be satisfied by anything else but to have a *Heart For God* is the only resource that will meet an empty Heart.

What does God say regarding the Search Of The Heart? As I read Psalm 139, I get answers to this question.

> "O LORD, *You have* searched me and known me. *You know* my downsitting and uprising; You understand my thoughts from afar. *You compass my path and 'my' lying down and are acquainted with all my ways.* There's not a word in my tongue, but, lo, O Lord, You know it altogether." (Psalm 139: 1-4—IBID)

Psalm 139 continually has me leading us along the path of Heart Thoughts. These thoughts come out as promises about how God has always looked out for us in The Past—He is looking out for us In The Present—and I see the promise of God's intent to continue looking out for us throughout time and eternity. It's the same caveat that we see in Genesis when God created Adam and Eve—Choose Life In God, and God Alone, and life can be LG (Life Is Good) *Ever-On (Forever)*—Choose to go it alone—and alone you will remain.

If I were a prospector, I would love to find PURE Gold just lying on the ground waiting for me to horde as much as I could carry—might this be too easy? Yes, but this is not how it is! On our Search For Gold, we find that finding it is one thing—making it pure, quite another thing! In 1 John 3: 1-3, John gives us a little picture of how God looks at us—long after the time of Adam and Eve in The Garden of Eden.

Behold, what manner of love the Father has conferred upon us, that we should be called the sons of God: therefore, the world doesn't know us because it knew Him not. Beloved, now are we the sons of God, and *it doesn't yet appear what we'll be*: but we know that, when He shall appear, we shall be like Him; for we shall see Him as He is. And everyone that has this hope in Him *purifies themselves*, even as He is pure. (1 John 3:1-3; KJV)

What was God leading up to in Psalm 139—David realized God had searched him out long before the period represented in Psalm 139. Was God Searching for a season of time after Creation like any other person? Did God plan things out, putting the pieces of the Puzzle of Life into just the right place at the proper time for all things to reach the climax of His strategy of the ages? It's often difficult to grasp a complete understanding of many things written in The Bible—the concept of God SEARCHING is one of these things.

And the Lord said unto Satan, 'Where did you come from?' Satan replied, 'from going to and fro in the earth and walking up and down in it.' And the Lord said unto Satan, 'have you considered My servant Job, that there is none like him in the earth, a perfect and an upright man, one that fears God and evil?' (Job 1:7-8' KJV-JBI)

God inquires of Satan about the matters he was pursuing regarding the Search Satan was on to find fault with Job—as well, it seems he was trying to find fault with God.

Then Satan answered the Lord and said, 'Does Job fear God for nothing? Haven't You hedged him and surrounded his house and all he has on every side? You have blessed the work of his hands and increased his worth in the land.' (Job 1: 9-10; KJV-JBI)

There was a lot of 'Searching' going on in the Book of Job! Someone was always searching to find faults and reasons to understand why a loving God allowed the testing of Job so harshly, just to prove Job was for real! Many folks think God should never put us to the test. I don't think God puts us to the test because He has doubts about us—but because we have doubts about ourselves.

In the Bible Book of Ezekiel, we see another portrait of *what seems like* God didn't always know what was going to happen at a particular time in history:

> I looked (searched) for someone from the crowd to build the fence and stand in the gap before Me to make the needed difference to keep Me from destroying the life that often grows into a patch of weeds—but I found nobody. (Ezekiel 22: 30; JBI)

Can we possibly understand the ways of God if He doesn't reveal Himself to us in a specific way? "I show you a mystery" (1 Corinthians 15: 51-53—). I know the Scriptural context is different here than what I suggest. Ephesians 1:9 says, "He made known to us the mystery of his will according to his good pleasure, which he purposed in Christ." In another place, The Bible says— "God kept some things back *to be a mystery* for a season of time—but now, The LORD shows us the hidden portions He once held back for that right season of time to appear." (Colossians 1:26; KJV)

In Isaiah 55, God says His ways are not our ways—so has anything we face in *our day*, or *any days since* Creation, ever been a mystery to God? *Methinks not!*

> My thoughts are not your thoughts, neither are your ways My ways, saith the Lord.
>
> The heavens are higher than the earth—in just the same way. My ways are loftier than your ways, and My thoughts than your thoughts.
>
> For as the rain comes down, as does the snow from heaven, and I don't remove them from you, but they water the earth and cause it to bud, so it gives seed to the sower, and bread to the eater: This is because My Word will never come back to *me empty-handed*! (Isaiah 55: 8-11; KJV)

It's not hard for me to understand that a MYSTERY is never understood until it's *searched out* or *someone reveals it to us*. When we search for and find the answer to the mystery, it's because someone left some clues behind. If it remained in hiding as if sealed off in or under a place in the Rocky Mountains of BC, buried beneath a mountain of more rocks—where's the hope of ever finding the answer? What are the chances of finding that Pure Jade, Gold, Silver—*unless someone maps out a path* to find the treasure?

However, I want to insert a mention of Jade here for interest's sake. Jade is tucked away inside stones, rocks, and even boulders. The rock's worth is not visible, only surmised (guessed at or speculated). One approach to knowing is to strike the rock with a hammer or sledgehammer because a jade stone will bounce back the hammer. Once we determine that the jade is in the boulder, stone, or rock, someone needs to cut a small hole in the stone. We can conclude that pursuing a search for Jade is no easy task—uncovering the Mystery is undoubtedly going to be a challenge! However, I suggest God knows where to look—He imbedded the Jade where it resides. If He is God, we cannot hide anything from His view: Scary Stuff—if we put it into the perspective of us mortals trying to get away with anything.

I don't necessarily want to say *I Am Leading Up To Something* as if only saying *we are here today*—and *we will be such and such in the end*. Although this is true in the Eternal Sense, there is a process by which we get to that Eternal sense in the *purest* form possible. Instead, in the most *present state,* I need to be saying I am leading us *through something* to get *to something* which will be the Best Case Scenario For All Our Labours In The Present! You are probably thinking, "What's he leading up to—What's he up to anyway?"

Physical Life has a correlating or associating factor with Spiritual Life! Let's look at eight factors in achieving *pure gold*! I found the process of refining gold on the following site [https://www.ehow.com/how_10024980_refine-gold-fire.html].

Hopefully, we'll begin to understand at least eight steps in the search for gold—however; I wish to add one step at the very top of the list: 'We have to find the gold first' in its raw form before we can insert it into the crucible, or container.

1] Insert the gold scraps and the flux into the crucible.

2] Put the crucible into the fire.

3] Stoke the fire until the heat reaches 1947.52 degrees Fahrenheit, which is the melting point of gold. The gold in the crucible will start to melt.

4] Take the crucible from the fire when the gold is molten.

5] Pour the molten gold into the mould and let it cool.

6] Separate the gold's base metals (copper, silver, iron, tin, lead, mercury, antimony). They'll float atop the mould.

7] Insert the gold into a *retort* with diluted nitric acid.

8] Pour off the nitric acid; pure gold remains.

(the physical process for making raw physical gold pure).

When we talk about the Spiritual Heart becoming Gold, we deal with gold's unusual concept. If we look at physical descriptions of entities we live with each day, we understand Spiritual things better. As we read the Bible, it becomes more apparent how parables help us understand 'challenging issues' better.

Today, we have many examples of people wanting our attention—Some are worth listening to, and others aren't. Often we think of some folks as Heroes—we may need to do a *credibility check*! In some respects, we all have Heroes; we may not think of some people as Heroes, but when we put one person ahead of the others on the *importance scale,* we suggest their measure of life is more significant than others. Let's stay within the same context when we are making comparisons. What comes out of our *hearts* is spoken through our mouths or by the things we do.

So, to stress a point on the word 'translated,' made earlier, we would say that because Enoch was a Good Person—God wanted to make him stand out for special recognition—put him on a pedestal in The Town Square! For us to understand Hebrews 11:5 any differently than him [Enoch] just having had 'An Extreme Makeover, or a Re-Do—' yes, we need to come to believe it was not a picture of simply being "WYSIWYG."

God lifted Enoch out of the misery of that time on earth. When we look back into The Greek (the authorship seems to imply Hebrews was written in Greek rather than what we may think—Hebrew) form from which Hebrews 11 was supposedly written—we see the word *translated,* sourced out from "Transposed."

"Transposed" gives us a clearer image of how the writer helps us understand. Initially, the verbs *swap* and *switch* come to mind. As I *reflect,* I think someone has changed residencies from earth to heaven without losing any sense of competency or ability. Death is not like this immediately, although it comes out in the Eternal purpose. When I think of Enoch's transposition, I see the story positioning me to understand God better—God took Enoch on as a part of His official team beside Him in heaven; for a particular function that he could no longer perform on earth.

"Reflective Faith" can help us understand more clearly.

Yes, I may be *Out On A Limb* here—I may Truly Be Out To Lunch. Please look at some synonyms for 'Transpose.'

"Commute, exchange, flip-flop, interchange, inverse, invert, move, put, relocate, shift, transfer, transmute (transform or change also fit here)."

We can use all these words to focus on anything we can think of as being movable in any fashion in the *earthly sense*. However, I want to take us out of the *temporal world* and translate, transpose, move, transfer, transmute, exchange, and relocate us into the second part of the theme mentioned above— "Translate" the *Spiritual Sense*.

To do this, we need to create, fashion, manufacture, order up—or understand a means of doing that is initially Out-Of-This-World—ethereal or non-earthly. Hebrews 11:1 tells us what this is.

"Now faith is the means of support we hope for, the proof of things we cannot see clearly." (Re. Hebrews 11: JBI)

How can we be taken out of this world apart from death and remain alive—in some respects, we could say it's the same as experiencing a translation. If this were the case, we would no longer be active in a fleshly way. The Spiritual World is otherworldly—not of the physicality we experience in our skin.

In our *Search For A Heart Of Gold—Not A Pot Of Gold*, please appreciate that there are 'Four Seasons' in the cycle of Creation—The Bible mentions Spring, Summer, and Winter. We know there are Four Seasons, and yes, The Bible mentions the third season, 'Fall or Autumn,' as 'The Harvest,' the seventh month—and other scriptures refer to The Fall Season. I don't think The Bibles says, 'Fall or Autumn' about this 'Season of the year.' However, it often refers to it in ways similar to the following—*So, folks*, be patient until the Lord's coming. See how the farmer waits for the precious fruit of the earth and is patient with it until it receives the early and the late rains. You also must be patient. Strengthen your hearts because the Lord's coming is near. (James 5:7-8; KJV-JBI)

The Rules of The Race have not changed. Our Race still operates under the same Rules as did the disciples of Jesus and all who had run before—OT Times. History *Is A Wonderful Word* emanating (oozing) from the experiential or practical life. Practical life is the stuff we usually manage without *FAITH*.

Over my years of writing, specific thoughts have captivated or attracted me to a particular theme of life that would be a part of my day to help me in my decision-making, sometimes for what may seem like minor issues or events. At other times, these moments of input into my spirit were majorly eventful in creating a *starting line* for what would be life-changing sessions—times I wouldn't have wanted to miss.

When I claim Inspiration for these inserts into my psyche, I often tend to feel as if there were some divine entity guiding my thoughts, in the process, directing my steps, or at least trying to get my attention. As I phrase these thoughts to express descriptive words, I try to evaluate the input rationally and spiritually to find the yardstick that will set a mark that I can depend upon to be clear and concise or *more to the point*.

Tomorrow Is Only A Day Away!

If Tomorrow Is Only A Day Away, we must sense 'Suddenness' to be of the nature of Reality which is more involved in our lives than just, 'Today Is All There Is!' Now Is The Time!

The Yesterdays of life brought about 'Today.' The Todays of our lives will, if we live on through another 'nighttime' of our lives, force us to accept the challenge of 'Tomorrow.' Tomorrow, if we extend the pattern, takes us through to the Future—Eternity. Do we have *Eternity In Our Hearts*?

Each day comes upon us every twenty-four hours. Every twenty-four-hour segment of time challenges us with new opportunities. As we've searched to see if we could have managed Yesterday better to affect change so Today would give us better results, we gained invaluable strength to seek God's help to facilitate the process. Who of us doesn't want life to be better today than yesterday played out?

SUDDENNESS presents quite a story! It pictures out in many words: astonishment, awe, bewilderment, consternation, curiosity, disappointment, miracle, shock, abruptness, bombshell, disillusion, eureka, godsend, miscalculation, phenomenon, precipitousness, prodigy, rarity, start, stupefaction, thunderbolt, whammy, wonderment, astoundment, curveball, eye-opener, unexpected and unforeseen—.

"REFLECTIVE FAITH" CAN HELP US THROUGH TOUGH TIMES.

"Reflective Faith" can help us *through* tough times—YES! So simply speaking—*What Is Reflective Faith*? Don't completely throw away the Past or the *Possibilities* and *Opportunities* of Today—Use it for its intended *purpose*! As we *Reflect*, we can better *Prepare* for TOMORROW!

◊ THE VISTA VIEW—THE OASIS ◊

Everything 'Tucked Away'(Ensconced) in Chapter Eight fits between Yesterday (History) & Tomorrow (The Future). Everything which is 'ensconced' (hidden, established, entrenched, installed) in Chapter Eight has a bearing on Yesterday, Today, and Tomorrow. These segments or seasons are all relevant in their historical participation time zone.

Spring, Summer, and Fall are Seasons of *Preparation*—Winter is when we hunker down to manage the harsh (tough, rough, bleak. severe, cruel—) season. If we toughen up in the Winter, we can welcome Spring from the resources we have thought through to best work through Spring, Summer, and Fall to ready ourselves once again for WINTER.

Caution is an excellent expenditure—If life seems only to pan out in the win column—and we believe nothing will ever change—we shouldn't throw caution to the wind! The Winter scenario focuses here on The Physical and The Spiritual sense. "Did we defeat Entropy?"

Consequences come whether we like them or not—we often face good outcomes, and then at times, we experience the harsh results of bad decisions. Entropy is a picture of beginning in a perfect state, and when we start to live through the tough times, things go downhill; perfection is always out of reach in the physical condition of Creation. (Ecclesiastes 1)

The song *Tomorrow* begins the first verse transliterated (Rewritten) like this in JBI (*Jacob Bergen Insight*) format—

We can be sure *Tomorrow* will be everything we want it to be. Yes, we will *Ever On* (*Forever*) have Sunshine and Roses as our 'Just Desert' (what we think we deserve because we are such friendly people)—You can bet on this! It is a 'Sure Bet!'—OR NOT—Methinks!

The first verse of *Tomorrow* presents a measure of 'false assurance,' a danger of 'misplaced reliance,' but there is also a degree of 'Faith' measured by purpose. What I like about this first verse of *Tomorrow* is—if our 'assurance,' not the 'false assurance,' is 'rightly placed,' we get to make a difference—By The Faith of The Son of God— "There Will Be Sunshine Tomorrow!"

Galatians 2:20 speaks of Paul's confidence in Christ when he says that 'persecution' comes, and it comes to me.' Paul follows with, "nevertheless;" he is still alive, but not in his strength, but in the power of what Jesus did for him. He says whatever he can do is because God has enough Faith for any challenge he may face. The truth is, God, in Jesus Christ, became human, suffered human frailties, and thereby allowed Him to understand us on the level of humanity!

While we think about *Tomorrow*, 'Doom & Gloom' threats try to deter us. However, Hope Rightly Placed is not Hope Deferred (Delayed). Who is The Son of God? JESUS! Who is our Blessed Hope? JESUS! "Looking for that 'Blessed Hope,' and the glorious appearing of the great God and our Saviour Jesus Christ; (Titus 2:13)

Presently, I'm thinking about Spider's Webs. The spider weaves the web with intent. The intent is to capture certain prey. The capture is not only with the intent to kill subjectively (feeling-based). The Spider has the *purpose* of survival in its sights as the motive for its project. The victim in the plot might feel unjustly dealt with—the victim's misplaced hope is also 'having the matter of survival' as motive enough to attack The Spider, or the victim may be out and about on some other task.

'Misplaced Hope' often does just that, leaving us to be caught up in the wind and sent packing in so far as making a difference is concerned. Instead of having Joy in The Journey, oppression and sorrow often leave us in the dust with only 'Grey Skies' in our sights. If we can foster 'A Stiff Upper Lip' and 'Grin and Bear It' by 'Faith In The Son Of God—JESUS, we will say again— "There Will Be Sunshine *Tomorrow*!"

These are the things between our Yesterdays and our Tomorrows—We call them TODAY! If we will hear The Voice of JESUS—TODAY—and *keep our Hearts soft and pliable*, we will be able to hang on until *Tomorrow*. (Hebrews 3:15) No matter what transpires, trying to leave us 'Hopelessly Stuck' on our difficulties, thinking our grey skies could never come 'Blue,' "There Will Be Sunshine *Tomorrow*!" If we set our eyes on JESUS, The Author and Finisher of our Faith—because of the JOY He saw ahead—we can also endure the crosses which may block the road at times—because we know 'The Detour Sign is Up!'

"Reflective Faith—" Might this be worth the effort?

For the people shall dwell in Zion at Jerusalem: thou shalt weep no more: he will be very gracious unto thee at the voice of thy cry; when He shall hear it, He will answer thee. And though the Lord give you the bread of adversity, and the water of affliction, yet shall not thy teachers be removed into a corner anymore, thine eyes shall see thy teachers: And thine ears shall hear a word behind thee, saying, This is the way, walk ye in it, when ye turn to the right hand, and when ye turn to the left. (Isaiah 30: 19-21; KJV)

The Heart Thoughts I have gleaned and shared here leave me with no option but to credit Charles Strouse and Martin Charnin for writing the song *Tomorrow* for The Musical "Annie—" was this not the case, I would have 'Suffered In The Loss of "*TOMORROW*!"

Many songs focus on Tomorrow in the title— "Tomorrow, Tomorrow Morning, Tomorrow Tomorrow, Come Tomorrow, Miss Tomorrow, Tomorrow's Dream, Tomorrow The World, Pave Your Way Into Tomorrow, Will You Still Love Me Tomorrow, Tomorrow Comes Today, They Shall Be Married Tomorrow, Yesterday's Tomorrow, Put It Off Until Tomorrow, Tomorrow Is Today, Yours Until Tomorrow, Goin' Home Tomorrow, 2 Days 'Til Tomorrow—. There are many more such songs; I'd love to pursue them all—but the message is clear enough in the above list.

I'll mention a few words of one more song that's often encouraged me— "*Many Things About Tomorrow I Don't Understand.*" Ira Stanphill wrote, "*I Don't Know About Tomorrow.*" We may not know everything about *Tomorrow*, but if we know Him Who has it in hand—we are in good stead—JESUS Has The Whole World IN HIS HANDS!

"Reflective Faith" can help us *through* tough times—YES! So simply speaking—*What Is Reflective Faith*? Don't completely throw away the Past or the *Possibilities* and *Opportunities* of Today—Use it for its intended *purpose*! As we *Reflect*, we can better *Prepare* for TOMORROW! (IBID)

WHAT'S NOT TO LOVE ABOUT TOMORROW?

I LOOK FORWARD TO *TOMORROW*!

Scriptures In Part Three Front Matter
—A Serious Search—
Jeremiah 29:13
Heart Sense
Matthew 11: 28-29; 1 Peter 5:7; Ephesians 3:20
Matthew 11:28-29

Part Three

A Serious Search

FOR A HEART OF GOLD?

FOR A POT OF GOLD?

OR

FOR THE HEART OF GOD?

"Where Will We Search For The Heart of God?"

As we live through the channels of everyday life in the present—we live in ambiguity (doubt). The 'Conundrum Arena' is 'problematic,' it's a world of mystery.' We might find ourselves puzzled in our decision-making; we realize we are riddled, inundated, or overwhelmed by the rules of our nations as they expect us to change the way we have learned to live as we grew up. We face the challenge of switching lanes on the highway of living life, and we feel as if we are posing or posturing as one thing while living another.

The channels (stations, networks, frequencies, canals, and or conduits) of life are incredibly varied—one channel declares everything to be white—another channel submits or *proposes* everything is black—. The forces of life offer more and more other living scenarios for us to consider—not even only to contemplate— they try to 'enforce' their newly concocted belief system on everyone who thinks differently than they do! God—Whomever He is (I have no qualms about Who He is—) either doesn't exist or is not the least bit interested in whether we listen and or adhere to His 'rule set' for living.

Hey—Let's Get Serious! When we notice the sky is blue and cloudless and the sunshine rules the day, we know it won't rain. It may rain on our parade—the plans we humans make for how life and living for that day will pan out. Are those wet drops held back until the cosmological, environmental, meteorological, or climactic conditions change? Do the clouds come to physically 'rain on our parade?'

The winds of change bring with them a horde of differing elements. As we move along to receive the words of this writer (me) and others, or not? —we need to expect to confront a multitude of choices and decisions about life on our planet and the world to come!

"WHERE WILL WE SEARCH FOR THE HEART OF GOD?"

OR

WILL WE?

When you search for Me intently—
When you set your Heart on Me—
There's no doubt you will find Me!
(Jeremiah 29:13)

My People, I'm fully aware of you
My every thought focuses on you—
Throughout your day and your night—
My watchful eyes will guide your steps—
Peace—Not evil; this is My Heart for you!
I'll provide an ending for you
That which you may not see—
When you're in the throes of distress—
Of the darkness of the night!
(Jeremiah 29:11)

HEART SENSE
Lord; I Know You Hear My Prayer

———————————◊———————————

LORD—MY HEART IS AN OPEN BOOK. I wait longingly for my Heart to be more like Your Heart! Miracles still happen! "Come unto Me, all ye that labour and are heavy laden, and I will give you rest. Take My yoke upon you and learn of Me; because "I Am" meek and lowly in heart: and ye shall find rest unto your souls." (Matthew 11:28-29; KJV-JBI)

Part One of this book began with *The Shepherd's Landing and The Hills and the Plains.* In Part Three of *Searching For A Heart of Gold,* I surrender to the question, *Where Will We Search For The Heart of God*? The answer lies in "Him Who is able—to keep me from falling or failing (Ephesians 3:20)." 'This Challenge' will be my attempt at changing lanes on life's highway!

Cast all your care upon Him; because He cares for and about you. (1 Peter 5:7)

When I think about the word 'Cast,' I think about something like YouTube, where I found a song or movie—it is nice to have it handy on my cell phone, but much more enjoyable when, through this convenience, I can project (cast) it onto the big 58-inch screen of my Samsung Smart TV. When I think of the word 'Cast,' concerning the Bible, verse (1 Peter 5:7), I see myself as encouraged to put my cares onto 'The Big Guy,' JESUS, where I see all my issues as more manageable—God, through His Holy Spirit, helps me through the problems!

Stay Tuned Seriously Through Part Three—
Moving Yet Farther Afield—
The Clincher—

PART FOUR—THE HEART OF GOD!

He Searched For Us—Why Would We Not Search For Him?
"To Him Who does exceedingly more than we ask or think—
His power also works in us."—He Is Worthy! (RE. Ephesians 3:20)

Some Serious Stuff! (*Heart Sense Continued*)

The Irish Potato Famine pictures a season of seriousness; so great was its impact for seven years. Another name for it was The Great Hunger—it began in 1845. Phytophthora was a fungus-like organism called "infestans." This infestation plagued the Irish much longer than was bearable—as if any plague, virus, disease—is comfortable even for a short while. The Irish faced severe issues, as were many other problems since 'The Beginning!' 'The Beginning,' depending on who we believe, is also in question!

[Just an Insert of Note—I'm thinking now of the War In Ukraine]

This Great Hunger was devastating to the potato crop, which was a mainstay for Ireland, and its effect on Ireland's population was tragic. About a million people died from starvation and other causes related to the famine; at least as many or more left Ireland, their ancestral home, and became refugees elsewhere.

Speaking of 'serious stuff,' we need not backtrack far from the season of life we are facing while I've been writing this portion. 'Covid-19 is about two years in,' since it began in China [so we hear], around October —November 2019. I've tried to get a number for the death count and other consequences, but it's hard to nail it down—everyone suggests different stats in this regard—though it's in the multi-millions. Covid-19 is either a reality or a circus. As to the effectiveness of the 'vaccines,' this also divvies up into the divisive arena—.

As we live through the channels of everyday life in the present—we live Problemlematic Lives. 'The Conundrum Arena' is problematic. It's a world of mystery; we find ourselves puzzled in our decision-making; we realize we are riddled, inundated, or overwhelmed by the rules of our nations as they expect us to change the way we have learned to live as we grew up. We face the challenge of switching lanes on the highway of living life, and we feel as if we are posing or posturing as one thing and living another. (*IBID*)

Causes—what are they? Effects—What are they? What defines Cause and Effect?

Cause and effect relate to connections and or links between one thing or another. Activity and Outcome are the mixtures we get to show us 'Cause and Development.' One cause leads to many consequences when all is said and done.

Fundamentally, it's one thing to be serious about the afflictions we endure, quite another if we are careless (reckless or negligent). We are in trouble if we care less about dealing with these problems to eliminate the plague (virus)—we're a 'done deal!' To be unsuccessful in dealing with Covid-19 leaves us bankrupt emotionally and financially—Eternally, failure leaves us in The 'Conundrum Arena' indefinitely.

We have not even considered the leading cause and effect problem.' We've not looked at The First Cause of life itself. Some folks *propose* 'Evolution,' some suggest 'God' as The First Cause— I advocate The latter—God, as the 'solution! It's not as simple to just say, "let's bring God into the picture; wave our hands and expect the problem to go away on its own."

In Effect, "The Die Is Cast—" The place, The Garden of Eden, is the beginning of our sorrows! We chose death over life! God said, OK, when this season of life we decided on is over, we'll get back to The Tree of Life instead of the Tree of Knowledge of Good and Evil. Some folks chose to have *'Eternity In Their Hearts* [for the moment].' The consequences of sin sickened them; they repented, asked forgiveness from God, and left behind their wickedness. While on Earth, we'll know the entire 'effect' of The First Cause—Jesus; He dealt with the most Serious Issue of all Eternity!

> Here's The Invite: "Come unto Me, all ye that labour and are heavy laden, and I will give you rest. Take My yoke upon you and learn of Me; for "I AM" meek and lowly in 'Heart:' and ye shall find rest unto your 'Souls.'"
> (Matthew 11:28-29; KJV)

Towards the finale of *Searching For A Heart of Gold*, there will be an RSVP (*Answer, Reply*) to fill out your decision about the Invitation to Go God's Way!

Life Is A Serious Entity!
LET'S GET SERIOUS!

Scriptures In Chapter Nine
Life Is A Serious Entity
[Let's Get Serious]
Ecclesiastes 1:6-7; Romans 1
Romans 1: 14-25
Ecclesiastes 1:6
Ecclesiastes 1:6
John 3:8; Isaiah 55:12; Nehemiah 8:10;
Hebrews 12: 1-2
The Vista View—The Oasis
Psalm 139: 1-4
Psalm 139; Psalm 139:1-4; Titus 2:13
Psalm 139:1
Heart Sense

Chapter Nine

Life Is A Serious Entity

———————————◊———————————

O Lord, You searched me through and through. Sitting or standing [it matters not]—You know my thoughts—even surrounding me while I lie down. You saturate me with Your presence. Before I think of an idea, You know the next word I will speak. (Psalm 139: 1-4; JBI)

We get to live LIFE only once in the lifespan unveiled, revealed, or shown to us on Planet Earth as we know it now. The Psalms, Proverbs, and Ecclesiastes are three Books of The Bible dealing distinctly with life 'Straight Up!' The writers give us 'Reel After Reel of Episodes of Real Life' settings from which we're well able to live life to the fullest possible degree!

In the day in which we live, access is hardly an imposition anymore—even in Non-Developing Countries, cell phones are highly possible. Many of these cell phones are of the Relic variety we now call Dumb Phones. However, as time passes and technology increases at more and more speed than ever before, the possibilities for Non-Developing Countries to be more able to use what we call Smart Phones also becomes more likely.

As technology leads us into the future, living life in the context to which we've become accustomed becomes easier. Though this is true, it's not the mega means or the best means from which we launch out on a successful Journey to get from Birth Through Life as we know it. Even if technology was the best and only means available to us, it could never transport us from Birth Through To Eternity.

If we only had hope in this life, we may try to cope alone— Us and Our 'Techno-Wizardry' (Technology and Magic)! Life leads us on a Journey of believing we don't need God! I cannot follow this pattern! Many other folks worldwide believe God is the only way to get us through LIFE!

"The wind goes toward the south and quickly turns again and heads north; it whirls about continually—the wind returns according to its circuits (as in electricity). All the rivers run into the sea without filling it to the brim; the rivers always return from whence they came in the first place." (Ecclesiastes 1:6&7; JBI)

This passage by Solomon (so we think) contains a fitting phrase regarding my thoughts concerning 'Where Will We Search For The Heart of God; Or Will We?' "All the rivers run into the sea, yet the sea is not full; unto the place from whence the rivers come, thither [there] they return (KJV)." I gather from this phrase that Solomon believed something outside of his present understanding was responsible for the path rivers choose.

As I read this portion of Scripture, I readily acknowledge 'God sees' the development and direction of every purpose taken by humankind—whether the motive of the 'plan maker' in human capacity is right or honourable for making a positive difference—or not.

Every human endeavour will make a difference in someone's life; every effort will not necessarily make the kind of difference that will make life better for someone else along Life's Journey! No *purpose* under the sun escapes the notice of God!

Ecclesiastes 1:6-7 emphasizes the wind, sea, rivers, direction, and *purpose*—. Let's look at the wind for a few moments—it's imperative to remember the importance of 'The Wind of The Spirit—The Spirit of God,' which guides us through life; if this is our security blanket for our God-given lives. Please hear the following phrase with this in mind—.

"The wind goes south and turns north; it whirls about continually, and the wind returns according to 'His' circuits [back to God]."

I believe God has a mind of His own—and that Rightly So! For this to even be close to being in the perception of others, they would first need to believe God exists—this is not easy for someone whose history never included a 'Christian Context.' In Romans Chapter One, the Bible tells us that even if our parents never Searched for God, none of us have an excuse for not finding Him. The Heart or Voice of God displays itself in many ways.

Please, let's listen to The Past for some of the significant insights that can still today, after so many years, help us balance the books of life enough to avoid the dangers that living brings us! Many voices in The Real World—and Planet Earth is the Real World—cry out for our allegiance. *Every Wind of Change Throughout History*—every new thought, false scale or measuring rod of some transaction or another will bring a judgment or consequence.

"I'm indebted to the Greeks and the Barbarians—to the wise and the unwise.

I am ready to preach the gospel to you in Rome—*with all my heart.*

Why? Because I'm not ashamed of the gospel of Christ! It's within the power of God to save everyone who believes. This message is first to the Jew but also meant for the Greek.

The righteousness of God reveals itself from faith to faith—just like The Bible says, "the just shall live by faith."

The wrath of God reveals itself from heaven against all ungodliness and unrighteousness of men (people), who think of truth in unrighteous ways—because that which we can know of God shows itself in them as well, because God has shown it unto them. From The Beginning of 'The World—' the invisible things of God show themselves clearly because of the things God made—even His eternal Power and The Godhead reveal themselves; 'so there are no excuses:' Because, when they knew God, they glorified Him not as God, neither were thankful; but became vain in their imaginations, and their foolish heart became dark.

These people thought of themselves as wise; they were, in fact, fools. They imagined God to be Immoral, comparing Him to the likes of humanity, birds, four-footed beasts, and creeping things.

So God allowed them to live their unclean lives, to dishonour their bodies between themselves. These folks suggested God lied, and they worshiped and served the creature more than The Creator, Who is blessed forever. Amen."
(Romans 1: 14-25; KJV)

The Bible tells us God isn't a man—He cannot lie!

Many quotes overflow the cup's brim about how women *change* their minds so often that it's hard to determine what they want. From personal experience (said tongue in cheek—Just Kidding), there's a measure of truth in this. However, we don't talk about men who follow the same pattern—men may be just as undecided, but possibly we don't admit it—ask our wives! I am trying to be as diplomatic as tolerance rules would allow. We all do *change* differently. I wrestle with 'change' as everyone else does.

"The wind goes Southward, then it turns around and goes Northward. It whirls busily—returning on the path from which it came. All the rivers go into the ocean, yet it's not full; like the wind, they go back to where they began." (This is the first phrase in Ecclesiastes 1:6; JBI).

Moving On is often a challenge for me because of my preference or inclination to cover many areas at one time—as if I'm on 1st Base of a Baseball Game—while I'm contemplating the pluses and minuses of getting to second base and onward to home plate to score the run. If, while on first base, I venture into La La Land—not prioritizing the running of the bases in the game to Reach Home Plate—I may never realize the importance and value of making a difference in the whole game. Do I need to do a 'reality check?'

"La La Land" definition according to Websters is—
"a euphoric, dreamlike mental state detached from the harsher realities of life."

'Where Will We Search For The Heart of God, Or Will We?' "The rivers run into the sea, yet the sea is not full; unto the place from whence the rivers come, they return. I gather from this phrase that Solomon believed something outside of his present understanding was responsible for the rivers' path."

I'm blessed to live in Invermere, BC, with The World Famous Rocky Mountains staring at me from where I sit on my West Side Facing Patio. The 'Where Factor' of *Searching For A Heart of Gold—Not A Pot of Gold*—and or *The Heart of God*—is huge in some respects—still, I consider the present advantage of my view to be advantageous for me. I don't personally wish to 'exchange' my venue for the Prairies of Saskatchewan or Manitoba [been there, done that]—I got my ticket for the Next Life—Heaven!

There are other places in Canada and or anywhere else in the world for that matter which for people other than myself, present an equally opportunistic (resourceful, blessed) domain (Field, or might I say, 'Field of Dreams') from which to begin the following search—

Where Will We Search For The Heart of God, Or Will We? Do we believe all rivers run into the sea? Does the sea ever fill up? Do rivers return to where they came from? Did Solomon think 'something' or Someone outside of his present understanding was responsible for the rivers' path? My guess is—Solomon was a pretty smart cookie—so The Bible tells us— "And Solomon's wisdom excelled the wisdom of all the children of the east country and all the wisdom of Egypt." (1 Kings 4:30; KJV)

Rarely, if ever, do rivers run a parallel, lateral, or unswerving course without wandering or meandering through crevasses or the differing slopes and curves of the landscapes of our lands. However, I wonder how other people find their way along the path of Least Resistance towards knowing 'How' and 'Where' to begin going "Where They Can Search For The Heart of God?" "All the rivers run into the sea, yet the sea is not full; unto the place from whence the rivers come, they return." [Like the winding Thames River].

'Water is Water' no matter where we live—with the same distinctive factors no matter where it is—apart from the additives we put into the water or the debris of the differing landscapes. Remove all the outside entities, and water holds all the same qualities or traits no matter where it flows. Initially, all water came from God's Creation—then rain maintained them. The rain maintains the rivers, lakes, oceans, and streams, whether in obscure places or elsewhere; it always returns to the atmosphere to gather in the clouds and returns 'again as rain!'

What's the makeup of water? Might this be a daft question? Everyone knows what water is—don't they? Water is wet— lifegiving and sustains the Planet on which we live. There are correct answers and wrong ones—maybe we'll find out.

Water consists of hydrogen and oxygen in vaporous, fluid, and stable states. Water is one of the most vital and bountiful compounds; it transpires as a liquid on Earth's surface under normal conditions, making it invaluable for human uses and as a plant and animal habitat. What would we do without water—.

Remember—rivers are rarely straight; finding two equal rivers of the same downhill sweep or width—is impossible in real-life, practical situations. In principle, a straight river would travel much faster—firstly, water in a meandering river loses force after every twist of a 'Bendy River.' Rivers don't have, postulate, or assume uniform bends; they're erratic—changeable. They show no definite patterns. If rivers were flawless, it would be a different story—in reality; it isn't. In theory, a straight river flows faster due to less loss of momentum; less resistance against the banks, but then again, we can't have a perfectly straight river.

'Are you up for The Challenge?' Try Life—not to imply in any way, shape, or form that 'Life' doesn't present us with 'Good Times.' However, it never flows evenly along like a channel we may build to exact specifications (as near to exact as possible), thereby creating, if you would, a straight river. When left to their native God-created flow (or, for some, in their opinion, an evolving evolutionary Godless miracle of existence), rivers are not straight.

We, the world's people, are most often affected by our physical environment's choices and decision-making abilities. In the best-case scenario, we assume a 'Spiritual' point of view in life. If we do our utmost to initiate a *Search For The Heart of God*—the *Search For The Heart of Gold*; or *The Pot of Gold*, the challenge may be refreshing. Failures often accompany some of the bends in the road of life because our motives may have taken a 'Detour!' Most of us have likely encountered a Detour or two.

Sometimes we need to change our course of direction in life because misinformation about our initial choice often diminishes our capabilities and preferences. Occasionally we change the course of our initial God intended direction because we thought we had failed in our attempts at success—maybe we did; perhaps we didn't. Maybe God knew we needed to take what we saw as a failure—as only a detour which would save 'our' lives and the lives of others He scoped out for special duty opposed to 'Spiritual Death!'

> "The wind goes toward the south, then turns about unto the north; it whirls continually and returns according to his circuits. All the rivers run into the sea, yet the sea is not full; unto the place from whence the rivers come, thither (there) they return." (Ecclesiastes 1:6-7; KJV)

The wind blows on its course at will, so to speak—you hear its sound, but you can't tell where it came from or where it ends up—everyone born of the Spirit is like this. (John 3:8; KJV)

Yes—the wind has a mind of its own, so it seems to us. We hear the noise it makes as it whistles through the trees, our homes, the hills, and the plains in every conceivable physical avenue. We feel we know when it comes from the North, South, East, or West. Just when it feels like it's blowing a Warm South Wind, it takes a turn and suggests we made a mistake because it darts at us from the West. The Wind can be a confusing entity.

The Bible takes the lead (The Bible has Dibbs on this) in relating The Wind to Spiritual things. The Bible gives us a physical picture to help us understand a Spiritual Truth and or Consequence. As we begin to understand the Wind we know of physically, the writer of John throws in another means of moving us along in a somewhat different direction in our *Search For A Heart of Gold— Our Search For A Pot of Gold—Our Search For The Heart of God*! We know this as The Wind of The Spirit! This Wind blows through our Heart—The Soul of our being—It's God-Breathed!

At the outset of this book, *Part One, The Shepherd's Landing—The Hills and The Plains,* I began with this—

The Trees of The Field Shall Clap Their Hands:

"For ye shall go out with joy and be led forth with peace—the mountains and the hills shall break forth before you into singing, and all the trees of the field shall clap their hands." (Isaiah 55:12; KJV)

Then he said to them (the people), go your way—eat the fat, drink the sweet and send portions to those for whom no provisions exist—this day is holy to God—also, don't be sorry, because the joy of the Lord is your strength. (Nehemiah 8:10; KJV)

The Sound of Music by Richard Rodgers—lyrics by Oscar Hammerstein II—and a book by Howard Lindsay and Russel Crouse concentrate on Maria von Trapp's memoir—the Trapp Family Singers. Austria is the venue—the story is of Maria, a governess to a large family—she considered being a nun. She loved children, and their widowed father, Captain von Trapp.

Captain von Trapp had to join the German navy; he opposed the Nazis. He, Maria, and the children escaped to Austria. *Edelweiss* was one of many songs from the musical; *My Favorite Things*, *Climb Ev'ry Mountain*, *Do-Re-Mi*—and of course, title song *The Sound of Music* topped the list.

As I peruse *The Sound of Music*, the Scriptures just stated above come alive in my Spirit—as the Wind of The Spirit blows gently over my demeanour and courses through every avenue of my psyche (mind). I find myself amongst the Trees Of The Field, Clapping My Hands to the melodies of *The Sound of God's Music*.

There is a unison—a harmony suggested in strains of the above Scripture—Unity brings Joy, Peace, Singing and Clapping!

"The hills will break out before you into singing, and all the trees of the field shall clap their hands." (Isaiah 55:12; KJV)

When people unite in *purpose*, they make beautiful music together. I wonder if we will ever experience anything like The Sound of Music shouts out to us—In This Life? Probably not! However, there's a day in the offing, an ethereal season, an out-of-this-world experience that The Bible tells us about—when Jesus comes back—Yes, "Comes Back!" He came once in the past, and most people never knew Who He was, but when Jesus comes again, everybody will know He is— 'King of Kings,' LORD OF LORDS! What A Day That Will Be! The option of this Joyful Day remains open if we accept the INVITE before our last breath on Planet Earth!

CELEBRATION RUNS DEEP WITHIN US IN REAL LIVING!

We'll never find the true *Heart of Gold* if it's the *Pot of Gold* we're intent on acquiring—it may seem like a bold and unwarranted statement—it might be so in the minds of many folks. Who am I to say people will never achieve to the fullest extent if they are only intently seeking THE GOLD! I'm Not The Final Judge!

Even if we acquire 'it all in the material sense; if others aren't part of our 'inclusion' to make a difference, I'd say our 'Reach For The Heart of Gold May Be Lacking Bigtime!' As I go through the Forbes List of The Wealthiest Persons on The Planet, at least one person especially comes to mind today, "Vladimir Putin" —many more fit the bill. History will record whether they are making a Heart of Gold Difference in the lives of others in a positive way!

Is the '*Heart of Gold*' the same in the sense of this book as it is in *The Heart of God*? How about I leave my audience, 'You' and the other people respectively, to answer this question yourselves. We all have personal rights. We all must choose whether white is white, black is black, or whether or not they are whatever any one of us says they are. Added to this, I need to ask, "What's the guideline for making these decisions for ourselves?" Are there any guidelines in this regard? Is The Golden Rule of Humankind enough to cover the bases regarding these thoughts? Is there a 'Hierarchy' of evolutionary, natural progression, common-sense direction—or a Spiritual God-Centred Golden Rule for Life on Planet Earth?

'What About My Humble Opinion?' To be on track in our *Search For A Heart of Gold*, a *True Heart of Gold* as I pattern it, we may need to put aside some of our hard-core opinions. What about our actions about how Real Life activates? What about our 'Hope' in and for other people—one 'ensconced' (established) by a 'Hard Core Hope' which we may not understand to the nth degree?

A great cloud of witnesses surrounds u*s*—let's chuck every weight and the sin which so quickly deters us. Let's *run with patience* the race set before us, *looking* unto Jesus the Author and Finisher of our faith, who for the joy before Him *endured the cross*, *despising the shame*, now sits at the right hand of the throne of God. (Hebrews 12: 1-2; JBI)

Suppose we position ourselves in 'humanly possible' ways to make a difference in someone else's life; as we face the difficulty of understanding and facilitating the issues of life ourselves, will that suffice? Will we be in good stead to achieve Spiritually, or 'Barely Make-it Through—Spiritually?' We may become better persons in the process, even to the extent of reaping life's challenges with a freer, less complicated attitude about life!

Then if we allow God—Jesus Christ—The Holy Spirit of God, The Wind of The Spirit—to lead us along through the tough spots—there are extended promises and bonuses waiting for us at the end of the physicality of the life, which we experience on this planet! *In My Heart There Rings A Melody* and *The Sound of Music* extend to us unique sensations of love and community, which binds us together.

LET'S GET SERIOUS

THERE'S NO OTHER WAY
TO GET THE JOB DONE!

◊ THE VISTA VIEW—THE OASIS ◊

Life Is A Serious Entity

LORD, the sincerity of Your search for me, involving every element of my personhood, overwhelms me at every moment of my day—often when I least expect anything. I'm *sufficiently suffonsified*—feeling it, as I do, the warm blood coursing through my veins, and these moments send me to You, even in my dark times. (Sentiments From—Psalm 139: 1-4—JBI)

"We Get To Live 'LIFE'" only once in the lifespan unveiled, revealed, or shown to us on Planet Earth as we know it now. The Psalms, Proverbs and Ecclesiastes are three Books of The Bible dealing with life 'Straight Up!' The writers give us 'Reel After Reel Of Episodes Of Real Life' scenarios from which we can live life to the fullest possible degree! There are no answers to the mysteries of life apart from You, LORD!

Today, we live in times where even the poorest of the poor seem to have access to cell phone technology. Admission to advanced technology is no hassle anymore. Many of these cell phones are of the 'Relic' variety we now call 'Dumb Phones.' Still, as time goes by and knowledge increases faster than ever before, the prospects or 'likelihoods' for Non-Developing Country's usage of 'Smart Phones' also increases.

As 'Technology' (for one) 'Leads' us into the future—living life in the context to which we've become accustomed—life becomes more effortless. Though this is true, it's not the mega means or the best means from which we launch out on a successful 'Journey' from *Birth Through Life* to get where we're going. Even if technology was the best and only means we had at our *beck and call*, it could never get us through from *Birth Through To Eternity*.

If we only had hope in this life—perhaps we can manage the Day-To-Day on our own—Us and Our Knowledge Base! Time can lead us on a Long Ride—believing we don't need God! I can't follow this course! Many people globally recognize God is The Only Way *to get through this* LIFE—. Many Do Not! Encouraging people to embrace a makeover is no simple issue.

Looking seriously from Both Sides Now demands a decisive (crucial, pivotal, final, essential, vital—) engagement. 'This Is Serious Stuff!' My main concern in this book is to represent *heart matter*—illustrating the *physical heart* comparatively [relatively]; a 'Bird's Eye' (Vista View) of what it's like to *begin to grasp* what the 'Spiritual Heart'entails—this is vital.

We should also begin to realize there are Two Hearts on the conveyor or sorting belt—A Good Heart and a Bad Heart. Personally—I may think I have dibs on judging another person's heart of intent for life because 'I think I have,' by the classification of 'Good and Bad,' set parameters by which all people should abide. Though I'm not the judge—God is! That said, not everybody believes God exists—if He does, He's not concerned about how we live day-to-day.

Listed in literary fiction and published in 1940, we find a gem called *The Heart Is A Lonely Hunter* by Carson McCullers. Carson lived from 1917 to 1967. She was only fifty years old. Nonetheless, age wasn't a barrier for her as she wrote a Heart Telling Story of fiction, reflecting *life as we know it* with the possibility of attaining *the life we all want*. I gleaned some of her thoughts from page 184 (Kindle Edition). I echo or applaud Carson McCullers words in the following—in the context of the book.

"Jake's [not speaking about me—but could be] blood vessels pulsated uncontrollably; he struggled to contain a proper decorum while his mouth twitched and the words he wanted to say didn't respond to his mental command. His body winced about in his chair as he began to process words he felt were imperative to the *Heart of Life*—he urged his lips to speak—then, in a gruff voice, said the following words." (My words echo those of Carson McCullers.)

"This is how it is—there's no sense being angry; seems nothing we do is of any value; this is what it looks like to me. Reality holds our only hope in its grasp. If enough unknowing people, who are aloof from the truth, learn the real truth, it will not make any sense to fight for truth anymore. All we need do is to tell folks the truth. If this is all we can do, how do we do it from the drive for truth within us and do it as effectively as possible to keep folks from falling into a quagmire of *same old same old* useless lifestyles— while still saying, *Everything Is A Heart Matter!*" (My words echo those of Carson McCullers.)

"O Lord, You've examined me and formed me."

As I read these opening words of Psalm 139, I crave to see *"Lonely Hunter"* as a current descriptor of those early thoughts. If I think of God as 'Lonely,' all by Himself somewhere up there in the whole universal picture of time as we know and the time of infinity before we came into view, I fear I will be doing God an injustice. God is God—the sense of 'Loneliness,' which is *a subjective human* emotion as I see it—these aren't feelings subject to His nature.

Although tempted in all the points, as are humans, He did so without sinning. Jesus was in the form of 'The Son of Man.' As Jesus, God with us, He never was without the objectivity of the total characteristics of Godhood! Having journeyed with people physically on this planet allowed Him to understand the *make-up of humanity* to the nth degree—After-All, He Created Us!

LORD, *You've* combed me and _know_ when I'm sitting or rising. You understand every possible avenue of thought I may have, without difficulty—from an infinite distance. You see the scope of my journey. Even when I'm just lying around for a respite, You're aware of all my intentions—Good and Bad! Because, there's not a word in my tongue, but that You LORD, know it from beginning to end! (—Psalm 139: 1-4; JBI)

Many thoughts arrive at my *cognitive domain* while doing a *Search For Myself* as I break down David's feelings about how God looks at us with the *intent* or *heart* to present His best for us in this life— 'Methinks it goes beyond life as we know it!'

I often backtrack to see how life was before I was born, not before God existed; He always existed! I look at *Today*—what it is as I live; as we live—I still see God (as He always has since creation and before creation) daily doing Life with us! Then, while looking towards the *Tomorrow* (a reference to the song), I can't yet fully realize assurance until it arrives—as I stretch my eyes to the ethereal (otherworldly) beyond the earthly. Within my Heart of Hearts, I know God *prepared* All We Need way ahead of our arrival (*as He did in Creation*). Past, Present, and Future—this is what I see in the first four verses of Psalm 139.

Life Is A Serious Entity—Yes, It Is! However, let's not think the word 'Serious' means there's 'No Hope!

JESUS IS THE BLESSED HOPE! (Titus 2:13)

TODAY I wrestle with the leadership traits of many leaders worldwide. TODAY I rethink The Headliner of Leaders, Who TODAY, March 1, 2022, feel the pain of doing the right thing to alleviate the pain of Ukraine and others who innocently (in the sense of physical war against them) experience the "Mega Pain" inflicted by "One Man"—Vladimir Putin.

I'll form Two Columns; the 1st —*Leaders Of Worthy Renown*—the 2nd —*Other Leaders—Ring Leaders!* There's a necessary breakdown *Ringleaders* present—Two Scenarios—Two Leadership Styles. Thesarus.com offers synonyms looking like the following—SYNONYMS FOR Leader—chief, commander, director, head, manager, ruler, President, boss, captain, conductor, controller, counsellor, shepherd, skipper, superintendent, superior, ringleader—and the list of candidates for 'Leader' is lengthy.

The list of SYNONYMS FOR Ringleader—is much the same; only the perspective leads to a sinister or disturbing direction; presenting—instigator, mastermind, troublemaker, agitator, inciter, noncooperator, provocative agent, rabble-rouser—. Again, the list is nearly endless; the consensus for me is that of being a Ring Leader In A Circus—offering a display of a considerable assortment of entities—Human and Animal.

Column One—*Leaders Of Worthy Renown*—Within this column, we can only place people who Lead with Integrity, Compassion, Concern, and the proper intent to Lead By The God-Given Golden Rule—this is my take on the Subject.

Column Two— *Other Leaders—Ring Leaders*! Within this Column, I will assign every other semblance of what we might call Leaders! The main Headline I will attribute to this consortium or group of folks is *Leaders Unworthy Of Renown*—People Who Are More Selfie Motivated! [Psalm 139 Headline is—].

O LORD, THOU HAST SEARCHED ME AND KNOWN ME.

Even if I don't have the right or capacity to name names and sort out the Quality of The Leaders of The World—Political, Religious, or Otherwise—God Does! If I consider the "Food For Thought Theme," this thought constantly challenges me!

HEART SENSE
Let The Winds Blow

◊

WIND CAN BE A SERIOUSLY DESTRUCTIVE FORCE—We need only look back at what's happened recently—Windstorm 'Ida' just began to lessen, and 'Larry' invaded the East Coast. The Atlantic Hurricane Season runs the course of this danger zone every year. Every year the folks contend with hurricanes on the East Coast—the Atlantic Ocean is at times an 'Angry Beast!'

Not only does 'Wind' affect us physically—though I've never experienced 'Hurricane Force Destruction,' I've seen what 'Wind' does as it brings with it rain deluges coming in buckets instead of droplets. Hail comes down as if someone was blasting us with baseballs as if shot out of an array of cannons. This summer, where I live in Invermere, BC, Canada, we had a storm that most folks said they'd never seen here in The Windermere Valley. I thought I was hard done by because it totalled 'I thought,' my beautiful array of hanging plants.

As destructive as The Windstorms are in their horrendous attack on land, things, and people—it seems after The Storm subsides, people get busy fixing the damage physically. People often begin to repair emotionally, although every Hurricane Season permanently takes the "*Wind Out Of The Sails*" Of Some People!

In the storm we had, where I thought my hanging plants were scrap heap bound, I cleaned up the damage, and low and behold, it wasn't long before I saw before my eyes how God brought the life of the roots back to the surface of the plants and buds and flowers began to encourage me with their blooms! How *Great* it is when Hope Springs Eternal when the 'death-knell' is near! Most of the time, the "Tomorrow—" of Life resurges to rise again as desuetude, destruction, or virtual extinction to make a new path of existence—even a path of New Hope!

Let's Look At Chapter Ten—
THE WINDS AND CLOUDS OF THE HEART

Scriptures In Chapter Ten
The Winds and The Clouds of The Heart
[Our Insecurities and The Freedom of God!]
John 3:8
Nahum 1: 3-5
Job 32 & 37
Job 32); Job 37:1-24
Job 38; Job 38-41; Job 3-27; Nahum 1:3-5; Job 1:3-5
Psalm 139: 23-24
The Vista View–The Oasis
John 3: 8-9
Hebrews 12
Jeremiah 29:11
Heart Sense
Psalm 19: 1-14

Chapter Ten

The Winds And Clouds
Of The Heart

◊

WHITHER SHALL I GO FROM THY SPIRIT?—
Where can I run from Your Presence? I can't
escape to Heaven or Hell for a getaway. Before the dawn
breaks, I don't know in totality what it will highlight—LORD,
You already know! Suppose I abide in the ultimate parts of the
sea, thinking everything's 'intact' for me to live safely—What
Then? If I desired to hide from You, LORD, darkness wouldn't
suffice. My reins are in Your hands. Before I was in my
mother's womb, You knew 'The Lot of Life' there's to know
about me [then, now and forever]! (Psalm 139: 7-13; JBI)

Life seems to dictate *Insecurity*! We face diffidence (self-
doubt) head-on, moment by moment. Our mental capacity is
overwhelmed and or overloaded—saturated with *insecurities* today
and tomorrow—Or life can bathe us in a Sea of Opportunities to
make a difference—the challenge to do so requires a resource we
must, I repeat, must be ready to engage. Along with every challenge
comes the opposition's bid, which might present the 'ultimate
internal and external' *War of The Worlds* yet unknown!

WHAT ABOUT OUR INSECURITIES AND THE FREEDOM OF GOD!

A week ago, we experienced a deluge of rain, wind, and hail
alien to anything I remember! Seemingly out of nowhere, as sudden
as the twinkle of an eye, this storm was akin to a chaotic *tropical
storm*. This blast of inclement weather was a warning from the *cloud
cover* up above Our Town—Invermere, BC; it scolded us for a solid
thirty minutes. Although this doesn't sound like something similar
to a significant storm, it damaged much plant life as the 'Windows
of Heaven Opened!' Life gets serious at unsuspecting moments.

"The wind blows at will; it may sound brutal, but 'we humans' can't assess where it initiated or determine its Final Destination—everyone moved by the Spirit of God is like this." (John 3:8; JBI)

Jesus speaks here about the lack of understanding Nicodemus had about being *Born Again*. He wonders how someone can physically replay the natural birth of a person entering and coming out of the mother's womb. "The wind strikes its targets at will. The sound of the wind in our ears—doesn't help us entirely realize its resource. Each person who is Born Again—Born of The Spirit, pans out like this." (John 3:8; JBI)]

The Lord doesn't employ rage quickly; He's powerful—wickedness won't prevail in His plans. He has His way in wind and storm; clouds—are as sand underfoot. He admonishes the sea, makes it dry—and dries up the rivers. Bashan wilts—Carmel and the flower of Lebanon fade. The mountains tremble before Him. The hills melt down—the earth burns in His presence. When God's fury surfaces, the world and its people face the same consequences. (Nahum 1:3-5; JBI)

We explored *wind* in Chapter Nine [and the wind is so elusive it's hard to corner it and say we've now controlled the wind]; now, we'll think about clouds and wind as roomies in Chapter Ten. We expect to expose ourselves to their connection in the Spiritual Sense as we examine these marvels in a tangible sense. As much as Psalm 139 gives us a clear picture of God's Magnitude, Excellence, and Sovereignty, Job Chapter Thirty-Seven delivers much the same message. The whole of The Bible leaves us without the option of *denial* when it comes to The Magnitude, Excellence, and Sovereignty of God! (Job 32 & 37)

Sometimes I write in a somewhat rigid perspective, implying my firm belief in the *Truth*, the *Whole Truth*, and nothing but the *Truth*. However, I think I always allow you, my readership, to choose for yourselves Whom or What you think about the matters of Faith. In my view, nothing ever existed in actuality before it burst forth in the Spiritual Realm. The Spiritual Realm is all about God—Having created *humankind* from the most profound longing within Himself, God allows His Spirit (Spirituality) to reside in us!

'Talking about 'Spirituality,' I wish to present Job Chapter 37 as a JBI (Jacob Bergen Insight) paraphrase and the KJV Translation of The Bible. In this way, you are the spark that keeps me faithful to scripture. By intent, I try to stay loyal to God's Word—*when* I fail in this attempt, please forgive me.

I've heard the expressions of the Heart of one of Job's friends (Elihu) in Job Thirty-six. Having begun his dialogue, discourse, or diatribe, if you would, in Job 32, Elihu continues in Job 37 as if there's no Chapter definition to break into another train of thought.

I tremble somewhat—my speech may be slightly impaired, unsafe, or out of sync. (*JBI*)

At this also, my heart trembleth and is moved out of his place. (*KJV*)

Job, listen closely as God's incredible (overwhelming) voice reverberates (rings) in your ears. It comes directly from God's Heart into your ears. (*JBI*)

Hear the noise of His voice attentively and the sound that goeth out of His mouth. (KJV)

Job, Almighty God's in control—what He wants to accomplish, He sends along the way throughout Earth, like lightning skates across the Heavens. (*JBI*)

He directeth it under the *absolute* heaven and His lightning unto the ends of the earth. (*KJV*)

Once God sends His Word and Plans worldwide, no one can foil them—no one can silence God's voice, like it or not! (*JBI*)

After it, a voice roareth; He thundereth with the voice of His excellency, and He will not stay them when His voice *echoes*. (*KJV*)

Don't expect to understand everything God has done or will yet do—no one can beat God when He decides to do what He does. The thunder of the voice of God will be marvellous to some folks, and many will not have the *Spiritual* capacity to grasp it. We should never doubt the authority with which God has and will always get the job done! (*JBI*)

God thundereth marvellously with His voice; great things doeth He, which we cannot comprehend! (*KJV*)

WHAT ABOUT OUR INSECURITIES
AND THE FREEDOM OF GOD?

The environment is powered by the strength of God's Word—happening at His will—the snow, rain and hail exist to supply fodder to meet the earth's needs. [Who knows better about the conditions we humans have than God]. Often we think we are at the controls—this is a big mistake. (*JBI*)

He saith to the snow, 'Be thou on the earth;' likewise to His strength's slight and significant rain. (*KJV*)

No one can raise their hand against God and get away with it! Every *person* will know God is *alive and well* because He purposed it to be so! (*JBI*)

He sealeth up the hand of every man (*person*) that all men (*people*) may know His work. (*KJV*)

At some time, all the animals will go to their homes—staying there at the command of God. (*JBI*)

Then the beasts go into dens and remain in their places (*KJV*)

God has unique directive sources set aside in His Universe, each in their directional coordinates—like the compass declares North, South, East and West. The tumultuous (whirlwind) weather comes from the South because of sudden pressure changes (often heat-related); cold weather comes from the northern sector. (JBI)

Out of the south cometh the whirlwind, and cold out of the north. (*KJV*)

God breathed the breath of life into humankind. He also causes the frost by His breath; the scope (size, width, scale or extent) of the rivers, lakes, and oceans—by His Word, they are heightened or lessened. (*JBI*)

By the breath of God, frost *comes*, and the breadth of the waters is straitened. (*KJV*)

Clouds release rain when they fail to hold the moisture evaporating from the earth; God breaks up dark clouds to be fluffy bright clouds as if speaking to us. (*JBI*)

Also by watering He wearieth the thick *cloud*; He scattereth His bright *cloud*, (*KJV*)

God changes the clouds patterned path at His will to achieve what He knows we need to nourish all of His creation. (*JBI*)

And it is turned round about by His counsels, that they may do whatsoever He commandeth them upon the face of the world in the earth. *(KJV)*

The reasoning of God is His to articulate (convey) in whatever way He chooses—for improvement to adjust land use—and or even to show His mercy in some way. (*JBI*)

He causeth it to come, whether for correction—or *His* land—or *His* mercy. *(KJV)*

Listen up, Job; stop long enough to fully realize the great hand of God at work on the earth for us and for what lay ahead. (*JBI*)

Hearken unto this, O Job; stand still and consider the wondrous works of God. (*KJV*)

Were you in Heaven with God when He created everything—and made *even the clouds* to be as light? Do you realize the magnitude of God's knowledge when He balanced everything in the universe to suit every purpose He had in mind to sustain all life? Even such things as clouds that are only crystallized vapour and change with atmospheric pressure are at God's command. Notice how we are warmed when we get a south wind, which seems to silence the worldly noise. Job, did you help fashion strength for the red-hot universe? (*JBI*)

Dost thou know when God disposed (placed) them and caused the light of His *cloud* to shine? Dost thou 'know' the balancing's of the *clouds*, the wondrous works of Him who is perfect in knowledge. How thy garments are warm when He quieteth the earth by the south wind? Hast thou with Him spread out the sky, which is strong and as a molten looking glass? (*KJV*)

Teach us what we shall say unto Him, for we cannot order our speech *because of* darkness. Shall it be told Him that I speak? If a man *speaks*, surely he shall be swallowed up. And now men (people) see not the bright light—in the clouds, but the wind passeth and cleanseth them. Fairweather cometh out of the north; with God is fearsome majesty. '*Concerning* the Almighty,' we cannot find Him out; He is excellent in power, *judgment* and abounding in justice; He will not afflict. *Therefore, men* [people] fear Him (*KJV*).

Why did God take such care in fashioning everything in Creation? It was always about us Created beings—and so done in The Image of God. We're allowed to have the Character of God built up within us for the task He asked us to look after on earth. He's given us every tool for the job. We looked much at wind in Chapter Nine. Now, In Chapter Ten, Clouds with the wind. Question—? Does God have the Sovereignty to choose how to manage His world?

We all enjoy Sunshine; whether it's the physical burning ball of fire in the sky or the Sunshine of His love displayed so vividly, we cannot resist wanting to do His bidding. Let a few dark *cloud*s waft into *our* world of only Sunshine and Roses, and we go all to pieces thinking God doesn't love us anymore because we messed up big time!

How do we address the *clouds* of life which will come? Trust me! The clouds will make their appearance betimes. Many folks honestly think they have the answer to all life's ills—some may have, and some don't! Many people believe we don't need God's help to get through life during the Cloudy Days [maybe even the Covid-19 Days] we endure. It seems like this kind of *issue-resolving help* never entirely '*Cuts The Mustard*' when we deal with the issues of managing life—and with 'Where Will We Spend Eternity?'

IS THE ANSWER BLOWN IN THE WIND?

"When we realize we are living in uncertainty, we should admit the same. It's of great value to know we don't know the answers to different questions. This attitude of mind—uncertainty—is vital to the scientist, and it's this attitude of mind that the student must first acquire." (*Richard P. Feynman*)

REALITY SEEMS TO INSERT ITSELF INTO LIFE!

Abraham Lincoln and others opened the door of communication and tolerance enough to say we can live with each other lovingly and productively if our heart condition says *everybody is equal*. God never created our hearts for us to discriminate based on colour. He made the path He laid out for us to have any chance of survival—and expected us to follow that path. There's never any hesitancy on God's part about knowing what's best for us!

Ever since decision-making became part of our natural makeup, we humans have been in trouble. On that Unfortunate Day [of sorts], we made the biggest mistake of our existence on Planet Earth. As we began to *Search For Our Pot of Gold*—so to speak, *The Heart of Gold* concept began to lose ground. If that's not enough, our *Search For The Heart of God* fell to the back of the line of importance because we thought we knew better than God!

In the first place, it was people's disobedience in The Garden of Eden which caused us all to take a wrong turn in life. Rather than *peace and prosperity* in the hands of God, people chose the knowledge in which they set their plan in place; we can see where that got us. Searching for something can be exciting— invigorating on the one hand and flooded with frustration and fear if it involves losing something of value.

In The Garden of Eden, Adam and Eve experienced one of the most significant losses of earth's time. A tremendous loss may come when we think about Eternity—if we lose or never get into a relationship with Christ. If we lose The Best of The Best we could've had if Adam and Eve had chosen *The Fruit of The Tree of Life* instead of *The Fruit of The Tree of The Knowledge of Good and Evil*, we'll have lost everything. Searching presents a twofold scenario. *Searching For A Heart of Gold* serves us best in this life!

No one's had a moment of peace 'Since That Fateful Day' [In The Garden of Eden]. God's intent was far richer in resource power and satisfaction with who and what He created us to be; rather than for what we settled. When people go on strike in the workforce, they often lose more than *the settlement* allows. By the time they tally all the costs, satisfaction might have been the better recourse to have taken [especially in a lengthy strike].

I don't think anybody is inferior because of how they believe. Did God think 'In The Beginning' that He would get out the whip to teach us a lesson we would never forget because we didn't obey Him? As we began searching for a replacement for what we lost—communion and camaraderie with God—we made Mega errors in the decision-making process. 'Time On Our Hands;' the terms we set to fill that time; could've been more productive for the sake of finding the Best of The Best in our *Search For The Heart of God*—opposed to a *Search for Only A Heart of Gold In This Life*, or *A Pot of Gold* we dug out of the ground for selfish intake.

Did we come out of the Garden of Eden Naked? Of Course Not! God didn't give us what we deserved: the heavy lash, a bleeding back, and the nakedness which might have had us face the chilling nighttime's 'in our nighties—' without a warm blanket. God provided us with a decent start—a wardrobe sufficient for the day in which Adam and Eve lived. Too often, we only see God as being a heavy-handed ogre who only wants to crush us like Goliath planned to do (Like Mr. Putin Is Doing To Ukraine) when he faced the little shepherd boy David. Is this what God had in mind before He carefully, lovingly, uniquely, and *purposefully* fashioned us in the foreground of Eternity past? Personally, 'I Don't Think So!'

Our hearts are wrong—that's why we have the issues we have today. Because the *takeoff* of the blueprint of and for life was all wrong, Adam and Eve gave out the incorrect parameters for sending out a proper value-based quote for acceptance to the humanity which was to come after them. We misunderstood what God said initially. We still do! The schematic of what kind of power source best-suited life in the day of these folk is why we needed resistors, capacitors, and inductors to allow for the fluctuations that frustrate life. We thought ourselves more powerful than we were.

If only life were so simple—we could figure out every problem we concocted because of our unbelief. Please realize that God already had it all figured out before He picked up the handful of soil that is the make-up of our existence. God used a unique soil, 'clay,' to make things like the pottery we see today and patterned after the things of the past with which our ancestors grew up. He was the Potter then; He formed the clay to fashion us; He can still change us from what we are without Him in our lives—but it's His Way or The Highway in the opposite direction! We never seem to learn; *It Ain't Over Until The Cows Come Home!*

Is The Answer Blown In The Wind? Do Clouds Relate To Us On The Spiritual Level?

We looked at Job 37, where Elihu, a friend of Job, tries to answer some of Jobs' questions about why life happened for him as they did. Before this, three of Jobs' other friends fitted him with wrong answers for his atrocious dilemma. If we pour everything from Job Chapter One through Chapter Thirty-one into a pill capsule, much of Jobs' life pans out as One Huge Cloudy Day.

A pill capsule has many tiny particles, like grains of sand. A tablet form of a pill is like an assortment of fine granules of sand, solidly packed to a more complex structure than a capsule. However, each of these does the same job in the same way. Every grain or particle plays a part in a time-release fashion to enable the employment of healing or bringing relief of pain to the action level for the patient. We are all patients in the Hospital Of Life (HOL— not AWOL). The hospital is where Doctors and Nurses assist in getting us fit for what comes after death.

Packaging pills into time capsules rightly covers the bases from Home Plate to Home Plate again. Our Birth represents the starting line—death presents our exit. The stuff in-between is like the granules of sand in the pill or capsule—we call this Life! Each grain has its task to accomplish and bring success to the journey's end. There are no shortcuts! If we begin the Game of Life, we'll experience closure. We often try all sorts of life extension enterprises to forgo closure—The End Is Still The End!

Job 38 begins with an answer we don't often recognize enough for its value. God, *The Answer-Man*, doesn't answer like the natural wind that blows in every direction, helter-skelter, blowing dust and debris about as if someone's out of control and demolishing everything in its path— 'A Wind Blown Wrecking Crew!' [Somewhat like some of Job's friends previous to Chapter Thirty-Seven]. I believe Elihu was on a better track than some other friends of Job. Elihu didn't have the same effect on Job as were the results of '*Answer-Man*,' God. It took Four Chapters—38-41, for Job to get the message. It took Thirty-Seven Chapters of Job, through the Hell and High-Water of Job's sufferings—including Job's Ten Speeches from Job Chapter 3—Chapter 27. All the advice of unwise friends; and how Job 1-2 presents us with Job's two tests to understand God in the proper framework, were part of Job's Journey. I suggest that Job had quite a Cloudy Day in his life span. We might say Job had a *Bad Hair Day*!

God never used the 'Answer Is Blown In The Wind Scenario' to address Job's issues, nor does He use this method with us. When the *clouds* roll into our projection of having a *cloudless day*, can physical and emotional—entities ruin our attitude? Is it the wind and the shadow of atmospheric pressure changes that ruin our day? In many cases, these conditions play havoc with our plans.

Often, our day is bouncing along nicely—everything is as if it were 'Coming Up Roses!' Do emotional issues change the Whether Or Not (not weather) pattern of our plans? Whether Or Not we face adversity doesn't make a hoot of difference in 'Whether Or Not' we'll have to carry on with life—no matter what reality it offers us. Unless life is so hard to carry on with—that we choose to exchange dying for living by choice—life is a 'given' and needs to continue—in our *Search For A Heart of Gold*.

If God didn't use the *'The Answer Is Blown In The Wind* Scenario' in the Job scenario, 'What did He use?' God used *'The Wind of The Spirit Scenario'* in the Job Scenario. The Human Rational pattern of working all things for the good is different from God's pattern in Job's life and the pattern He'll use in the 'take' (the acceptance factor) of our lives.

Was Job *Searching For A Heart of Gold* as Chapter One began? As I look carefully at Job at the beginning of his story, I See A Blessed Man! As we focus on the accumulation of Job's wealth, it may appear he might or must've been *Searching For Gold*—else (*otherwise*), why was he so rich? Might *The Pot of Gold* 'At Rainbow's End' have been the priority of this man from 'The Land of Uz?'

As we read into Chapter One, *The Evidence Declares The Verdict.*' Josh McDowell wrote *Evidence That Demands A Verdict* (*Publisher: Thomas Nelson; Revised edition (Oct. 13, 1999)*). In 2017 Josh McDowell and his son Sean McDowell wrote an update to this— *Evidence That Demands a Verdict: Life-Changing Truth for a Skeptical World.*

For just a moment (a Selah [Meditative] Moment), let's note the minor difference between 'Declares' and 'Demands.' 'Declares' is clear—[Affirms, Claims, and Proclaims—], saying, "I Am Sure of what I say, or that which announces something." 'Demands' is much the same in the context of the whole. However, 'Demands' seems to say, *You'll do it 'MY' way*! I wish to add the perspective of 'Calling For and or Requesting' the word 'Declare.' Chapter One of Job clearly defines Job's priority in his *Search For The Heart of God*! "His substance also was seven thousand sheep and three thousand camels, five hundred yokes of oxen, five hundred she asses, and <u>a very great household</u>; so that this man was the greatest of all the men (people) of the east."

"Job's sons feasted in their houses, everyone on his specified day, and sent and called for their three sisters to eat and drink with them. And it was so, when the days of their feasting were gone about, that Job sent and sanctified them, and rose early in the morning, and offered burnt offerings according to the number of them all: for Job said, It may be that my sons have sinned, and cursed God in their hearts. Thus did Job continually." (Job 1:3-5; KJV)

God blessed Job, not as if Job was 'selfishly' *Searching For A Pot Of Gold*! When we set proper priorities, the Blessing of God follows. I don't suggest everything which follows will be without challenges. As we take in the 'overall' trend of life's journey—looking for how life might have taken adverse turns which wouldn't have produced the desired fruit of our Heart, 'We Can Declare The Blessing of God, as seen in 'Results.'

Was there ever a time when Job wondered what was going on? I'm sure Job had his druthers concerning how he wished and prayed life wouldn't turn on him as it did. He faced extreme pressures from his family (his wife, for one); he had to deal with a continual diatribe (tirade, rant and criticism—) from his friends about how he must've been living life wrongly. The outcome of his life would've differed if he'd thrown in the towel as his wife suggested.

After all, was said and done and he'd had his little talk with Jesus, Job's final response looked like this in Job 42: 1-6; KJV—.

"Then Job answered the LORD and said, I know You can do everything and that we cannot keep any secret from You. Who is he that hideth counsel without knowledge? Therefore, I uttered that *I understood not*; things too wonderful for me, which *I knew not*. Hear, pray, and speak; I will demand of Thee and declare You unto me. I have heard of Thee by the ear's hearing, but now mine eye seeth Thee. Wherefore *I abhor myself and repent* in dust and ashes. If this were always our acknowledgement before God—What Then?"

After an overall 'Search' of his heart while trudging at times along his life's Journey; repenting for not understanding what was happening and why; Job 'committed' his own will to rest under the Wings of God's best for him. Please look at *a slight diversion* from The Book of Job to how David responded after he had undergone a few trials and tribulations—

> Search me, O God, and know my heart: try me, and know my thoughts: And see if there be any wicked way in me and lead me in the way everlasting. (Psalm 139:23-24; KJV)

As we search out life's many ways like we do, it's necessary to look hard and fast at how our priorities line up with God's priorities. God wants to make us more like Jesus; we want God to become more like us, desiring the things for ourselves—God never works from our point of view. If only God understood us—He Does! If only God could see we need to make our own decisions about life without input from Him—He Does! However, we can insist on doing life our way, but God loves us too much not to show us The Better Way To Go At Life! [Haven't We Tried It Our Way Long Enough?] Most everybody knows the story of Adam and Eve; God showed them the right way but let them decide if this is what they wanted or not. History tells the story— The *evidence declared the verdict*! In the final court of appeal, Adam and Eve were *guilty as charged*.

Both Sides Now (by Joni Mitchel) is a song that speaks clearly to us about how we need to look at life. I wish I could cast (put on the screen of my writing here) the lyrics of *Both Sides Now* for you. Copyrights and other difficulties restrain me from doing so. However, you can look up the lyrics and even listen to the song on YouTube for yourself. That said, I'll chance-fitting thoughts of my own alongside those of Joni Mitchel.

As we look at verse one of *Both Side Now*, we see what we want with rose-coloured glasses—we think of niceties, 'demanding' we want those compared to their opposites. We look at clouds thinking they'll bring these goodies to us; instead, the clouds give us an array of things—rain, wind, inclement weather, gloominess— some of these things, rain, for instance, are good for us even when we want the sunshine of the day, so we can *bask* instead of running for cover. The presentation of *Both Sides Now* reveals our make-up—also some of the blemishes needing touch-ups.

According to Joni, it seems 'clouds' only block the sunshine. Clouds offer to rain on us; they snow on us; they keep us from having fun; the shadows of the sky (clouds) get in our way. I've looked at clouds from different angles; I only see the ruses *illusions* reveal to us—I don't understand why we need the Clouds!

I feel I have to fake life—making folks think I'm living in the lap of luxury—having a hoot; when the festivities are over, folks think I'm great, 'I gave them a laugh—' but they have no idea how the clouds get me down when I'm alone. I try not to be honest because folks may not like me as much.

Love comes out much the same—I look at it like I look at clouds—sometimes, I have to fake it when the clouds get in the way. Yes, illusions may reach out to me throughout the day, but the outcome is the same at the day's end. Disappointments rule my life. I've looked at life this way much too often. Not every day is like the doldrums I've shared.

Old friends are acting strange towards me—they think I've changed from the happy-go-lucky person I was in their view. We win some and lose some while living every day with a mixture of Sun and Cloud. As I live life knowing I'll win some and lose some, I often recall the illusions of life more than the positives that come from a mix of Sun and Cloud. I don't get it. I can't seem to understand life in all of *its fullness*! Yes, I've looked at life, love, and clouds from two sides—I often think *The Jury Is Still Out On The Verdict*!

We all love a sunny day—for some of us, we like it *not being too hot or too cold*; for others, 'Bring It On!' Cloudy Days can negatively affect our mentality. We think the beauty of 'any one day' wraps up in the sunshine and the blue sky. The Bible challenges us to see Clouds to allow us to see the beauty of God in the whole scope of life as it plays out because of what our search has garnered. Was our search about *Gold* an entire *Pot of Gold*? Was our search about the *Heart of Gold* which was the *Heart of God*?

If we can transmit *The Heart of God* through Sunshine and Clouds, we especially feel the presence of God—rather, shall I say WE KNOW THE PRESENCE OF GOD IN A SPECIAL WAY? As we study the Bible, we'll see that the 'Cloudy Days' of the Bible characters built character. Many of the old-timers, Biblical people, may have failed more miserably than they already did, had they not experienced cloudy and sunny days on their journey. Yes, I would rather have the Blue Skies—but in retrospect, I can see more clearly that the dark times in my life built a character I never would've had—were it not for the clouds that came. I often try to Pray Away my cloudy days—As A Christ Follower: Should I do this?

THE WINDS AND THE CLOUDS OF CHANGE
OFTEN AFFECT US ADVERSELY WHEN WE
PLACE THEM ALONGSIDE THE PLAN GOD HAS
FOR US TO FOLLOW.

I know the thoughts that I think toward you, saith the Lord, thoughts of peace, and not of evil, to give you an expected end. (Jeremiah 29:11; KJV)

◊ THE VISTA VIEW—THE OASIS ◊

The Winds of Change are Challenging

In and of itself, 'Wind' isn't a bad thing. After a hot day, a fresh evening breeze is refreshing—let that breeze show us its flipside (ugly side) and our attitude 'Changes' instantly. *The Winds of Change* challenge us to redirect our 'attentions to duty.' A beautiful flower garden attracts different audiences—people, hummingbirds (I saw my first hummingbird 2022 May 3, it waited until May 11, 2022, to sit and have a suitable feed), and bees—. We make haste to attend to duty to protect our investments—so it should be when we face 'Winds of Adversity.'

Though we use the 'same' words (wind and clouds) to describe two differing entities—*Physical and Spiritual*—presenting identical scenarios (calm and reassuring or disturbing and or upsetting), there's a world of differences involved when we assess them in their bailiwick (field). Physical 'wind and cloud' affect our mood, but it doesn't change our eternal destiny. A physical wind is necessary at differing times. The wind brings the leaves down off their comfortable homes on the branches of the trees in the fall. When the leaves begin changing colour from a great green to another beautiful arrangement of browns, orange, and red—because they've served well their destined season of *purpose*, we know that we're supposed to begin *preparing* for the next season—*Winter*.

Chapter Ten has been working hard to clarify the words 'Wind and Cloud' within two differing contexts—yet, the same context in another sense. If you're not yet completely confused, I'm bordering on confusion to get my message across with clarity—different because the characteristics of wind and cloud each have their unique season and or *purpose*—Physical and Spiritual. There are always Two Columns of Beliefs Systems in life.

The context comes full circle and declares that we cannot have one without the other. The Breath of Life is both Physical and Spiritual—by the choices offered in both. Life DEMANDS Choice, and Choice DEMANDS Direction—Physical and Spiritual. Wind affects the Clouds—causing the clouds to move as the wind commands them to flutter or dash speedily. Everything in life affects something else along the course of life 'Directionally.'

The Clouds themselves also influence the Wind—there are definite connections between the two. When we have a Cloudy Day, we'll have a measure of Wind—How much depends on other factors; we'll leave this thought to stand alone, at least for now. We shouldn't have winds on a clear day; these may be our thoughts—not so! All atmospheric conditions relate to each other at one time or another—The Wind of The Spirit.

> The wind bloweth where it listeth, and thou hearest the sound thereof, but cannot tell whence it cometh, and whither it goeth—so is everyone born of the Spirit. Nicodemus answered and said unto him, How can these things be? (John 3:8-9; KJV) Nicodemus lacked the necessary understanding to grasp a mystery that existed in the past over these matters—the mystery continues today.

I have said much about Physical things so far—this is by direct intent. *Sailing Winds* can be pleasant or disastrous—we cannot sail a boat without wind; we will never get anywhere. The 'Wind' is all about 'Direction,' and let me 'Introduce' The Refreshing Wind of the Spirit. You ask, 'what may this be?' Good Question. Wise, knowledgeable people of the past have tried to fashion all the correct answers—and failed to some degree.

The Bible tells us God is a Spirit, and we need to "Worship Him in Spirit and Truth!" Here's that word 'Spirit' again. If 'Spirit' is all God was and is about, we'd never have been able to understand or know God because what we saw blowing around helter-skelter in the atmosphere and blowing all around us in and through the trees—wouldn't have told us THE STORY of God's Love!

Enter—JESUS! Now we see 'Physicality' again, but not just 'Physicality.' The Physical part of God is Jesus—God The Father, God The Son, God The Holy Spirit. Jesus, the son of man, came with a divine *purpose* of Heart. John 3:16 says God sent His only begotten Son because of the Love Factor.

There was a directive here to carry the message of Love to a creation still future—it existed before the Creation of The Foundations of the World. Jesus came to make sense of it all for us. The Sad News is that the majority rejected Jesus back in the day, and the majority still rejects Him—of this, I cannot make any sense! Having to choose our path seems to have been our nemesis.

Someone came to tell us The Story of Love—it had to happen just as it did. When first created, we messed up miserably, disobeying God's command to Choose Life because a wrong choice here would produce 'Death.' Annihilation was our just desert (our deserved portion of creation), but God's Love changed all that.

When Jesus fulfilled His Earthly *Purpose* by showing us all about God, he gave us another chance at Eternal Life. By dying a death that had to be as it was, to bring us any Hope, by forgiving us—this is all we needed to accept God's offer by repenting (being sorry and asking for help—forgiveness). I'll offer more about this in R.S.V.P.

Jesus died on The Cross, nearly finishing the job. Yes, as He drew His final breath while on the cross, Jesus said—"IT IS FINISHED;" only one thing remained (not Taking Away Anything From Jesus's Words, "IT IS FINISHED.")—Jesus had to return to His seat in the Throne Room of Heaven, and allow the following: "And I will pray to the Father, and He shall give you another Comforter, that He may abide with you forever." (John 14;16; KJV)

Enter— "The Wind of The Spirit!" Might I add—

"The Refreshing, Cloudless, Wind of The Spirit!"

I 'Pray Bigtime' that I've made some things clear in Chapter Ten, which will help us as we travel in Chapter Eleven and onward. One Season always follows another—we have The Four Seasons: Spring, Summer, Autumn and Winter. Then it begins again and again—Spring ETC. Each of these couldn't exist Physically or Spiritually without one another.

Much of what we've looked at is the story of people. The Story of God Precedes The Story of People! My previous book is *Everybody: Everybody Is A Somebody*. If all I've ever written only expresses one thing, it's "THAT PEOPLE ARE IMPORTANT!"

If this weren't the case, God would've never initiated The Creation of anything. He could've just existed in Heaven floating around ethereally on a Celestial Cloud—with the breezes of the heavens to cool Him on those Hot Sultry Days. God would've had a lot fewer problems without our presence. However—Hebrews 12 tells us why He did what He did on the cross. It wasn't all about God like it is about us regarding the satisfaction factor.

We also are surrounded by a great 'cloud' of witnesses. So, let's lay aside every weight and the obstructions that try to put us out of the race. Let's run with patience—the race planned out before us. In so doing, let's look unto Jesus, The Author and Finisher of our faith. Now Get This Finishing Line—

"Jesus—Who for the joy waiting ahead of Him, endured the cross—despised the shame—and the sat down at the right hand of the throne of God." (Re. Hebrews 12)

It turns out it wasn't all about Him—Jesus saw the Finished Portrait, and it gave Him Joy compared to none other when He saw that we'd be satisfied! It has always been about us, as far as Jesus is concerned! Won't you consider Him—Jesus, who suffered a great degree of suffering around The Via Dolorosa, assuming it was as if it were His sin—the Person Who never sinned, becoming sin for us. Then The Scripture reads—"lest ye be wearied and faint in your minds." Who was looking out for Number One? Jesus. Who was Numero Uno? Yes, as far as Jesus was concerned, it was us!

For God—It's Always Been About PEOPLE!

For many years I've had a book in the works called—

"It's People—Passion and People!"

It May Never Get Done!

But Let's Move on to

Chapter Eleven

HEART SENSE
LORD, I Know You're Up There

◊

THE HEAVENS DECLARE THE GLORY OF GOD and the firmament showeth His handiwork. Day unto day uttereth speech, and night unto night showeth knowledge. There's no speech or language where we can't hear their voice. Their line is gone out through all the earth, and their words to the end of the world. In them hath He set a tabernacle for the sun, as a bridegroom coming out of His chamber, and rejoiceth as a strong man to run a race. His going forth is from the end of heaven, and His circuit unto its ends. There's nothing hidden from the heat thereof.

The law of the Lord is perfect, converting the soul: the testimony of the Lord is sure, making wise the simple. The statutes of the Lord are right, rejoicing the heart: the commandment of the Lord is pure, enlightening the eyes. The fear of the Lord is clean, enduring forever—the judgments of the Lord are true and righteous altogether. 'More to be desired than gold, yea, than much fine gold:' sweeter also than honey and the honeycomb. Moreover, Thy servant should hear the warning echoed here by them, and there's great reward in keeping them.

Who can understand His errors? Cleanse Thou me from secret faults. Keep back Thy servant from presumptuous sins; let them not have dominion over me: then shall I be upright, and I shall be innocent from *the great transgression*.

"Let the words of my mouth, and the meditation of my heart, be acceptable in Thy sight, O Lord, my strength, and my Redeemer." (Psalm 19: 1-14; KJV & JBI)

While we are *Searching For The Heart of God—*
What makes more sense than to acknowledge God for Who He is!

Scriptures In Chapter Eleven
John 3: 1-2
Genesis 2: 17; John 3: 1-2
John 3: 3-10
Psalm 139
Ecclesiastes 3; Hebrews 11
Ecclesiastes 12: 1-7; Ecclesiastes 1: 12-15
Mark 12: 28-34; 2 Timothy 2: 15
The Vista View—The Oasis
Philippians; 4-9
Ecclesiastes 12: 13-14
Heart Sense
1 John 3; Psalm 51;1 John 3; Jeremiah 17:9

Chapter Eleven

The Vault—The World—

---◊---

—SEARCHING OUR DOMAIN—

SEARCHING FOR ANYTHING PRESENTS A CHALLENGE. The spur of the moment often sends us on a chase. Looking amongst our stuff or all around the world in hopes of finding just anything at all—requires determination. To 'Search Without *Purpose*' is ludicrous (nonsensical)!'

"THE VAULT"—Isn't only part of the title of Chapter Eleven; I've preferred THE VAULT—to be the title of my next book, [scheduled for release in 2024—this is tentative, and LORD Willing!]. I'll continue The Search Process of Life in the many formations or seasons 'Life' presents. I'll not voluntarily give Life away, so I know this Search process will not be futile! My *Purpose* is always, and will continue to be—To Reach Out And Touch Someone!

It's easy to get into a frenzy when we look doggedly (tenaciously) for that misplaced something. Sometimes I search for something I've given away—thinking it's still somewhere in my domain. Sometimes I'm looking for something I've junked—while thinking, Why would I throw that out? Yes, *SEARCHING* can be laborious or painstaking. Yes, life can be a challenge, even if we choose to do life like God intends to involve us in life's plain old living aspect!

In another sense, Searching can be pleasurable and rewarding—if *Purpose* is the target. Without *Purpose,* life is futile. Imagine getting up every morning not knowing what the day will bring in any sense of the thought. I've often reminded myself of the Bill Murray movie *Groundhog Day*. Every Morning at 6 AM, Phil Conners (Bill Murry) awakes cloudy-eyed or bewildered at first because he knows he already lived this day *Yesterday*! When he 'gets it,' he establishes a *Purpose* for the day before him.

Preconceived ideas of normal are varied. Many people who, because of their physical circumstance—health, mental capacity (not necessarily because of any wrong they've done, and sometimes because of wrong choices) and other reasons out of my reach to explain in simplicity, live without *Purpose*. Living without Purpose may be near to being like a death sentence. What does life look like to any one of us without *A Reason For Living?*

Understandably it's tough to rationalize 'how we can help someone living in the dire *No Hope Scenario?*' As I realize I can only do so much to help people through the issues of life they encounter—it may frustrate me. At some point and in some fashion, *everyone* who has the mental capacity to do so needs to find an avenue by which they can generate *the purpose* for their life's journey.

I don't say this without a deep sense of compassion. Over time, our 'senses' may dampen (diminish). With the increase of technology and the increase of an 'everyone for themselves philosophy—' accepting folks who by choice have no clue about *The Being of God*, and those people without the willingness to acknowledge God for His *Want To* for a personal one-on-one relationship with everyone on Planet Earth—these are mega challenges. Without 'The Missing Link' in place, we may fail to understand if we don't seek hard after God—we may never '*Get It*!'

A loss of hope accelerates the picture of life to being out of whack when it comes to knowing why we're *searching*! What if we were to make God's initial will for creation [people] our Number One *Purpose*? Do we even know why God created us?

It's unconscionable to think God created the world without *Purpose*. If we don't believe God exists, or if He does, but He cares little or nothing about our concerns, then my words concerning God creating with His *Purpose* may not matter to you. If we believe He cares about the 'minutest' moments of our existence, it's easier to think of the universe and everything this entails as distinctively set apart for us!

If God created the world and everything in it for 'us,' think about how *Valuable* we must be to Him as He completes the list in His Day-Timer! If we take a moment to think about *the people* this entails—professing Christians are certainly on His Bucket List! Isn't this true for the 'us' I mention here?

If God cares so much about the people who acknowledge Him as LORD—and He does; if we believe The Bible to be His Word to 'us'—and it is; this is a good thing. I'm thankful for His GREAT Love! John 3:16 is a verse in The Bible with which many non-Christians are well-versed—even these folks often reflect on these words. Christians and non-Christians are often confronted in public by John 3:16—we see it plastered on billboards and the like worldwide.

Nicodemus, in John 3, seems wise enough, as a ruler of the Jews during the time Jesus walked on earth— as The Son of Man, The Son of God, 'God with us,' The Word of God—but he had questions—Vs's 1&2 suggest questioning—without stating them as such. Let's not get off track here—it's not wrong to have questions; it's wrong to persist in error when the truth stares us in the face! In fairness to people who don't understand the simplicity of the message of Jesus, faith being the avenue to this, I say, "Just Look At The Whole Story!" Nicodemus was 'smart' enough to recognize the presence of God in a given situation. If Jesus was as important as Nicodemus seemed to think He was—what do we make of the following words?

There was a man of the Pharisees named Nicodemus, a ruler of the Jews—he came to Jesus at nighttime and said unto him, Rabbi, we know that You are a teacher come from God— for nobody can do these miracles that You do, except God be with him. (A picture of realization).

God so loved the world, that He gave His only begotten Son, that whosoever believeth in Him should not perish, but have everlasting life." God didn't send His Son into the world to condemn the world, but that the world through Him might get saved. Those who believe in Him need not face condemnation—they have a chance. Non-believers have no place where God resides because of the confession of their unbelief in the name of the only begotten Son of God.

Herein lies the condemnation—light came into the world, and people, as people often do, loved darkness rather than light—Why? Because their deeds were evil. Everyone who does evil hates the 'light' and doesn't consider the 'light' for fear of rebuke. (John 3: 1-2; 3:16 (KJV-JBI))

Those who believe truth counts for something—are at least walking in the direction of the light—they seem to realize they have Someone to answer to at the end of the Journey.

Do these words suggest Jesus was *only* talking about The Christian World? If Jesus invited the Whole World, good and bad people (look at this by your definition if you would)—what does this say about how much Jesus wants a relationship with all people everywhere. Genesis Chapter Two leaves the page open for opportunity—for 'us' to choose what we will do with what God gave us in The Beginning. The consequences of choice are clear—God never left 'us' in the dark concerning His *Commands—His Promises*, and He won't shut the door to hearts yearning for Him. We 'The People' are the problem—we balk at everything we don't fully understand accordingly—if we don't get our way.

The tree of the knowledge of good and evil wasn't for us—God left the option open for us to decide on the other side of life than He wanted us to choose. God told Adam and Eve it was dangerous—the road would have many 'mines' and 'roadblocks,' which He knew we couldn't handle. In effect, God said, if and when you eat the fruit of 'this tree,' you will begin to die— "thou shalt surely die." (Genesis 2: 17; JBI)

Nicodemus spoke to Jesus in John 3, 1&2 with questions in his heart but didn't yet ask the questions. God respects our heartfelt questions, knowing we are on a *Search*!

Jesus answered and said unto him, Verily, verily, I say unto thee, Except a man be born again, he cannot see the kingdom of God. (Now come the questions)—Nicodemus saith unto him, How can a man be born when he is old? Can he enter his mother's womb for the second time and be born?

Jesus answered, Verily, verily, I say unto thee, Except a man (person) be born of water and the Spirit, he (they) cannot enter into the kingdom of God. That which is born of the flesh is flesh, and that which is born of the Spirit is spirit. Marvel not that I said unto thee, Ye must be born again. The wind bloweth where it listeth, and thou hearest the sound thereof, but *can't tell* whence it cometh, and whither it goeth: so is <u>everyone</u> that's born of the Spirit.

Nicodemus answered and said unto him, How can these things be? (Jesus answered and said unto him)

Now Jesus answered Nicodemus with a question. There was *no outburst* in John 3—not a one-way street; it was a conversation—a conversation allows for the opportunity of one side to convince the other side with a persuasive answer.

Art thou a master of Israel, and knowest not these things? Verily, I say unto you—we speak that we do know, and testify that we have seen, and ye receive not our witness. If I have told you earthly things, and ye believe not, how shall ye believe if I tell you of heavenly things? And no man (no one) hath ascended to heaven, but He came down from heaven, even the Son of Man. And as Moses *raised* the serpent in the wilderness, even so, must the Son of Man 'be lifted'—that whosoever believeth in Him should not perish but have eternal life. (John 3:3-10; KJV)

Purpose needs to be *Power-Driven,* or it cannot work. Every *purpose* under the sun has defined seasons from which to extend the features of that *purpose.* When Solomon wrote Ecclesiastes, he must've been in touch with the *Wind of The Spirit* [so to speak], enough for even him to understand—he seems to have read between the lines—trying to get the people of the day to understand!

We often refer to Solomon as the wisest person in history—apart from Jesus! As I study the seasons of the life of this personage—this *somebody,* I seriously wonder why he was in the running for top billing as 'Celebrity Of All Time' as far as being the wisest person in history. It's not my intent to get down and dirty about his *affairs* (no pun intended); I just needed to explain that he made many bad choices too!

So, to the degree of living life in the day-to-day compared to 'us,' I'll simply say we have much the same characteristics as Solomon—we can dither with each other on the 'wisdom issue.' Solomon did have a *Season of Wisdom* for which we must acknowledge him—please listen to it carefully as if he were speaking to us in person. If we hear what Solomon tells us, we will be the better person for the time spent.

"There's a season for every *purpose* under heaven: A time to be born and a time to die. There's a time to lay in the crop and take off the harvest. Sometimes evil needs to give an accounting for healing to come. Some things need to undergo a facelift or see a new building rise from the ground up. After we demolish a structure, we hardly ever rebuild it to the exact specifications as the old one.

Often we weep because grief is heavily upon us, and at other times we laugh because joy grew from our time of weeping—Go Figure. When life follows the proper course and repentance for our wrong living comes, it's time to dance! There are times to clear the field of stones—and use them to build structures.

There are times to accept the inevitable and seasons to reject doubtful ambitions. Times are when we suffer losses, but the flip side is that we'll also establish profitable ventures. Often, we need to hang onto what we have, but betimes, we need to give away what we seem to cherish most. We need to know when to speak ['know' when to 'hold em' and 'know' when to 'fold-em!' (Kenny Rodgers)] and when to 'Zip The Lip!' There are times when we should speak out on a matter—and at other times, we should 'Love Our Way' through the conflict—Peace Often Comes Easier In This Case!"

"What profit hath he that worketh in that wherein he laboureth? I have seen the travail that God gave to people to work in their field.

He hath made everything beautiful in His time (season): also he hath set the world in their heart so that no one can find out the work that God maketh from the beginning to the end.

I know that there's no good in them, but for a man to rejoice and do good in his life. Everyone should eat and drink and enjoy the 'good' of all their labour—it's a gift from God.

I know that whatever God does, it will be forever. God will not add anything, once put into action on His part, and take nothing away—God allows some hard things so we will recognize His Sovereignty."

"The things that we observe of the past are the same things we face today—and the future is much like what we've already experienced. God considers as necessary, the history which already was. I saw the place of judgment under the sun, that wickedness was there; and the establishment of righteousness, that iniquity was there."

[We judge based on what we hear and see—God judges based on what He knows! (Psalm 139)]

"I thought to myself, 'God shall judge the righteous and the wicked,' for there is a season for every *purpose* and work.

Again, I seriously considered the state of disrepair people were in back in the day and their condition today. God wanted people to learn from their mistakes back in time, and He wants the same for folks in our day.

Death does not have favourites. People and animals breathe the same air—people and animals, each having the breath of Life God made available in The Beginning—all die at one time or the other, in one way or the other. Solomon observed many things as he wrote Ecclesiastes—after looking intently at the facts, he surmised that all is vanity. From his perspective, he didn't see much hope."

I'm glad The Bible shares The Hope God promised to many of those people listed in Hebrews 11—in The Hall of Fame of Faith. Solomon only saw hopelessness—God turned the tables on that philosophy when in the fullness of time, Jesus, God with us, came and made Hope available to all who believed in The Gospel of Salvation. In John Chapter Three, Jesus tried to help Nicodemus understand through His talk about *The Wind of The Spirit*. We have many examples of questions answered with God's wisdom!

"All go unto one place; all are of the dust, and all turn to dust again. Who knows the spirit of a person? Solomon says the 'spirit' of people goes upward—and the 'spirit' of the beast goes downward to the earth?

Wherefore I perceive that there is nothing better than that a man [person] should rejoice in his [their] works; for that is his [their]portion: for who shall bring him [them] to see what shall be after him [them]?" (I've shared thoughts in and out of the actual scriptures from Ecclesiastes 3; some KJV and Some JBI)

None of us come to wisdom such as this by just lackadaisically or reluctantly *Searching Out Life to find the Hidden Treasure* [so to speak]. By searching for God, we see the truth in this regard—God never hides the truth—Never Ever! We see ever so clearly from Ecclesiastes 3 that God is a fearsome contender for truth. As we read more in my book, we need to latch onto the treasures of life—and live out the promises of God!

"Vanity of vanities, saith the Preacher, vanity of vanities; all is vanity. What profit hath a man of all his labour which he taketh under the sun?" (The Preacher!) Solomon begins his sermon by looking at what he considers an exercise in futility. "I, the Preacher, was king over Israel in Jerusalem. And I gave my heart to *seek and search* out by wisdom concerning all things done under heaven—this sore travail hath God given to the sons of man to practise. I have seen all the works done under the sun; behold, all is vanity and vexation of spirit. The crooked paths cannot be made straight, and we cannot number the wants we have before us." (As per Ecclesiastes 1: 12-15)

Think about The Thames River Again—As per *Bridging The Gap* (*Two Books Ago by Jacob Bergen*)

The end of Ecclesiastes presents these observations, highlighted as Words of Wisdom! Solomon lived 75-80 years—give or take. He lived life day-to-day just like us—only in a more elegant manner and often more indiscreet, unwise, or careless fashion. Yet, like us, he observed the sun coming up in the morning and the sun going down in the evening.

Just like for us, there were still only twenty-four hours in the day (—time and chance happeneth to them all—Ecclesiastes 9:11) to get done what needed to get done in his life—he still needed the breath of life to accomplish everything God put in his path to travel. Please look at the finishing touches of Ecclesiastes.

"Remember now thy Creator in the days of thy youth, while the evil days come not, nor the years draw nigh when thou shalt say, I have no pleasure in them.

While the sun, or the light, or the moon, or the stars, be not darkened, nor the clouds return after the rain: in the day when the keepers of the house shall tremble, and the strong men shall bow themselves, and the grinders cease because they are few, and those that look out of the windows see darkness—and the doors shall close in the streets.

When the grinding sound is low, he shall rise at the bird's voice, and the daughter's merriment shall cease.

Also, when they shall be afraid of that which is high, fears shall be in the way. The almond tree shall flourish—and the grasshopper shall be a burden. Desire shall fail—because people die, going where death takes them."

("Remember to Remember Often!")

"The mourners go about the streets—the golden bowl breaks, the pitcher breaks at the fountain, or the wheel breaks at the cistern. Then shall the dust return to the earth as it was: and the spirit shall return unto God Who gave it." (Thoughts in and around Ecclesiastes 12: 1-7)

The Bible is a Vault of sorts. The Bible is a storage space of information for *Eternal Purpose*—often, it's only about nine inches by six inches by two inches and holds just less than eight-hundred thousand words. Yet, as I see it, every directive for the necessity of life on Planet Earth and Eternal Life displays vividly within the pages of "This Vault." According to my research, the Bible is still the most sold book globally. More and more books are becoming contenders for the top spot—this, in my perspective, is a sad thing and will be a 'sadder' day if The Scriptures 'Surrender The Hill!'

It's hard to determine the actual most extensive World Vault in size. The largest Gold Vault in the World is The Federal Reserve Bank in New York City. Is the size of a Vault the most crucial factor? Many Vaults show themselves as the most Impenetrable Vaults in The World. We even have the Doomsday Vault—it's a seed bank set to be a reserve for holding every important seed to sustain life if the Doomsday Clock runs down to zero—I understand this to be a case in point.

History records *Gold* to be one of the most prized possessions on Earth. When *Gold* is fully processed, it highlights itself as a sign of affluence and strength. Gold is not usually just lying around on the ground, ready to be picked up by every passer-by—we have to work hard to get it in the raw form and then process it to become the Gold Bars we see stored in Vaults. There's more Gold kept in Vaults than there is any more in the ground for its mining.

When I think of the world's 'largest' Vault, I think firstly of Fort Knox. However, as per a Vault of Gold, this is not the case. Manhattan, New York, houses the most extensive Gold Vault globally; this Vault is five stories beneath The Federal Reserve Bank. Apart from an act of God [in my opinion], it's impenetrable by undesirable outside forces. It houses three-hundred and fifty billion dollars of value in Gold.

Searching is not a big issue in a vault if we want to find something. A vault contains only so much room—we can only put a limited amount of things in a 'vault.' Even if the vault is as massive as the Largest One In The World, it's not the size of The World.

Even if we had access to these large 'Lockers,' we could cover the distance within such a 'vault' in a given time slot. It would be a manageable search, yielding a display of a vast amount of wealth in visual form. If this *Pile of Wealth* stays Eternally Planted on the floor, it'll never make a difference in even one person's life for Eternal Value Sake.

So, where does the Value of *A Search For The Heart of Gold—Not A Pot of Gold* lay? We can search and find this valuable commodity; we can stockpile the knowledge we gain from a successful search for product knowledge; then we come to a fork in the Road of Our Search, one which Demands a DECISION!

What does the fork in the road look like as we approach the Road Less Travelled and The Road Well Traveled? Put yourself into a visual world for a moment. If you can walk a path that has a fork in the road, try to imagine or fit these scenarios into what that arena of life suggests, and consider, think about it—will you get any farther than where you are at now at this fork or crossroad—what will you do next?

For that matter, either you or I will make camp at this junction for the rest of earthly time, or we'll take one road and plan to have our campout at our targeted journey's end. No matter which life road we assume, there'll be a Journey's End. As we fathom or understand life as we know it physically [as opposed to Spiritually], we know 'Death' is this End Of Road setting. On the Spiritual [as opposed to the physical], 'Death' is only a part of The Journey's End.

Suppose the 'World Is Our Domain' in so far as to what degree we involve ourselves in the life God wants for us to live. With technology and the resources of people who will reach out to do some of what we cannot do, we often need to support others, and in so doing, we are a part of The Great Commission. We're not the lesser person if we're not confronting people about their status of believing in God or Not—twenty-four seven. I think everyone should be involving themselves in things for the benefit of others presently and eternally.

Searching requires Physicality whether we are *Searching For Gold*, fortunes of any mineral or fundamental value, a life mate, searching for the prospect of having children, and much more! Physicality is also essential for us to conjure up, summon, or scope out to travel along the Spiritual Fork Of The Road of Life. Physicality and Spirituality must walk hand in hand, but our choice will put us on track with our Creator God or take us onto the other road where our selfish ambitions will rule our options and lives. Opportunities present challenges—Minor and Major ones.

God did for us what we couldn't do for ourselves—how does this view out for us as we *Search For A Heart of Gold: Not A Pot of Gold?* Added to this, how do things play out in our *Search For The Heart of God?*

'Vaulting' (spring-boarding) to get somewhere—a jump or distance—is not an exercise for the feeble-hearted. All of us have moments when we are not as strong in certain seasons of life as we know we ought to be—this does not determine the overall level of our Spirituality. When we are weak, He [God The Father, Jesus, The Holy Spirit—GOD] comes alongside us to carry us through that season to the next after being comforted and strengthened by God To Go The Distance! Elijah's story is a case in point—if we study it throughout his journey.

While thinking about Vaulting or Spring Boarding, we imagine getting over a space or an obstacle. A Steeplechase Course is one way for us to get to where we are going—while avoiding some of the pitfalls we would need to endure if we walked through *feet on the ground.* Walking through a minefield is hazardous, to say the least—however, we can carry out this task successfully with the proper tools and much care. At Journey's End, we come out stronger for having managed our way through the tough times.

I'm not suggesting we strap on a backpack and head for the nearest or most distant MINEFIELD! Some people train arduously to manage minefields—many folks can attain this level of expertise (know-how, proficiency or skill in this area). Though not everyone fits the bill to take this road, everyone should travel on one route or another [Physically and Spiritually]. Physicality is not an option—this is all of us; Spirituality is an option. By the birthright condition of choice, we all find ourselves at the crossroads of the fork in the road when we consider serving the world around us.

We'll never attain a value level of the riches of life on God's plan if we never venture out on a Search For The Heart of Gold. Because of an inheritance, we may attain or get *A Pot of Gold*—by hard work in the direction of wealth, by choice, we may get *A Pot of Gold*; these may include *A Pot of Gold* but miss the point by a 'country mile' (usually an uncalculated distance).

What's missing if our *Search is for The Pot of Gold* alone is the operative and keyword in this book and every book I've written—HEART! We will always have a Physical Heart as long as we live; sadly, not everyone has a Spiritual Heart. As mentioned often throughout this book, choosing between only the Physical Heart and realizing The Spiritual Heart for the Eternity most of us seem to want, must be decided here on earth while still living the Physical Life.

Realizing the Spiritual Heart, *A Heart of Gold*—amounts to being on a *Search For The Heart of God*! A Search For The Heart of God never comes accidentally.

> Study to show yourself approved unto God, a workman that needeth not to be ashamed, rightly dividing the word of truth. (2 Timothy 2:15; KJV)

"One scribe came, he heard people reasoning together, perceiving he had answered them well, he asked, 'Which is the first commandment of all?' Jesus answered him, 'The first commandments is, Hear, O Israel; The Lord, our God, is one Lord: You shall love the Lord thy God with all thy heart, and with all your soul, and with all your mind, and with all your strength—this is the first commandment and Greatest Commandment."

Secondly, you shall love your neighbour as you would love yourself. No commandments are more significant than these. The scribe said to Him, well said Master, You have spoken the truth: Yes, we know there is one God; and there is none other than He: And to love Him with all the heart has to give, and with all the understanding, and with all the soul, and with all the strength, and to love his neighbour as himself, this is more than all whole burnt offerings and sacrifices. When Jesus saw the scribe answer discreetly, He said to him, You are not far from the kingdom of God. After this, nobody dared ask him any more questions." (Mark 12: 28-34; KJV-JBI)

—TWO PRINCIPLES THAT ARE IMPERATIVE TO A SUCCESSFUL SEARCH ARE—

—KNOWING WE ARE ALIVE—
&
—KNOWING WE HAVE A PURPOSE—

Know Who You Are Looking For and Search For Him With All Your Heart! Knowing This Source to Be The Ultimate Reason For Living—Is like Gold in your Vault.

Once You Know Who You Are Looking For and Acknowledge Him With All Your Heart and Strength—Set Out To Accomplish What He Sought For From The Beginning of Time!

If we seek to fulfill only the Physical, we will always be disappointed and or unfulfilled—If we seek First The Spiritual, The End Result will be a Reward greater than our understanding!

◊ THE VISTA VIEW—THE OASIS ◊

Jeff Bezos, Elon Musk, Bill Gates, and Warren Buffet—couldn't purchase the amount of Gold stored in TFRB (The Federal Reserve Bank).

No matter how much Gold there is in the storehouses of the World—in the ground, in the water, or in our pockets—it still leaves at least one question unanswered: Is it enough to meet our eternal expectations in our quest for infinite satisfaction?

I Suggest A Big NO!

Resources—it seems that we can't live with them, and we can't live without them. What do I mean when I say we can't live with them? Resources are the *Bread of Life*—so isn't it a given that we can *or will* always live with our resources? True, they are a given; but what leaves resources somewhat in doubt is that we are never satisfied with how many we accrue. The Rolling Stones sang—*I Can't Get No Satisfaction*— '*I Try, Try, Try*!' It's no use—it isn't working. It comes down to where we place our trust to get satisfied.

When we say— "resources, we can't live without them,"—we put a wrap on the issue because our dependency is not on How Many Resources We Have—but on Who Is The Supplier Of Those Resources! When the bank is empty, there is no means to back up the suppliers' promises or commitments to look out for us. In this case, we are dealing with Physicality—When we need to trust the Spirituality aspect—God! Leastwise that is my story, and I'm sticking to this line.

Well, I better give due diligence to finishing Chapter Eleven here in *The Vista View—The Oasis*—this means that I'm looking over what I've written in Chapter Eleven—*The View* as I've stated my thoughts for you to check over for yourselves.

The second part of the heading of this finishing portion is *The Oasis*. Until we take some time to "*Smell The Coffee*," so to speak, and *make and tak*e the time to reflect and take a few sips of our coffee or tea—and have some 'thinking time,' we have no resource to set a working time to begin fixing the issues we need to handle.

You know that the issues we are dealing with in Chapter Eleven are what the title suggests—*The Vault—The World—*. *The Vault*, which I suggest is The Bible, holds all we'll ever need to come up with The Answer that will help us through the issues we face daily—if not moment by moment at times; these are surprises we can better live without!

I'm not brave enough to say I have all the answers or that you should have all the answers as committed followers of Jesus Christ. But [and this is often a "Big Pain In The Butt"], if we can hook up with the Trust Factor, The Bible, and what it encourages us to do—without our excuses, we will be on the right track as far as facilitating the use of the resources available to us! Please, let's listen together to a few verses from The Vault—The Bible.

Rejoice in the Lord always—I repeat it, Rejoice. Let's be moderate in all things to allow people to see we lead by example—not just our words. Let's note that Jesus is coming again, and we want to be ready when He does come.

Part of the challenge is— don't get so wound up about everything. Part of the answer is to be thankful for what we have already; tell God (requesting in prayer) what we feel (subjectively) is holding up the progress of life being as it should be; and with this kind of trust in God, we can find peace amid the storms of life we have no control over. Jesus Is The Answer To Life's Issues—!

The guidelines are in doing—whatever is truthful, honest, and morally right things and looking to accomplish things on our path with pure intentions. We can all see clearly which things around us are lovely, of good report, virtuous (honourable), and praiseworthy.

If we think about these things as we attempt to walk in a right relationship with our Lord Jesus Christ, we will have a Peace that is not easily understood if we are trying to do life independently. We learn many things *right and wrong* from watching others—keep Jesus in focus, not only other people. Yes, there are worthy people to follow as leaders—find these folks. (Philippians 4: 4-9' KJV-JBI)

We've looked at Ecclesiastes many times in *Searching For The Heart Of Gold; Not A Pot Of Gold*. Why do I feel that this was necessary? Well—many life lessons mentioned in Ecclesiastes for us are ready for us even today—and that by some Wise Person, in this case, some Wise Guy named Solomon! In Chapter Eleven, I garnered food for thought that I don't neglect or take lightly. If we live life successfully, we all need to follow some Great Guidelines.

I know that we make many mega mistakes—I know that Solomon made numerous huge mistakes—Solomon also knew that he was not always on top of things—as we also realize about ourselves if we open our eyes and ears to The Truth! As we peruse Ecclesiastes, we find at least one of the "Big Pluses" concerning finding some answers for successful living. Please hear what Solomon realized after he'd surveyed his tenure on this planet—

Let us hear the conclusion of the whole matter—Fear God and keep his commandments, for this is the entire duty of every person. For God shall bring every work into judgment—every secret thing, whether good or evil (Ecclesiastes 12: 13-14; KJV).

The Bible [The Vault]—has a few good pointers to get us through life, through to when we end earth's destiny—and onward through the Destiny of Eternity!

The Vault—by Jacob Bergen

Chapter Eleven here is a Preview
[Wait For The Book] (Hopefully 2023-24)

Chasing After God—What's This Like?

Let's Find Out In Chapter Twelve
Please Stay With Me!

HEART SENSE
Lord—Hear My Unending Prayer

————————————◊————————————

MY HEART IS DECEITFUL ON ITS OWN!
(Jeremiah 17:9)

LORD, Fashion a new Heart inside of me, one that glows with the radiance of Your Love! The 'Wonder of You,' created in me, would indeed be A Miracle of Transition from what I am now to what I will be when I see You from my current vantage point—Just As You Are! (Psalm 51 & 1John 3; JBI)

Transform the way I look at life so that I will recognize the durability of Your love, LORD. LORD, the devotion of Your thoughts towards me from before anything You shaped, I long to know this; I want to know You More.

"Look at what kind of love the Father is sending our way, even to call us His children. As we look more like Jesus, the people opposite our belief won't know us anymore because we differ in too many ways—basically in the form of our relationship with God in The Person of Jesus The Christ."

Right now, we are not yet at that perfect place where sin will no longer taunt us to give up on Jesus. When Jesus comes back, He will take us to the place where we will forever 'BE' with Him—and The Bible says we will 'BE' like Jesus. Because we will see with differing eyes—we will see Jesus as He is—we will see Him differently than we have ever imagined Him to 'BE.'

As this is the case, we will begin *preparing* for that day by shaking off the cares of this world that attach themselves to us and drag us down—The Bible says, We will make ourselves purer because that is what Jesus is—PURE!" (1 John 3; JBI)

Scriptures In Chapter Twelve
Genesis 1: 1-5; Genesis 1; John 1; John 3:16
John 1: 1-5; Psalm 139
Hebrews 13:5
1 Corinthians 2
Matthew 9: 1-13
The Vista View—The Oasis
Matthew 22: 35
Matthew 22: 37-40

Chapter Twelve

Chasing After God
What's This Like?

THE NUMBER ONE SOLD BOOK of all time has about 800,000 recorded Words. As I Searched Google and Bing, it amazed me that I was hard-pressed to find an immediate recognition by the masses that The Bible was and is indeed The Number One Best Selling Book Of All Time. Guinness World Records admits to The Bible topping the list at an estimated 5 Billion copies.

I Googled "And The Number One Bestselling Book of all time is—" and without much ado, the list immediately veers away from Guinness's listing of The Bible in the 5 Billion (not knowing what year this estimate came about) section to many others listing in and around 500 Million. Yes, Guinness stands out atop for me— kudos to them for the attempt to put The Bible where it belongs.

When I Search the topic of 'Books,' the central theme on the value scale is making a difference in the lives of 'All' People Everywhere. It's virtually impossible to find consensus about how many written books there are and who holds the Numero Uno spot; the list carries on into oblivion—as far as I can determine.

People were 'Created' [as far as I'm concerned, I have never reneged on my belief about this]. If I'm to be inclusive in the sense that even God, *In The Beginning*, allowed us to choose *what we would believe*; in the 'sense' that Jesus said in John 3:16— "That Whosoever Believeth," At least I'll try to be as inclusive as God! When I say, "people were Created, or came from some other source," I'm saying that there may be someone reading 'this book' and looking at the overall picture of what I'm talking about and be thinking differently than what I think. Communication sources create the "Different Strokes For Different Folks" choice factor.

While I'm *Searching For The Heart of Gold*, firstly in myself, I wonder if I am guilty of placing the importance level of God in the Person of Jesus Christ into a state of Anonymity. Because of my everyday lifestyle, I may be implying Ambiguity, Obscurity, and *'Insignificance.'* Sometimes, I wonder how the rest of the People of the World—Believers in God or Non-Believers in God—fit into the picture of "Ambiguity" about The Bible.

[For argument's sake and the *purpose* of reaching a consensus, could we all use The Bible as a *Testing Benchmark*? What would be the answer if we suggested an opinion from our perspective and shared our beliefs in the same context? "How Is The World Doing In So Far as sorting out the 'insignificance' and uncertainty issues I Spoke about Previously?] WOW! This paragraph, from the word "For" at the beginning—to the word "Previously," suggests a *'Huge Picture'* (*sixty-one words*). We face a Big Issue, *with innumerable problems*!

God Chasing After Us—Us Chasing After God—HMMM? Each four-word phrase has equal letters and words. Each four-word *turn of phrase* houses the *'same words.'* So, 'should each phrase have the same perspective, leading us into the same context?'

God Chasing After Us suggests a few things: God loves us so much He doesn't want to live without us—for me, this is clear from John 3:16. From the human perception, I liken these thoughts to the setting of one person chasing after another person to form a lasting relationship—(Marriage between a man and a woman).

Another situation stares me in the face as if saying, "I saw what you did; it was wrong and or criminal, and I'm going to hunt you down and whip you into shape." In The Beginning—The Garden of Eden comes to mind. [This is not an inviting scenario]—this is an easy picture to grasp because we can liken it to the Physical *'Cops and Robbers'* scenario of life as a reality we can clearly understand. *God Chasing After Us* because He Loves Us—begs the question: 'Why would He or Why should He Love Us? Why would He or why should He Chase Us? We Messed Up—this is a no-brainer unless we have a Love Relationship With Him!

God might be Chasing Us is to *Help Us To Be More Like Him*—Not to make us Little Gods, but to build us up or help us have the desire (that which He shows us by His Love) to be like Him—to have the character He has—and Love others as He first loved us!

Us Chasing After God also has a few different perspectives to consider. The question which comes to mind looks like this: *Why would we Chase After God?* The short answer—one already answered—is Because *He First Loved Us!*

Us Chasing After God may look different for each of us in our manners of questioning *Why We Would Want Any Part of God.* Many folks believe in God in some fashion. Many think of God as some entity that is somewhat the same as the thoughts of Evolution. They may say that He is the 'Opening Line,' as is the first cell coming into existence and expanding from there to all we have throughout time. In this plot, God may be part of The Beginning but not the Initiator of all things—maybe He spoke Creation into being, making 'People' the unique feature of His Creation. For many folks Chasing After God looks like we're just a bunch of animals foraging for a living—Finito! (There's also much to see in John 1 about God in The Person of Jesus Christ!)

Us Chasing After God may leave us as just wanting all the 'goodies—' having the power to be the dominating force of life with everything around us. Selfie Mode is a huge part of life as we know it 'Today!' The way we picture ourselves Chasing After God is often so varied and indistinguishable, leaving us feeling God is no more Special than the rest of us.

Chasing After God—What's This Like? My prayer is that the pages lying ahead will instill in us a desire to experience more than life may have offered us in the past—to *know God* for all He's Worth—as we move forward—DOING LIFE! I pray God won't only be The Opening Line of every moment of our lives but that He will be The Bottom Line reason for *Life Itself* on a Personal Relational Level!

Life Is A Precious Gift! Life should never be just something scrolling swiftly through nature—the universe—like a stiff wind does while knocking down everything in its path—leaving destruction in the wake. Yes—Life Is A Precious Gift! Life shouldn't ever be like strolling through the park and looking towards the Exit—as if "Let's Just Get It Done—" after our entrance.

While *Doing Life,* we need to take some time to smell and taste the coffee, smell the roses, and engage with what straddles, toddles, ambles, meanders—along the same path as the one we're *Basking In!*

Chasing After God—What's This Like?

In the beginning, God created the heavens and the earth. And the earth was without form, and void, and darkness was upon the face of the deep. And the Spirit of God moved upon the face of the waters. And God said, Let there be light: and there was light. And God saw the light, that it was good: and God divided the light from the darkness. And God called the light Day, and the darkness he called Night. And the evening and the morning were the first day. (Genesis 1: 1-5; KJV)

We just read the 'Opening Line' of the Genesis (Beginnings) of Creation. Though Genesis 1 is the 'Opening Line' of The Whole Bible, it has a particular phrase ensconced in verse 1— "In The Beginning God."

[————]

In The Beginning, God!

[————]

I'm *Purposefully* leaving some separation between the lines here to help us understand there is A Huge Separation *of* Sorts [while at the same time—no Separation] between God and Humankind! I've *Purposefully* drawn out the First Four Words of The Opening Line of Genesis, not to separate God from Creation—but to recognize that God *was and is* before all time *as we understand time*.

"Without Him was nothing made; that was made!"

I've always thought of The Gospel of John Chapter One as being a Direct Connective [like coordinating conjunctions such as For, And, Nor, But, Or, Yet, and So (Fanboys is an Acrostic)] Chronology (Record)] with Genesis—I call it The New Testament Genesis.

FANBOYS is a word spelled downward.

F-for
A-and
N-nor
B-but
O-or
Y-yet
S-so

The apostle John, son of Zebedee, brother of James, called a "Son of Thunder" and called *the disciple Jesus loved,* is the 'man' (person) responsible for the clarity of thought in John 1:1. Jesus links with—The Word, God, Creator (without him was not anything made that was made) to The first four Words of Genesis 1:1.

"In The Beginning, God—."

The naysayers queried John about his status and the rank of Jesus because He was unsettling [intentionally or unintentionally?] the naysayers—to this, John answered—.

> And this is the record of John when the Jews sent priests and Levites from Jerusalem to ask him, Who art thou? And he confessed and denied not; but confessed, I am not the Christ. (John 1:19; KJV)

> "*Us Chasing After God* also has a few different perspectives to consider. The question which comes to mind looks like this: *Why would we Chase After God?* The short answer—one already answered—is Because *He First Loved Us*! (*IBID*)

Here's the thing—here's the question, "*Why would we Chase After God?*" Well, the answer may begin like this; the following is how I finished Chapter Eleven (*The Vault—The World—*) in preparation for Chapter Twelve (Chasing After God—What's This Like)—

<u>Two principles that are imperative to a successful Search are— Knowing You Are Alive & Knowing You Have A Purpose</u>

> Know *Who* you are looking for and search for *Him* with all your heart! Knowing this *Source* to be *The Ultimate Reason For Living*—Is like Gold in your Vault.

Once You Know Who You Are Looking For and Acknowledge Him With All Your Heart and Strength—Set Out To Accomplish What He Sought For From The Beginning of Time!

Suppose we seek to fulfill only the Physical. In that case, we will always be disappointed and or unfulfilled—If we seek First The Spiritual, The *End Result* will be a reward more significant than our understanding!

Why wouldn't we *Chase After God? Why don't we Chase Hard After God?* Does evidence demand a verdict? Historical testimony reveals the magnitude of God in *Physical* ways—as The Son of Man; the evidence is insurmountable. The result is that the Bible tells us how much God 'loved' and still 'loves' us (John 3:16). Why is the following question even in our hearts or on our lips?

"Why would we Chase After God?"

Please look at some of The Magnitude of God with me—.

In the beginning, the Word (Jesus) was with God, and the Word was God. The same was at the beginning with God. He made all things; without Him was not anything made. In Him was life, and the life was the light of men. And the light shineth in darkness; and the darkness comprehended it not.
(John 1: 1-5; KJV)

I reference Psalm 139 many times. It's a continual backdrop—in *Searching For A Heart of Gold; Not A Pot of Gold.* Psalm 139 is a power-packed setting that speaks to the Magnitude of God— it's a stark reminder of Who God Always Was. It sharpens our knowledge base as to Who God Is Today. Added to this, Psalm 139 and the entire scriptures continually point us to Who God Wants To Be For Us As We Struggle In Life. We are without an excuse for why we should want to chase *after God.* If we let Him, God can change Our *Want* (Desire)!

After John 1 links us to Genesis 1, *John* continues in a historical context, telling us more about Jesus—God With Us. (John 1: 6-18) John always pointed to Jesus and Who He Was and Is! Desire is a Powerful Emotion—subjective and often misdirected by hurts and fears. When we keep our eyes on the ball, we are objective, but even then, sometimes, we drift aimlessly and lose our way.

Slow Fade—by Casting Crowns stories (tells) about when we lose the integrity of faithfulness in a marital relationship—it's here we drift (a loss of the truth, honour, and goodness—drifting is a process) by taking a second look when a blind eye should be the choice we make—. The issues and consequences are the same when we have a relationship with Christ. The backsliding steps lead to a broken relationship on our part—us drawing away from God and His integrity and faithfulness! Fading Away into the crowd is to lose the reality of error—it's devastating.

The 'Opening Line' of Genesis includes much more than observing a few verses but meanders through The Garden of Eden. From the time Adam and Eve entranced The Garden of God—to Leaving the Garden of Eden through an unintended Exit Gate—they were running adrift—A Slow Fade. *Paradise Lost* leaves us considering many decisions, possibly more than we anticipated making on The Long Road. Adam and Eve took their eye off the ball. They should've employed a *Blind Eye* philosophy when the devil pointed out that what he said was a better road to handle than the one God suggested was The Only Way!

The 'Opening Line' was just that—The Beginning. The 'Opening Line' would've been sufficient to meet every expectation and need. If Adam and Eve had listened to God instead of the devil, 'The Opening Line' and 'The Bottom Line' would have merged [linked]—as if being one road—not two lanes. There never would've been a "Road Less Travelled." The Roads Less Travelled and The Road Not Taken would never again have presented a Crossroad—A Valley of Decision.

The Opening Line as opposed to the Bottom line—What are the differences? In simple terms, we might say 'The Opening Line' is The Beginning and The 'Bottom Line' and the 'Closing Line' is The Ending or Final Result or The Final Answer. As I theorize, delve or dig further towards the "Bottom Line" of this book, *Searching For A Heart of Gold*, I pray I'm not exploring a 'Bottomless Pit!'

In Bridging The Gap, my Fourth Book, I presented the setting of Building A Physical Bridge and how it relates to Building Bridges of Reality insofar as connecting two sides of a Gap—Physically, Emotionally, and Spiritually. I asked myself, 'Why build a Bridge?'—What Do We Accomplish By It?—Are there times we think trudging through physical territory or paddling over a river to get to the other side would suffice?

With these thoughts in our rear-view mirror, I'd like for us to look at 'Life' in these ways. Hence I speak about the Opening Line and The Bottomline (Closing Line). As I do so, I know that where we have a beginning, we'll have an end—this includes every entity or 'Every Created Thing;' aside from God. God is Eternal, Everlasting, and Ethereal—[He was The Son of Man, human] while at the same time, we say He remained God.

God never left us flopping in the wind; He never leaves us in the dark; He will never leave us as if blown in the wind. The promise of God's Word to us—always carries the day.

> Let your conversation be without covetousness, and be content with such things as ye have: for he hath said, I will never leave thee, nor forsake thee. (Hebrews 13:5; KJV)

At the beginning of any *Human Endeavor*, or might I say that when we were born, we were incapable of making decisions—rational or otherwise. The act of having wisdom was foreign to us—the process of receiving and or processing wisdom came to us as an initial seed at the hand of someone else—from here, the responsibility factor of our growth in understanding fell on us. We might think here about The Opening Line.

Once we receive a gift (See *Chapter 11—Twin Towers of The Heart*), it's ours. Whether accepted thankfully or begrudgingly, how we receive this gift [wisdom] is within our grasp or our accountability to manage well. These things become the *Middle Portion* of what we do with the Life we receive at birth. This period varies for each of us. I doubt anyone has lived precisely the same amount of time down to the nanosecond.

I believe God has always been in control of the issue of being human—even though this presents a mega host of Questions. Did God manufacture the DNA and RNA of every person who has ever lived so uniquely that not one of us is the same as our counterpart? If Forensic Science is reliable—my query about God's part in creating humanity must be correct, or we couldn't count on the usage of DNA results enough to say we got it one-hundred percent right! I'm just thinking again—when I do so, I'm dangerous! I've been talking about part of the 'Middle Portion' of the space between The 'Opening Line' and The 'Bottom Line or Closing Line,' which is a necessary part of the realities we endure.

The 'Bottom Line includes time spent on this Earth as we know it! However, according to many belief systems, there's Life After Death—Physical death of the human body on Planet Earth is inevitable! There are some exceptions to my thoughts about what different belief systems believe—one exception is Atheists; because they don't believe in God! Is it necessary to believe in something to have a relevant opinion? Good Question?

When it comes to matters of Wisdom, the Bible has quite a story to tell—better said would be to say The Bible has no 'tale' to tell but lays out The Way It Is! The Bible speaks about *The Way We Were*—In Retrospect, It Told Us What We Would Face In Life—these items and more are told to us as facts we need to accept by Faith because we weren't there. History records life as it was, but to be honest—maybe what we call *the facts*—are fudged [doctored] (I don't worry much about this stuff). For me, there are enough concerns about *today* to deal with without soliciting unwarranted theories—. Someone said, "Don't Sweat The Small Stuff!"

And I, brethren, when I came to you, came not with excellency of speech or wisdom, declaring unto you the testimony of God. I determined not to know anything among you, save Jesus Christ and Him crucified. And I was with you in weakness, fear, and trembling. My speech and preaching were not with enticing words of man's wisdom but in demonstration of the Spirit and of power: that your faith should not stand in the understanding of men [other people] but the power of God.

Howbeit we speak wisdom among them that are perfect: yet not the knowledge of this world, nor the princes of this world that come to nought: but we talk about the wisdom of God in a mystery, even the hidden wisdom, which God ordained before the world unto our glory: Which none of the princes of this world knew: for had they learned it, they would not have crucified the Lord of glory.

But as it is written, Eye hath not seen, nor ear heard, neither have entered into man's (people's) heart, the things God hath prepared for them that love Him. But God hath revealed them unto us by his Spirit: for the Spirit searcheth all things, yea, the deep things of God. For what man knoweth the things of a man, save the spirit of man which is in him? even so, the things of God knoweth no man, but the Spirit of God.

Now we have received, not the spirit of the world, but the spirit of God; that we might know the things that are freely given to us of God. We also speak, not in the words which man's [people's] wisdom teacheth, but which the Holy Ghost teacheth; comparing spiritual things with spiritual.

But the natural man receiveth, not the things of the Spirit of God: for they are foolishness unto him: neither can he know them, because they are spiritually discerned. But he that is spiritual judgeth all things, yet he is judged of no man [nobody]. For who hath known the mind of the Lord, that he may instruct Him? but we have the mind of Christ. (1 Corinthians 2; KJV)

The writer Paul might have been saying, "I may not be the sharpest knife in the drawer," when it comes to *Wisdom* about what is said. What Paul said then might come out to us as him saying, he didn't intend to meddle in our business; it seems to me that his most significant concern was that we would know all there is to know about Jesus. Paul openly declared he was weak *physically* and trembled even though he had something to add to what we already knew about Wisdom. As per what I feel he was saying, I think he was telling us not to try to figure out Spiritual things by human measures; but to rely on The Word of God to be our guide. What better Guide could we utilize?

Paul suggests that as Spiritual beings, people who have accepted The Way of The Cross; The I Am The Way, The Truth, and The Life (Jesus) as our Personal Saviour, in a living moment by moment way—we have access to the Wisdom from Above!

The things which have entered our hearts concerning Jesus; those things that history told us about; the depth of the workings of God; these are things that people who don't have a relationship with God in The Person of Jesus will not grasp unless they come into a relationship with God in this way.

The Bible tells us that God clearly shows us through his written Word, and our acceptance of it by faith, without reservation (not stupidly or foolishly), that we can understand the true wisdom through the things He has said in the distant past and through what He said and did in the Personage of Jesus Christ, and God's Spirit!

To the person who cares nothing about God, we're fools— this person has no means by which to have Wisdom concerning Spiritual things. Who's our 'Boss?' Is the wisdom of the unbeliever great enough—proficient, competent, or experienced enough to tell God what is right and what is wrong? Who in this world of those who don't know Christ—know the mind of the God—believers can have the mind of Christ through Faith!

We have four boys, and they constantly phone us on Special Days on The Calendar—like Birthdays. On my 75th. Birthday one of our sons came from Calgary with a surprise visit. These times are precious. The visit was great—too short, but it was a blessing for me as I turned the three-quarters of a century mark.

Part of what made it special was when we prayed together before he left for a few days of Fly Fishing in Fernie, BC. My wife prayed, and then our son prayed—part of his prayer said, "Thank You LORD that *You Chased After Us*!" This pleasant reminder was significant because on this same day I was writing Chapter Twelve—*Chasing After God—What's This Like?*

Our son had no idea that this was the Day's Topic for me. The Lord reminded me again that I was where I was supposed to be in the use of the Gifts He has given me to write for this very day. I'd been writing about what it's like, in my opinion, to be on a Search For God!

What does it look like to be on a Search For God? In my reference to The Bible and what it feels like in the deepest part of my soul to know I can communicate with The God of Everything about 'Everything' essential to me in my Search For Him—Chasing Him For All I'm Worth, is a Book Story all its own! I'm worth plenty according to God—the same goes for you!

"What books have the best record of Changing Lives— having made the difference between Life and Death?"

I understand that most writers most likely felt they had a story to tell—throughout history. As quickly as these thoughts came, I searched for who wrote the first novel and when they wrote the book. I did this because I could distinguish between fact and fiction in this way. My interest is geared more toward non-fiction than fiction—each genre has its rightful place—this said, I believe anything derived from being or developed as fictional had a factual origin. No story sets itself—somebody's *body was involved*; hence we have the objective.

Each Author, fiction or factual, had something brewing within their psyche—something that had to escape the prison within the human mind, ready to write the story. Knowing that computers were not even on the market, I surmise that ink and quill were the tools of the trade to accomplish the dreams of these early writers.

My search suggests the *First Novel Author* was a lady by the name of Murasaki Shikibu. She was Japanese, and she penned the First Novel of recorded time in 1007. *"The Tale of Genji,"* tells a simple truth to life type of story—life is about being wise enough to work through it; as I see it, a life without love is empty and or void of the reason to live. I assume Murasaki Shikibu captured these thoughts well enough as she penned about a thousand pages to tell her *Novel Story* (Unique Story).

I've just purchased the Abridged (shortened) Kindle Version of *The Tale of Genji* and expect to browse it for some general insight. *The Tale of Genji* is an ancient Love Story about a Prince searching for Love and Wisdom. The original version worded out at over 1000 pages and 54 Chapters. [I expect the book you are reading to be less extensive.]

The novel is the unique idea of telling life stories hypothetically. In the writing of a Novel, the writer visualizes a theme and may even have real people in mind—*they change the names to protect the innocent.* We have books that weave a fictional story into a background of real places—New York, Paris, China, London—I think especially of Edward Rutherford—Author of Books by these names (Places). We might think of these as literal historical accounts of how life was—.

Just yesterday, my ninety-six-year-old friend Fred wrote a few words similar to the following— "Life is like us walking in the sand and leaving our footprints, and then the wind coming along and covering our tracks." My words are changed slightly from Fred's, but he gave me copyrights to express his thoughts—he said I should use this in my book. This stately gentleman said he wanted the people who read what he wrote to figure out what he meant by it. That's also what I like to do when I write. However, I can't resist interpreting the meaning here because it's relevant to what I'm trying to say.

We do life expecting to make a difference—significantly, but sometimes, as happens at times, it turns out insignificantly. It seems we get to know *we have been there*, thinking someone will notice we've existed and along comes a breeze or a stiff wind and covers our tracks! No one ever knows we lived. I think this is extremely sad. In my previous book—*Everybody: Everybody Is A Somebody*, I stress how important we are by Right Of Birth!

History—The factual; Non-fiction is like this. How far back will anyone of us think daily to gain from the experience of the people who thought to make a difference in some small way— seemingly, nobody ever notices!

Back to *The Tale of Genji* for a moment—in Japanese, Genji means "Two Beginnings." I briefly discussed the writing of *Novels*. I acknowledge their rightful place in history as being relevant and or essential! For my intent here, this will suffice. What I wish to draw from *Genji* is its meaning—.

Two Beginnings!

Literally and or Historically, "Two Beginnings" cannot exist together about how everything came to be what we have or are today. However, there are many theories surrounding *Beginnings*. Fact or fiction—none of us were there at *The Beginning*—for every one of us, there is a considerable degree of needed Faith even to try to put the Whole Story together!

At the moment, it's not my intention to broach this subject. At the moment we have at hand, I wish to feature the historical impact The Bible has made so far as a factor in *Changing Lives*! My bias likely shows Big Time—After 75 years of living Life, I will say that The Bible has always led me on the Right and Only Course sufficient to the end for managing Life Now and for Tomorrow.

And The Number One Bestselling Book of all time is?

—————————————!

After much research on the subject of The Bible—to find an answer to the question of relevance for the day we live in, it's generally acknowledged that The Bible is The Numero Uno Best Seller of recorded time. We know that many of those Bibles bought were not for personal usage. In the first place, people bought The Bible because of its value for personal growth. Then because of the seen value in this regard, people began to buy The Bible to give to other people because of the difference it made in the Life of the original purchaser. The numbers are enormous when we think about this, and therefore, there must be a Solid Reason to believe it has a Great Measure of Importance for leading people to God! It's one thing to direct folks to God; another challenge to grow them in God!

And The Number One Book of All Time In So Far As Making A Difference In Changing Lives is?

—————————!

The Oldest Books as declared to be by those who search out these things is— *1. Etruscan Gold Book – c. 600 BCE.* I have no intention of disputing this with anyone. When we search the matter of references to the question of Which Is The Number One Best Selling Book of All Time, most come to one conclusion.

"How Stuff Works" gives us twenty-one choices to consider—*Don Quixote* tops this list. Following this, we have *Xinhua Zidian.* Number three is *A Tale of Two Cities*; then we have *The Lord of the Rings*, followed by *Harry Potter and the Sorcerer's Stone*, in the fifth position in the race. In sixth place, we find Agatha Christie's book, *And Then There Were None.*

However, this is not the end of the story—The Rest Of The Story Is— "And The Story Never Ends!" There are books relating to The Story Never Ends, and I'll leave us with that thought Regarding the book issue for now.

As Chapter Twelve Title openly states, the Idea of *Chasing After God—What's That Like*—will continue indirectly. I still have much Food For Thought to layout on The Table as an outlay fitted for The Survival of The Hopeful! The Hopeful are those who believe God is The Answer—Yes. It doesn't stop here—The Bible tells us God isn't there only for The Hopeful—but He is also Totally interested in The Hopeless—! Many folks think God could not be interested in them—God loved the whole world.

And he entered into a ship, passed over, and came into his city. And, behold, they brought to Him a man sick of the palsy, lying on a bed: and Jesus seeing their faith, said unto the sick of the palsy; Son, be of good cheer; I forgive your sins.

And, behold, certain scribes said within themselves, This man blasphemeth. And Jesus knowing their thoughts, said, Wherefore think ye evil in your hearts? Which is easier to say, I forgive your sins, or say, Arise, and walk? So you may know that the Son of man hath power on earth to forgive sins, (then saith he to the sick of the palsy) Arise, take up thy bed, and go unto thine house.

And He arose and departed to his house. But when the multitudes saw it, they marvelled and glorified God, which had given such power unto men. And as Jesus passed forth from thence, he saw a man, named Matthew, sitting at the receipt of custom: and he saith unto him, Follow Me. And he arose and followed Him.

And it came to pass, as Jesus sat at meat in the house, behold, many publicans and sinners came and sat down with Him and His disciples. And when the Pharisees saw it, they said unto His disciples, Why eateth your Master with publicans and sinners?

But when Jesus heard that, He said unto them, They that be whole need not a physician, but they that are sick. But go ye and learn what that meaneth, I will have mercy, not sacrifice: for 'I AM' not come to call the righteous, but sinners to repentance. (Mathew 9: 1-13; KJV)

It comes across clearly that Jesus is interested in saving those lost in Hopelessness. Jesus is interested in the folks He already has onside—in that they can assist in carrying the necessary tools to bring healing to those presently outside The Kingdom. Everybody in The Kingdom is part of the solution—each one of us in this position has some responsibility—the available tools are many.

◊ THE VISTA VIEW—THE OASIS ◊

AS WE CHASE AFTER THE HEART OF GOD, 'our personal' *Heart of Gold* and or *Pot of Gold purposes* may adjust to the whole scenario to read—*Searching For The Heart of God*! Life as we see it is often a hodgepodge of everything but God, at least the things we may present outwardly in our day-to-day actions.

My summation of Chapter Twelve's detail is much about how we treat The Creator, Our Saviour, Jesus, The Captain of The Ship of Life, The Captain of Our Salvation—if we've accepted Him as LORD and Saviour. Many books garner more attention for the residents of the world than does the Bible—The Bible is The Info Package for the whole of Life and Eternity.

Eternity—What does Eternity look like?

In the *Story of Mankind,* Hendrik van Loon paints a vivid picture that's not hard to understand. He wrote it for his grandchildren—this book received a medal for being a wonderful 'Book Contribution' in league with child literature.

Hendrik van Loon's words concerning 'Eternity' look like this—.

"HIGH Up in the North in the land called Svithjod; there stands a rock. It is a hundred miles high and a hundred miles wide. Once every thousand years, a little bird comes to this rock to sharpen its beak. When the rock has thus been worn away, then a single day of eternity will have gone by."

How do our day-to-day lives map out in the light of *Eternity*? While looking inwardly at my life—I realize that I need to adjust the Map of my Day-To-Day to reflect better on what God had in mind when He created or mapped out time on earth. God saw us in His Image and Likeness in the light of 'Eternity—' Please read again some verses which I have often brought reference to:

Then, a lawyer asked Him a question, tempting Him, saying, Master, which is the great commandment in the law? (Matthew 22:35) These words are a good 'starting point' question for us as we Search!

255

AND THE FINAL ANSWER IS!

> Jesus said unto him, Thou shalt love the Lord thy God with all thy heart, and with all thy soul, and with all thy mind. This is the first and great commandment. And the second is like it; Thou shalt love thy neighbour as thyself. On these two commandments hang all the law and the prophets.
> (Matthew 22: 37-40)

One of my main trains of thought in Chapter Twelve concerns when we *Search Out Books Of Importance* on Google—. Yes, in most cases, The Bible is mentioned as holding The Title of Having The Most Print Copies In History—but is it openly held to be the Most Important Book ever written—by the general population?

As we *Chase After The Heart of God,* we realize *He First Chased After 'us.'* If we are on track to living life on this planet to the full—we'll see that the rewards of *Life In Eternity* are greater because we'll be living life in the presence of Jesus; our Creator and LORD! Do I have a vivid imagination—or is this The Way, The Truth, and The Life? Jesus said— "I Am The Way, The Truth, and The Life!" Can we and or do we believe this?

I pray that Chapter Twelve has been a jumping-off point to take in the rest of this book—beginning with Part Four and Chapter Thirteen—*Out On A Limb*!

See You There!

Part Four
The Heart Of God—The Clincher!

GOD SEARCHED FOR US—Why Wouldn't We Desire To Search For Him? When I say The Heart of God Is The Clincher, I'm not suggesting we've gone the distance of *Searching For A Heart of Gold; Not The Pot of Gold*—in this book [There's Still Much Distance To Travel In The Unseen Arena Of Life].

God is beyond our comprehension insofar as the totality of why God does certain things in ways we may question—we often question God's intent vehemently, violently, or passionately. We will fail every time if we try to understand God in full measure as to these things. However, God allows us to know Him personally—relationally—not withholding anything He knows is best for us.

Though I say, "God is beyond our comprehension insofar as the totality of why God does certain things in ways we may question (IBID)," the answer lies in the Scriptures.

I wish you'd fully understood the degree of responsibility I carry concerning You—and the many I have never met. These folks need the consolation of The Scriptures as much as those I've preached to at other times. There's comfort in knowing the fullness of God's love and experiencing the togetherness the love of God brings to us as we receive His Love. Many of you folks at Colosse, Laodicea, and others know about the riches of the full assurance of understanding in Christ. The acknowledgement of the mystery of God—the Father and Christ, holds all the treasures of wisdom and knowledge—it's available to everyone—but we need to share it with those who don't know these truths.

I need to share what some see as hidden mysteries to determine who are false teachers coming only to acquire what they have no right to receive. Even when I'm not alongside you physically, I'm thinking joyfully about you and how you are managing your Faith Journey.

As ye have therefore received Christ Jesus the Lord, so walk ye in Him: Rooted and built up in Him, and established in the faith, as I have taught you at other times—always overflowing in life with thanksgiving.

Watch Out! Don't let anyone turn your heads from what I've taught you in how God alone in Jesus Christ can lead you effectively. Some preachers will twist The Scripture to their benefit, hoping to catch some of you unaware, through deceitful viewpoints as if making you 'slaves' of their making—not being as Christ would teach you.

If, as we do life, we grasp all God has for us in The Person of The Father, The Son Jesus, and The Holy Spirit of God, we are closer to being thoroughly committed to Christ. Knowing God is All-Powerful—in control of all things, gives us hope because we link ourselves to His purpose, and because of this, we try to walk more in His ways than in the ways the secular world does life. Because of Christ's death and resurrection, we are as if buried with Him, not yet being perfect, but on the way there. (Thoughts I glean from Colossians 2)

So as we move along, God may ask us to go *Out On A Limb*! Hey—I fully understand the consequences of going *Out On A Limb* on anything. It can be Dangerous—at the same time, Adventurous—Challenging. Yes, but being in a relationship with God, Jesus—Will Be Worth The Reach!

The remainder of *Searching For A Heart of Gold; Not A Pot of Gold* will be more of an invitation to join me as we try to find out how much God loves us! Everything God *purposed* for us from before time as we know it; before He Created anything, relies on The Love Of God!

God so loved the world, that He gave His only begotten Son, that whosoever believeth in Him should not perish, but have everlasting life. (John 3:16)

I've shared much on material things—physicality or carnality are issues we cannot avoid in this life. Many of our struggles relate directly to the fact that we came into this life reliant on someone else. If we were God, we wouldn't have this problem—however, we are not God, and we do have this problem.

It's of necessity that we look at our fleshly existence before we ever attempt to travel a Spiritual Journey—because we are as if *Jars of Clay*, and God is Spirit—non-earthly. The Spiritual concept of life came into the mix as an added option to our Birth—one which we access by choice.

But we have this treasure in earthen vessels, that the excellency of the power may be of God, not of us. We are troubled on every side, yet not distressed; we are perplexed, but not in despair; persecuted, but not forsaken; cast down, but not destroyed; always bearing about in the body the dying of the Lord Jesus, that the life also of Jesus might be made manifest in our body. (2 Corinthians 4:7-10)

As we begin to 'move in on' *Searching For The Heart of God*—where the *Pot of Gold* isn't as important to us anymore, the Spiritual Aspect of things is something we need to pursue. Letting go of some of the Earthly Treasures we try hard to keep on the string is no easy task. We have this thing in the back of our minds;' what will I do in case of an emergency if my *Pot of Gold* isn't as vast as The Larger Vaults many other people have?

The Short Answer, and The Long Answer, fit within the enclosure of God's Answer —"Cast all your cares on Me—because I care for you!" (1 Peter 5:7)

Remember I'm Human LORD—Remind Me, Remind Me Oh LORD! As I wrap this intro to Part Four, I'm thinking ahead to Chapter Nineteen—I'm Reminded of The Song "Remind Me, Dear LORD!" I plan to elaborate on this in *Searching For The Heart of God*—Chapter Nineteen.

Stay tuned for Heart Sense!

Scriptures In Front Matter of Part Four
Colossians 2
Heart Sense
Psalm 34: 8; Psalm 45; John 10: 27; Matthew 5: 8
Jeremiah 1:9; Isaiah 6:7; Luke 8: 45; 1 Peter 5: 7
Heart Sense
Scriptures In Chapter Thirteen
James 4:8; Hebrews 4: 12
Hebrews 4: 12-16
1 Corinthians 13: 9-13
Matthew 22: 32-40
John 15: 11
Romans 1: 13-32
Psalm 51: 1-13
Psalm 139: 1-6; Matthew 22: 32-40
Genesis 1: 26-28; Genesis 2: 5-25
The Vista View—The Oasis
Mark 1: 35
Psalm 23

HEART SENSE
Lord; Hear My Prayer

––––––––––––––––––– ◊ –––––––––––––––––––

CHAPTER THIRTEEN sets me on course to reach out—to wind down because I may have topped the mountain. I don't say that the rest of what I share is less significant than what I've written previously. My thoughts here are as if I climbed to treetop along the trunk only, with a one-way purpose of reaching the top of an Elm tree or the like, compared to Coniferous and or Evergreen Tree.

If this were my attack, I would've missed many exciting adventures and skirted a few dangers. The 'Trunk' offers more safety than do the branches. Branches may stem out broader and more robust as they leave the main stem—but as they extend to length, they narrow down and are less stable in holding weight. As we explore the trunk, we see the value it contains—it's the source from which the branches get their strength. It takes more than just one part of the tree to have full force and endurance.

The Five Senses of the Heart is part of Nancy Ruegg's Blogging Sight. I was excited to read this blog because I often relate things to our Fives Physical Senses throughout my writing. For Four of the Five Senses, Nancy offered a verse of Scripture to connect to the Spiritual Sector as she wrote her blog.

Taste— "Taste and see that The LORD is good!" (Psalm 34:8).

Smell— "All thy garments smell of myrrh, and aloes, and cassia—." (Psalm 45)

Hearing— "My sheep listen to my voice; I know them, and they follow Me." (John 10:27)

Touch— Nancy Ruegg does not give a specific verse, but she relates how God touches her as she meditates on the Psalms in Praise and Worship.

Sight— "Blessed are the pure in heart, for they will see God" (Matthew 5:8)

So I pulled out the Fourth Sense *Touch* and looked at it as a matter of interest—needing some exploration. One website says there are fifty-six mentions of Touch in The Bible. I wish to share a few and make a few remarks concerning them.

> Then the Lord stretched out His hand and touched my mouth, and the Lord said to me, behold, I have put My words in your mouth. (Jeremiah 1:9)

Here we find an incident where Jesus touched Jeremiah to use him for His *purposes*—this is a picture that Isaiah shares about God's Touch in forgiving sin.

> Then flew one of the seraphims unto me, having a live coal in his hand, which he had taken with the tongs from off the altar: And he laid it upon my mouth, and said, Lo, this hath touched your lips; with this, I took away your iniquity and removed your sin. (Isaiah 6:7)

> And Jesus said, Who touched Me? When all denied, Peter and they that were with him said, Master, the multitude throng Thee and press Thee, and sayest Thou, Who touched Me? (Luke 8:45)

God notices when we reach out to Touch Him in our time of need. Jesus wants to be there in times like these; He also wants us to touch Him for many reasons. 1 Peter 5:7 tells us to "cast all our cares on Jesus because He cares for us!"

I surmise that 'touch' is essential to Jesus. As Nancy Ruegg mentioned in her blog, she's refreshed when she reaches out to praise and worship God—this is the primary acknowledgment we can offer God. But God never turns a deaf ear [*hearing*] when we reach for help or the many other reasons we muster up.

I may be on an *Alter Course* from that of many other people. I'm an Author, so I have a different set of interests, but this does not lessen them, nor are other people's callings insignificant. We may sometimes be Out On A Limb to execute Life's issues, which crop up more often than expected, no matter our giftings or callings.

STAY TUNED FOR *Out On A Limb!*

Chapter Thirteen

Out On A Limb

―――――――――――――――◊―――――――――――――――

GOD'S WORD IS 'TO THE POINT,'—A Double-Edged Sword—It cuts out the worthless things and makes way for New Growth. God's Word takes care of the unfavourable aspects of life—When God clears the way, His purposes come to fruition; it may not be Today; it may not be Tomorrow; nonetheless—It Will Happen! Let's not forget one of the main themes running the course throughout our term—Preparation, Purpose, Progress, and Preservation!

Someone said, "*If You Build It, he Will Come*" (*A Field of Dreams*). As I understand The Bible, it reads like this in a specific place, "Come close to God, and He will come close to you!" (JBI)

Draw nigh to God, and He will draw nigh to you. Cleanse your hands, ye sinners (I didn't call you sinners [*sounds harsh*], Jesus's Brother did; he wrote the Book of James); and purify your hearts, ye double-minded. (James 4:8)

Please notice how the word 'double-minded' comes into play here in James 4:8. This suggestion surfaces again in Hebrews 4:12; when it uses the hyphenated word *two-edged*, in effect' (essentially or in truth) saying, *double-edged*—I'm thinking, double-minded to bring the two passages together in a somewhat conjunctive (unions 'For, And, Nor, But, Or, Yet, So') or connective way. God often makes these connections in The Bible while at the same time keeping the assignment in the context of the placement of the original words.

God's Word is quick, powerful, and sharper than any two-edged sword, piercing even to the dividing asunder of soul and spirit, the joints and marrow, and is a discerner of the *thoughts* and *intents* of the HEART. (Hebrews 4:12)

GOD'S WORD—DIVIDES RIGHT FROM WRONG!

The factual story of the Garden of Eden clears the way as an example of separating Right from Wrong for us to position ourselves to make the right choices. Our efforts to *Search For A Heart of Gold; Not A Pot of Gold—will likely fail every time* if we never get this RIGHT!

"God is beyond our comprehension insofar as the totality of why God does certain things in ways we may question—we often question God's intent vehemently, violently, or passionately. We'll fail every time if we try to understand God in full measure as to these things. However, God allows us to know Him personally so that He will not withhold anything He knows is best for us." *(IBID)*"

An old [and I emphasize Old to represent the possibility of a Greater Wisdom about life than I may have in some things (he is 96 years old)] friend of mine shared a quip he wrote with me, which reads as follows:

"Life: We leave tracks in the sand—and the wind comes along and covers our tracks." (by permission of Fred Franchuk Sr.)

"The evil that men do lives after them; the good is often interred with their bones—" (Julius Caesar, Mark Antony)

It often seems the wind of life doesn't cover the tracks of life we make when we harm other people in the process—most often, people can't hide these evil deeds indefinitely—they always seem to come back to haunt the aggressor. [Case in point—all the people who hurt others in the pursuit of their sexual preferences—all the innocent indigenous children of The Residential Schools killed because others did not have the Right Sense of Right and Wrong! And The list Seems Never To End.] In Canada, we remember The Indigenousness Folks in at least one way—by wearing Orange; there are also other ways to acknowledge these folks.

God's Word is quick, powerful, and sharper than any two-edged sword, piercing even to the dividing asunder of soul and spirit, the joints and marrow, and is a discerner of the thoughts and intents of the heart.

Neither is there any creature that is not visible (evident) in His sight—but all things are naked and opened unto His eyes with whom we have to do. Seeing then (so then) that we have a great High Priest that went into the heavens, Jesus the Son of God, let us hold fast to our profession. We don't have an untouchable High Priest without feelings for our infirmities; but was in all points tempted like as we are, yet without sin. So, therefore come boldly unto the throne of grace, that we may obtain mercy and find *grace to help* in time of need. (Hebrews 4: 12-16)

Yesterday a familiar Scripture came to mind somewhat out of the blue—this passage gave me a good look at Charity. I know that sometimes I neglect the feelings of others—not looking at them compassionately but judgementally—thinking they should be able to do better.

For we know in part, and we prophesy in part. But when that which is perfect comes, that which is in part shall be done away. When I was a child, I spoke as a child, I understood as a child, I thought as a child: but when I grew up, I put away childish things. We see through a glass, darkly; but then face to face: now I know in part; but then shall I know even as I'm known. And now abideth faith, hope, charity, but the greatest of these is charity. (1 Corinthians 13: 9-13; KJV)

Last night I dreamt about children; I don't know if there's any relevance in this for me regarding where I'm at in writing *Searching For A Heart of Gold; Not A Pot of Gold*—or for that matter, Chapter Thirteen—our present position. However, it seems everything leads to another story—Let's Look At The Rest of The Story.

As I think in retrospect—tree climbing comes front and center. As a child, we generally didn't venture *Out On A Limb* in what we thought of as a Major Disaster Zone—if we did, there was always a chance of danger befalling us and us breaking something! However, we went ahead and did a little climbing anyway; we projected ourselves a little too far along a branch at times—one which may have been a bit thin. It's much easier to understand these things when we take the time to observe the things around us.

Art Linkletter hosted a show years ago, and the favourite line was, "Kids Say The Darndest Things." Kids say the darndest things—but they also do the darndest things. Can I tell you a secret?—Adults also do some of the darndest things—this isn't a secret; the thing is, we are not always honest enough to admit to the *Big Boners* we pull.

We cannot get through the process of life without ever being in a position where we must choose between Pleading Innocence or Pleading The Fifth—where we should admit to The Guilty Plea. Suppose we Search our Hearts and admit guilt when it is due. In that case, we also need forgiveness from one source or another—putting us into a precarious situation and causing us to look over what the circumstances of wrongdoing are telling us. We got *Out On A Limb* a little farther than we should have in a situation such as described and or in one of a million more issues in which we would have been better off not getting involved! Sometimes it's hard for us to decide whether or not to step into situations that may be costly.

The following thought came to me on July 13/2021. I was dreaming that my wife, another lady and I had a writing project before us; I couldn't get going on it, and I was about to quit; the girls' reprimanded me for my decision and so on—hence, what came out of it was the title *Out On A Limb*.

Out On A Limb presents many avenues and thought perspectives to figure things out. What does it mean when someone tells us they went *Out On A Limb*—?

What does it mean when someone says they went '*Out On A Limb*' to be there for us?

What does it mean when someone says they went '*Out On A Limb*' to be the best they could be as a person?

What does it mean when someone says they went '*Out On A Limb*' to find the best job to provide for their family—?

What does it mean when someone says they went '*Out On A Limb*' to be the best CHRISTIAN they could be—and what does it mean to be a CHRISTIAN? [*Check out some of Martin Lloyd Jones's Preaching in Spiritual Depression*]?

What does it mean when someone says they went '*Out On A Limb*' to be all they feel and or know about what God expects of them—?

As we continue in this Chapter, I'll try to set the stage for Chapter Nineteen— *"Searching For The Heart Of God!"* Every physical entity has more than one road to explore. The first mention usually presents the context of the moment—the perspective we have when we say what we are thinking; this should always be the first venture to delve into if there is any doubt about what the communicator is trying to present. Please follow along with me as I express some of the relevant thoughts I have as I'm writing about issues concerning our having a better focus as we Search for God!

If while I'm talking about *Searching For A Heart of Gold*, I say *I'm going up a tree* on the matter, it simply means I'm exploring the many facets of how to go about Searching For How I Can Best Present A Pure Heart To Those Around Me—. If we follow the Heart of God and wish to live it out, the best answer I can give you comes from Matthew 22, featuring verses 32-40—I refer to these words often. One of my Pastors said he often made references to some of the same things because people tend 'to leak.' It's like having a hole in our jeans pocket and putting our loose change in that pocket—we shouldn't start to wonder where our money is when we dip our hand into our pocket—OUR LOOT IS GONE! So, The Final Answer Plays Out Here—.

I'm the God of Abraham, Isaac, and the God of Jacob? God is not the God of the dead but the living. And when the multitude heard this, they were astonished at His doctrine. But when the Pharisees had heard that He had put the Sadducees to silence, they were gathered together. Then, a lawyer asked Him a question, tempting Him, saying, Master, which is the great commandment in the law? Jesus said unto him, <u>Thou shalt love the Lord thy God with all thy heart, and with all thy soul, and with all thy mind. This is the first and great commandment.</u> And the second is like it; Thou shalt love thy neighbour as thyself. On these two commandments hang all the law and the prophets.

Thou shalt love the Lord thy God with all thy heart, and with all thy soul, and with all thy mind. This is the first and great commandment.

To find out where we "Lost It" [Our Peace of Mind], we need to check back to when we had "Our Peace of Mind."

So, when I am beginning to talk or write about a specific theme and in the midst of so doing, I say, "I Am Going Up A Tree" while doing this, I am not going outside to begin climbing a tree! So you see, when we stay on course, in context, we can use analogies (parallels) such as described to bring clarity—as parables do. Still, we can get confused if we don't remain attentive to the speaker or writer—or life itself as it plays out!

I'm Going Up A Tree—'I Am!' Genesis speaks to us of Two Trees—The Tree of Life (JESUS The First and Best Choice) and The Tree of The Knowledge of Good and Evil (Our Selfie Interests; Not The Best Choice). Let's take an extended journey with the folks of every generation of time since then, through the many years this entails. We come to *a specific pl*ace, preordained from before the world came to be as we have it today. History is imperative for us to grasp everything The Bible speaks of 'to us!'

The Journey—how inclusive this has been for so many people. Every Generation, Every Person—needed to make choices concerning Whom they would serve! The Tunnel of Life has often been dark. However, there has always been a LIGHT at the end of that tunnel—The LIGHT has always been JESUS!

Speaking of this—JESUS takes me to John 15, The Story of JESUS being The Vine. This morning my wife and I got up early, as usual, to take in some online Church as we do every Sunday from First Baptist Church Naples in Southern Florida at 7:30 AM Mountain Time. My day began to take shape as I heard the song *The Goodness of* God (You Are Faithful) because, throughout the night, the theme of God being Faithful was running through my Spirit.

It turns out that this wasn't enough to kick start my day as I was *preparing* to continue writing Chapter Thirteen, *Out On A Limb*. As we turned to the next Church Online, one we also watch every Sunday morning, First Baptist Church of Jacksonville, Florida, there was a streaming issue, and we could not get the Online Service. So, we went to our Third Stop, a little farther North (556 KM North and a little West) of Jacksonville, Florida.

As always, God planned my specific writing needs. At *First Baptist Church Atlanta,* one of the songs was—*The Goodness of God* (You Are Faithful). I don't plan out my writing schedule this precisely—God always seems to take care of this for me! I never hear 'An Audible,' it's just that I always get a nudge to move along.

If this wasn't enough, I thought it was—Pastor Anthony George opened The Word to John 15: 11. It was here that God nailed it down for me because Chapter Thirteen, *Out On A Limb*, right where we are now, was where I needed to take the baton and run the next leg of my present Journey of writing this book.

John Fifteen has been one of my favourite go-to places in The Bible when I was thinking and writing about Who JESUS IS! When The Bible speaks of Jesus as The Vine, it says that this is the source from which the branches stem out, and the offshoots continue their growth and bear fruit. Fruit doesn't grow out of the Trunk of a fruit tree—the Trunk produces The Branches—they bear The Fruit! The Pattern is—God; In Jesus; By The Holy Spirit; Through Us As His Disciples!

If the branches bore no fruit, there would be no need to call it a tree. If this were the case and the tree had only a Stalk or Trunk, it may as well be a Totem Pole [dead wood—except for telling the story a Totem Pole tells, but it bears no leaves and or fruit]. Palm Trees do not have branches such as what we think of as branches, but they still bear fruit. I think of a Palm Tree, and I see it as topped with Palm Leaves, coconuts, figs—and I think firstly of it as only covering the Trunk, like a hat covering a bald head.

The Palm Tree is far from fruitless when the season is suitable for the fruit to bud and grow. Palm Trees grow a variety of fruits—coconuts, figs, fruit for making wine and jellies, and even using the fruit of the Palm Tree for medicinal reasons. We use the Saw Palmetto or The Serenoa to give hope health-wise in certain times of need. Palm Oil also comes from particular Palm fruits. So trees without a specific set of branches coming from the trunk from the lower parts of the tree are still in the hopeful position of being Fruit Bearing.

Next door to where we live, the folks managing Mount Nelson Place cut down some Elm Trees. The tree *Butchers* (Surgeons) left stumps about four feet high. One would think this to be the end of life in those trees—not so! Not too long after the tree massacre, new growth began to spurt out of the stumps, and many new '*Little Branches*' found their way out of the prison within the stump. Was it the stump (trunk) that was the life-giving resource for the sustenance required to be a fruit-bearing tree—or is there another resource from which the tree grows?

More than once, when the upper growth of my plants suffered damage somehow, I thought—'End of Story!' Not So! Time and some TLC proved me wrong most times. I realized that if the plant's root is undamaged and managed with proper nutrients and water and sunshine for warmth, we'll soon see new growth budding above the soil's surface. All this is the said same for trees of all kinds. Every type of tree has unique characteristics—however, every tree has needs similar to every other tree to grow to its full potential—needing watering, food, and sunshine—.

The analogies (comparisons) of the physical, the earthly, and the temporal—that I present always turn my attention to the Spiritual segment of our 'Eternal' existence. As for me, *Life Is Always Both Physical and Spiritual!* Without Physicality, the Spiritual could never exist for humanity. Spirituality preceded Physicality—according to my research of Eternity' past.

The Bible tells us God is a SPIRIT—and those of us who have engaged in a Spiritual Relationship with God must be of this mindset and live as though this is Factual (Physicality In A Sense)—*The Way, The Truth, and The Life*! Jesus came to earth physically for reasons we may not so quickly grasp.

Unless Jesus came as The Son of Man, we would never have gotten the message. The Bible tells us that God built a picture of us being able to understand Him even if there was no personal representation, such as The Son of Man, The Son of God, The Holy Spirit, God The Father.

Now I would not have you ignorant brethren that frequently I purposed to come unto you (but was let hitherto) that I might have some fruit among you, even as among other Gentiles. I'm indebted to the Greeks and the Barbarians, the wise and the unwise—I'll preach the gospel to the Romans. I'm not ashamed of the gospel of Christ: for it is the power of God unto salvation to everyone that believeth; to the Jew first, and also to the Greek. For therein is the righteousness of God revealed from faith to faith. According to the Scriptures, *the just* shall live by faith. For the wrath of God is revealed from heaven against all ungodliness and unrighteousness of men, who hold the truth in unrighteousness—because that which we can know of God is manifest in them; for God hath showed it unto them.

For the invisible things of him from the creation of the world are seen, being understood by created things, even His eternal power and Godhead; so that they are without excuse: Because that, when they knew God, they glorified Him not as God, neither were thankful; but became vain in their imaginations, darkness showed up in their foolish heart. Professing themselves to be wise, they became fools and changed the glory of the incorruptible God into an image made like a corruptible person and to birds, four-footed beasts, and creeping things. God also gave them up to uncleanness through the lusts of their hearts. He allowed them to dishonour their bodies between themselves—who changed the truth of God into a lie and worshipped and served the creature more than the Creator—Amen.

For this cause, God gave them up unto vile affections: for even their women did change the natural use into that which is against nature: And likewise, also the men, leaving the natural use of the woman, burned in their lust one toward another; men with men working that which is unseemly, and receiving in themselves that recompense of their error which was meet. These folks didn't like to retain God in their knowledge. God gave them over to a reprobate mind to do those things which are not convenient; being filled with all unrighteousness, fornication, wickedness, covetousness, maliciousness; full of envy, murder, debate, deceit, malignity; whisperers, backbiters, haters of God, despiteful, proud, boasters, inventors of evil things, disobedient to parents, without understanding, covenant-breakers, without natural affection, implacable, unmerciful: Who knowing the judgment of God, that they which commit such things are worthy of death, not only do the same but have pleasure in them that do them. (Romans 1: 13-32)

Scripture expects everyone to be wise enough to recognize God through the things He made. God desires for us to have a personal bond with Him. He's The God of Creation. God was never, and is not now ever fearful that we the people, humanity, will ever be wise enough to do the job only He can do! If this were to happen, and it will never happen, we would still not be God—God would still consider us friends.

Searching For A Heart of Gold; Not A Pot of Gold—ties in perfectly with *Searching For The Heart of God.* If we eliminate the words "*of Gold; Not A Pot of Gold*" from the title, we get right into the crux of the whole plan of Salvation. When we import "*Searching For A Heart*" from the title, our search reaches God's intended purpose before He created anything Physical—Right Relationship with the *God of Eternity*—Past, Present and Future.

The Garden of Eden tells us this story. God came personally to The Garden, inviting Adam and Eve (US) into perfect harmony with Him. God told US Heaven on Earth was ours for the taking— All we had to do was Trust He had our best interest in mind—and listen to what He asked of US!

However, we messed up and chose Knowledge over Relationship; this necessitated implementation (application) of The Plan of Salvation—but Salvation could not come until sin was paid for in full—offering a Plan requiring our acceptance. The Paid In Full Poster—God Posted This On The Cross of Calvary!

> According to Thy lovingkindness, have mercy upon me, O God: the multitude of Thy tender mercies blot out my transgressions. Wash me thoroughly from mine iniquity, and cleanse me from my sin. For I acknowledge my transgressions: and my sin is ever before me. Against Thee, Thee only, have I sinned, and done this evil in Thy sight: that Thou might be justified when Thou speakest, and be clear when Thou judgest. Behold, I was shaped in iniquity, and my mother conceived me in sin.
>
> Behold, Thou desirest truth in the inward parts: and in the hidden part Thou shalt make me know wisdom. Purge me with hyssop, and I shall be clean: wash me, and I shall be whiter than snow. Make me hear joy and gladness; so that the bones You have broken may rejoice. Hide Thy face from my sins and blot out all mine iniquities.
>
> Create a clean heart in me, O God, and renew a right spirit within me. Cast me not away from Thy presence, and take not Thy Holy Spirit from me. Restore the joy of Thy salvation, and uphold me with Thy free spirit. Then will I teach transgressors Thy ways, and sinners shall be converted unto Thee. (Psalm 51: 1-13; KJV)

God searched for us before we ever had a clue to look for Him! David was—Shepherd Boy; King; Runaway; Adulterer, and much more—God still considered him "A Man After His Own HEART!" How could this be when so much junk piled up on David's ledger? When David realized the gravity of his sin, he *sorrowed* for the infraction. He sought to make amends; he asked for God's forgiveness—more than once; as we look at the scale of David's downtimes, there seemed to be a continual waffling in David's lifestyle. Let's see how David came back at God again and again. David continually recognized WHO GOD IS!

O Lord, You have searched me and known me. You know my downsitting and mine uprising; You understand my thought afar off. You compassest my path and lying down and are acquainted with all my ways. There is no word in my tongue, but, lo, O Lord, You know it altogether. You beset me behind and before and laid Your hand upon me. Such knowledge is too incredible for me; it is high, and I cannot understand these things. (Psalm 139: 1-6)

As we consider the Scriptures we've looked at in our Search—For Life, Vitality, Goodness, God—we get a straight shot at the HEART of the whole matter of life from beginning to end in the following verses in Matthew 22: 32-40—

I'm the God of Abraham, Isaac, and the God of Jacob? God is not the God of the dead but the living. And when the multitude heard this, they were astonished at His doctrine. But when the Pharisees had heard that He had put the Sadducees to silence, they were gathered together. Then one of them, which was a lawyer, asked Him a question, tempting Him, and saying,

Master, which is the great commandment in the law?

Jesus said unto him, Thou shalt love the Lord thy God with all thy heart, and with all thy soul, and with all thy mind. This is the first and great commandment. And the second is like, unto it, Thou shalt love thy neighbour as thyself. On these two commandments hang all the law and the prophets.

What-can-make-a-tree-deadly—SINFUL?

One of the reasons people plant trees in their yards is to enhance their surroundings. Why are trees beautiful? We usually notice as we observe trees—their stature, leaves, fruit, and colour as it changes in the seasons of the year and other things. Many folks admire the branches and leaves, thinking they are the focal point. A tree without limbs is a big stump—possibly dangerous and most often unsightly or ugly.

The *Limbs* of a tree offer us a picture of each their individuality insofar as each species has differing kinds of personality characteristics. Tree Surgeons or Arborists consider the branches, leaves, flowers, and seeds as tools to identify tree groups—each tree has its unique shape. Tree branches naturally grow out of their trunk; they grow in strange and exciting directions—adding quality to the yard; buds, blooms, and colour— are part of what trees offer to enhance our space.

Trees are much more in so many ways—they provide shade for those hot sunny days, which are good, but the sun beating us into the submission of the excessive Ultra-violet rays—is often uncomfortable and even dangerous. We can enjoy the warmth of the sun while at the same time enjoying the cool of the shade. Trees— what an excellent addition God gave us when He thought up the concept and reality of TREES!

Trees have leaves, palm branches—if they have no fruit; yet *the leaves are the fruit* of those trees. So, what is the fruit we speak of—it's whatever the tree produces. Is the sap of a tree Fruit? Well, I would say so. Sap can produce honey—whatever a tree makes is like the saying, *The Fruit of Our Labor*. The fruit that is the outgrowth of a tree comes out pure; the fruit is tainted or spoiled by environmental conditions and circumstances it faces as it grows to enhance our empty spaces.

In our *Search For A Heart of Gold; Not A Pot of God*; if the End Result is our *Search For The Heart of God*, this is the ultimate desire of God for us! A *Search For A Heart of Gold; Not A Pot of Gold* is not in and of itself a statement that applies only to The Heart of a person who has a personal Born Again Relationship with God in The Person of Jesus Christ. The primary directive of the first part of the creation of humankind was for us to be like JESUS! Attempting to be like Jesus became what often seems like a 'Never-Ending-Story—Journey' based on Faith and Hope!

Some folks who care little or nothing about God—Who He is or what He wants for all created Humanity, are exceptional people. All of life was in the Hands of God In The Beginning. The Bible says God took dirt from the ground and formed us to be a person, and in God's own Words, *the first person was a man.* I make no apologies for sharing this—this is what God says, and I believe it—not to make women of lesser value in their skin. God took the same care in handling a rib from Adam and creating The Beauty He called WOMAN! *No Woman should ever be valued less because God made her second!*

And God said, Let us make man in Our image, after Our likeness: and let them have dominion over the fish of the sea, and over the fowl of the air, and over the cattle, and over the whole earth, and over every creeping thing that creepeth upon the earth. So God created man in His image, in the image of God created he him; male and female created He them. And God blessed them, and said unto them, be fruitful, multiply, replenish the earth, and subdue it: and have dominion over the fish of the sea, and over the fowl of the air and every living thing that moveth upon the earth. (Genesis 1: 26-28; KJV)

And every plant of the field before it was in the earth, and every herb of the field before it grew: for the Lord God had not caused it to rain upon the earth, and there was not a man to till the ground. But there went up a mist from the earth and watered the whole face of the ground. And the Lord God formed man of the dust of the ground and breathed into his nostrils the breath of life; and man became a living soul.

And the Lord God planted a garden eastward in Eden, and there He put the man He had formed. And out of the ground made the Lord God grow every tree that is pleasant to the sight, and good for food; the tree of life also in the garden, and the tree of knowledge of good and evil. And a river went out of Eden to water the garden; it was parted and became into four heads from thence. The first name is Pison: that is it which compasseth the whole land of Havilah, where there is gold; and the gold of that land is good: there is bdellium and the onyx stone.

And the name of the second river is Gihon: the same is it that compasseth the whole land of Ethiopia. And the name of the third river is Hiddekel: that is it which goeth toward the east of Assyria. And the fourth river is the Euphrates. And the Lord God took the man and put him into the garden of Eden to dress it and to keep it. And the Lord God commanded the man, saying, Of every tree of the garden thou mayest freely eat: But of the tree of the knowledge of good and evil, thou shalt not eat of it: for in the day that thou eatest thereof thou shalt surely die.

And the Lord God said, It is not good that the man should be alone; I will make him a help meet for him. And out of the ground, the Lord God formed every beast of the field and every fowl of the air; and brought them unto Adam to see what he would call them: and whatsoever Adam called every living creature, that was the name thereof. And Adam gave names to all cattle, the fowl of the air, and every beast of the field. But as for Adam, he didn't have a physical helper.

And the Lord God caused a deep sleep to fall upon Adam, and he slept: He took one of his ribs and closed up the flesh instead. And the rib, which the Lord God had taken from man, made He a woman and brought her unto the man. And Adam said, This is now bone of my bones, and flesh of my flesh: she shall be called Woman because she was taken out of Man. Therefore, a man shall leave his father and his mother and cleave unto his wife: and they shall be one flesh. And they were both naked, the man and his wife, and were not ashamed. (Genesis 2: 5-25; KJV)

So here we have the Record of Humankind; Personhood—Man and Woman!

Going *Out On A Limb* on issues is never an easy road. It matters not if we look at Life Physically or Spiritually; *Life Can and Will Be Hard At Times*. Life became harder than was initially intended by God in The Garden of Eden because we were puzzled by what the Trees offered us! Adam and Eve should have observed God better in their quality time with Him!

The difficulties we face as we do life are like travelling the branches of the many trees of life—and the many avenues of choice we must decide on for the present, and the tomorrow we have not yet seen. Once we have climbed to the treetop or any distance higher than the trunk, we must also venture down the tree. While looking down is often more challenging for us because we see all the dangers we have already faced going upward, going downward is also a necessity.

We are exploring up and down until we analyze every segment—while tree climbing, mountain climbing—while *Searching For A Heart of Gold; Not A Pot of Gold*—or while *Searching For The Heart of God*—Searching is often exhilarating when we are Searching for Treasure. However, if we are searching for something we've lost—it's often more frustrating than thrilling—until we find the treasured lost item; then, the jubilation begins after the Search.

These and more present the dangers of going *out on a limb* farther than Physically or Spiritually safe to do! Do we need to explain these things further to satisfy our mental peace of mind? Or is it better yet if we live life in such a fashion, other people will notice we have a more settled Peace of Mind since we were Born Again than we had before we began a relationship with Jesus Christ?

We get to live LIFE only once—in the lifespan unveiled, revealed, or shown to us on Planet Earth as we know it now. The Psalms, Proverbs, and Ecclesiastes are three Books of The Bible dealing with life 'Straight Up!' The writers give us 'Reel After Reel of Episodes to Real Life' scenarios from which we are WELL ABLE to live life to the fullest possible degree! This search for the Treasure of God's Word is, for me, *Always* exhilarating!

I like Freedom of Choice. My penchant or fondness for The Selfie Desire for the flesh—the skin in which I was born is noteworthy. I may make bad choices about what I deem the liberty God allows us. In every facet of the life we face, the Freedom Of Choice may cause us trepidation from time to time—Especially Today in October 2021!

In the day we live, access is hardly an imposition anymore—even in 'Non-Developing Countries,' cell phones are highly possible. Many of these cell phones are of the 'Relic' variety we now call 'Dumb Phones.'

However, as time passes and technology increases faster than ever before, the possibilities for 'Non-Developing Countries' to be more able to use what we call 'Smart Phones' also becomes more likely.

As technology leads us into the future, living life in the context to which we've become accustomed becomes more manageable. Though this is true, this is not the mega means or the best means we launch out on a successful 'Journey' to get from 'Birth Through Life' as we know life. Even if technology was the only means we had at our beck and call, it could never get us through from 'Birth Through To Eternity.'

If we only had hope in this life, we might think we could manage the 'Day-To-Day on our own— 'Us and Our Technology!' Life leads us on a Journey of believing that we do not need God! I cannot follow this pattern! Many other folks worldwide believe God is the only way for us to get through LIFE!

DARE WE GO—

OUT ON A LIMB—

AS WE SEARCH FOR GOD?

Jesus is The Trunk—He Supplies The Resources through The Holy Spirit—The Branches (The Disciples; US) come from The Trunk—!

◊ THE VISTA VIEW—THE OASIS ◊

Where Will We Search For The Heart of God?" If we've decided to acknowledge God in The Person of Jesus Christ to be all we'll ever need for our sustenance in this present world, we'll readily realize our need for some alone time.

Respite is essential. It's necessary not only for Christians but also for all who wish to keep their sanity in the business of life. However, for the Christ Follower to continue a vital flow of connectedness with Jesus, they must maintain and grow in their spirituality or relationship with God. Jesus had His Time of respite—it looked in part as the following—so it is essential for believers, as Christ Followers, to follow His example! There is no better example of love than what Jesus laid out on the cross.

And in the morning, rising a great while before day, He went out and departed into a solitary place and prayed.
(Mark 1: 35; KJV)

The business of our world more or less demands that we make time to pull back for some respite. Respite is not only "Lazy Time," although it will include this—but in the quiet time we call *Respite*, we are open to hearing The Holy Spirit of God speak to us. If you are not a Christ Follower, and you are reading this book, I recommend two things—that you still take time to be alone, away from the cares of the world that life itself demands—to take a deep breath and look at what life needs to be to keep your sanity intact. Secondly, if you haven't yet given Jesus a good look—do so; you may be surprised and encouraged to form a relationship with Him!

We looked at being *Out On A Limb* in Chapter Thirteen, and there are many ways to look at this theme. Firstly—If we are *Out On A Limb* alone and overburdened by what life offers, we may place too much of the weight of that burden on the branch, and it will break, and we will suffer the consequences.

Secondly—If we are *Out On A Limb* alone, we have no one with whom we can share the weight of the burden, and the stress of two people on the same limb may be less because they can share the space proportionately. If we take a massive chance of accomplishing an enormous venture, we need the help of others.

My wife and I watch an old TV Series called *Leave It To Beaver*. One such episode had Beaver (Theodore Cleaver) sitting on a tree limb with a girl. Beaver got teased because of this; his friends accused him of having a 'Girl Friend,' which was true, he being a boy and the girl being a girl, and them being friends made the girl a 'Girl Friend.' Beaver faced some dire consequences because of his situation.

After the School Principal took the matter in hand to solve the consequences and the effects of relationship issues, which the teacher explained about this matter of life, another friend took the chance to share a place with the same girl on the same Tree Limb. It turns out that being *Out On A Limb* was not such a bad idea—If one's perspective is in the right place.

There are many places and times we need to share quiet times with others to allow our perspective of life to stay intact. Going Out On A Limb has its place; we need to face challenges to grow physically, emotionally, and spiritually. I challenge everyone who can do so "To Do So" from time to time. Much of the time, life is only about the general day-to-day stuff of "Doing Life!" However, we need to get a little risky (not Risqué— verging on impropriety or indecency) from time to time!

We may need to look at the horizon lying before us, into the future, *Not Venturing Out On A Limb* but sitting at an Oasis—for Oasis Time. Think of the Desert—hankering for "Cool Water." Another thing I think of when an Oasis comes to mind is a setting of Palm Trees for some welcome shade after bearing the brunt of the Hot Desert Sun. Whichever way you look at the prospect of an Oasis, let me share my favourite display of an Oasis again—

"The Lord is my Shepherd; I shall not want. He makes me lie down in green pastures: He leads me beside the still waters. He restoreth my soul: He leads me in the paths of righteousness for His name's sake. Yea, though I walk through the valley of the shadow of death, I will fear no evil: for You are with me; Your rod and Your staff comfort me. You prepare a table before me in the presence of mine enemies: You anoint my head with oil; my cup runs over. Surely goodness and mercy shall follow me all the days of my life: and I will dwell in the house of the Lord forever." (Psalm 23; KJV)

Please realize—I have no intention of suggesting All Of Life is only about the pressures of life and the burdens we carry through life as if that's all we have available on the table before us. If this is all you have, you may need to sit *with someone* else at The Oasis because you've already fallen off the Tree Branch. You need help—and the only place you can find the assistance you need is to share your burden with someone.

I know we need God With Skin On—When this is your requirement, find that someone! Please consider sitting at Your Oasis and Just Having A Serious Little Talk With Jesus! —this may be where your relationship will best be able to get on track.

Let's Move On To—
What Was I Thinking—And Why?

Scriptures In Chapter Fourteen
Heart Sense
Philippians 4: 6-7; Philippians 4:8
John 4: 1-52; John 4: 40-44; John 4:4
Romans 12: 2; Romans 8: 5-6; Colossians 3:2
Jeremiah 29: 11
Genesis 1:31
Ecclesiastes 1: 1-11
Matthew 16: 1-3
Ecclesiastes 11
The Vista View—The Oasis

HEART SENSE
Here We Go—More Questions.

————————————◊————————————

IF I WAS TO ASK YOU—You who are a Christian, "What's the first thought you had regarding Becoming A Christ Follower—" What would You Answer? [Your Answer>————————————————]

Let's turn the tables, and because I'm a Christian, you ask me—"What's the first thought you had or have regarding *Becoming A Christ Follower*—"

Would My answer be with a Question—Or Could I Answer Without Any Hesitancy?

If My Answer was blanked out in White, and I said 'I will give you my answer later after you have considered your answer— Would both of our answers be in a question form looking like the following—"Who Is Jesus?" If we answered like this as a professed Christ-follower, there's room to wonder if we did indeed have a relationship with Jesus!

If we asked the non-believer the same question [—*"What's the first thought you'd have if I shared with you regarding Becoming A Christ Follower*—"] there would be just cause for them to ask, "Who Is Jesus? Would this be the first question they would broach before they gave us an answer?

Here's a Question—*"What is the Answer we might think the Non-believer might have?"* [Your Answer>————————]

Let's try to justify these questions as we move into the body of Chapter Fourteen. The world appears to us as *jampacked* with Questions about anything and everything. The hard part worldwide now, and always has been, is finding unanimity on The Answer!

Before we get to Chapter Fourteen, let's look at Psalms 108 and think carefully about what it says—let's see if the answer might more easily come from what David wrote here.

As I begin to read Psalm 108, I find material ensconced (Tucked Away) in the first six verses that are the nucleus or kernel of hope for me to desire a relationship with God in The Person Of Jesus Christ!

"O God, my heart is fixed; I will sing and give praise, even with my glory. Awake, psaltery and harp: I myself will awake early. I will praise thee, O LORD, among the people: I will sing praises unto thee among the nations. <u>For thy mercy is great above the heavens</u>—and <u>thy truth reacheth unto the clouds.</u> Be thou exalted, O God, above the heavens: and thy glory above all the earth; <u>that thy beloved (me) may be delivered</u>—save with thy right hand, and answer me."

Three things [actually four] that attract me in these six verses are—God has mercy on us mere human beings; God always tells the Truth; we can count on His promise of Deliverance—and number four is—For this, we need to praise God to no end!

"Through God, we shall do valiantly: for He it is that shall tread down our enemies." (Psalm 108:13 KJV)

Yesterday, my wife and I watched "The Perfect Game." It was about some Mexican kids who formed a baseball team—it was a GREAT movie! After playing a series of tournaments and remaining undefeated, they came to the Final Game against those considered the absolute best team in Little League—What chance did this makeshift team have against these odds?

The Mexican team had a Pastor who prayed for them and read Psalms 108 to them—this hope carried them through to victory. Someone asked why he read Psalm 108—his reply was, "Because Major League Baseballs had a 108 double stitches to sew the cowhide on the ball cover."

Sometimes we only need a small window of hope to accomplish Great Things when God is on our side—when it seems the challenge is too great—if we trust God; give Him Due Diligence (acknowledgment), we can defeat The Giant!

I JUST FELT IT APROPOS TO SHARE THIS—
AS AN ENTRANCE OF IMPORTANCE TO CHAPTER
FOURTEEN AS WE CONSIDER WHY WE WOULD
CHOOSE TO PICK JESUS
TO SAVE US WHEN WE HAD NO HOPE!

Chapter Fourteen

What Was I Thinking—And Why?

—————————————— ◊ ——————————————

FINALLY—FOLKS: Let's think about the things God is thinking concerning what our lives should look like if we are trying to wear *The Badge Of Peace*! Think About It—Is it True? Is it Honest? Is it Just? Is it Pure? Is it Lovely? Does What I Am Thinking Present Like A Good Report Card? Is What I Am Thinking a picture of God's Moral Value? If My Thoughts Are Praiseworthy—I NEED TO THINK ON THESE THINGS! (Philippians 4:8; JBI)

"Don't worry about the things which are of no concern to our immediacy—the nearness of life to affect you adversely, which will leave you without Peace. God made provision for these things through Jesus' death and resurrection—Leave the worries in The Hands of God. Don't worry about *ANYTHING*.

We need to take the things of concern seriously enough to deal with them as Jesus would deal with them—by praying; trusting that God cares enough to help us through this *toughie* as He does with little things. Be Thankful for all God has already done; be confident He can *Do It Again*! God knows everything about our problem—YES! Share it with Him anyway.

As we go through the *Valley of Sorts*, we ought to let The Peace of God fill our Heart and Mind through what Jesus has done and what He has promised to do through the process of Trusting Him!" (Philippians 4:6&7)

Adventures are often a venture or trip into unknown territory. If our Adventure is a journey into a previously explored area, we usually know what our day will be like—that said, we should always be on the *Lookout* for the unexpected. The 'Unexpected' doesn't necessarily represent awful news; it's great if it isn't, but it can be an adverse experience for those expecting perfection in the Adventure; Expect The Unexpected—Be On The Lookout!

TAKE A LOOK

This morning, I woke up bright-*eyed and bushy-tailed*—well, I woke up, but 'bright-eyed and bushy-tailed,' I Don't Think So! However, as the day began to *dawn* on me, I began to get inspired. With this in mind, I'll be downloading my thoughts of what I feel God is saying to me and unloading my beliefs on you! Some days we are not as perky. First off, when dawn breaks, we grasp the day opening before us—Hopefully.

This expression [*bright-eyed and bushy-tailed*] means to be enthusiastic, often unnaturally so, mainly when others are less than keen.

We use this phrase [*bright-eyed and bushy-tailed*] when referring to somebody who is uncommonly aware and cheerful first thing in the morning—while most folks remain tired from sleep for just a bit farther into the day. The reference stated above can be used at any time of the day, when some people are more UP than others; it shows by their excitement.

"The secret of genius is to carry the spirit of the child into old age, which means never losing your enthusiasm." (*Aldous Huxley*)

"There is only one corner of the universe you can be certain of improving, and that's yourself." (*Aldous Huxley*)

Quotes present a world of information and insight in short quips. In this my first episode of "Lookout," I'm backgrounding the launch of said heading by presenting "The Understory" of what lay ahead in future installments of "Lookout."

Understory— "is a layer of vegetation beneath the main canopy." My interpretation of Understory is simply a matter of *prepping* us for what lies ahead.

If I've tempted you enough in this *First Segment*, I expect you will come back another day. *Bet your bottom dollar 'Tomorrow' is only a day away!* ("Lookout"—by Jacob Bergen; First Edition) [If you're interested, I'll send you a copy—*jcbbergen@gmail.com*].

Jesus chose to leave Judaea, where it seems people believed in Him. At Galilee, He said He must go through Samaria— (John 4: 1-52; 40-44). What was He thinking? Life is different in our world today than it was two-thousand years ago, but everything is the same, only different! We need to understand people more in-depth.

As we study Scripture, it's clear that Jews and Samaritans didn't have much use for each other—Jesus was a Jew; so what was He thinking when He said He *"must needs go through Samaria"* (John 4:4)? As I see it, it was all about *The Purpose of Finishing The Course* of the journey that it was His part to enact while He was on earth as The Son of Man!

In one sense, Jesus was *Searching For A Heart of Gold—Not A Pot of Gold.* Because He was on a journey to do The Father's will, it necessitated Him to do some difficult things for the rest of the folks of His earthly culture to understand. Jesus was not confused! Jesus had not lost anything! The way I see it, Jesus was leaving us an example of what we need to look forward to while living our Life!

Jesus was on *The Lookout* for achieving The Plan, which was in place before time as we know it existed! As we Search For The Meaning of Life, we have *Lookout Points* from which we set the stage—prepping for the rest of Our Journey. The Bible always points us towards engaging in *Right Thinking*—if we are on track to fulfill God's will for our earthly tenure, addressing this desire God has for His children is part of the package we involve ourselves in to move forward in our Walk With God.

Don't be fitted into the principles of this world—be transformed by renewing your mind, that by testing, you may discern what the will of God is, what is good and acceptable and perfect. (Romans 12:2)

We should set our minds on things that are more than our present comprehension, not on the physicality's of our world. (Colossians 3:2)

People agreeing to earthly things place their thinking mode on the things of the flesh. Those who commit themselves to the Spirit focus their heart's capacity on the things of the Spirit. To trust in earthly things is to head for spiritual death, but putting trust in the Spirit is life and peace. (Romans 8: 5-6)

I Am telling you that I'm aware of the plans I've laid out for you— My heart for you is in your best interest—may evil always be too distant from you to affect you in any way. My plan for you includes a positive future—A Hope-Filled Future. (Jeremiah 29:11; JBI)

When He shared these and other Words with us through many of His other Faithful Servants, what was God thinking? Have we, ['*Still Living Believing Christians,*'] been entirely on track with The God of All Creation? Think about It; He is—The Eternal One— From Everlasting to Everlasting—Eternal; Immortal; Invisible God. Do we reflect *The Visible God*, Jesus, by the Love of Christ, to those around us?

Is the answer to *Chasing After God*—blown in the wind of Time or Time Change? Sports is one entity that presents a different picture today than it once did, in how people dissect everything differently from how the populace did *Back In The Day*! The 'Whiteout Phrase' [Re The Winnipeg Jets Games] is offensive to some cultures because it doesn't present a picture of tolerance towards other cultures or a picture of Inclusion. (Right Or Wrong?)

There are teams like the Cleveland Indians, the Boston Red Socks—and different things like black or white, with these things in their names—many of them feel the pressure to change all of history from which they chose specific words for various reasons—not because of race ETC. I wonder— 'Are There Not Any Defining Issues considered acceptable anymore?

While being sympathetic, I wonder if we might not find something offensive in nearly every word in the Thesaurus. Should we change every dictionary, Bible, and book writing, at least those noted in a specific context, with proper or good-intentioned hearts!

Have we 'stated' things with innocent intent in the language we have grown up through—without someone taking personal offence because they feel assaulted! Are we so sensitive to every aspect of life, leaving no room for 'Grace and Mercy?' Yes, we need to address assaults directed at so-*called minorities* and the like. Are we overacting on many issues—thereby causing other problems of disunity? When we are all on the same page—just seeing everybody as "A Person"—This would be Heaven on earth! [My previous book was *Everybody; Everybody Is A Somebody*].

What once was acceptable isn't good enough or compelling enough to save the day. I believe we will rue the day we changed what was once right and good enough [this part of history] because God set it in place and looked back at what He had done and said it was good; in effect saying, "What I Have Made Is Good Enough To Carry The Day!"

And God saw everything He'd made, and, behold, it was very good. And the evening and the morning were the sixth day. (Genesis 1:31)

We can readily see cries for self-gratification in our proximity and across the whole earth—God declared the world as "*Very Good.*" This satisfaction is often out of our reach—*we think*; because of one incident in The Garden of Eden. I May Say Huge; others may say, "What's The Big Deal:" "God Said What?" "So God said, Thou shalt not—partake of one of the two special trees in the middle of The Garden of Eden; He just didn't want us to have any fun!"

Yet, having now gotten our way, we, the people continue the cry; *we are not having fun yet; we want more for ourselves*. So, God gave people everything they needed; this should have been *satisfying,* but it didn't suffice well enough for us. The more we've gotten, the less satisfied we are and the weaker we've become!

Liberalism (not meant to 'Flog' the Liberal Party) as a tenet (principle), or seemingly by consensus, captures the political agenda across our countries. Our leaders make plans and entrench them into the law of the land. Even when the decrees are in proper context, our freedom of speech gets challenged in the courts.

Our constitutions state that we are all created equal and can believe what we wish—under moral guidelines (my interpretation). God gave us the liberty of CHOICE! Yes! What we do with it is on us!

Is *Searching For A Heart of Gold; Not A Pot of Gold* a larger picture for each of us on the personal and or corporate level than we expected, or more than we can handle if we are genuinely committed to God? After all, if God created everything, He is responsible for the outcome—Right? —this was God's Best For Us Plan, but He knew that if He gave us a Choice of Direction For Life, there would be a glitch—SIN!

God knew He would have to deal with the sin issue—hence Jesus came to create The Way, The Truth, and The Life. Jesus became human, and as a human, He could feel our pain—and suffer human death—paying for our SIN in this way. Do we understand the magnitude of this?

However, certain seemingly new things are not new; we rework them to sound new; they challenge me to look again at the facts of history and The Bible to find the proper balance—there is always a right balance. Just as in the measurement of weight, the scale of justice throughout eternity will not fail to give an accurate account. We need to look over *Our Accounts* (our beliefs) for Another Internal Review Of Our Hearts.

Vanity of vanities, saith the Preacher, vanity of vanities; all is vanity. What profit hath a man of all his labour, which he taketh under the sun? One generation passes away, and another comes, but the earth abides forever.

The sun rises, goes down, and hurries to its place where it arose. The wind goes southward and turns about unto the north; it whirls continually, and the wind returns according to its circuits. All the rivers run into the sea, yet the ocean's not full; unto the place from whence the rivers come, they return.

The thing that hath been is that which shall be, and that which is done is that which shall be done: and there is no new thing under the sun.

Is there anything of which it may be said, See, this is new? It hath been already of old time, which was before us.

There is no remembrance of former things; neither shall there be any remembrance of things that are to come with those that shall come after.

(Ecclesiastes 1:1-11)

AND THE SEARCH CONTINUES!

Initially [in the Bible], in The Garden of Eden, people disobeyed God and ate from the *Tree of The Knowledge of Good and Evil*—it's the same today. It couldn't be stopped by human hands then, and history proves it's been unstoppable now and for all earthly existence as we presently live life. However, we keep trying to outmaneuver God!

So, why would we think we can solve all the problems with a 'General Answer' to all the questions 'Blowing In The Wind?' Jesus dealt with life issues in the face of the day's opposition.

The Pharisees and the Sadducees came to tempt Him and desired Him to show them a sign from heaven. He answered—ye say it will be fair weather when it is evening, for the sky is red. And in the morning, it will be foul weather today, for the sky is red and lowering. O ye hypocrites, ye can discern the face of the sky; but can ye not discern the signs of the times. (Matthew 16: 1-3)

Curious thought: 'Blowing In The Wind.' It carries a pejorative [harsh and disapproving] tone in one sense and hope in another way. I'll do okay if I experience a favourable wind in my sails. If I see a 'Red Sky' in the morning and look for calm winds for my sailing pleasure, I may be in for a rude awakening.

The disparaging view—the harsh disapproving verbiage we get when we acknowledge only God as the ultimate answer—seems impossible to convey to a person on the opposite side of our view that God is the Final Answer! The excellent source to keep us from floundering along in the wind to catch up to the Twenty-Dollar Bill that caught our eye as we were living life as we knew it—is still "Blowing Around In The Wind." We may never get the fair winds we so desire until Jesus comes back into the picture to help us out.

Do we need to question the 'sin' entity? What is sin anyway? Does it lie open on the table as disobedience, lying, cheating, stealing, hating, unfaithful, adultery, inappropriate sexual sins, or murder—? I am against sin; however, I fall into a category of sinfulness when I don't obey God's word; I continue doing wrong; being unholy—sin is the breaking of God's law—are we diminishing God's law?

The story of sin has been, and always is, one of such contention, dispute and or debate it seems the universe cannot come to grips with it or come up with an answer fitting every description of it. I don't know if enough books are available to help us get it right; what's sin and what constitutes not sinning. I cannot include enough information in this short book to guarantee I'll have presented every correct answer to the questions that abound. No one living today has the smarts to do so all the time.

However, we can use a few hard and fast rules to get the picture reasonably close to being right—be objective, not subjective. If we are to solve the problems of life and the intrinsic or primary value of each person ever born [came into this life with], we might need to recognize what value is and demands of us—how we manage our lives as we age—day by day, moment by moment.

We might look at the many belief systems concerning morality, relativity, or dependence—believing that right and wrong are not a matter of objectivity [absolute values] but based on partiality (our viewpoint) because of the particular circumstances or culture we were born into, or not.

When it comes down to bottom-line scenarios, we balk at anything that does not align with our subjective life slant. Try claiming God is all we need in a theatre of people; *you will need God's help to survive the onslaught*!

One of the many belief systems is secular humanism [materialistic or temporal, as everything made by human hands will perish at some point]. This belief says human reason and ethical, philosophical, or moral issues don't depend upon any belief system that espouses or adopts God as the authority on the subject. Do we need to follow these guidelines to be in an absolute proper position with life and or the universe for our decision-making process to sustain life and eternity?

Atheism is the old term we know. It and its close relative, New Atheism, are big-ticket items today. Hence, we have gone from plain old atheism (believing there is no God) to New Atheism. New Atheism maintains the old but goes further by saying there can be no respect for anybody who believes in God; thus, they try to take away the right of freedom of conscience and belief as ensconced in our constitutions. Their disdain has increased to say that religion is not *simply wrong*; a religion of any kind is evil in its very inception, no matter the origin it embraces.

Agnosticism says that we are not sure about anything besides what is physically before our eyes, which we can feel or touch. Admittedly or not, 'they are saying they are unsure about being unsure.' The bottom line is that Agnostics are saying there are no reasonable grounds for a belief in God or the non-existence of God. In The Beginning, they have their right by God's choice—we all have free will, but not everything is 'right!'

Another issue that has been with us for eons is the one of Evolution. The Big Bang Theory is a big topic of this belief. Many atheists are in this camp; there are also some Theistic Evolutionists; who believe God may have used evolution to bring about all of what we have in our universe. I'm not trying to discredit anyone in these camps; I'm just proposing my own biases of beliefs as I see them. Somehow, even though we disagree adamantly about the methods other folks endear to us, we need to exhibit God's love!

Evolution in its basic form says the evolvement (evolving) of everything began from a single cell that came from nothing. It just appeared. Some folks say this happened from a form of gravity— they say it existed before or along with the nothing that preceded everything.

What a 'Power Packed (my attempt at some humour)' cell this must have been. Yes, again, some Christians believe in an evolutionary process where God's still involved, differing from the many atheists who passionately believe that anything like a God or Supreme Designer had nothing to do with Creation or the appearance of everything. I realize that whatever I see, whether in my hand or what lies in nature or the universe above, had its initiation at the hands of Someone, or at least had a beginning powerful enough to be the Beginning and the End.

Accordingly, *Time and Chance* alone were the progenitors (forerunners) of all we see. It all falls into the hands of Mister, Madame, MS, It, They— [to try to be politically correct, tolerant], and I'm not sure what tomorrow's name for gender will be; we will figure it out—I guess, or not? If not, we'll be more troublesome to each other.

Christianity: As a Christ Follower, I look to the Bible to reference all we know about Christianity. However, to debate the above subjects, as I read in the book *Can We Be Good Without God, Paul Chamberlain* is only one resource; it's also theory-based because it requires faith. All other belief systems require faith; nobody was there at the inauguration of the very beginning of everything to see it coming into existence. However, when Paul Chamberlain finishes his conversations with the participants of his book, the results cast reasonable doubt on the other belief systems because of the balancing act of Moral Objectivity and Moral Subjectivity.

The whole matter of debate between people who hold differing views about anything and everything only asks everyone to take an unbiased look at the topic, look at the Pros and Cons to see which one makes the most sense from a logical platform. The Occam's Razor Principles suggest that the *Simplest Answer* most often proves to be the most efficient way to garner the truth on any matter to decide anything.

The God scenario requires faith to believe God is Who He says He is; God will do what He said and says He will do. These folks accept Him personally as their Guide for Life, with the expectation of everlasting life after death, the one God provided for us because 'Jesus' paid off the entire debt of us living our lives for ourselves and the temporal desires of the flesh.

Many of the other Belief Systems say they are not faith-based. These folks believe they can decide what to expect after they die using Common Sense Reasoning. These people base their theory on the feeling they have within their psyche and spirit—Subjectivity. Objectivity [trust and faith-based, detaching ourselves from the entity of emotions, and entrusting ourselves to The God Who offers Love as the avenue of eternal life; not feelings] is the opposite of subjectivity.

You may say, "Love is a feeling." What we often call 'Love' may be a feeling. Love is not a feeling; love is a fact. If love is evident in life, it produces more than feelings to determine an action. We love God because He showed us how to love. We access this belief system by accepting Jesus Christ as God in the flesh—He came to guide us through life's rough spots. I highly recommend reading, *Can We Be Good Without God?* (Paul Chamberlain).

The Answer is Blown-In the Wind: OR NOT?

These discussions fall into one place as we Search For The Heart of Gold—The Heart of God!

Brian Doerksen sings the lyrics to the song titled *Everlasting*, saying God is from the beginning to the end around and around in a circle—without beginning and an ending—He Is God ALWAYS! Eternal, immortal, invisible God. Our world suggests a spirit of flippancy, almost a boldness to say, "Who Cares About This God Thing?"

Our world grasps at everything blown into our space in this wind of time we live in—for the things it feels are new and will finally satisfy that insatiable inner craving only the initial life-giver could supply. A life force that propels us on, day by day, to keep reaching for that something that seems to blow around in the wind is part of a tangled mess that includes every belief system concocted by humankind. Some 'God,' or other entity that may yet be unknown, seems to be the answer. When we experience the physical winds, it gives us cause to reflect on the Spiritual World—Jesus used the *wind similarity* when He talked to Nicodemus.

The morality, which was once the norm, is *Gone With the Wind!* Methinks the answer we are looking for is not just blown in by any wind of doctrine, rule, principle, or dogma.

What Was I Thinking—And Why?

When I came across negative things while on Life's Journey to find my Pot of Gold—Did I find what I was looking for in this regard? Or, might God have placed a Detour on this path to affect a Change in My Desire—one which may have proposed that I begin *Searching For A Heart of Gold.* Now I have cause to find a LOOKOUT POINT from which I can assess all the options for their Right and Wrong presentations and end up *Searching For The Heart of God*!

I'm thankful that God placed a few obstacles on the Road of Life, so I would need to stop abruptly to evaluate life's conditions for my future. The Detours often meant I might not arrive at my planned destination—if I did, it would take just a little or a lot more time for me to be able to say I Got A Second Chance—or a Third Chance or even more; to make a wiser decision about the Tomorrows ahead of me!

Cast thy bread upon the waters: for thou shalt find it after many days. Give a portion to seven and eight, for thou knowest not what evil shall be upon the earth.

If the clouds are full of rain, they empty themselves upon the earth: and if the tree falls toward the south, or the north, in the place where the tree falleth, it shall be. He that observeth the *wind* (natural winds) shall not sow; he that regardeth the clouds shall not reap.

Thou knowest not what is the way of the spirit, nor how the bones do grow in her womb with child: even so, thou knowest not the works of God who maketh all. In the morning sow thy seed, and in the evening withhold not thine hand: for thou knowest not whether shall prosper, either this or that, or whether they both shall be alike good.

Truly the light is sweet, and a pleasant thing it is for the eyes to behold the sun: But if a man lives many years and rejoice in them all; yet let him remember the days of darkness; for they shall be many. All that cometh is vanity.

Rejoice, O young man, in thy youth; and let thy heart cheer thee in the days of thy youth, and walk in the ways of thine heart, and in the sight of thine eyes: but know thou, that for all these things God will bring thee into judgment. Therefore remove sorrow from thy heart and put away evil from thy flesh: childhood and youth are vanities. (Ecclesiastes 11)

It should be easier to decide on our daily lives; distance is not an issue. We are reasonably sure of our intended result as we plan for tomorrow. A red sky in the evening suggests fair winds ahead. A Red Sky in the morning may mean a windy day lies ahead, warning those planning to go sailing to be cautious.

Looking at longer-term planning, we cannot depend on the "Red Sky in the Evening "or" Red Skies in the Morning scenario." These are only in place for our Day-To-Day plans. When we're trying to determine our destiny and or the successes for the months ahead, such as the Seasons of The Year, Spring, Summer, Autumn, and Winter, we can rely on a market we can predict accurately.

The Stock Market is a good commodity with which we can watch the Financial Markets fluctuate. Looking at weather patterns for the months or years ahead is hard—for which we employ meteorologists; some folks swear by the Farmers Almanac.

It's scary to try to predict Political Futures. There are seemingly many more variables to consider. Faith and Trust are a couple of the fair measures we depend on; it might rely primarily on WHOM we put our Faith and Trust. If our Faith and Trust change like the wind by the promises of the prospective political people in the running, we need to be extremely careful. History portrays the list of errors politicians [and the rest of us] make at times.

Like the weather, no matter which predictive means we use, some variables are subjectively based. These are feely-based agendas—usually not founded on *Objective* (factual) outlines, but primarily *THEORY BASED*!

HOW WILL WE GARNER THE BEST PRACTICES FOR ANYTHING FUTURE-BASED?

Futures Markets are Public Massacres; everybody is fighting for the lead—wrapping up the winning bid. Leaders do this to use their newly secured wares on the buyer's list of participants in the whole market for financial gain. The future is hard to predict; leaders promise a bright future they cannot control based on today's outlook.

The problem is that nobody can agree on anything long enough to make the promised *future* come alive within the awaited timeline. THEN THERE'S THE SPIRITUAL WORLD!

Stay Tuned For Reality
If You Build It Properly—
It Will Come!

"What Was I Thinking—And Why?"

◊ THE VISTA VIEW—THE OASIS ◊

Some people live in the zone of *I Still Believe—The Russ Taff Story on YouTube—*. This video is a good resource for an imperfect person who still tries to leave their burden of sin in the hands of God.

I Still Believe
Shame Was His Prison
Love Set Him Free

As we get further into what we consider a *Closer Walk With Jesus,* are we getting closer to a love relationship with people who don't seem to be as "CHRISTIAN AS WE THINK WE ARE?"

Does our *Search For The Heart of Gold—Not A Pot of Gold*—include people struggling big time in their daily walk to present themselves as becoming More Like Jesus? Do we see their mistakes as struggles that say to the world of *"Christians—Born Again* people" that these Strugglers who claim to Still Believe—Are just like us who Claim to be the Elect of God?

Some people have a tremendous yearning to reach out and touch people who live all the Wrongs of Life! Many Entertainers, Christians and Non-Believers spread themselves *too thin* to Reach People. Whether they are right or wrong in their relationship with God—is there something within them that's all right in God's eyes because He uses everything for His Eternal Purpose?

Some secular artists sing words that often seem to come from The Heart of God Himself, which sometimes touches my heart. Did God or Did God Not, Give Living Breath To All Humankind—and beyond—to every living thing to fall into a place of purpose within His Original Plan?

HEART SENSE
Lord, What About Difficult Times?

$\Diamond$

WHEN YOU PASS THROUGH THE WATERS, I will be with you; through the rivers, they shall not overwhelm you; when you walk through the fire, it will not burn you, and the flame shall not consume you. (Isaiah 43:2)

For I, the LORD your God, hold your right hand; it is I who say to you, "Fear not, I am the one who helps you." (Isaiah 41:13)

Fear not, for I am with you; be not dismayed, for I am your God; I will strengthen you, help you, and uphold you with My righteous right hand. (Isaiah 41:10)

The LORD is my shepherd; I shall not want. He makes me lie down in green pastures. He leads me beside still waters. He restores my soul. He leads me in paths of righteousness for his name's sake. (Psalm 23.1-3)

He will tend his flock like a shepherd; gather the lambs in His arms; carry them in His bosom, and gently lead those with young. (Isaiah 40:11)

Scriptures In Chapter Fifteen
Heart Sense
Isaiah 43: 2; Isaiah 41: 13; Isaiah 41: 10; Isaiah 40: 11
Psalm 23: 1-3;
1 John 4: 15-19
Hebrews 11; Matthew 8: 25-27
Psalm 119: 105; Hebrews 11:1;
Ephesians 6:10-19; Psalm 139: 1-6
James 4: 8; Isaiah 55: 6-7
The Vista View—The Oasis
Psalm 23; John 4: 24
1 Peter 5:7

Chapter Fifteen

Does God Really Care About Our Day-To-Day Living?

⸻◊⸻

WHOSOEVER SHALL CONFESS THAT JESUS IS THE SON OF GOD, God dwelleth in them. And we have known and believed the love that God hath to us. God is love, and he that dwelleth in love dwelleth in God, and God in him. Herein is our love made perfect, that we may have boldness in the day of judgment: because as He is, so are we in this world. There is no fear in love, but perfect love casteth out fear: because fear hath torment. He that feareth is not made perfect in love. We love Him because He first loved us. (1 John 4: 15-19)

As we understand more about Jesus—Who He is, The Son of God—we realize that God takes up residence within our spirit. It becomes as if living physically in the dwelling—house, apartment, tent, log cabin, or any other semblance of what we call the home we live in on Planet Earth.

If someone lives in our home after they've grown to a certain age, there are some reasons. Usually, when a daughter or son gets to a certain age, they feel the urgent need to get out on their own— thinking our home's restraints as parents are placing on them are too demanding.

Sometimes the children stay at home on and on and on—. The *strain on the parents* makes '*them*' want to get out and run away from the constant pressures of raising the children who are now adults. These *new adults* need to be on their own to learn about the Reality of Life. We continue loving each other, so we hope and pray, but our home becomes too small to include each other's physical and emotional desires. Birds put their young out of the nest *when it's time* to leave home.

Relationships are valuable—they can be *'great' if each of us knows of the 'need' for the other party in the connection to have their space*. God never pushes us out of His Nest of Love and Care— He Has A Big House (Not 'The Big House-Prison')! He is always as close as the mention of His name when we call out to Him. He's always this near, even when we leave Him out of our Day-To-Day Living. We may not feel assured of this because we depend *wrongly* on subjective or felt mechanisms—Insecurities. God doesn't function subjectively but objectively.

Facts are more important to God than our feelings. Faith, True Faith, never works based on emotions. If this were the case and God created us with this in mind, creation might have been a futile effort on God's part. Hebrews Eleven tells this story better than I could ever hope to express. Let's look for a moment at some of the words of Hebrews Eleven—. For starters, verse one says:

> Now faith is the <u>substance</u> of things hoped for, the <u>evidence</u> of things not seen. (Hebrews 11:1)

Please take note of the Fifth word in verse one—*Substance*. I have never encountered anything substantive or essential that was subjective (*individual, personal, biased, skewed*—) or feeling-based. In Hebrews 11:1, the word Faith is self-descriptive and or self-evident. We struggle with the word *Faith* because, as the Bible tells us in another place, why we fight back—when it says, *Oh You of Little Faith*. Please look further into Faith's substance and what it often seems like as we *Don It* as our *Weapons of Warfare*. *Substance and Evidence are as if being the same word.*

> And his disciples came to Him and awoke Him, saying, Lord, save us: we perish. And He saith unto them, why are ye fearful, <u>O ye of little faith</u>? Then He arose and rebuked the winds and the sea, and there was a great calm. But the men marvelled, saying, what manner of man is this, that even the winds and the sea obey Him! (Matthew 8:25-27)

Take Note—Faith here in these verses pictures out in this specific context and perspective as *LITTLE*! The context here sees the disciples struggling for the Hope of Survival because they felt [subjectively, or because of feelings and or emotions] they were in BIG TROUBLE!

If the Faith in a particular context of living our lives is LITTLE [small]—the implication or suggestion of an answer to fix *small faith* is that *our confidence needs to increase.* How do we do this? Scripture is clear as to how to do this in Psalm 119:5, as it's in the whole of Psalm 119 plus mega more places in the Bible. Along with the reading of the Word of God, we need to talk to God! We call this PRAYER!

Thy word is a lamp unto my feet and a light unto my path. (Psalm 119:105)

Another implication I see is, *We Need To TRUST GOD!* What does TRUST suggest? Trust suggests we can conclude the deed is A Done Deal! Trust forms *the connection* between *asking God for help in a time of need and seeing Jesus walking on water to come and help us.* If I switched places with the disciples on this night experience of a storm so overwhelming, and "If I Was Scared," [and there's no IF involved], and I saw someone walking on water to come to my rescue, I think I might begin to see Hope of Survival. *I suppose* I could see a measure of TRUST building within me. Think about it—under normal conditions, we don't see people walking on the raging sea—might we be able to TRUST that help is in The Offing?

So when we think back to the words "O ye of little faith." We ought to realize we need to build this Faith to become self-evident—Big As Life! Let's look again at Hebrews 11:1—.

Now faith is the substance of things hoped for, the evidence of things not seen. (Hebrews 11:1)

The weapons we need to enact this act of increasing Our Faith *shine brightly* in Ephesians 6: 10-19—.

"Finally, my brethren (folks), be strong in the Lord and the power of His might. Put on the whole armour of God, that ye may be able to stand against the devil's wiles. We don't wrestle against flesh and blood, but against principalities, against powers, against the rulers of the darkness of this world, against spiritual wickedness in high places. Wherefore take unto you the whole armour of God, that ye may be able to withstand in the evil day, and having done all, to stand.

Stand therefore, having your loins girt about with truth, and having on the breastplate of righteousness—your feet shod with the preparation of the gospel of peace; above all, take on the shield of faith, wherewith ye shall be able to quench all the fiery darts of the wicked.

And take the helmet of salvation, and the sword of the Spirit, which is the word of God: Praying always with all prayer and supplication in the Spirit and watching thereunto with all perseverance and supplication for all saints; and for me, that I will speak effectively, that I may open my mouth boldly, to make known the mystery of the gospel."

Once we realize there is a means for building Faith's stamina, which can move the mountains of doubt and the inabilities we in our strength to do so—don't have, we have the direction before us. The *how-to* of getting the job of building Faith within our Spiritual Personhood when life gets hard—[and it does get hard at times] lies in large part in Ephesians 6: 10-19. These are not the only realizations we need to encounter.

Please follow me to one of my favourite passages in the Bible, Psalm 139. We will offer a maximum concentration on this passage as a Sermon in Chapter Eighteen to finish the 'just' of *Searching For A Heart of Gold: Not A Pot of Gold*. But as a prelude to that, let me highlight a little of Psalm 139 here. As we think about the *toughie* it is to begin or continue the Walk of Faith—in the light of Hebrews Eleven and those die-hard participants of the Journey of Faith—let's overview Psalm 139: 1-6:

O Lord, You have searched me and known me. You know when I sit and when I stand. You understand my thoughts from afar. You search out my path, watch over me when I'm lying down, and are familiar with all my ways. There's not a word in my tongue, but you know it well, lo, O Lord. You've surrounded me and laid Your hand upon me. Such knowledge is too incredible for me; it's too hard to grasp. *The wonder of it all overwhelms me*!

Please Realize—Please Remember—God knows all about our Struggles Today—He has always known how life would be because of the wrong turn we took in The Garden of Eden.

There's an old Spiritual called, *There's Not A Friend Like The Lowly Jesus*. It stresses the picture of our struggles being taken care of by Jesus as we Trust Him because we have a relationship with Him. In other words, the songwriter says, *Jesus Knows* that not a day will go by that He will not think about us—He will lead us through the tough times by His Holy Spirit. Jesus will be a Friend until The End! No one can replace Jesus as the Friend above all friends.

> "For there is not a word in my tongue, but, lo, O Lord, Thou knowest it altogether." (IBID)

> "Such knowledge is too wonderful for me; it is high, I cannot attain unto it." (IBID)

As we work our way through life, we NEED To Come To The Place of Faith and trust where nothing will shake us—we NEED To Realize the self-evidence of the Whole of Scripture (The Bible) as having the sufficiency to carry the day! The Bible begins in Genesis as being Self-Descriptive from the Get-go—when it says, In The Beginning GOD! There are no other options throughout Eternity for the assurance of getting to our desired destination than GOD! When we get to Chapter Eighteen, I intend to present a clear picture of God's Sufficiency, and it will 'practically' curl your straight hair!

Please, let me say that all of us will need Absolution, Forgiveness, Amnesty, Acquittal, Mercy, Pardon and Release from our inability to fully TRUST God all the time—because of our HUMANITY.

> Seek ye the Lord while He is openly calling, call ye upon Him while He is near: Let the wicked forsake his way, and the unrighteous man his thoughts: and let him return unto the Lord, and The Lord God will have mercy upon him; and to our God, for He will abundantly pardon. (Isaiah 55:6-7)

> Draw nigh to God, and He will draw nigh to you. Cleanse your hands, ye sinners; and purify your hearts, ye double-minded. (James 4:8)

The Bible passages I relate to are all *Invitational* in that they point to Jesus! We'll post this clearly in The R.S.V.P. later!

God never pushes us out of the nest like a parental bird does—except in the sense that God sends us out *at the right time*, believing He has taught us enough so that we by Faith can continue to not only survive but to flourish *when it is time to leave the nest*.

Most of us are *searching* for something—we usually have an idea about what we are exploring. Some of the material things we search for are—our car keys, our wallet, the clothing we thought we still had [but gave away because we outgrew them], craft patterns (re my wife), [and sometimes our kids—they're not material things].

It is one thing to know what we are Searching for—it is quite another thing to realize we are missing something. The search isn't easy when searching for that something (satisfaction in life on the emotional level) that seems to elude or escape. Sometimes, because we believe that when this something stares us in the face realistically—we don't know if we could handle or manage the reality—this something captures imagery of failure in our minds.

Our Chapter Fifteen title looks like this— *"Does God Really Care About Our Day-To-Day Living?"* If there's such an entity as GOD, why would He care for me—I'm just *a distant* product of His imagination. I'm part of His creative thinking; part of a kingdom effort to cause people to bow to Him in some form of reverence we don't grasp because the concept of God is so much higher than what we, with our infantile minds, can picture out to where we would even want to be like Him!

If God didn't become human in one sense—how could we begin to understand why He would love us and want something more for us than even we could imagine.

I Can Only Imagine, by Bart Millard, sends me a message about how The Love of God can come to us. As I peruse or examine for myself—within the parameters of my heart, what it may be like to understand why God Does Care About My Day-To-Day Living, I'm overwhelmed. I try to pursue or follow the instincts of The Holy Spirit as He guides me through the process of A Search Second To None—*A Search For The Heart of God*!

As Your Glory Surrounds Me—

My Imagination Soars High!

And The Strength of Realization Consumes me!

One of the most intense thoughts—instead, I should say One Of The Most Intense Questions We Have in this mixed-up world of ours is—

Does God Really Care About Our Day-To-Day Living?

I don't consider it a fluke, accident, mistake, coincidence, by chance—that I titled this Chapter as I did. We often ask this question from both sides of the fence. The non-believer asks, If God Cares So Much About People, why does He allow so much pain and suffering? If we think about it, it's reasonable to realize this is a fair question. We may lose our way if our concept of God is that He is supposed to be a good God if we cannot see the fruits. If we don't value God for Who He is—caring about every conceivable aspect of the world and the people in the world He created, Faith is not at work in us because we choose not to believe what God said. '*If Indeed He Created Anything At All*;' if our ideal of God is only about the goodness He is supposed to represent, how can we think differently. God's goodness is available to all people. (John 3:16)

If God looked at one person's needs, and that person was not the least concerned about his neighbour, he did everything possible to make that person's life unbearable—which side should God decide to favour? Might this not be why God, as He is said to have done, created the world, then chose to set the Guideline of Choice by placing two trees in the Garden of Eden from which to determine the direction we would travel. We decide on the Good and or The Evil which happens in our world. God doesn't cause the evil of our world; some folks think He causes our afflictions.

Now, we get to another sticky issue which Christians [those on The Other Side of The Fence] also ask—

Does God Really Care About Our Day-To-Day Living?

We, those people just described as Christians, sometimes ask, "Does God Really Care?" When we are in difficult straits (a sticky situation), we ask this question, which we think is fair. We believe it's a fair question because we decided to follow Christ and often suffer for Christ, so we feel we are more deserving than those who openly reject Jesus! We were born through the same process—we began from a seed of equality.

Scripture says, "God rains on the just and the unjust." This statement sheds some light on the issue—but doesn't always cut it for us. No matter how we tend to slice it, giving God the upper hand, there's always a bit of a nudge saying— "Why Me, LORD?"

Every word I write leads us closer to where I will try to bring a bit more closure to the question, "Does God Really Care About Our Day-To-Day Living?" If He is God, isn't He so much more superior to anything we peons [pardon the use of the word peon] think about the situation?

Suppose God looked down His nose at us because He is so much Superior to us, calling us drudges, only farmhands, gophers, labourers, peasants, serfs, servants, enslaved people, and unskilled labourers. The Bible says He is a Loving God—could this be true if He treated us like I just laid out.

Then how could He say He loves us—John 3:16

But God does not think of us like this.

God just wants us to be thankful and appreciate Him for Who He is and what He Has Done!

God lets us make up our minds about what we would believe and which way we would choose to go!

GOD WANTS US TO CAST OUR CARES ON HIM!

◊ THE VISTA VIEW—THE OASIS ◊

As we soak up the refreshing elements of *Psalm Twenty-Three* at the Oasis, we get to see *in part* how much God Does Care For Us—I say *In Part* because the whole of Scripture backs up these thoughts repeatedly! These times of Reflection and Respite are essential if we expect to have an *enduring relationship* with God in The Person of Jesus and in The Fellowship of The Holy Spirit, which Jesus sent to earth when He left to return to The Majesty on High in Heaven when He ascended after His *resurrection*.

The Holy Spirit now took the place and or position Jesus held while on earth. The Holy Spirit became The *Comforter and Caregiver* we would need throughout our tenure on earth. While Jesus was in our world on earth, He fulfilled this position as He met with people in His physical body. God, being a Spirit, as The Bible tells us in John 4:24—and God, Who showed Himself to us in The Person of Jesus as The Son of Man and The Son of God, cared for and comforted the people He moved amongst daily.

> God is a Spirit: and they who worship Him must worship Him in spirit and truth. (John 4:24)

God, The Holy Spirit, took this position when Jesus left us physically to carry on this work in a Greater Way by moving amongst the Whole World as The Spirit of God—To be The Comforter, Our Caregiver—and to point to everything Jesus said and did. The Holy Spirit also convinces us that we need to experience more than Physicality in our birth—. When we extend the Word SPIRIT to Spiritual Things, we see that The Holy Spirit would be The Director of these things for us and in us. Because of this, God needed to *convince* (convict) us that we are sinners in need of God's saving grace through Salvation.

When we do a "Vista View [Look Over Where We Are At]," we may understand that we need Oasis Moments in life to keep it all together—because life itself turns down so many avenues that we often struggle to know which road to travel. Robert Frost illustrated this well In *The Road Not Taken*. When we get to those inevitable crossroads in life, we must, I repeat, stop at least for a moment to make a decision—This is what Oasis Moments allow us to do! Without ever taking time to smell the roses, we will falter.

The Road Not Taken

By Robert Frost

Two roads diverged in a yellow wood,
And sorry I could not travel both
And be one traveller, long I stood
And looked down one as far as I could
To where it bent in the undergrowth;

Then took the other, as just as fair,
And having perhaps the better claim,
Because it was grassy and wanted wear;
Though as for that, the passing there
Had worn them really about the same,

After we've taken some time at an Oasis of one making or another, it's usually not in a physical desert; still, it's usually at one of our "WILDERNESS MOMENTS" in plain old living life we have the resources to make better decisions.

We need to *Make The Time* to *Take The Time* to be refreshed in this way for God's purpose for us to be complete in every way as we enjoy life to the full! There are no shortcuts—as much as we like to think we can *shortcut* the challenging life moments—circumvent or go around those *character-building lessons* Life Offers Us! I say, Offers Us because we can ignore these life lessons, and *we will*, I Repeat, WE WILL suffer the consequences for trying to avoid Life's Challenging Moments.

Does Jesus Care?

I Know He Cares!

Cast all your care upon Him;

Because He cares for you.

(1 Peter 5:7)

HEART SENSE
Lord, What About Our Stature Or Need?

———————————◊———————————

WHO OF US CAN ADD A CUBIT—(17.71654) inches, or even an inch to our height—just by thinking we can? Why do we worry so much about having enough clothes to wear and the latest greatest craze in clothing—just look out at the flowers in the field—they bloom well because God supplies the ingredients for their growth—no worries. Solomon, in all his glory, didn't look this good.

If God can and does watch out for the things He created—will He not take care of them today and tomorrow if we trust Him? Have A Little Faith! So, let's not worry about what we will eat, drink, and wear—God knows what we need (*Not Necessarily Ready to satisfy our wants*).

"But seek ye first the kingdom of God and His righteousness, and all these things shall be added unto you.

Take therefore no thought for the morrow: for the morrow shall take thought for the things of itself. Sufficient unto the day is the evil thereof." (Matthew 6: 27-34)

Scriptures In Chapter Sixteen
Heart Sense
Matthew 6: 27-34
1 John 4: 1-21
Genesis 1: 9-13
Genesis 1:3
Matthew 22: 34-40
Psalm 139
The Vista View—The Oasis
Hebrews 12:1

Chapter Sixteen

Why Should I Care About What God Thinks?

---◊---

THE BIBLE HAS EVERY RESOURCE NECESSARY TO GET US THROUGH THIS LIFE TO THE NEXT!

BELOVED, BELIEVE NOT EVERY SPIRIT, but try the spirits to see or not whether they are of God: because many false prophets are gone out into the world. With this know ye the Spirit of God: Every spirit that confesses that Jesus Christ has come in the flesh is of God.

Every spirit that confesses not that Jesus Christ has come in the flesh is not of God: and this is that spirit of antichrist, of which ye have heard that it should come; and even now already is it in the world.

"Ye are of God, little children, and have overcome them: because greater is He in you than in the world. Therefore, they are of the world: they speak of the world, and the world heareth them. We are of God: he that knoweth God heareth us; folks who aren't of God don't hear us. As a result, we know the spirit of truth and error.

Beloved, let us love one another: love is of God, and everyone that loveth is born of God and knows God. He that loveth not knoweth not God; for God is love. In this was manifested the love of God toward us because that God sent His only begotten Son into the world that we might live through Him. Herein is love, not that we loved God, but that He loved us and sent His Son to pay the price for our sins.

If God so loved us, Beloved, we ought also to love one another. No man hath seen God at any time. God dwelleth in us if we love one another, and He perfects His love in us. Now we know that we dwell in Him, and He in us, because He hath given us of His Spirit, and we have seen and do testify that the Father sent the Son to be the Savior of the world.

Whosoever shall confess that Jesus is the Son of God, God dwelleth in Him, and he in God. And we have known and believed the love that God hath to us. God is love, and He that dwelleth in love dwelleth in God, and God in him. Herein is our love made perfect, that we may have boldness in the day of judgment: because as He is, so are we in this world. There is no fear in love, but perfect love casteth out fear: because fear hath torment. He that feareth is not made perfect in love."

"WE LOVE HIM BECAUSE HE FIRST LOVED US."

"If a someone says, they love God, and hate their siblings, they are liars: for he that loveth not his brother whom he hath seen, how can he love God whom he hath not seen? And we have this commandment from Him that he who loveth God also loves his brother." (1 John 4:1-21)

At my inception, I was just a handful of dirt—in one sense, not of much value when I look out at the earth in nature occupied by much more impurity today than the wholesome soil God created In The Beginning!

Evolutionists say we came from some Melting Pot of Soup from which came The Ape—and developed exponentially (aggressively, determinately, expanding, increasing, growing, rampantly, spreading, wantonly) to become the magnificent specimen of the humanity we see walking about Planet Earth! Dirt may have been included or mixed into the Melting Pot of Civilization!

The first mineral God made was dirt. Dirt is a lesser item, as we think about Gold. (mind you, farmers place a considerable value on dirt. If the dirt on their farmland is full of weeds and otherwise useless, something needs to be done about it to restore it) (IBID—From This Book's Introduction).

And God said, Let the waters under the heaven be gathered together unto one place, and let the dry land appear: and it was so. And God called the dry land Earth, and the gathering together of the waters called he Seas: and God saw that it was good.

> And God said, Let the earth bring forth grass, the herb yielding seed, and the fruit tree yielding fruit after his kind, whose source is in itself, upon the earth: and it was so. And the earth brought forth grass, the herb yielding seed after his kind, and the tree yielding fruit, whose origin was in itself, after his kind: and God saw that it was good. And the evening and the morning were the third day. (Genesis 1 9-13)

We see the earliest record of 'dirt' in The Bible, God's Word to us, on the third day of recorded history. It seems like it's more significant initially than 'Gold.' I'm sure God had a reason to record this first; maybe because we needed to understand that 'He made us from dust and to dust, we would return. We are human, but God is superior. He displayed His understanding to us in the simplest way possible. He became one of us, yet, without the flaws (sin) we brought upon ourselves in The Garden of Eden.'

We often think that when God made dirt, He must've been unaware that we would disobey Him in the Garden of Eden. This thought is often confusing to us because we think, 'if God was aware of this, why did He even give us the concept of choice and put us in this vulnerable state of fleshly humanity—where we are prone to make mistakes over, and over, and over again!'

God's overall purpose was for things to grow—this includes folks like us. God made the soil a vital issue; He made minerals in this soil; He made Gold necessary in His plan in creation. God did this not only to get us excited about the beauty and glitter of gold, but by looking forward, He saw our value. He knew we'd have needs; one of those needs is MONEY. Bartering was one of the means of handling financial matters and the survival aspect of living. People wanted wealth and personal worth beyond the soil beneath their feet.

More than this, God had a plan for and around the mineral we call 'Gold.' The value of Gold in this world has always been immense. Oil is almost the lifeblood of our planet; it's almost as if it's in our veins instead of the blood of life God created within us. What will we ever do when we run out of the oil God also created, and why did He create oil? In every aspect of the life and living part of creation He made, God prepared everything well in advance of our arrival from the soil He made in Genesis 1:3.

Blood is more than an element for our physical survival. The Bible says that without the shedding of blood, Jesus's blood, there wasn't going to be a pathway for us to get to the eternity we did not deserve when we rejected God's input into our lives for our benefit in The Garden of Eden. (Where are the most significant oil reserves in history found? Some folks have thought it to be in Iraq. I don't know this for a fact. However, the Middle East has been where we have mainly considered as being the crux or heart of the place we depend upon for this mineral: Black Gold!)

So, in our search for Gold, do we remember we are drawn from or lifted out from the soil formed by God to become more than we were for God's purpose on earth. *We are the vessels* in the Potter's hand, *not the Potter*; *we are the creation, not the Creator*; we did not initiate life; God did! As we think of the commodity we call Gold, we ought to consider it more than a physical reality. Pure Gold comes from being purified in the fire!

Physical reality is what we have become accustomed to, so much so we often forget God in the whole process of life as we know it. You Know—we've grown accustomed to believing it's "All About Us!" God had us in His thoughts before forming anything (earth and all the other system of the universe). Everything He created apart from us was because of us and for us.

However, before we get too proud, remember it was not for 'us' individually as much as for *us* corporately; yes, it was for us to be something for someone else. Wow! If that doesn't take the 'lead' (the mineral) out of our pencil!

The English language can be complicated. We can misinterpret communications if we don't consider the context when using certain words. In my opinion, LEAD (the mineral) should read LED. But, used in its other form, L E A D, to LEAD someone down the Garden Path, is another context entirely.

Mathew 22:34-40 puts much of the *US* thing into perspective—the proper context. If we want life to be all it can be, God says we need to put Him first in everything we do. We need to put all our strength, energy, and other resources into loving Him first. In one respect, this is a tall order because we cannot see God physically. The Bible tells us we must believe in Him, do what He has scoped out as the best-case scenario—then life will be all it can be!

Second to this and in much the same context, God says we need to love our neighbour in the same way. So what remains as the 'Subject' matter of the context?—God Is! The 'Complement' seems to be that God will be enough for us to get through life in the most desirable way. Here is the KICKER!

He that loveth not knoweth not God; for is love.

Do we have time? Every one of us is so busy! Can we afford to waste our time? I don't think so. The time *From Here To Eternity, Life*—is so short. The time of ETERNITY is ENDLESS!

High in the North in a land called Svithjod, there is a mountain. It is a hundred miles long and a hundred miles high, and once every thousand years, a little bird comes to this mountain to sharpen its beak. When the mountain has thus been worn away, a single day of eternity will have passed. (Hendrik Willem van Loon's History of Mankind [published 1922])

God also gave us the promise of a 'Street of Gold—' for down the pike! Here is a commitment that can provide us with hope to get over our flaws and become more than we are in the present. The promise of the future God gives us hinges on two things— Firstly, we need to know in Whom we believe; Secondly, we need to stay on track to keep *Searching For A Heart Of Gold* in front of us at all times. Our Search insofar as me writing this book, and you, while reading this book, needs direct focus. 'The Right Overall Perspective' is "God— and all He Is;" then, within our guide (the rest of 'US' and our STUFF), we'll be able to say, IT'S ALL GOOD—For God Is Good!

And He said to him, "Why are you asking Me about what is good? There is only One who is good; but if you wish to enter into life, keep the commandments." (Mathew 19:17)

Think About It!

We know God is above all (if we have a relationship with Him), Creator, The First and The Last—nothing existed before Him, and nothing will live after Him or without Him—We are lowly compared to God! He gave of Himself JESUS—.

How could we not care about God?

WHY SHOULD I CARE WHAT GOD THINKS?

Because He Cares What I Think!

Psalm 139

Oh God—When I was out of the reach of any other source of help—You searched for me and found me—when I'm sitting in my Lazy Boy or anywhere else, you know when I hoist myself reluctantly from my sitting place when You ask me to do a little something for You! You know what I'm thinking at all times. You surround me at all times—while I'm sleeping or awake.

Before I even think to speak of anything, You know all about it—and when I'm thinking wrong things, You caution me to Think It Over Again Before I Speak It—This is in my best interest. As I move out onto The Road of Life, to do Your will, You anoint me to accomplish Great Things wherever I go.

All the knowledge You allow me to partake of is too incredible in scope for me to fully grasp!

◊ THE VISTA VIEW—THE OASIS ◊

Part Four (Part Four Wrap-up)

The Heart Of God—The Clincher!

Part Four houses Four Chapters from which I drew many thoughts of our continuance in *Searching For A Heart of Gold; Not A Pot of Gold*—Ultimately leading us to function relationally in *Our Search For The Heart Of God*!

Chapter Thirteen is *Out On A Limb*; Chapter Fourteen Is *What Was I Thinking—And Why?* Chapter Fifteen is, *Does God Really Care About Our Day-To-Day?* Chapter Sixteen is *Why Should I Care About What God Thinks?* Parts One Through Part Four cover much about us Prepping for The Final Assault To Take The Hill!

To "Assault The Hill" is to make an Offensive Charge— Onward and Upwards— As if being The Charge Up San Juan Hill on July 1/1898 (In The Spanish American War). I picture the scene as us laying aside every hindrance to getting the job done!

> Wherefore seeing we also are compassed (surrounded) about with so great a cloud of witnesses, let us lay aside every weight, and the sin which doth so easily beset us, and let us run with patience the race set before us. (Hebrews 12:1)

God Is The Clincher of our every need. The determining Factor of Winning The Day—Conquering The Hill—The Clincher for us is—To Lay It All Down, in so far as we can do so—to fulfill our part in The Relationship With God In The Person of Jesus Christ—by The Power of The Holy Spirit of God!

To Wrap Up Part Four—Let's Think About Growing In God's Plan—Growing To Be More Like Him In Every Way Possible. There's an individual aspect to this plan, and there is a corporate segment involved in following this plan and purpose. Each of us has Personal Responsibilities to carry out in the process. Each of us has Corporate Responsibilities to carry out with other Christ Followers; we have responsibilities to be a part of the Journey To Include Our Fellowperson who is not a Christ Follower.

Scriptures In Part Five Front Matter
Psalm 139
Heart Sense
Proverbs 8: 5; Proverbs 3: 11-15

Part Five

Searching For The Heart of God!

Something I've Often Wanted To Do Is Preach Psalm 139.
—Why Would I Want To Do This?—

In doing this in a manner in which Good Preaching is most effective (transparent), I'd need to begin with a Story of Part of my Life which is Most Relational to The Exegesis of The Passage of Scripture which will be the Theme of The Sermon—In This Case, It Is Psalm 139—.

If God Wants To Search For Me;
Why Would I Not Want To Search For Him?

LET'S FILL UP ON SEARCHING FOR THE HEART OF GOD

We need answers in a world of mixed emotions and perceptions about life. When the eternity we think of doesn't seem to be panning out as we believe it should—when a season of life is seemingly all about us—we need to know God exists and know what He most sincerely wants for us in a relational sense—What's Our Part To Play?

—God IS—
The Omni-Relational God
Semper Fidelus!
Always Faithful!
Always Loyal

HEART SENSE
Oh, If Only We Could Define Simplicity!

––––––––––––– ◊ –––––––––––––

O YE SIMPLE [not simple-minded—those who mind common sense in simple manners of understanding]: understand wisdom. And, ye fools (those folks who always seem to want to scrap about the common sense things that other people suggest as the best pattern of living), be ye of an understanding heart. (Proverbs 8:5)

Occam's razor

Occam's razor suggests the most straightforward answer is most often correct—although this is an oversimplification. The 'correct' interpretation is that we shouldn't needlessly multiply the wordage of things to explain them in more detail than necessary to get the message across in a conversation.

Common sense begins to make sense as we study The Book of Proverbs in The Bible. Common Sense does not seem to come as naturally as we might expect it should. There are too many voices of contention (opinion) in today's world—contending (insisting) that everything is truthful, even if it's proven to be a bald-faced, bold-faced or barefaced lie! Common sense needs operative developmental skills in play to get the most significant benefit from the contributor.

My son, despise not the chastening of the Lord; neither be weary of His correction: For whom the Lord loveth He correcteth; even as a father the son in whom He delighteth. Happy is the man who finds wisdom and the man who gets understanding—for the merchandise of it is better than the merchandise of silver and the gain thereof than fine gold. She is more precious than rubies: and all the things thou canst desire are not to be compared unto her. (Proverbs 3: 11-15)

In Chapters Seventeen and Eighteen—
Let's Seek To Find Wisdom [Common-Sense!]

Scriptures In Chapter Seventeen
Isaiah 52
Psalm 23
Psalm 23
Psalm 23; Psalm 78
Psalm 78:1-52
Jeremiah 17:9; John 3:16
Hebrews 12:1; Hebrews 12:1-2;
1 John 3:1-3; Jeremiah 12:5
Psalm 139:1-4
Psalm 139:1-4
Psalm 139:7-13
Isaiah 9:6
Hebrews 12:2-3
James 4:8; Hebrews 4:12; Matthew 28:6-7
Philippians 4:8; Philippians 4:6-7
1 John 4:15-19; Revelation 1:7-9
John 3:15-17
The Vista View—The Oasis
Ephesians 6:18-19

CHAPTER SEVENTEEN—[SUMMARY OF CHAPTERS 1-16]

Our Troubles Will Fade Away

––––––––––––––––––––––––––––––––– ◊ –––––––––––––––––––––––––––––––––

Summary of Chapter One—*The Lay of The Land*
Our Troubles Will Fade 'As we take a Refreshing Time-Out!'

HOW LOVELY ARE THE FEET OF THOSE WHO BRING GOOD NEWS down from the mountain top where they meet You LORD; as they share Your heart, showing us Your plans to love and guide us. How beautiful thoughts of peace as they bring good news to weary pilgrims. (Isaiah 52). [—The Preparation—]

Chapter One is vital for the strength and energy to express my reliance or trust in The One Who matters most for any success I may have to commit to paper what I wish to say at length. Let's not let fear deter us because words like 'at length' [wordily] are long-winded. I know sometimes *more* is overkill.

My Hope, My Heart—acknowledges The God Source as the only resource for strength enough to carry out anything of eternal value. My Creator, God The Father, God in The Person of Jesus Christ, through the avenue of God The Holy Spirit, is how I agree to *get* what I have inside of me—to share.

Robin Mark sings the song *Be Unto Your Name*; he expresses his heart with words parallel to *us being a moment*; "God is forever." Robin suggests God is forever in the eternal past; Mr. Mark acknowledges God with *heart words* expressing themselves as Love—reigning for eternity. Robin declares God to be "Holy, Almighty, and Worthy." These are my sentiments as well!

Jesus is the freely given payment to allow us a chance at eternal salvation. We are broken containers; God is the Potter who repairs these vessels if we only ask Him to fix our *sinful condition*.

EVERY STORY HAS AN ENTRY OR *PREPARATION POINT—PREPPING FOR ETERNITY* TAKES A LIFETIME!

Summary of Chapter Two—*Surveying The Land*
Our Troubles Will Fade when Jesus Leads The Way!

THE LORD IS MY SHEPHERD; I shall not want. He maketh me to lie down in green pastures: He leads me beside the still waters. He restores my soul: He leads me in the paths of righteousness for His name's sake. Even if I walk through the valley of the shadow of death, I will fear no evil: for You are with me; Your rod and staff they comfort me. (Psalm 23)

You *prepare* a table before me in the presence of my enemies: You anoint my head with oil; my cup runs over. Surely goodness and mercy shall follow me all the days of my life: and I will dwell in the house of the Lord forever. (Psalms 23)

While reflecting on *The Lay Of The Land,* it becomes clear— The LORD is The One who wants His best for us. The Green Pastures of Psalms 23 allow us to grasp a complete sense of God's love. It breaks down for us into bite-size pieces. We all know that our digestive system doesn't work so well if we gobble our food down. [—The Purpose—]

Chapter Two, *Surveying The Land,* comes as a Preparatory Layout [the next step to come] after Chapter One, *The Lay Of The Land*—Chapter Two lays out the steps after Chapters One and Two. Chapter Three is *The LORD Is My Shepherd*—before we can begin building on a foundation, we need to mark out the boundary lines and elevations to get to the next step in the process—nothing ever gets made without some parameters to define the entity.

We need to find the best place to pour the Foundation and find The Source of supply for furthering the project. The Foundation we have before us in this book—Is God. Beforehand we had to observe the whole project to decide whether it was worth the effort and if it would be a value-added subject to pursue. When life throws us a *curve,* and we miss hitting the ball too many times, we need HELP to learn how to hit a CURVEBALL! God is the One Who will support us.

EVERY STORY SHOULD HAVE PREPARATION AND PURPOSE— OTHERWISE, WHAT'S THE POINT OF TELLING ANYBODY ANYTHING! I'M TRYING TO DEVELOP PREPARATION AND PURPOSE—THROUGHOUT THIS BOOK! GOD ALWAYS HAD A PLAN— HE STILL HAS A PLAN TODAY!

Summary of Chapter Three—*The LORD Is My Shepherd*

Our Troubles Will Fade when 'we let go and Let God take Charge!'

WHILE REFLECTING on the first two chapters, I see God as The One who wants His best for us. Ahead of us are the 'Green Pastures' which Psalms 23 allows us to grasp in the most profound sense:

THE LORD IS MY SHEPHERD; I SHALL NOT WANT. He maketh me to lie down in green pastures: He leadeth me beside the still waters. [He restoreth my soul: He leadeth me in the paths of righteousness for His name's sake. Yea, though I walk through the valley of the shadow of death, I will fear no evil: for Thou art with me; Thy rod and Thy staff they comfort me]. Thou preparest a table before me in the presence of my enemies: thou anointest my head with oil; my cup runneth over. Goodness and mercy will Always follow me: and I will dwell in the house of the Lord forever. (Psalms 23)

[—The Progress—]

We begin at The Oasis of Psalm 23 by being refreshed in The Green Pastures and taking in the Refreshing Waters—' breathtaking aura [atmosphere]. Then as we move into verses three and four, we begin to make progress after we'd been out on the parching effects of our 'Desert Journey.'

What more can I say about Psalms 23 to explain the context [there are numerous contexts in a book]. The setting or predetermined framework [not parameters that suggest limits or walls that do not allow us to connect to the rest of the content of The Bible or portion thereof] of this passage does not need explaining. Psalms 23 is famous. *The Lord Is My Shepherd* on Amazon.ca search bar for books gives us four-hundred choices. The Information Highway is an endless Journey of Resources. One subject leads to another, and The Short Road soon becomes The Long Road!

AS I BEGIN TO SURVEY (AS IN SURVEYING THE LAND), I SEE THE PRESENTATIONS ARE MULTI-INCLUSIVE OF MANY THOUGHT ASPECTS. "AND AS WE MOVE ON, THE STORY NEVER ENDS!" (SONG BY WRITER (S) MICHAEL MATOSIC, ARI LEFF, MIKE ELIZONDO, MICHAEL POLLACK, JOHATHAN SIMPSON—).

Summary of Chapter Four—*Led By The Shepherd*
Our Troubles Will Fade 'In The Shepherd's Presence at The Oasis!'
WE'VE LOOKED AT SOME OF PSALM 23—taking some of it apart piece by piece, but the end has not yet become 'Total Insight' as we begin Chapter Four, *Led By The Shepherd*. We've 'sighted' many particulars of this passage—yet the end is not 'In Sight—' The depth of 'Knowledge' and 'Insightful' helps often remains undiscovered. [—Preservation—]

Please look at Psalm 78 (JBI—Jacob Bergen Insight Version)? The Scriptures to follow are in my words and thoughts as I glean the King James Version—don't take them to be the actual KJV by the author of Psalm 78. As we read scripture, we all think about what the Scripture means for us in the day we live now, keeping the context of Scripture intact. It is easy to take anything out of context—easy to change the perspective to suit our bent.

However, to stay true to the context—we shouldn't think God said something He didn't say. Many thoughts flood my mind as I write—this is the challenge of most writers. We try to bring in a Bird's Eye View like that of an Eagle, who has one of the keenest eyesight's of all birds—this is the vantage point I hope to use as best I can to transfer the thoughts scripture, I tag as "JBI." The Eagle has a special place in my heart!

Listen Up, Folks—We need to Perk up our ears. We need to notice what's going on in the life around us, with an eye open to what may lay ahead of us—this is needful to live life successfully!

I'll be speaking in and about tones, mental hues, varieties of characters, and pictures so we can get the most up-to-date information available. If we Listen Up, the past will become the present for us in so far as giving us sufficient INSIGHT to be able to confront and or manage whatever jumps out of the bush to halt our progress. Adversity often strikes in a moment while we move about nonchalantly—. Let's not ever let Adversity change the pattern of Faith recorded in The Bible. After we've learned about God's Faithfulness in times past, we also need to be taught to accept that life is much the same for us all.

We shouldn't hide all God has done, is doing, and yet is planning to do in our day. The things we learn from our children, grandchildren, and great-grandchildren are rewarding. God's strength and beautiful words stand out plainly; for this, we will Praise God All The Days of Our Lives in the hope that the generations following us will also continue remembering God and never cease to Praise Him Always as they walk in His ways.

God established His presence in the People of The Past—Abraham, Isaac, Jacob—He expected they would pass the torch to those who would live after them. God has done all this and more, so all people everywhere would not forget Him and how He made way for them in places they would otherwise have feared beyond the measure of being fit to travel. He made His will and Laws clear, so the responsibility is ours.

God noticed when many of the past generations were a little stubborn, and in fact, they were often obstinate and inflexible—so He used desperate measures to change their minds. Their hearts of unbelief often deterred them from following God's ways—this was to their detriment, loss, and injury.

Ephraim, armed and so-called ready, turned and ran away on the day of conflict—they broke their bond with God and balked at walking with God. They quickly forgot the wonders God performed with and for them—down the line, down through the land of Egypt.

When Israel came up against their enemy at the Red Sea, with Pharoah hot on their heels, God opened up the Sea. God dried up the ocean floor so they could manage their steps without dragging their feet through mud—allowing them safe passage to the other side, even though they sometimes thought the wall of water would come crashing down upon them!

As they looked behind them, this same water came down on Pharaoh's hordes [army], which for a time gave the people a heart of thanksgiving. God provided a cloud to lead them during the day—at nighttime, He lit the way for them with a pillar of fire, as if led by a tour guide. How much more intense could life have been in favour of God's way! God held nothing back while He showed His love for them.

While these folks were in the wilderness, God split the rocks so the people could draw water from deep down, as well; He caused water to run like a river for them to be satisfied—not leaving them dehydrated. Then, as if God would have killed them off by hunger, they bent God's wishes and will out of context; they continually complained and went against God's laws. They taunted God, doubting He could supply their wants and needs—the thirst for their needs should have exceeded the lust of their heart.

God was angry, but He still supplied food and water—but the people's taste buds—God's gift of sustenance according to His dietary plan never satisfied the people. When He gave them bread, they wanted meat— 'The Story Never Ends'—so it seems. The folks never reasonably believed God had their best interest at heart, so they did not trust He would save them from their enemy and might I add, keep them from themselves.

God taught them a lesson from time to time for the good of the whole. He killed off the "Fat Cats" (pardon the possible intolerance, no offence intended); even this did not deter the people from distrusting God; they continued their diatribe of sinful lusts for forty years in the wilderness. (Psalm 78 1-52)

In their own hands, 'Trouble Followed Them Like A Plague.' After many got killed, they returned for a time, so to speak [as if this was true repentance, it doesn't look like it to me]. Because it seemed like they said the proper thing tongue in cheek, they flattered God with their mouths, but their heart was not right—they were a bunch of Flip-Floppers. They openly acknowledged God as the "Rock of Their Defense," their Saviour, when they were in 'Big Trouble!'

Even amid all the STUFF these folks pulled—here's God, reaching out His arm of 'Strength and Compassion' when the next wave hit them square in the face. He, being the loving God He is, forgave them. He didn't eradicate them—though they deserved payback. God remembered they were only human; they needed reminding from time to time—nothing has changed; we are in the same boat.

THERE'S NO END TO THE BIBLE'S STORIES; WE LIVE MANY STORIES TODAY NOT YET WRITTEN IN THE BIBLE.

Summary of Chapter Five—*Searching For The Heart!*
Our Troubles Will Fade 'In the excitement of Searching For God.'

IN PART ONE—We looked at The Lay Of The Land; Surveying The Land; The LORD Is My Shepherd, and Led By The Shepherd.

Now, let's plunge a little farther into 'The Matter Of The Heart!' The King James Bible records "HEART" '884' times. The book of Psalms records the word "HEART" '130' times—this is 14.7058823529% (1 out of nearly seven times. 'Heart' is mentioned in The Bible; it's in The Psalms) of all '884' references in The Bible. They say there are 783137 words in the KJV. So this tells us HEART is mentioned 0.0165999053% of the time out of all the words in the KJV. So, if and when we are interested in studying THE HEART, not the blood-pumping organ in the physical body, but the HEART which Jeremiah talks about— 'Take Heart!'

"The heart is deceitful above all things, and desperately wicked: who can know it?" (Jeremiah 17:9)

The Biblical references to the Heart are not physically orientated (housed)—and just as obvious, at least to me, is that not all the mentions of the Heart in The Bible say the Heart is always in disrepair or as unfavourable as it seems Jeremiah suggests. If we miss the context of what someone is talking about in whatever dialogue they are addressing any subject, whatever it is—in this case, 'It's The Heart,' we often tend to end up with troublesome conversations or negotiations.

Let's look at a few references to the 'Heart' in The Psalms. Many of them will overlap in context anyway, but I want to look at some of them; I often present Scriptures as JBI—*Jacob Bergen Insight*, not the actual KJV words. I'm not trying to lessen the impact of the original, so please read them for yourselves in the version you read. My thoughts are just that— "My Thoughts!"

ONE OF THE MOST COMFORTING STORIES IN THE BIBLE IS PSALM TWENTY-THREE. LIKE JOHN 3:16, MOST PEOPLE HAVE HEARD OF THE 23RD. PSALM. IF WE TURN A DEAF EAR TO THESE SCRIPTURES, HOPELESSNESS IS NEAR! GOD ALWAYS HAD A PLAN—HE STILL HAS A PLAN TODAY! IT'S UP TO US TO SEARCH FOR WHAT GOD SAID IN HIS WORD!

<u>Summary of Chapter Six</u>—Finding The Heart— Then What?

Our Troubles Will Fade 'If we put other folks on the Priority List over ourselves!'

DOES ANYONE REMEMBER The Bumper Sticker— "I FOUND IT?" There are many seasons in life for each of us. Each season differs from the last, and things change as the seasons change.

Have people ever really lived Through Life Completely while they lived and breathed? I'm not just asking, 'will we ever have lived through life just because we were born into it and died at birth—Will We Ever Have Lived Through Life!' To have lived Through Life means we have gone Through numerous seasons of time where the present Season of Life Today is diametrically (entirely) different than what we experienced yesterday. By Yesterday, I don't necessarily mean the day just passed—like only hours behind us!

"I Found It" Bumper Stickers were a product of the 60s. When a person became a Christ Follower, they wanted to tell the world around them of their Newfound Faith. So it seems one of these folks started the "I Found It" craze or trend by making up Bumper Stickers to announce to the world that they were on a New Track of Life, meaning something was wrong on the inside of their life—this was true then and is true now as well. Now begins letting this HEART' grow to become stronger each day. These folks didn't quit living a natural life—they just added the Spiritual Life.

Perfection wasn't resident at any time in the process! When someone experiences the "I Found It" encounter, it only means their Old Heart of not believing God in the person of Jesus Christ is working on an about-face scenario. Now Jesus, who personally died, took the guilt and shame associated with that Old Life and its Heart of Unbelief and said, "I Will Take The Punishment For The Harm This Old Life Created." The Biblical term for this experience is being "Born Again," thereby creating a NEW HEART!

LIKE THE FOUR SEASONS OF THE CALENDAR YEAR, THE MAIN STORY OF OUR LIVES CHANGES—OUR BIRTH STARTED THINGS PHYSICALLY. GOD IS UNCHANGEABLE! HE'S ALWAYS KNOWN THE STORY!

Summary of Chapter Seven—What Then—? Steeplechasing—.

Our Troubles Will Fade 'If we stay the course on the Steeplechase Horse!'

FASTENING OUR GAZE ON JESUS, The One Who authored our shot at Faith; The One Who not only began for us this journey, He perfected it so we can Run The Race Set Before Us, as given to us long before our birth. God knew each of us before He ever created anything else! If we never achieved any importance or recognition for anything else, the fact that God knew us before we were born is enough of an "Importance Factor" for me! (Re Hebrews 12:2)

Jesus braved the cross; again, because of what He saw as laying ahead, as a possibility for us—To Become Something! This thought seemed to bring Jesus a huge Joy Factor. When Jesus finished His course of life as The Son of Man, His humanity completed, He took His rightful position as God, in all this represents, in the Throne Room of God. One day we will know more about The Throne Room Of God!

Behold, what manner of love the Father hath bestowed upon us, that we should be called the sons of God: therefore, the world knoweth us not, because it knew Him not. Beloved, now are we the sons of God, and it doth not yet appear what we shall be: but we know that, when He shall appear, we shall be like Him; for we shall see Him as He is. And every man that hath this hope in Him purifies themselves, even as He is pure. (1 John 3: 1-3)

So, because of what I've looked at sparsely in Hebrews and 1 John, I flip back from Hebrews 12: 2 to verse one—to help us see the background of the setting. So, as we are in The Race of Our Lives, we need to shed any hindrances [such as obstinate objectors to truth], and we must Run With Enduring Resolve to win not against each other but the foe of honest living [the devil]. We should realize that God set The Rules for The Race (Re Hebrews 12:1).

EUGENE PETERSEN'S BOOK, RUN WITH THE HORSES—PRESENTS US WITH A GREAT STORY ABOUT LEARNING TO ENDURE WHEN THE HARD TIMES COME. (JEREMIAH 12:5)

Summary of Chapter Eight—*Tomorrow Is Only A Day Away*.

Our Troubles Will Fade 'If we learn not to fret over the Yesterdays we thought we should've experienced.'

O LORD, THOU HAST SEARCHED ME AND KNOWN ME. Thou knowest my downsitting and mine uprising; thou understandest my thought afar off. Thou compassest my path and 'my' lying down, and art acquainted with all my ways. There is no word in my tongue, but, lo, O Lord, Thou knowest it. (Psalm 139: 1-4)

There are huge differences between Yesterday and Today. Though they are only hours apart (up to twenty-four hours)—they present mega entities. It is imperative to deal with each new day differently than yesterday! We can never reclaim Yesterday, though it's just One Day Behind Us On The Calendar—it's gone! The overall Agenda we had Yesterday may be the same as Today. Let's look at the weather patterns; they are not the same; it may just be that Yesterday was sunny and today is cloudy; it may be that Today is a degree or two different than it was Yesterday—up or down one way or another.

My mood this morning isn't precisely the same today as yesterday at this exact time. As I'm writing these words and thinking about my mood, it's different today than yesterday at the same hour of the day. Yesterday was Easter Sunday—Yesterday, as I was trying to be in the right MOOD for Easter Sunday, Resurrection Day, I was allowing the Yesterday of Yesterday to impact the Mood I was trying to create for Easter Sunday.

As Good Friday ended, I began to think about The Disciples of Jesus and The Saturday they were now having. It saddened me when I put myself [as much as is possible] in their shoes for a while—because they'd just lost the dearest friend they ever had in this life. The disciples and others felt the world had ended. Jesus told them what would happen, but somehow they hadn't noticed in advance of the now!

IMAGINE THE STORY WE MIGHT HAVE SHARED IF WE'D BEEN THERE THAT EASTER WEEKEND—THEN TRANSPORTED TO LIFE IN THE PRESENT! WOULD WE HAVE HELD BACK BECAUSE WE FAILED SO BADLY?

Summary of Chapter Nine—*Life Is A Serious Entity.*
Our Troubles Will Fade 'If our concentration or focus sees us sitting at the feet of Jesus!'

O LORD, YOU SEARCHED ME THROUGH AND THROUGH. You know my thoughts, even surrounding me while I lie down, whether sitting or standing. You saturate me with Your presence. Before I think of an idea, You know the next word I will speak. (Psalm 139: 1-4)

We get to live LIFE only once in the lifespan unveiled, revealed, or shown to us on Planet Earth as we know it now. The Psalms, Proverbs, and Ecclesiastes are three Books of The Bible dealing distinctly with life 'Straight Up!' The writers give us 'Reel After Reel of Episodes of Real Life' settings from which we are Well Able to live LIFE to the fullest possible degree! There's much more to living life than just a Quick Fix.

In the day in which we live, access is hardly an imposition anymore—even in Non-Developing Countries, cell phones are highly possible. Many of these cell phones are of the Relic variety we now call Dumb Phones. However, as time passes and technology increases at more and more speed than ever before, the possibilities for Non-Developing Countries to be more able to use what we call Smart Phones also becomes more likely.

As technology leads us into the future, living life in the context to which we've become accustomed becomes easier. Though this is true, it's not the mega means or the best means from which we launch out on a successful Journey to get from Birth Through Life as we know it. Even if technology was the best and only means available to us, it could never transport us from Birth Through To Eternity.

If we only had hope in this life, we may try to cope alone—Us and Our 'Techno-Wizardry' (Technology and Magic)! Life leads us on a journey of believing we don't need God! I cannot follow this pattern! Many other folks worldwide believe God is the only way to get us through LIFE!

OUR STORY IS LIKE A MOVIE REEL—MANY SCENES FILL THE DURATION OF THE EPIC STORYLINE. SOME SEASONS SEE US WIN THE GOLD—OTHER SCENES ARE CLIPS OF DISASTER—WE ARE DEAD LAST!

<u>Summary of Chapter Ten</u>—The Winds And The Clouds Of The Heart.

Our Troubles Will Fade 'If we had access to an open Bank Vault at day's end!'

WHITHER SHALL I GO FROM THY SPIRIT? Where can I run from Your Presence? I can't escape to Heaven or Hell for a getaway. Before the dawn breaks, I don't know in totality what it will highlight—LORD, You already know! Suppose I abide in the ultimate parts of the sea; everything is 'intact' for me to live safely. If I desired to hide from You, LORD, darkness wouldn't suffice. My reins are in Your hands. Before I was in my mother's womb, You knew everything there is to know about me then and forever! (Psalm 139: 7-13)

Life seems to dictate *Insecurity*! We face diffidence (self-doubt) head-on moment by moment. Our mental capacity is overwhelmed and or overloaded—saturated with *insecurities* today and tomorrow—Or life can bathe us in a Sea of Opportunities to make a difference—the challenge to do so requires a resource we must, I repeat, must be ready to engage. Along with every challenge comes the opposition's bid, which might present the 'ultimate internal and external' *War of The Worlds* yet unknown!

A week ago, we experienced a deluge of rain, wind, and hail alien to anything I remember, going back at least fifty years—*maybe never*! Seemingly out of nowhere, as sudden as the twinkle of an eye, this storm was akin to a chaotic *tropical storm* as I could imagine. This blast of inclement weather was a warning from the *cloud cover* up above Our Town—Invermere, BC; it scolded us for a solid thirty minutes. Although this may not sound like something analogous or similar to a significant storm, it damaged much plant life as the 'Windows of Heaven Opened!' Life gets serious for us at an unsuspecting moment—Yes, as if it were a *hurricane or the like*. I've never lived through a storm equivalent to a hurricane—many folks have; recovery is possible.

ARE WE READY TO SHARE OUR CONVERSION STORY WHEN THE MOMENT ARISES? YESTERDAY, I SHARED MY CONVERSION STORY WITH MY NINETY-SEVEN-YEAR-OLD FRIEND. I TOLD HIM THAT WHEN I WAS TWELVE YEARS OLD—MY SISTER, BROTHER, AND TWO COUSINS WERE PLAYING CHURCH—PLAYTIME GOT SERIOUS, AND WE ALL COMMITTED OUR LIVES TO CHRIST!

Summary of Chapter Eleven—*The Vault—The World.*
Our Troubles Will Fade 'If our good times far outweigh the bad!'

SEARCHING FOR ANYTHING PRESENTS A CHALLENGE. The spur of the moment often sends us on a chase. Looking amongst our stuff or all around the world in hopes of finding just anything at all—requires determination. To 'Search Without *Purpose*' is ludicrous (nonsensical)!' Our world is full of people who seemingly have no purpose in having fruitful lives.

"*The Vault*"—Is not only part of the title of Chapter Eleven; I've preferred *The Vault*—to be the title of my next book, [scheduled for release in 2024—this is tentative, and LORD Willing!]. I'll continue The Search Process of Life in the many formations or seasons 'Life' presents. I'll not voluntarily give 'Life" away, so I know this Search process will not be futile! My '*Purpose*' is always, and will continue to be—*To Reach Out And Touch Someone!*

It's easy to get into a frenzy when we look doggedly (tenaciously) for that *misplaced something*. Sometimes I search for something I've given away—thinking it's still somewhere in my domain. Sometimes I'm looking for something I've junked—while thinking, *Why would I throw that out?* Yes, *SEARCHING* can be *laborious or painstaking.* Yes, '*Life Can Be A Challenge*' as well, even if we choose to do life in the way God intends for us to involve ourselves in life's plain old living aspect!

In another sense, Searching *can be* pleasurable and rewarding—if *Purpose* is the target. Without *Purpose,* life is futile. Imagine getting up *every morning* not knowing what the day will bring in any sense of the thought. I often remind myself of the Bill Murray movie *Groundhog Day. Every Morning* at 6 AM, Phil Conners (Bill Murry) awakes cloudy-eyed or bewildered at first because he knows he already lived this day *Yesterday!* When he 'gets it,' he establishes a *Purpose* for the day before him.

THE GREATEST STORY EVER TOLD—WHAT MIGHT THIS BE FOR YOU? FOR ME, IT'S— "UNTO US A CHILD IS BORN, A SON IS GIVEN; THE GOVERNMENT WILL BE ON HIS SHOULDER; HIS NAME WILL BE CALLED WONDERFUL, COUNSELLOR, THE MIGHTY GOD, THE EVERLASTING FATHER, THE PRINCE OF PEACE." (ISAIAH 9:6)

Summary of Chapter Twelve—*Chasing After God—What's This Like?*

Our Troubles Will Fade 'If we chase The Right Dream!'

THE NUMBER ONE SOLD BOOK of all time has about 800,000 recorded Words. As I Searched Google and Bing, it amazed me that I was hard-pressed to find an immediate recognition by the masses that The Bible was and is indeed The Number One Best Selling Book Of All Time. Guinness World Records admits to The Bible topping the list at an estimated 5 Billion copies.

I Googled "And The Number One Bestselling Book of all time is—" and without much ado, the list immediately veers away from Guinness's listing of The Bible in the 5 Billion (not knowing what year this estimate came about) section to many others listing in and around 500 Million. Yes, Guinness stands out atop for me—kudos to them for the attempt to put The Bible where it belongs.

When I Search the topic of 'Books,' the central theme on the value scale is making a difference in the lives of 'All' People Everywhere; I'm immediately disappointed by the choices that take precedence. It's virtually impossible to find consensus about how many written books there are and who holds the Numero Uno spot; the list carries on into oblivion—as far as I can determine.

People were 'Created' [as far as I'm concerned, I have never reneged on my belief about this]. If I'm to be inclusive in the sense that even God, *In The Beginning*, allowed us to choose *what we would believe*; in the 'sense' that Jesus said in John 3:16— "That Whosoever Believeth," At least I'll try to be as inclusive as God! When I say, "people were Created, or came from some other source," I'm saying that there may be someone reading 'this book' and looking at the overall picture of what I'm talking about and be thinking differently than what I think [this is their choice, to think differently—right or wrong]. Communication sources create the "Different Strokes For Different Folks" choice factor.

ANOTHER GREAT STORY IS—JESUS, THE AUTHOR AND FINISHER OF OUR FAITH, ENDURED THE CROSS TO PAY FOR OUR SINS—HE DID IT JOYFULLY BECAUSE HE SAW WHAT HIS SACRIFICE WOULD DO FOR 'US.' WHAT JESUS DID FOR US WAS TO ENCOURAGE US TO CARRY ON WHEN THE GOING GOT TOUGH! (HEBREW 12: 2-3)

Summary of Chapter Thirteen—*Out On A Limb.*
Our Troubles Will Fade 'When Jesus sits *Out On A Limb* with us.'

GOD'S WORD IS 'TO THE POINT,' and intense— God's Word is like a Double-Edged Sword—when swept forward, it cuts out the worthless things, and when pulled back, it opens the way for New Growth. God's Word takes care of the unfavourable aspects of life—He causes the favourable things to come forth. When God clears the way, His *purposes* come to fruition; it may not be Today; it may not be Tomorrow; nonetheless—It Will Happen! Let's not forget one of the main themes running the course throughout our "Read—" *Preparation, Purpose, Progress, and Preservation*!

Someone said, "*If You Build It, he Will Come*" (*A Field of Dreams*). As I understand The Bible, it reads like this in a specific place, "Come close to God, and He will come close to you!" (JBI)

"Draw nigh to God, and He will draw nigh to you. Cleanse your hands, ye sinners; and purify your hearts, ye double-minded." (James 4:8)

Please notice how the word 'double-minded' comes into play here in James 4:8. This suggestion surfaces again in Hebrews 4;12—when it uses the hyphenated word *two-edged*, in effect' (essentially or in truth) saying, *double-edged*—I'm thinking, double-minded to bring the two passages together in a somewhat conjunctive (unions 'For, And, Nor, But, Or, Yet, So') or connective ways.—God often makes these connections in The Bible—while at the same time keeping the assignment in the context of the placement of the original words. God's word will not return to Him empty of fulfilling His Purpose!

God's Word is quick, powerful, and sharper than any two-edged sword, piercing even to the dividing asunder of soul and spirit, the joints and marrow, and is a discerner of the thoughts and intents of the heart. (Hebrews 4:12)

THIS STORY NEVER ENDS—HE IS NOT HERE: FOR HE IS RISEN, AS HE SAID. COME, SEE THE PLACE WHERE THE LORD LAY. AND GO QUICKLY AND TELL HIS DISCIPLES THAT HE HAS RISEN FROM THE DEAD; BEHOLD, HE GOETH BEFORE YOU INTO GALILEE; THERE SHALL YE SEE HIM: LO, I HAVE TOLD YOU. (MATTHEW 28: 6-7)

Summary of Chapter Fourteen—*What Was I Thinking—And Why?*

Our Troubles Will Fade 'When we go Through The Valley of Despair—If we fix our eyes on Jesus!'

FINALLY—FOLKS: Let's think about the things God is thinking concerning what our lives should look like if we are trying to wear *The Badge Of Peace*! Think About It—Is it True? Is it Honest? Is it Just? Is it Pure? Is it Lovely? Does What I Am Thinking Present Like A Good Report Card? Is What I Am Thinking a picture of God's Moral Value? If My Thoughts Are Praiseworthy—I NEED TO THINK ON THESE THINGS! (Philippians 4:8; JBI)

"Don't worry about the things which are of no concern to the immediacy of the nearness of life to affect you adversely in a way which will leave you without Peace. God made provision for these things through Jesus' death and resurrection—Leave the worries in The Hands of God. Don't worry about *ANYTHING*.

We need to take the things of concern seriously enough to deal with them as Jesus would deal with them—by praying; trusting that God cares enough to help us through this *toughie* as He does with little things. Be Thankful for all God has already done; be confident He can *Do It Again*! God knows everything about our problem—YES! Share it with Him anyway.

As we go through the *Valley of Sorts*, we ought to let The Peace of God fill our Heart and Mind through what Jesus has done and what He has promised to do through the process of Trusting Him!" (Philippians 4:6&7)

Adventures are often a venture or trip into unknown territory. If our Adventure is a journey into a previously explored area, we usually know what our day will be like—that said, we should always be on the *Lookout* for the unexpected. The 'Unexpected' does not necessarily represent bad news; it's great if it isn't, but it can be an adverse experience—Be On The Lookout!

WE HAVE MORE OF THE GREATEST STORY EVER TOLD—NOW, THE DISCIPLES WATCHED AS JESUS ASCENDED HEAVENWARD IN A CLOUD, AND HE WAS SOON OUT OF THEIR SIGHT. JESUS' DISCIPLES LOOKED STEADFASTLY TOWARD HEAVEN AS HE WENT UP—IN WONDERMENT!

Summary of Chapter Fifteen—*Does God Really Care About Our Day-To-Day Living?*

Our Troubles Will Fade 'When the Hope of seeing Jesus builds up within us because of The Promises Jesus made—this will be a Banner Day!'

WHOSOEVER SHALL CONFESS THAT JESUS IS THE SON OF GOD, God dwelleth in him. And we have known and believed the love that God hath to us. God is love, and he that dwelleth in love dwelleth in God, and God in him. Herein is our love made perfect, that we may have boldness in the day of judgment: because as He is, so are we in this world. There is no fear in love, but perfect love casteth out fear: because fear hath torment. He that feareth is not made perfect in love. We love Him because He first loved us. (1 John 4: 15-19)

As we understand more about Jesus—Who He is, The Son of God—we realize that God takes up residence within our spirit. It becomes as if living physically in the dwelling—house, apartment, tent, log cabin, or any other semblance of what we call the home we live in on Planet Earth.

If someone lives in our home after they grow to a certain age, there are some reasons. Usually, when a daughter or son gets to a certain age, they feel the urgent need to get out on their own— thinking our home's restraints as parents are placing on them are too demanding.

Sometimes the children stay at home on and on and on—. The *strain on the parents* makes '*them*' want to get out and run away from the constant pressures of raising the children who are now adults. These *new adults* need to be on their own to learn about the Reality of Life. We continue loving each other, so we hope and pray, but our home becomes too small to include each other's physical and emotional desires. Birds put their young out of the nest *when it's time* to leave home.

THE PROMISES OF STORYTIME KEEP COMING—JESUS SAID HE WOULD NEVER LEAVE US OR FORSAKE US. "BEHOLD, HE COMETH WITH CLOUDS, AND EVERY EYE SHALL SEE HIM, AND THEY ALSO WHICH PIERCED HIM: AND ALL KINDREDS OF THE EARTH SHALL WAIL BECAUSE OF HIM. EVEN SO, AMEN." (REVELATION 1: 7-9)

Summary of Chapter Sixteen—*Why Should I Care About What God Thinks?*

Our Troubles Will Fade 'When we see Jesus face to face!'

BELOVED, BELIEVE NOT EVERY SPIRIT, but try the spirits to see or not whether they are of God: because many false prophets are gone out into the world. With this know ye the Spirit of God: Every spirit that confesses that Jesus Christ has come in the flesh is of God.

Every spirit that confesses not that Jesus Christ has come in the flesh is not of God: and this is that spirit of antichrist, of which ye have heard that it should come; and even now already is it in the world.

"Ye are of God, little children, and have overcome them: because greater is He in you than in the world. Therefore, they are of the world: they speak of the world, and the world heareth them. We are of God: he that knoweth God heareth us; he is not of God heareth not us. As a result, we know the spirit of truth and error.

Beloved, let us love one another: love is of God, and everyone that loveth is born of God and knows God. He that loveth not knoweth not God; for God is love. In this was manifested the love of God toward us because that God sent His only begotten Son into the world that we might live through Him. Herein is love, not that we loved God, but that He loved us and sent His Son to pay the price for our sins.

If God so loved us, Beloved, we ought also to love one another. No man hath seen God at any time. God dwelleth in us if we love one another, and He perfects His love in us. Now we know that we dwell in Him, and He in us, because He hath given us of His Spirit, and we have seen and do testify that the Father sent the Son to be the Savior of the world.

WE ALL KNOW THIS STORY—"THAT WHOSOEVER BELIEVETH IN HIM SHOULD NOT PERISH, BUT HAVE ETERNAL LIFE. GOD SO LOVED THE WORLD, THAT HE GAVE HIS ONLY BEGOTTEN SON, THAT WHOSOEVER BELIEVETH IN HIM SHOULD NOT PERISH, BUT HAVE EVERLASTING LIFE. GOD SENT NOT HIS SON INTO THE WORLD TO CONDEMN THE WORLD, BUT THAT THE WORLD THROUGH HIM MIGHT BE SAVED." (JOHN 3:15-17)

◊ THE VISTA VIEW—THE OASIS ◊

Praying always with all prayer and supplication in the Spirit and watching thereunto with all perseverance and supplication for all saints; and for me, that my words will be those which God has imparted unto me—that I may open my mouth boldly, to make known the mystery of the gospel. (Ephesians 6: 18-19)

"As I write, I'm in a continual Prayer Meeting with God. I want to make sure I'm not saying something out of line with what God had already spoken to translators who wrote The Bible to be what we have in the many translations, which can honestly serve as what the original writers meant when they wrote what they wrote.

Mysteries are often hard to articulate. When it comes to discerning and presenting the mystery of The Gospel of God, which I cannot claim to understand fully—Some things remain a mystery—but I'm satisfied by Faith in God that I don't need to know everything. God has always been in charge, and that is enough for me!" (Ephesians 6: 18-19—JBI)

I've just presented Chapter Seventeen's first page of Chapters One—Sixteen [with minor changes]. My thoughts are that after having read nearly three-hundred and fifty pages from the Cover onward, not everything will be as fresh as when you first read each page in the *Understory* of Page 320 (The End of Chapter Sixteen).

Chapter Seventeen brings some of that fodder to the fore as we begin Part Five. Chapter Eighteen—Parts One To Part Four is a Four-Part Series—A Sermon! From *The Cover Through Chapter Sixteen* of *Searching For A heart of Gold; Not A Pot of Gold—* [*Searching For The Heart of God*].

I often rephrase Bible Passages from the King James Version of The Bible. I pray that as people read my reworded paraphrases, in what I think of as plainer language—[these words I've used are those that I felt were thoughts I've gleaned from The KJV], they've gleaned an understanding they might otherwise have missed. Preachers do this all the time as they Preach Their Sermons.

This book is not a Series of Sermons—Chapters 1-16 can lead to Sermons. *Watch out in Part Five!* I'm Not A Preacher, though I have Preached—consider me as Preaching in Part Five!

HEART SENSE
We Start Young & End Up Old!

—————————————◊—————————————

HEART SENSE TELLS ME that Life can only be proper when God's Word is at The Front of The Line. Psalm 119 is a Jam-Packed Emphasis on Words about God's Word and how it effectively changes lives.

Wherewithal shall a young man cleanse his way? By taking heed to live according to Thy word. I have sought Thee wholeheartedly: O let me not wander from Thy commandments. Thy word have I hid in mine heart, that I might not sin against Thee. Blessed art Thou, O LORD: teach me Thy statutes. With my lips have I declared all the judgments of Thy mouth. I have rejoiced in the way of thy testimonies, as much as in all riches. I will meditate in Thy precepts and have respect unto Thy ways. I will delight myself in Thy statutes: I will not forget Thy word. (Psalm 119:9-15)

Here's the thing—we can talk about how we need to walk in The Presence of God. We can pay lip service so much so that it looks like we are as close as anyone could be to a right relationship with God. But if we aren't honest about it in our hearts [no judgement intended—I'm the same as everybody else—"I'm Only Human Too"], God Knows All About This Part of Our Lives.

O LORD, Thou hast searched me and known me. Thou knowest my downsitting and mine uprising; Thou understandest my thought afar off. Thou compassest my path and lying down, and art acquainted with all my ways. There is no word in my tongue, but, lo, O LORD, Thou knowest it. (Psalm 139: 1-4)

LORD, I understand how diligently You search for the *pure heart* of those You've created! You know absolutely everything about us, and that's scary. It matters not if I'm walking along a path or lying down—You are right there beside us. Then, when I open my mouth, You know even before I say anything—if I will honour You with my words or not! (Re JBI on Psalm 139: 1-4)

Next! THE SERMON—Part One—*by Jacob Bergen*

347

Scriptures In Chapter Eighteen—The Sermon—Part One
Heart Sense
Psalm 119:9-15; Psalm 139:1-4
Psalm 139
Romans 10
Proverbs 3:5-6
Psalm 139
Romans 10:13-17
2 Timothy 4:1-8; Psalm 139:1-6
Habakkuk 2; Philippians 4:13; Psalm 139
Psalm 139; 2 Corinthians 3:2-3; John 3:16
2 Corinthians 3:2-3; Psalm 139
Psalm 139
Psalm 51
Psalm 51:1-13
Psalm 139; Psalm 51

Chapter Eighteen

The Sermon—Part One

PSALM ONE HUNDRED & THIRTY-NINE

(Dedicated To Biblical Truth-Sayers—Not Nay-sayers)

While Preaching "THE SERMON," Clarifying My Sermon is uppermost in my mind—I need to Story-Out [Write-Up] a part of life that is *most relational* to the Explanation of The Passage of Scripture which will be The Sermon's Theme—Psalm 139.

ABOVE ALL!—EXPERIENCE GOD!

I'm not sure when Psalm 139 became such an integral part of The Bible for me. I tend to experience *Where* and *When* Moments. These times always lead me to be *By The Still Waters* [Psalm Twenty-Three]. As I live out the—Who, What, When, Where, Why, and How, of how GOD gets my attention—mystery accosts me. Again and again, The Central Resource of LIFE and all The Realities Life Presents, Challenge Me Greatly. What would life look like if we never had any challenges to deal with throughout the journey of our lives?

From about five to seven years back now, I've been minded (inclined) to Preach a Sermon on Psalm One-Hundred and Thirty-Nine. Being I might never have the chance to do so from *The Public Platform*, I decided to benefit from and outfit myself for this "God Allowed Moment Experience (G.A.M.E.)" to Sermonize Psalm 139 from my perspective *In The Context* of this book!

"If I ever Preach a Sermon Again," I would like to Preach Psalm One-Hundred and Thirty-Nine. The operative or active word is *AGAIN*. I've preached a time or two, or three—over time. Since I was about twelve or so, I thought I might be a Preacher—It Never Happened in the fashion of being considered a *Regular, Called By God Pulpit Preacher of The Word!*

However, What Is A Preacher Anyway—simply put, it's just someone willing to tell the Stories and Events of The Bible. The Old Hymn *Tell Me The Story of Jesus* says it well. Another Hymn that relates well here is *I Love To Tell The Story*. This song endears us to travel a Road Of Commitment! Commitment To What? Well—[*A Long Pause Is In Order—A SELAH MOMENT—*] a Commitment to be a part of fulfilling the command of Jesus to Go Into All The World and Preach The Gospel To Every Nation.

I'm aware that most people have never put their faith in Jesus Christ as Savior of the World. Jesus—The One Who Once Forgave—and still forgives us if we choose to allow Him into our lives in the relational sense, is still available to Everyone! The Bible calls us all to be Preachers—we aren't all Preachers in the *Sense We Think Of As What A Preacher Is*—A Pulpiteer! No matter who we are, *Everybody; Everybody Is A Somebody*! [Published 2018]

The Bible clarifies our need to equip [outfit] ourselves for the scenario of Preaching The Word—*Telling The Story of Jesus*—Travelling The Road of Commitment. With this in mind, I endeavour to Preach Psalm 139 in '*SFAHOG; NAPOG*' [*Searching For A Heart Of Gold; Not A Pot Of Gold*] to Journey this Narrow Road on My Bucket List! Writing— 'Getting It Out There' is One of My Commitments For Fulfilling The Great Commission—Your Road Of Commitment might differ—It's not up to me to judge. As part of this *Sermon or Sermon Series,* please allow me an 'insertion point' for one of the Greatest Preachers of all time, [at least second to Jesus Himself], to input his thoughts—Paul is the man!

Brethren, my heart's desire and prayer to God for Israel is that they might get saved. For I bear them record that they have a zeal of God, *but* <u>not according to knowledge</u>. For they being ignorant of God's righteousness, and going about to establish their righteousness, <u>have not submitted</u> <u>themselves</u> unto the righteousness of God.

For Christ is the end of the law for righteousness to everyone that believeth. For Moses describes the righteousness of the law, that the man [person] who doeth those things shall live by them. But the righteousness of faith speaketh on this wise, Say not in thine heart, *Who* shall ascend into heaven? (that is, to bring Christ down from above:)

Or Who shall descend into the deep? (that is, to bring up Christ again from the dead.) But what saith it? The word is nigh thee, even in thy mouth, and in thy heart: that is, the word of faith, which we <u>Preach</u>;

> If thou shalt confess with thy mouth the Lord Jesus and believe in thine heart that God hath raised Him from the dead, thou shalt be saved. For with the heart, man [people] believe unto righteousness; and confession is made unto salvation [*with the mouth*].

For the scripture saith, *Whosoever* believeth on Him shall not be ashamed. There's no difference between the Jew and the Greek. The same Lord is rich unto all that call upon Him. For whosoever shall call upon the name of the Lord shall be saved.

How then shall they call on Him in whom they have not believed? How shall they believe in Him of whom they have not heard? And how shall they hear without a <u>Preacher</u>? And how shall they <u>Preach</u>, except someone sends them? As it's written, How beautiful are the feet of those that <u>Preach</u> the gospel of peace and bring glad tidings of good things! <u>But they have not all obeyed the gospel</u>. For Esaias saith, Lord, who hath believed our report?

So then faith cometh by hearing and hearing by the word of God. But I say, Have they not heard? Yes, indeed, their sound went into all the earth, and their words unto the ends of the world. But I say, Did not Israel know? First Moses saith, I will provoke you to jealousy by them that are no people, and by a foolish nation, I will anger you. Esaias is very bold, and saith, I was found of them that sought Me not; I was made manifest unto them that asked not after Me. But to Israel he saith, I have stretched forth My hands unto a disobedient and gainsaying people all day long. (Romans 10)

"However, What Is A Preacher Anyway—simply put, it's just someone willing to tell the Stories and Events of The Bible. The Old Hymn *Tell Me The Story of Jesus* says it well. Another Hymn that relates well here is *I Love To Tell The Story*. This song *endears* us to travel a Road Of Commitment!" (*IBID*)"

Endear can be a complicated word—or it can be as simple as trusting God by faith—Simply Pushing *The Easy Button of God!*

> Trust in the Lord with all thine heart; and lean not unto thine own understanding. In all thy ways acknowledge Him, and He shall direct thy paths. (Proverbs 3: 5-6)

In my way of looking at things, *The Easy Button* breaks into at least two columns—Faith in God Alone and The Reality of The Temporal [In which we all must live].

I'll start with *The Reality of The Temporal* and wrap these thoughts up with *Faith In God Alone.* I like to begin explanations with The Reality of Our Present Age and Nail it down by covering the 'Why' question and saying— "because God Said SO!" In so doing, please allow me the time to share some Thesaurus Thoughts from Thesarus.com. Please thoroughly observe the following *Stack of Words* 'relating' to Endear:

> Endear: Allure, appeal to, bait, beckon, beguile, bewitch, bring, captivate, charm, come on, court, drag, draw, enchant, engage, enthral, entice, entrance, exert influence, fascinate, freak out, give the come-on, go over big, grab, hook, induce, interest, intrigue, persuade, invite, kill, knock dead, knock out, lure, magnetize, make a hit with, mousetrap, pull, rope in, score, seduce, send, slay, solicit, spellbind, steer, suck in, sweep off one's feet, tempt, turn on, vamp—WOW.

> Couple these above connections with the 'actual' Synonyms for *Endear*, and it looks like this— captivate, cherish, attach, bind, charm, engage, prize, treasure, value, win—.

Words like these synonyms and related words often seem more manageable for us to understand than the Simplicity of Faith God asks of us—song writer (Marijohn Wilkin) says— *I'm Only Human—I'm Just A Woman.* We are just human—woman, man, child—it matters not. As we live and breathe, we are temporal—the Reality [complete understanding] of all God said in The Bible may escape us at times. So we ask for, and God gives us the mercy and grace we need to get us through this season of reality we call our Humanity.

Marijohn Wilkin is a name I never recalled hearing until today. As I searched in an offhand way about this in my Sermon Chapter on Psalm 139, I found Marijohn Wilkin and the song *One Day At A Time*. Though I'd heard the song many times, the first time probably by Kris Kristofferson, it came alive for me today. While in search mode, I also came across the song *LORD Let Me Leave A Song*—by Marijohn Wilken.

Marijohn Wilkin was a huge Country Music success, but she suffered from depression and feelings that Life was not worth living. In and around 1970, she, as they say, "Found Religion" and became a New Person—following through with the term being Born Again. Then began some of the songs I like best—*One Day At A Time*; *LORD* (Co-Written with Kris Kristofferson)—*LORD, Let Me Leave A Song*.

I began with *The Reality of The Temporal* and now wrap up these thoughts in the other picture of The Two Columns I spoke of—*Faith In God Alone*.

The simplicity of Faith began in Marijohn —it changed her life. One moment, she's lost hope in the throes of despair; another moment has her saved from the dumpster—*Amazing Grace,* by John Newton, shares his experience of being salvaged by Faith. Many people's testimonies tell the same story as John Newton and Marijohn Wilken—Extensively So!

In the song *LORD, Let Me Leave A Song*, Marijohn Wilken expresses thoughts like—some folks leaving riches—others leave behind written thoughts by Paul The Apostle—but the saddest thing 'stories-out' like someone who leaves nothing of value for the sustenance of family, friends, and the world they could affect for change if they had the *Heart* to leave something good behind; like—

> Friends, Romans, countrymen, lend me your ears;
> I come to bury Caesar, not to praise him.
> The evil that men do lives after them;
> The good is oft interred with their bones;
> So let it be with Caesar. The noble Brutus
> Hath told you Caesar was ambitious:
> If it were so, it was a grievous fault,
> And grievously hath Caesar answer'd it. (Julius Caesar)

The stuff some of us leave behind is like a shadow cast on the sidewalk of life as we live it—in a single nanosecond moment, it's gone. The cry of Marijohn Wilkin in her song is to leave something lasting—something tangible, so she wanted to leave a song behind because songs are so inclusive of relationships. She alludes to what we do as servants to others—it should last beyond our lives.

Marijohn was an artist of songs. I hope I'm '*thought of*' as an artist of words—all the rest of you have the challenge and opportunity to do so as well, but everyone won't follow our artistry; there's such a reservoir of giftings in this world it's impossible to cast a number on them. For some folks, the most extraordinary artistry or gift they have may just to be a good neighbour and maybe offer a hand-up to a thirsty beggar or another hurting soul. So if we are *Just Human*—whatever that looks like for us as we endure Planet Earth, how can we understand the Simplicity of Faith In God? Faith is believing something we cannot see is alive! I refer back again to—

"However, What Is A Preacher Anyways—simply put, it's just someone willing to tell the Stories and Events of The Bible. The Old Hymn *Tell Me The Story of Jesus* says it well. Another Hymn that relates well here is *I Love To Tell The Story*. This song <u>endears</u> us to travel The Road Of Commitment!" (*IBID*)"

Faith wraps us up in hearing The Story of Jesus and His love. Faith is the act of believing the Story He Told. Faith is living The Story of Jesus—but it doesn't stop there: *Tell me the Story of Jesus*—write on my Heart every Word. We need to love to share this story as we live in so many different deportments—departments and seasons of life—share as you have received: FREELY.

We believe in the breath of life; we cannot see it—the wind will blow things about like the leaves on the trees in the fall after the frost loosens their grip on the stem. The leaves will fall when the wind blows (Side Bar: '*When The Wind Blow, The Cradle Will Rock—Rock-A-Bye Baby!*'). After this, we know the snow will come—in the colder climates. The tropical climates still have a winter season; the folks there don't think so. They may not see the change that fall and winter present, but folks from the colder climates spend the winter in the tropics.

As I see it, it's still a change—a change of attitude about life as they know it in the Frosty Fields of the North. Whether we see it or not, there are Four Seasons of the year—trust me on this one. We'll see changes in our lives year by year. Faith always requires us to believe in something we don't see. Creation or Evolution; both require Faith—not one of us was at the 'Beginning,' no matter which belief system we follow. We spend too much time disputing—not enough time looking at what God wants from us!

In Chapter Eighteen [*The Sermon—Parts One to Four*], I intend to be clear about my message—Sometimes analyzing my thoughts as per the scriptures I'm presenting—in the pattern of 'line by line' study and interpretation of The Bible.

The other side of Bible Study, which we often confuse with Exegesis (Explanation), is Eisegesis. *Eisegesis* is the pattern of interpreting a text, such as a biblical text and doing so by targeting ideas—and using scriptures as examples of said same. For instance, writing a book thematically and applying The Scriptures, like doing the writing in a Parable way—is not necessarily wrong; it's a matter of context. Today, there are so many contrary voices that it's hard to get at the truth. Schemes of every genre plague us on every hand. Please Believe The True Story.

> For whosoever shall call upon the name of the Lord shall be saved. How then shall they call on Him in whom they have not believed? And how shall they believe in Him of whom they have not heard? How shall they hear without a Preacher? And how shall they preach, except someone sends them? Someone said, How beautiful are the feet of those that preach the gospel of peace and bring glad tidings of good things! But they have not all obeyed the gospel. For Esaias saith, Lord, who hath believed our report (is anybody listening)? So, faith cometh by hearing and hearing by the word of God. (Romans 10: 13-17)

"I'm Thinking Again—" Maybe I'm in a Danger Zone Again! [Maybe I'm being factious (controversial)]—Let God Be The Judge of My Intentions. I think about Fiction (Fictitious—Imaginary) and Non-fictional Works (True Stories). Some folks read mostly Fiction; this is their forte; I like Non-Fiction; this is my bias, proclivity or desire. I struggle big time when I begin a book of fiction—No offence to those who read fiction—just not my forte.

Timothy—a student of the Apostle Paul; had a Heart for The Word of God. Paul spoke the following words to his young study.

I charge thee therefore before God, and the Lord Jesus Christ, who shall judge the quick and the dead at His appearing and His kingdom; Preach the word; be instant in season, out of season; reprove, rebuke, exhort with all longsuffering and doctrine. For the time will come when they will not endure sound doctrine; but after their lusts shall they heap to themselves teachers, having itching ears; and they shall turn away their ears from the truth and turn to fables.

But watch thou in all things, endure afflictions, do the work of an evangelist (Preacher), make full proof of thy ministry. For (because) I am now ready to be offered, and the time of my departure is at hand. I have fought a good fight; I have finished my course, I have kept 'The Faith:' Henceforth there is laid up for me a crown of righteousness, which the Lord, The Righteous Judge, shall give me at that day: and not to me only, but unto all of them also that love His appearing.

David wrote Psalm 139; Realization and Reality are front and center throughout this Psalm. Let's see Psalm 139 as a Prayer and the declaration of a Realization that's often hard to grasp. In the First Person sense, we often reflect a personal narrative, like when the writer tells a story or relates to their own experience. This perspective is the writer's point of view, becoming the focal point. What we find in Psalm 139 is—First-person pronouns are I [*1 Time*], we [*none*], me [*5 times*], us, [*none*] my, [*6 Times*] myself, [*None*] mine, [*One Time*] our, [*None*] ours [*None*] and ourselves [*None*]— in Psalm 139: 1-6 they are as noted.

With these thoughts in mind, let's look at the personal pronouns relevant to Psalm 139: 1-6. Part One—Psalm 139 as a Sermon will focus on Verses 1-6 for starters as an intro into Part Two of this as a Sermon Miniseries. But before I do, I need to do what I stated in the Intro of this Chapter—

"As I do this in a manner in which Good Preaching is most effective (transparent), I need to begin with a Story of Part of my Life which is Most Relational to The Exegesis of The Passage of Scripture which will be the Theme of The Sermon—In This Case, It Is Psalm 139—." (*IBID*)

Here Goes—

My Testimony

Being born in 1946 makes me a *Baby Boomer*—and Proud Of It! *Why do I say this?* It sounds out of sync—As per how I [personal pronoun as per David in Psalm 139: 1-6] feel. I'm proud of being a Baby Boomer—it's where I was supposed to be so I could be in the right place at the right time for the Rest of The Story of My Life to become "The Rest of The Story" of My Life and Testimony.

I'm thankful to be here today—If hope wasn't part of my Forte—If God hadn't 'been The Great 'I [Personal Pronoun accenting THE as a DEFINITE Article] Am,' there would've been no Hope! When I was about a month old, I experienced Double Pneumonia. My mom said I'd even stopped crying. Hope was nearly gone—But God!

My Mother prayed because there was nothing left to do but trust God—Pray. Doctors were not so handy. Hospitals were not so convenient. Dad was off working somewhere, so Mom had no transportation; God was all she had at the ready! Mom told God that if He healed Me (personal Pronoun as per Psalm 139: 1-6), Jacob Bergen, she would commit me to Him—The Great I Am! "God Showed!"

I've inherited some of what I am today. I've inherited bits and pieces of what I am from the people whose bloodline I've got in my genes. The character of God became evident in David, One of the Psalmists. Some of God's character breaths within us. We're "Made in The Image of God." I have specific characteristics or tendencies to do certain things in certain ways because of my parents and their parents before them. I am a "Bergen" because my Dad was a Bergen; his dad was a Bergen, and it goes back a long way. I cannot help being a "Bergen."

Being a "Bergen" isn't bad; it's good—but I don't have to be the same Bergen in every nature that every Bergen before me was. If my Great, Great, Great, Great Grandfather was not a person who outwardly showed emotions, this leaves me with no excuse for not finding the resources to make myself a better person in this way.

Over the years and through the many issues I went through, I would've come to a very different condition of life than I face today—if I hadn't made many important decisions. The matter of decision making is a Two-Part Story [and much more]—but please hear these two statements:

"I will" be responsible for physically making the final decision for my choices. (Habakkuk 2).

"I will" succeed in doing this because of my relationship with Jesus Christ. (Philippians 4:13)

Enough said about My Story here—More to come later in *About The Author* Portion. Personal Experience and Choice dictate how we will handle The Rest of The Story. After we've lived within the God-given Portion of Our Story, part of His Character also grows within us. We develop the remaining Story of Our Future by addressing the Realities of Life properly as they accost or approach us daily. Living Life successfully is a Two-Part Event: God and Us!

"As I do this in a manner in which Good Preaching is most effective, I need to begin with a Story of Part of my Life which is Most Relational to The Explanation of The Passage of Scripture which will be the Theme of THE SERMON—Psalm 139." (*IBID*)

I have just done this in part.

I'm not sure when Psalm 139 became such an integral part of The Bible for me. I tend to experience *Where* and *When* Moments. These times always lead me to be *By The Still Waters* [Psalm Twenty-Three]. As I live out the—Who, What, When, Where, Why, and How, of how GOD gets my attention—mystery accosts me. Repeatedly, The Central Resource of LIFE and all The Realities Life Presents, Challenge Me Greatly. (*IBID*)

ABOVE ALL! EXPERIENCE GOD!
A&E
NOW LET'S ACKNOWLEDGE GOD IN FULL FORCE—
HE IS ABOVE ALL!

His Word—Living (*Jesus The Living Word*)

Written (*The Bible as we have it*).

Added to the Story of Psalm 139, we can effectively insert a portion from Paul's writing when he says—

> Ye are our epistle written in our hearts, known and read of all men: Forasmuch as ye are manifestly declared to be the epistle of Christ ministered by us, written not with ink, but with the Spirit of the living God; not in tables of stone, but fleshy tables of the heart. (2 Corinthians 3:2-3)

"We are messages and or stories to be observed by the fellow persons in our world—both those closest to us like family, neighbours and friends and in the bigger picture—The Whole World. There are many avenues for each of us to explore to do so!

We are a Full Life Story as if on the New York Times Best Seller List—so let's not mess that up. It's not hard to 'blow it' if we are in it for ourselves alone. Let's not take the Personal Pronoun Approach overly seriously to the degree that we become selfies only. Like Psalm 139 says in presenting the personal pronouns as David used them. When we get 'intimate' [I'm not speaking of sexual intimacy here] with folks, there's a better chance of forming Relationships.

We are Real Life Stories to be Like Jesus Christ in fashion so much so the responsibility can be unbearable if we don't latch onto God full bore and let Him lead us by The Spirit of God in every facet of our lives. By the choices we make, we administer the authority of God to rule our lives— or we, by choice, don't give God Full Access to what was and still is His Property or Treasure—and that, from The Beginning!

Though our bodies came from the dust of the ground, we aren't now, nor have we ever been, just a handful of dirt. We were not just penned out, as if by Ink-Pen, set apart to be washed away as soon as we messed up. The history of God's Day-Timer recorded our Past, Present and Future. He made us to be more than just Stone Casts—ornaments sitting on a mantle, ready to be declared functional or not—and someday trash bound (Somewhat Re John 3:16).

Our being is more than just flesh and bone—we are destined for Greatness by Almighty God! Yes, we are as yet only human, but in The Heart of God, we exist as extensions of His love—it's up to us to accept the challenge." (2 Corinthians 3:2-3; JBI—Jacob Bergen Insight)

To get the picture in our mind of being just stone idols instead of being created as fleshly, feely, emotional beings, please carefully read the following. The masonry product we use for building quality, edging and or ornamental facing for buildings or other shapes is *Cast Stone*. We can make Cast Stone from white and grey cement, mass-produced or ordinary sands, carefully chosen scrunched sand—and inorganic colouring dyes to attain the desired colour. Though it's possible to make or change many things into something else—it's much harder to do a makeover on humans.

We experience "The Who, What, When, Where, Why and How of God." We are part of determining our position related to Him and us—we have a choice! The Central Resource of Life—The Realities of Life, present well in Psalm 139.

How we choose to do life makes us important or not. To be considered part of the Psalm 139 Story according to how God planned for our road of travel—and the twists and turns it would take—takes faith, trust and effort. God's plans are inclusive in many varied ways, so much so that we can take this Psalm '*Personal*' (as in the form of the personal pronoun fashion we looked at) and place our names and hearts in the same place David has in Psalm 139—and many other portions of The Psalms.

The Theme of Psalm 139 is that God is all-seeing, all-knowing, all-powerful, and present everywhere. God knows us, God is with us, and his greatest gift is to allow us to know him. (Author: David To the chief Musician, A Psalm of David).

LORD, Thou hast searched <u>me</u> and known <u>me</u>. Thou knowest <u>my</u> downsitting and <u>mine</u> uprising; Thou understandest <u>my</u> thoughts afar off. Thou compassest <u>my</u> path and <u>my</u> lying down, and art acquainted with all <u>my</u> ways. There is no word in <u>my</u> tongue, but, lo, O LORD, Thou knowest it. Thou hast beset <u>me</u> behind and before and laid Thine hand upon <u>me</u>. Such knowledge is too incredible for <u>me</u>; it's high, and <u>I</u> cannot attain that level. (Psalm 139: 1-6)

In these few verses of The Bible, we come to understand our frailty as humans while, at the same time, we can find Hope for the Realities we've faced, and for the shortcomings we'll all have to face down the road. Psalm 139 presents as a Two Column Story. In one column (Piece, Article—), the journalist, David, realizes the innate component of his makeup—Dirt. At the same time, he is whacked in the head by reality; he recognizes God as Someone who is At The Ready for him in his times of need—At All Times!

In The Second Column, we have God. God doesn't say a word in Psalm 139—He just sits back and LISTENS to David as he "Pours Out His Heart." God watches as David presents the Reality of Life as he sees it playing out for him. He watches David open his eyes to acknowledge the overriding presence of Himself being in the scope of David's Plan for Life.

'God Is' and presents Omnipotence, Omniscience, and Omnipresence—these are huge words; in simple terms, they just say God Is All-Powerful; God Knows Everything— "Period." 'God Is' present in the whole of His Creation—in that we can access Him anywhere and at any time we need Him! 'God Is' also Always (Omni) Personal—Personally Relational.

Let's look at what OMNI means in words that better present God's Greatness! Omni is a Prefix—a word, letter, or number placed before another to give a fuller picture—the prefix introduces the topic which it precedes—we might call 'Omni" a 'Headliner.'

When we say God is Omnipotent, we are simply saying He can do anything He wants to do without any help from us—though He chooses to use us to help facilitate or fulfill His Plans on this *mortal coil* we call Earth. Some adequate words related to this are— everything, whole, all, complete, overall, the total, all-inclusive, all-or-nothing; all-powerful, almighty, supreme, most high, preeminent, invincible, unconquerable, unstoppable! We could say much more to this, but the message is already evident.

When we say 'God Is' Omniscient, we simply say He is All-knowing, all-seeing, almighty, infinite, knowledgeable, preeminent, wise, intelligent, all-knowing, all-wise, well-informed, heavenly, celestial, deific, hallowed, divine blessed, immortal, boundless, deathless, everlasting, enduring, pervading, eternal illimitable, unlimited, endless, ceaseless—. God chooses to use us to help facilitate or fulfill His Plans on Planet Earth.

In these and many more earthly ways, His purpose is always Spiritual, Eternal—not just for today. The resources we have to explain God's attributes, characteristics, and qualities are nearly limitless as we see things. God sees way beyond what we can Only Imagine! We get the message, don't we?

If the description of Omnipotent and Omniscient isn't enough to explain Who and What 'God Is,' let's add—'God Is' Omnipresent—this looks like is that 'God Is'—ubiquitous, universal, general, global, prevalent, communal, pervading, worldwide, pervasive, extensive, rife, predominant, boundless, infinite, ubiquity everywhere, far-reaching, wall-to-wall, wide-ranging, present everywhere, all-pervasive, all-present, ever-present, all over, widespread, pandemic (a word we shudder to hear any more about in our world today), permeating, all-embracing!

Let's take in the whole scenario of Omnipotent, Omniscient, Omnipresent, and for the moment, add 'Omnirelational—' a word left undefined, which I conjured up in a *drifty mode mentally*. We could discard all the descriptive comments and 'simply' say that GOD IS ENOUGH! He is more than anything we could conjure up!

Any Message here must include, at least for me, Psalms 51 because it puts me in touch with my frailties and inabilities and puts my care into the hands of God where it belongs now and has continuously resided—(*OMNI*) be available to us.

> Have mercy upon me, O God, according to Thy lovingkindness—according to the multitude of Thy tender mercies blot out my transgressions. Wash me thoroughly from mine iniquity, and cleanse me from my sin. For I acknowledge my transgressions: and my sin is ever before me.

> Against Thee, Thee only, have I sinned, and done this evil in Thy sight: that Thou might be justified when Thou speakest, and be clear when Thou judgest. Behold, I was shaped in iniquity, and my mother conceived me in sin. Behold, Thou desirest truth in the inward parts: and in the hidden part Thou shalt make me know wisdom. Purge me with hyssop, and I shall be clean: wash me, and I shall be whiter than snow.

> Make me hear joy and gladness; that the bones Thou hast broken may rejoice. Hide Thy face from my sins and blot out all my iniquities.

Create in me a clean heart, O God, and renew a right spirit within me. Cast me not away from Thy presence and take not Thy Holy Spirit from me. Restore unto me the joy of Thy salvation and uphold me with Thy free spirit. Then will I teach transgressors Thy ways, and sinners shall be converted unto Thee. (Psalm 51: 1-13)

In the setting of these verses, we should find ourselves with open eyes and ears. Our Hearts and everything we could imagine to The Extended Possibilities only God can facilitate, manage, and or bring about for this World and The World to come—are ready for us—there for the taking!

If God Wants To Search For Me—Why Would I Not Want To Search For Him? In a world of mixed emotions and perceptions about Life and a Season of Eternity, is it problematic or a mixed bag for us to even try to figure out? God says I'll Take The Lead—You Follow, and everything will be JUST FINE; *"not 'just' fine."* When it seems the Eternity as we expect it to be—A Season Of Time when life is seemingly all about "US" as we perceive it—does not pan out; What Then?

Well, it's here we need to know Who and What God is; as we examine ourselves, we will begin to explore "US" shortly as we delve into Psalm 139. We just scratched the surface of Psalm 139 in sharing the first six verses to bring out Column One [Us] and Column Two [God], which help us begin to walk through this Chapter—*Parts One to Part Four.*

It's vital to know 'Who and What God' is—and 'When, Where, and Why' also confronts us as we try to figure God out. The question always surfaces as to 'How' can we get close enough in our skin to say—I KNOW HIM!

Yes, we need to know what God is and what He most sincerely wants for us in a relationship sense as we live within the humanity He created—what is our part to play?

God is The Omni-Relational God

Semper Fidelus!

Always Faithful!

Always Loyal

—God Never Fails—

There's a vivid picture to encapsulate (capture) as we open up to Psalm 139. I see a *Hungry Person* [David]; he's not starving for *Deer Steak Sandwich*; David is Hungering After A Fill-up of The Presence of God To Be Evident In His Life! Why? Because David realizes Who God Is!

As I approach the end of Part One of THE SERMON, a song comes *subtlety* (beautifully, cautiously, gracefully, softly, daintily) into my spirit. *"Pour Out My Heart"* (by Matt Redman).

I see David telling God, "I'm here LORD, down on my knees again—Here's My Heart LORD, I'm pouring it out before You as I melt before Your Awesome Presence." David knows God is listening. Even when David was in one of those 'Low Times,' which often plagued him (Psalms 51), he poured his heart into God.

> "Create in me a clean heart, O God, and renew a right spirit within me. Cast me not away from thy presence and take not thy holy spirit from me. Restore the joy of thy salvation and uphold me with thy free spirit."

I suggest we take an OASIS MOMENT here to reflect on the vast volume of information I've left for us to digest regarding Psalm 139. What we have just walked through is Part One of The Sermon Series of Chapter Eighteen—Psalm One-Hundred And Thirty-Nine—THE SERMON.

I will try to stick tightly to the actual twenty-four verses of the Chapter as I walk through in a manner that hopefully leaves us feeling like we are traversing The Twenty-Third Psalm.

The LORD Is My Shepherd

◊ THE VISTA VIEW—THE OASIS ◊

As I read Psalm 23, no matter which Bible Version I read, I feel like I'm at "THIS OASIS!" What am I before I reach this "PLAZA HOTEL" 'Off In The Desert?' Words that come to mind are: DEPLETED—of all physical resources; THIRSTY—near death's door physically and emotionally. SPIRITUALLY EMPTY—I haven't got a HOPE—Or So It Seems! Until—!

"God is good to Israel, to those with a clean heart. My fleet were almost gone; my steps had slipped a few paces. I was spiteful towards the foolish when I saw the success of those different than I thought was. These folks seem to defy death, but their strength appears firm. Trouble seems to be their middle name; they don't have other people's concerns. Pride hangs around them like a chain; they are dressed as if their garment was made of porcupine quills—no one can touch their heart or demeanour.

These folks already seem to have more than what desire can provide—they speak sharply about the oppression of others. They set their hearts against spiritual things, and they rattle on mindlessly as if they know it all—they say, how does God, if there is a God, know anything? How intelligent could He be?

I've tried so hard to please God, and what do I get for it? Every morning I wake up from this useless existence to do it again. If I say, I'll speak such and keep on keeping on, by suggesting an answer, I might offend someone. While trying to come to grips with the issues of life, it became too painful for me; until I went to an OASIS where I knew God would be—then I understood the end of those who did not call God their God and did not call out to Him!"— [*JBI; Jacob Bergen Insight as per Psalm 73*].

Chapter Eighteen The Sermon Part Two Scriptures

Heart Sense
Psalm 119; Isaiah 9:6
Psalm 139
Psalm 139; Psalm 23
Ezekiel 34: 1-31
Ezekiel 34; Psalm 23; Psalm 139:19-22; 1 Kings 19:2-8
1 Corinthians 2
Psalm 139
Psalm 139
Jeremiah 29:13; Psalm 139:3
Psalm 139; Psalm 23; Psalm 56:3-11
Psalm 139:6
The Vista View—The Oasis
Psalm 42:11; Romans 12:18
Psalm 56:4
Heart Sense
Psalm 139:7-13

HEART SENSE
Lord; Hear My Prayer

───────────────◊───────────────

HEART SENSE FOR THE SERMON—Part Two points us conclusively to the issue of Leadership. Psalm 119 offers a full slate of directives confirming to us, as God's servants, that we need to acknowledge Leadership—in this case, everything points *indisputably* to God as our *First Place Scenario Leader*

It's generally thought that Ezra The Priest wrote Psalm 119. Priests are leaders—but God is our Number One Leader. Psalm 119 firmly states the importance of The Word of God as it talks about The Law of The LORD, The Testimonies of The LORD, The Commands of The LORD, The Precepts of God, The Statutes of God, The Judgements of God, The Works of God, The Way of God, The Way of Truth and God's Word—. 'The Bible tells us that God magnified His Word above even His Name—in Psalm 138: 1-4.'

I will praise Thee with my whole heart: before the gods will I sing praise unto Thee. I will worship toward Thy holy temple and praise Thy name for Thy lovingkindness and truth: Thou hast magnified Thy WORD above all Thy name. In the day when I cried, Thou answerest me and strengthened me with strength in my soul. All the kings of the earth shall praise Thee, O LORD when they hear the words of Thy mouth.

God's Word is True! God's Word is Wonderful, His Word Counsels, He's The Mighty God, He's The Everlasting Father, and God's Word brings Peace. God's Word Teaches us all we'll ever need to get through the storms of life, and God's Word will get us through to Eternity—with Him!

For unto us a Child is born, God gave to us His Son: and the government shall be upon His shoulder: and His name shall be called Wonderful, Counsellor, The Mighty God, The Everlasting Father, The Prince of Peace. (Isaiah 9:6)

Heart Sense tells me that Life lived in proper union with God's Word will bear a magnitude of fruit, the mystery of which we might never understand—leastwise in our allotted time on the present earth.

Next! THE SERMON—Part Two—*by Jacob Bergen*

Chapter Eighteen

The Sermon—Part Two

◇

PSALM ONE HUNDRED & THIRTY-NINE

(Dedicated To Biblical Truth-Sayers—Not Nay-Sayers)

WE ARE ALL PREACHERS; we're not each on different levels value-wise; we all live our STORY differently. I dedicate Chapter Eighteen to Preachers—YES—because God calls some to Special Stories [Ministries and or the use of The Special Gift we each have to affect someone else for The Kingdom of God] in The Giving Out of The Scriptures Sense; to live out as leaders. Why? Because many people are more FOLLOWERS orientated, most people need to have a Headship [Like A Group of Warships heading into Battle—Like a Gaggle of Geese gathering at a predetermined place in time]. In a sense just described, we may call them Pastors, Teachers, and Missionaries.

Imagine this whole scenario by thinking about the Human Body—without our head (the Brain leads our Life) physically, the rest of our body is, in effect, useless. God holds Pastors more responsible. After all, they are Leaders in his Kingdom of Leaders because they become Shepherds. A Shepherd without an effective Leader is not much use, and they will lead their sheep blindly—The Blind Leading The Blind—leading to mega destruction in the end! So, if you desire to be in leadership—it isn't all Glory Road!

We are establishing an entry point to cast a Forward Focus on Psalm One-Hundred & Thirty-Nine. I could begin to do this by starting at verse 1 of Psalm 139, where it reads, *"O LORD, thou hast searched me, and known me."* All this is good, but though it says *'Thou hast'* and tells me there was a starting point, it does not give me the address of that beginning.

We could check out Genesis 1:1; it's the ultimate starting position of all God said and did in that 'Beginning.' It was and is the address for finding out Why we are Where we are today in the mess of sinfulness we find ourselves. We could rightly suggest this was the sufficient address for Psalm 139: 1

Genesis One led to the forwarding or mailing address outside The Garden of Eden. However, when I try to nail down the inception or birth point of what David explains to us in Psalm 139, I find The Genesis Story is a bit too distant for me to get the perspective nestled down gently enough to be invitational enough here.

At the moment, I don't wish to focus so much on the sinfulness aspect of Genesis. I want to address or start us in Psalm 139 in a fashion that will point to our need for refreshment and comfort for the time after we have served well and hard in our Walk With God.

Sometimes, I need a '*hand up*' instead of *Why Have You Not Done Better?* There are many Scriptures previous to Psalm 23 which will get us to where we need to go in the moment; however, My Heart seems fixed on Psalms 23 because this is where David, the author of Psalm 139, found what I am trying to get at here.

According to my search results, David was about thirty when he began his Kingship, and he ruled for forty years—making him about seventyish when he wrote Psalm 23. Some Scholars suggest David was elderly, which indicates that he was weary after all the battles he fought and all the threats to his leadership. It seems he needed an 'Oasis Point' to have the strength to move ahead. I feel it was here that David reflected on a quieter, more refreshing Selah Moment to fill his tank. In my opinion, this initiated the inception of Psalm 23 and augmented or enhanced the 23rd. Psalm.

Psalm 23

The Lord Is My Shepherd; I Shall Not Want.

What may I ask is sheep's focal point to keep them safe and secure? —The Shepherd. If I might use this trust, faith-based word to describe a flock of sheep, their confidence is one-sided or singularly focused. Whether we call it 'confidence' or 'instinct' doesn't matter much; sheep rely on a 'focal point' to survive!

We call Christians a "Flock." So, are we just a bunch of animals as described by atheistic doubters? Please, let's peruse a lengthy portion that hits on this point; let's try to deduce or understand how all this fits Psalm 139.

And the word of the Lord came unto me saying, Son of man, prophesy against the shepherds of Israel, prophesy, and say unto them, thus saith the Lord God unto the shepherds; woe be to the shepherds of Israel that do feed themselves! Should not the shepherds feed the flocks?

Ye eat the fat, and ye clothe you with the wool, ye kill them that are fed, but ye feed not the flock. The diseased have ye not strengthened, neither have ye healed that which was sick, neither have ye bound up that which was broken, neither have ye brought again that which was driven away, neither have ye sought that which was lost; but with force and with cruelty have ye ruled them. And they were scattered because there was no shepherd, and they became meat to all the beasts of the field when they were scattered.

My sheep wandered through all the mountains, and upon every high hill; yea, My flock was scattered upon all the face of the earth, and none did search or seek after them. Therefore, ye shepherds, hear the word of the Lord; as I live saith the Lord God, surely because My flock became a prey and My flock became meat to every beast of the field because there was no shepherd, neither did my shepherds search for My flock but the shepherds fed themselves and fed not my flock.

Therefore, O ye shepherds, hear the word of the Lord; thus saith the Lord God; behold, I'm against the shepherds; and I will require My flock at their hand and cause them to cease from feeding the flock; neither shall the shepherds feed themselves anymore for I will deliver My flock from their mouth that they may not be meat for them.

For thus saith the Lord God; behold, I, even I, will search My sheep and seek them out. As a shepherd seeketh out his flock in the day that he is among his scattered sheep, I will seek out My sheep and deliver them out of all places where they have been scattered in the cloudy and dark day— [God is The Shepherd that can and will lead according to His Eternal plan].

And I will bring them out from the people and gather them from the countries, and will bring them to their own land, and feed them upon the mountains of Israel by the rivers and in all the inhabited places of the country.

I will feed them in a good pasture and upon the high mountains of Israel shall their fold be; there shall they lie in "a good fold and in a fat pasture" shall they feed upon the mountains of Israel.

I will feed My flock and I will cause them to lie down saith the Lord God. I will seek that which was lost, and bring again that which was driven away, and will bind up that which was broken, and will strengthen that which was sick; but I will destroy the fat and the strong; I will feed them with judgment.

And as for you, O My flock, thus saith the Lord God; behold, I judge between cattle and cattle, between the rams and the he goats. Seemeth it a small thing unto you to have eaten up the good pasture, but ye must tread the residue of your pastures with your feet? You have drunk of the deep waters, but ye must foul the residue with your feet?

And as for My flock, they eat that which ye have trodden with your feet and they drink that which ye have fouled with your feet.

Therefore thus saith the Lord God unto them; behold, I, even I, will judge between the fat cattle and between the lean cattle. Because ye have thrust with side and shoulder, and pushed all the diseased with your horns, till ye have scattered them abroad; therefore will I save My flock and they shall no more be a prey and I will judge between cattle and cattle.

And I will set up one shepherd over them and he shall feed them, even my servant David; he shall feed them, and he shall be their shepherd. And I the Lord will be their God, and My servant David a prince among them; I the Lord have spoken it.

And I will make with them a covenant of peace and will cause the evil beasts to cease out of the land and they shall dwell safely in the wilderness, and sleep in the woods. And I will make them and the places around My hill a blessing; and I will cause the shower to come down in his season; "there shall be showers of blessing.

And the tree of the field shall yield her fruit, and the earth shall yield her increase, and they shall be safe in their land, and shall know that I am the Lord, when I have broken the bands of their yoke and delivered them out of the hand of those that served themselves of them. And they shall no more be a prey to the heathen, neither shall the beast of the land devour them; but they shall dwell safely, and "none shall make them afraid."

And I will raise a plant of renown for them, and they shall be no more consumed with hunger in the land, neither bear the shame of the heathen anymore. Thus shall they know that I the Lord their God am with them and that they, even the house of Israel, are my people, saith the Lord God. And ye My flock, the flock of My pasture, are men (and women), and I'm your God, saith the Lord God. (Ezekiel 34: 1-31—straight-forward KJV)

Ezekiel prophesied quite a mouthful; it's like he and David got together for a consult when David penned the words he did in Psalm 23; and, might I add, Psalm 139! Let's just read the rest of Psalm 23 within the context of Ezekiel 34 and move on with a Forward Focus.

"He maketh me to lie down in green pastures: He leadeth me beside the still waters. He restoreth my soul: He leadeth me in the paths of righteousness for His name's sake. Yea, though I walk through the valley of the shadow of death, I will fear no evil: Thou art with me; Thy rod and Thy staff comfort me. Thou preparest a table before me in the presence of mine enemies: Thou anointest my head with oil; my cup runneth over.

Surely goodness and mercy shall follow me all the days of my life: and I will dwell in the house of the Lord forever." (Psalm 23)

As I read Psalm 23—I feel I'm entering a Gated Community, only accessible if I have the Code. In the case of the Christian (Born Again' Person), it means people who have a Personal Relationship with Jesus; they have the Key or the Code. In my words, the Gated Community I speak of is "THE OASIS" we are exploring. We have a clear picture of how intimately God Searches us out to couple us to Himself Relationally. With these thoughts in mind, I'm thinking of how a Relationship includes having Fellowship with God!

After reading Ezekiel 34 and Psalm 23, apart from Psalm 139: 19-22—A person might quickly come to grips with almost everything in the rest of the verses— [succinctly or briefly].

God Cares About what He Created—God Cares About Us So Much—He spread much detail on the drawing board and sorted it all out to the Best Case Scenario!

<u>Psalm One Hundred & Thirty-Nine</u>

So, I've nestled down Psalm 139 into The 23rd Psalm as a Place Setting on the Dinner Table—and bedded it down for a refreshing respite. I've waded through Seventeen Chapters of Info Style Writing to get into some Deeper Heart Stuff—into Human Feelings and God's Feelings. I'm trying to blend at least Two Sections of The Book of The Psalms to be as if served up at a feast at The Oasis surrounded by Desert Sands, but feeling the whole world is now The Oasis.

As David is writing to the Chief Musician here in Psalm 139, it seems appropriate to begin with a song. A considerable volume of songs tells well the story of what David must have had in his heart when he wrote this Psalm and others. It reminded me of John Newton writing *Amazing Grace*. The story he tells in Amazing Grace clearly shows us the Love and Forgiving Heart of God so profoundly that he had trouble maintaining composure.

Just about now, I get a nudge—more like a heavy push as if saying— 'This Is My Time'—My Time to receive from God what Elijah so badly needed when he was on the run from Jezebel.

"And Ahab told Jezebel all that Elijah had done, and withal how he had slain all the prophets with the sword. Then Jezebel sent a messenger unto Elijah, saying, So let the gods do to me, and more if I make not thy life as the life of one of them by tomorrow about this time. And when he saw that, he arose, and went for his life, and came to Beersheba, which belongeth to Judah, and left his servant there. But he himself went a day's journey into the wilderness and came and sat down under a juniper tree: and he requested for himself that he might die; and said, <u>It is enough; now, O LORD, take away my life; for I am not better than my fathers.</u> And as he lay and slept under a juniper tree, behold, an angel touched him and said, "Arise and eat.""

"And he looked, and, behold, there was a cake baken on the coals, and a cruse of water at his head. And he did eat and drink and laid him down again. And the angel of the LORD came again the second time, touched him, and said, "Arise and eat; because the journey is too great for thee."

And he arose, and did eat and drink, and went in the strength of that meat forty days and forty nights unto Horeb the mount of God." (1 Kings 19: 1-8)

Let's put ourselves into a *Selah* moment for a while— 'Our Time Moment' and try to FEEL The Moment so that it's challenging to keep any sense of composure in this The Presence of God! As we sing vocally or in our spirit, the Heart Song which comes to bear in This Moment for each of us, let's open this Worship Session in The Presence of God with PRAISE. I am listening to a Shane and Shane song as presented by The Brooklyn Tabernacle Choir— ["PSALM 23 (Surely Goodness, Surely Mercy)" sung by the Brooklyn Tabernacle Choir].

"The Lord is my Shepherd I Shall Not Want"

In The Spirit of Praise, the song continues to do just that—Praise God!

[Then the words of their song point to a place where God has prepared an Oasis—Green Pastures in which to lie down for respite.]

A Mind of Soul Restoration focuses here as God leads Me on after My Hard Times in Victory for His Name's Sake— For me [*and you*] to carry the torch in Jesus's Name!

I want to post the song lyrics directly, but because of Copyright Laws and appreciation for other people's rights to their property, I will just leave you with access to this song at the following link.

"PSALM 23 (Surely Goodness, Surely Mercy)" sung by the Brooklyn Tabernacle Choir - YouTube

The song By The Rivers of Babylon also came into my spirit 'first thing' this morning and caused me to reflect on why my hard times come. Hard Times come to drive me to The Oasis—The Selah Reflection Moment—to lift my voice and Heart to Praise This Awesome God, which Psalm 139 brings to us. It not only shares the 'About Factor,' but with a willing spirit, it forces me to fall and Worship God from an almost hidden place deep within me!

As I write this portion, I enter into this My Moment before This Awesome God. I struggle somewhat to get into Psalm 139 because of the felt need to Prepare my Heart and Yours to Praise and Worship God first and foremost before we attempt to fulfill any of our Greatest dreams for God! Right now, it is tough for me to keep My Composure!

To the chief Musician, A Psalm of David.

So, <u>knowing</u> The Holy Spirit will fill our hearts with songs we worship God with, I'll now delve into The Meat of The WORD—The LIVING WORD—Think JESUS as we do!

The Heart of Worship

Psalm One Hundred & Thirty-Nine

O LORD, thou hast searched me and *known* me.

The 1st thought I have here of the many 'R' words I've stored is *Realization*. My Sense at the outset of this Psalm [139] is that when David wrote Psalm 23, he <u>Remembered</u> those times he had in the Sheep Fold [sheep pen] with his sheep. As I tag this thought to God [Who has us in His Sheep Fold], I see how God *Remembers* the times He has with us when we yield ourselves to Him in Worship— seeing us as just wanting more of Him! Not more stuff, but more of Him in just wanting to KNOW Him better at this moment than the moment just past. We attain awareness (realization) through Remembrance.

Behold, what manner of love the Father hath bestowed upon us, that we should be called the *children* [sons] of God: therefore (1 Cor. 2) the world knoweth us not, because it <u>knew</u> Him not. Beloved, now are we the sons [children]of God, and it doth not yet appear what we shall be: but we know that, <u>when He shall appear, we shall be like Him; for we shall see Him as He is</u>.

And *everyone* who hath this hope in Him purifieth *themselves*, [himself] even as He is pure. (1 John 3: 1-3)

2nd *God Searched for us*. In an Earthly Sense, I see God making a *Resolution* to Ransack [scour] all Life through Eternity— Past, Present, and Future—Just to find us who'd lost our way!

We've all probably lost something Very Dear to us—often something of immense physical value; something of a more human value, 'A Family' member—.' If we search hard, we may find this entity of Physical Value, which we may have just misplaced—and joy to overflowing comes for us at that moment! God cares not so much about the Physical things of life we have [Although I think He may]—the earthly things. I've said it before—we cannot have a Spiritual life until after we have Physicality—we are born as a child.

When we lose a Family Member [in death], we can search Planet Earth, and we will never find that person still alive. We can go to the graveside placement of this loved one; we don't lose them in this sense; we know where their remains are. They are lost to us in this life except for remaining in our Memory.

God cares a whole lot when we have lost a Family Member, and He helps us through our grieving process when we Worship Him! When we have a relationship with God, Jesus, through The Holy Spirit, we will again see this loved one who is still breathing the Breath of Real Life in The Eternity God has prepared for us. God can and has Searched for the lost sheep [us]. He can, does, and will find us and offer us Fellowship and a Relationship with Him for Eternity. Our part—accept His invitation to The Family of God!

The 3rd note here in Psalm 139: 1 is that God did not just search for us—and put us on one of His mantle shelves to look at us from time to time like a trophy. When God looks at All He has done, He says— "It Is Very Good!" In the 1st verse, David *realizes* one significant key element about God—God Wants To KNOW Us Intimately! God knows all about us! He ultimately cares about all we have reservations and apprehensions about in our hearts. We will come closer to understanding this as we move onward with a Forward Focus!

<u>Thou</u> *knowest* [*verb*] my downsitting and mine uprising, Thou understandest my thought afar off.

Verses 2 and 4 reacquaint us with the word Known (vs. 1) [verb (Past Tense)]. In verses two and four, we have *Knowest*, which represents a list of things God looks after in our lives in the present tense. The physicality of standing up and sitting down; these seem like such menial or tedious matters—we might think, 'Big Deal,' what's that got to do with life, in so far as being essential or not.

Well, wait until we can't do either, or we need to lay in bed twenty-four-seven—then we might *realize* how God even cares about these seemingly insignificant things. As long as we can stand and sit, we have the mobility to do many more necessary and even many exciting things: run, walk, skate, ski—. When we cannot stand up or sit down, even then, God can be there for us—this is where it gets contradictory as far as whether or not God cares. When we are disabled, *the evidence of us being in need is right on our doorstep*!

Maybe the answer here is not too exciting for us—but we can still Pray, Encourage someone else not to give up when they face the trials of accidents that may temporarily or permanently hinder their progress. There's a man I've read about and heard Preach, who has no arms, legs—Nick Vujicic. Another blind man I know of climbs mountains—Erik Weihenmayer: The Blind Adventurer Who Conquered Mount Everest And The Grand Canyon. Sure, I'd rather have all my faculties and live what I think of as everyday life—what's the Big Deal about being normal? These folks believe they are normal—I agree; when I see the example they leave us, it would be a shame to think of them as abnormal.

God even cares about these people because He has given them the ingenuity to figure out other means of accomplishing life in Big Ways.

Psalm 139: 2 offers another hard-to-understand mention— *Understanding* what people do and say when we are in physical contact with them—on the phone, texting, videos, photos, movies— and much more. Many folks believe in Telepathy; some say they have had this experience. 'What could we call this gift if it does exist;' I cannot cover this base with any understanding on the physical level, nor do I wish to dispute with anyone on the issue. There are many things *I don't understand*, and that's okay.

David, The Psalmist, understood the fact of telepathy—or might I just say David had been in touch with God often enough to tell us God even knows what we are thinking—a scary thought. To understand this, we need to believe in Someone or something without ever seeing that Person—and yes, God is a Person—JESUS. David says God not only *Knows* our thoughts from somewhere way out there [some say we'd have to be 'way out there' to believe this kind of stuff].

God knows what we are thinking; He knows WHY we consider what we are thinking. He understands our motive for believing what we are thinking. He knows the legitimacy of said same thoughts. He can help us work through the issues of those thoughts we hide from the public. "What An Awesome God we have or can have!"

There's a trilogy in verse one I don't want us to miss—. First— 'Thou—' represents us coming to where we acknowledge there is Someone Way out there somewhere, while at the same time, He is always present with us everywhere and always faithful to be there for us in our darkest hour. The Second Part of The Trilogy is He's not lazy—God says, "*But seek ye first the kingdom of God and his righteousness, and all these things shall be added unto you.*" (Matthew 6:33) God is semper-available! (Always Available)

Thirdly, God knows the difficulty we have in understanding the totality of His being.

Acknowledge God—Know He is always looking for the Lost Ones—He knows every circumstance we face in coming to decide whether or not to believe in Him. God knows these things from a time we cannot imagine—before the foundation of Everything.

The onus or responsibility to know God is on us to look for God in the many ways He shows Himself to Lost Humanity—He does reveal Himself; we need to be on the LOOKOUT!

> And ye shall seek Me and find Me when ye shall search for Me with all your heart. (Jeremiah 29:13)

> Thou compassest my path and my lying down, and art acquainted with all my ways. (Psalm 139:3)

LORD, You fasten Your eye on me every day—not on me alone but every part of Your Creation. As I leave my home, You prepare the first step before I make it—when I come home, You welcome me at the door. I feel David has these thoughts as he works *out* his feelings about God! Nothing we do escapes the care of God—we can prove this as we accept Him; these things display clarity.

> I will instruct thee and teach thee in the way which thou shalt go; I will guide thee with My eye. (Psalm 32:8)

> There's no word in my tongue, but, lo, O LORD, Thou knowest (verb) it *all together*. (Psalm 139: 4)

In one sense, I picture God in the framework of a *Verb*—He is always working things out for our overall good. We may think we can keep secrets from God—Not So! We may whisper a thought in another person's ear because we may be planning something on the '*Sly*;' God hears this, and He knows the motive of our Heart before we even whisper it. When we get to Verse seven, we'll listen to David asking where he could hide from God—if he even wanted to.

We can curb this inclination to hide because of how lavishly God provides *The Oasis* in the 'desert' of our days. When we look back to Psalm 23, —God spreads out the Banquet Buffet in the middle of The Desert—The Wasteland; He would do it if I were the only person in that place. I would need to proceed cautiously so as not to get a '*tummy ache*.' We might say—it's best to watch what we think to say.

> Thou hast beset (surrounded, overwhelmed) me behind and *before* and laid Thine hand upon me.

While amid our troubles—when we are in a quandary about many things happening in this messed up world we try to live peacefully within—David says God still has us in the palm of His Hands (laid thine hand upon me).

> What time I'm afraid, I will trust in Thee. I will praise His word; In God; I have put my trust; I will not fear what flesh can do unto me. Every day they wrest my words: all their thoughts are against me for evil. They gather together; they hide and mark my steps while waiting for my soul. Shall they escape by iniquity? in Thine anger cast down the people, O God.
> Thou tellest my wanderings: put my tears into thy bottle: are they not in Thy book? My Enemies Shall Turn Back when I cry unto you: this I know; for God is for me. In God will I praise His word: in the Lord will I praise His word. I have trusted God: I will not be afraid of what man (people) can do unto me. (Psalm 56:3-11)

LORD—PLEASE HELP ME UNDERSTAND HOW NEAR YOU ARE!

Such knowledge is too incredible for me; it is high, and I cannot attain it. (Psalm 139:6)

As I read this verse with which I will trek off to finish Part Two of Chapter Eighteen (of This Sermon Series) of *Searching For A Heart of Gold; Not A Pot of Gold*; while reaching for Part Three, I felt The Holy Spirit of God lead me to a George Beverly Shea song called, *The Wonder Of It All*. As I listened to it, my spirit began a meltdown in the presence of God—I thought, Oh, How Awesome is this God? We have the privilege of KNOWING HIM!

I hear words akin to the wonder of a sunset; if this isn't enough, thoughts of sunrise again the next day come alive within me. Bev. Shea then expresses something much Greater than even these manifestations—The Greatest Wonder of All is JESUS! God Loves Us! If this does not touch every fibre of our being, we may as well be a carved statue—not at the hands of God The Potter, but only at the hands of someone who can swing a hammer and chisel. God never used a hammer and chisel to make us—He took a handful of clay with His own hands, moulding us to fit with all of His characteristics—Love being the GREATEST CHARACTERISTIC!

Springtime, harvest, sky, sun, moon, and stars cannot hold a candle to The Wonder of Jesus!

Such knowledge is too outstanding for me; it is high, and I cannot contain it. (Psalm 139:6)

As I came to this place in writing these words, I began today with the song *I Sing Praises To Your Name* (by Terry MacAlmon March 10 Release 2000) ringing in my ears, and I proceeded to listen to it and sing it as a backdrop on Youtube all Day Long. I feel like I've gone to Heaven—If this is what Heaven will be like, all I'll want to do is Worship Jesus for Eternity!

◊ THE VISTA VIEW—THE OASIS ◊

—My Tribute To God!—
From Everlasting—To Everlasting
"You Are God!

—To You—

'THE WORLD'

"Why art thou cast down, O my soul? And why art thou disquieted within me? Hope thou in God: for I shall yet praise Him, who is the health of my countenance, and my God." (Psalm 42:11)

Why is the World Distraught (Troubled)? Why are we Troubled individually within ourselves Day-In and Day-Out? Why is there no Peace in The World that can Comfort Us? The Health of our appearance, expression, and the spirit within us can only *sufficiently be suffonsified* (weighed-out, determined or gauged) within a Relationship With Christ!

We are *hard-pressed* to find the phrase or expression 'sufficiently suffonsified' in our dictionaries or thesauruses. The term seems to be about a hundred years old—some say it came from The Upper Great Lakes (Ontario/Michigan), and it's thought initially to come from the phrase, "My sufficiency is suffonsified." The term suggests that if we have any more than this, we are of a greedy spirit of selfish desire!

The leadership of the World is in Trouble!
God In The Person of Jesus Christ Is The Answer!

My supposition or assumption is that we are following the wrong leaders as our eternal destiny is at stake. I realize we should follow the Leaders who have our best interest at heart; these are generally our elected Leaders—many do—and some do not. As far as the general rules of what is right to do and what is not right to do, how do we decide these things? Many of our relational problems stagnate on this platform.

As much as lieth in you, if possible, live peaceably with all people. (Romans 12: 18)

A MIND MOMENT

(RE THE BRIDGE)

[A Story I heard (I don't know where) and adjusted with my own words]

Once upon a time, two neighbours shared everything they had as they farmed their acres of land. There was a piece of property that separated their places, and being it was crown land, they kept it regularly with one intent or purpose so that their lives would equally share the beauty of life.

One day they had an argument that got out of proportion, and one of the men dug a trench that led from the river to form a waterway between them; it seemed the intent was to make a point that they no longer shared common ground.

The other man thought I'd not let this go unnoticed and hired someone to erect a massive fence along the property line of the waterway so that he would no longer have to look out over his neighbour's affairs: out of sight, out of mind; "I Guess."

He left the labourer behind while this man was away to build the fence. When he returned to see the finished work he had contracted out, constructing the barrier, he found that the labourer had made an attractive "Bridge."

He was angry and surprised that the contractor ignored the contract terms. However, as he looked over the "Bridge," he saw his neighbour coming across the bridge with his arms wide, thinking his neighbour had the bridge built to make amends.

"Bridging the Gap, What A Story Might This Be?"
(Excerpted From "Bridging The Gap" —by Jacob Bergen [Bridging The Gap: Bridges Have Fallen, Bridges Are Still Falling, Bascules of Hope: Bergen, Jacob, Bergen, Jacob: 9781537530871: Books - Amazon.ca]) (June 2018)

I recognize that these kinds of stories are possible today—they still happen! However, on the World Scene, Politically [and in other leadership roles of every genre], even when the Leaders have The Heart to live life as in our story, and they try to implement this sort of lifestyle, it's nearly impossible to enforce. I know of only One Answer! If Everyone in The Universe Lived By Following God's Standards— "I'll praise God's Word and trust Him—I'll not fear what people can do to me." (Psalm 56:4) [All Would Be Well!]

HEART SENSE

When I'm Thinking—'Poor Me'—Then What?

$\Diamond$

WHITHER SHALL I GO FROM THY SPIRIT? Whither shall I flee from Your presence? If I ascend into heaven, Thou art there: if I make my bed in hell, behold, Thou art there. If I take the wings of the morning and dwell in the uttermost parts of the sea; Even there shall Thy hand lead me, and Thy right hand shall hold me.

If I say, Surely the darkness shall cover me; even the night shall be light about me. Yea, the darkness hideth not from Thee, but the night shineth as the day: the darkness and the light are similar to Thee. Thou hast possessed my reins: Thou hast covered me in my mother's womb. (Psalm 139:7-13)

In the light of the hard times [is it only 'hard times' when we are unprepared?], we too often face—possibly when we have not made provision for the tough days we'll meet, then what will be our course of action? Psalms 139: 7-13 set a pattern that can help us. Let's call this action, *One of Dependency On The Giver of Enough.*

The first question gets right to the point—

Whither shall I go from Thy spirit?

Where can I run away from God because it seems like He's nowhere near me!

The next question is—Why? If I've prepared for these Hard Times, is there even an option for me in my mind—to run away, and where would I run if I did?

STAY TUNED!

Chapter Eighteen The Sermon Part Three Scriptures
Psalm 139:7
2 Corinthians 1:1-12
Psalm 23
Psalm 91:11; Psalm 139:7; Psalm 103
Psalm 139:19-22; Psalm 23
Psalm 139; Psalm 51
Psalm 139
Psalm 139
Psalm 139
Genesis 1:1-5; Psalm 139; Psalm 103:1-5
Romans 8:28
Psalm 139
The Vista View—The Oasis
Psalm 139
Psalm 139:7-13; 2 Timothy 2:15; Galatians 6
Heart Sense
Lamentations 3:22; Genesis 32:10

Chapter Eighteen

The Sermon—Part Three

―――――――――――――◊――――――――――――――

Psalm One Hundred & Thirty-Nine

(Dedicated To Biblical Truth-Sayers—Not Nay-Sayers)

Life finds us feeling a little peaked at times from beginning to end. We may feel *a little poorly* when Life presents too many twists and turns or detours for our liking. If we think this is only true today, we need to think again! Undoubtedly we face so many issues trying to get through life. Maybe this is the issue—*we are just trying to get through life* instead of honouring the One Who can take us through life. God, the Life-Giver, desires more than we can imagine to move us to where we can appreciate Life itself because of Him. More than any generation from the beginning of time, we try to fit life into our plan instead of God's Plan!

POOR ME!

> Whither shall I go from Thy spirit? or whither shall I flee from Thy presence? (Psalm 139:7)

The song "Singing The Blues" (I Never Felt More Like Running Away), released in 1956, is a Melvin Endsley song. As I continued here with *My Sermon* on Psalm 139:7, this song had me backtracking to thoughts that speak well to this verse's words.

Many of us had *Heartaches By The Number* while growing up—so Ray Price seemed to think when he sang *Heartaches By The Number* (Written by Harlan Howard and released in 1959) about his woman problems. Women's or men's issues are only one of the problems of life which have us feeling like we want to run away from it all. Many parents felt like this as they watched helplessly as their children strayed to experience the pitfalls on the Road to Their Perceived Happiness.

The Bible speaks to this puzzle over and over again. Psalm 139:7 sees David addressing the issues I mention in songs by Melvin Endsley and sung by Ray Price and others (Written by Harlan Howard). Songs like these fit in well in light of the hard times [*is it only 'hard times' when we are unprepared?*] we face too often— possibly when we have not made proper provision for the challenging days ahead of us.

    Paul, an apostle of Jesus Christ by the will of God, and Timothy our brother, unto the church of God which is at Corinth, with all the saints which are in all Achaia: Grace be to you and peace from God our Father, and the Lord Jesus Christ.

    Blessed be God, even the Father of our Lord Jesus Christ, the Father of mercies, and The God of all comfort; Who comforteth us in all our tribulation, that we may be able to comfort them which are in any trouble, by the comfort wherewith we ourselves are comforted of God.

    For as the sufferings of Christ abound in us, so our consolation also aboundeth by Christ. And whether we be afflicted, it is for your consolation and salvation, which is effectual in the enduring of the same sufferings we also suffer: or whether we be comforted, it is for your consolation and salvation.

    And our hope of you is steadfast, knowing that as ye are partakers of the sufferings, so shall ye be also of the consolation. For we would not, brethren, have you ignorant of our trouble which came to us in Asia, that we were pressed out of measure, above strength, insomuch that we despaired even of life:

    But we had the sentence of death in ourselves, that we should not trust in ourselves, but in God which raiseth the dead. He delivered us from so great an end, and doth provide through whom we trust—He will yet deliver us; ye also helping together by prayer for us, that for the gift bestowed upon us using many people—thanks be given by many on our behalf.

    For our rejoicing is this, the testimony of our conscience, that in simplicity and godly sincerity, not with fleshly wisdom, but by the grace of God, we have had our conversation in the world, and more abundantly to you-ward. (2 Corinthians 1: 1-12)

As I read these verses, I return to Psalm 23; I can take a Deep Breath of fresh cool air from the Hot Desert Sun and Heat thereof to take My Moment, My Selah Moment [as The Psalms often present these Oasis Moments]. When Life gets tough—hard to get a handle on—where else could I turn to for respite?

As I see the troubles listed by the songwriters and the consolation of Psalm 23, I wonder why the needs cannot or will not find the desired relief at The Oasis—because we either want to keep living in squalor or don't trust God—ETC.

Melvin Endsley speaks about 'singing the blues' and 'crying all night' because of 'lost love.' He didn't think he would ever lose a firm grip on what he thought he had. It seemed like nothing was going right—in fact, he felt 'everything was on the wrong track.' The moon and stars were becoming 'lightless;' his bucket list of 'dreams' saw the 'hole in the bucket' drain everything he surmised he'd had for so long. In his lyrics, Melvin Endsley imagined all he had left was to cry all the time and run away to where Life would be better—I guess!

Harlan Howard had much the same mindset when he wrote *Heartaches By The Number*. He mentioned when his love left him, and he alluded to the pain of this moment [this was Heartache Number One]. Then when he thought he had his prayers answered and his love came back, he was under the illusion she came back to make a go of their relationship. His lover had other ideas about the relationship—Heartache Number Two.

Harlan talked about Troubles—he had a hard time counting the many troubles; they were near unnumberable—you think you got problems? According to this songwriter, his lady friend loved him less every day, and the heartache he felt made him feel he loved her more— [seems to be a story where someone is a 'glutton for punishment'].

Yes, Heartaches—they seem numberless. There's no winning number—no matter how many tickets you buy on the Lottery of Love, Ya can't win! Then comes another turn at the wheel of life, and you've thought you finally just won the LOTO—Lucky Number Three was going to be The Big One—his girl called and said she was coming back—this time, 'To Stay.' At that moment, life got Good Again—Not So! We sometimes feel "We Got This" as we're in between the ups and downs of life.

In the words of his song, Mr. Howard says something to the effect [affect] of him waiting for his gal to show up on his doorstep, but she never showed—to the tune of 'she must have forgotten where he lived,' and got lost because as it turns out, it was only Heartache Number Three which showed up in his life. It seems three may not have been enough for him—in his *Hope Portfolio;* he said if he stopped counting, his World Would End!

We can enter The Hope Portfolio—not of the making of Melvin Endsley or Harlan Howard or another Human Being, but The Hope Package God Provides. God's hope package will lead us through many Psalms of Encouragement to Keep On Keeping On when life seems Hopeless!

One Great Psalm of Comfort is—

He shall give His angels charge over thee, to keep (guard) thee in all thy ways. (Psalm 91: 11)

There are one hundred & fifty Psalms. Many of them deliver Poor Me Stories of episodes in the life of David and others. Many of these Psalms encourage us to Worship and Praise God for all He is Worth—this puts us on track for being able to 'Get Going When The Going Gets Tough!'

We could look at many Psalms that illustrate how David felt and worked through his downtimes; I've already shared many of these in many ways; The 23rd Psalm is the favourite Comfort Psalm for many folks—it's one of mine! As we move along with the theme of this book *Searching For A Heart of Gold; Not A Pot of Gold*—in effect (affect) *Searching For The Heart of God*—Psalm 139 is one of The Tickets For Admission.

Maybe I should read Psalm 139:7 like this—

[Even if I wanted to, but I don't], "Whither (Where) shall I go from Thy spirit? —Whither (Where) shall I flee from Thy presence?" (Psalm 139:7)

When we look at the benefits of Psalm 139 [and Psalm 23], we might also check Psalm 103—

"Bless the Lord, O my soul: and all that is within me, bless His holy name. Bless the Lord, O my soul, and forget not all His benefits:"

God forgives all your iniquities and heals all your diseases. He redeems your life from destruction. He crowns you with lovingkindness and tender mercies. God satisfies your mouth with good things and renews your youth like the eagle. [Our God is so complete!]

The Lord executeth righteousness and judgment for all the oppressed. He made known His ways unto Moses, His acts unto the children of Israel. The Lord is merciful and gracious, slow to anger, and plenteous in mercy. He'll not always chide, nor will He keep His anger forever. He hath not dealt with us after our sins; nor rewarded us according to our iniquities.

As heaven is high above the earth, so great is His mercy toward them that fear Him. As far as the east is from the west, so far hath He removed our transgressions from us.

Like a father pitieth his children, so the Lord pitieth them that fear Him. For He knoweth our frame; He remembereth that we are dust. As for man (people), his (their) days are as grass: as a flower of the field, so *they* flourish.

The wind passeth over it, and it is gone, and the place shall know it no more. But the mercy of the Lord is from everlasting to everlasting upon them that fear Him, and His righteousness unto children's children; to such as keep His covenant, and to those that remember his commandments to do them.

The Lord hath prepared His throne in the heavens, and His kingdom ruleth 'Over All.' Bless the Lord, ye His angels, that excel in strength, that do His commandments, hearkening unto the voice of His word. Bless ye the Lord, all ye His hosts; ye ministers of His, that do His pleasure. Bless the Lord, all His works in all places of His dominion: bless the Lord, O my soul.

In Psalm 139:7, David doesn't seem to suggest he's in the position that many of the illustrations I've highlighted seem to indicate—Hard Times. If we look at the perspective and or context of his words here, we can readily see David has already realized Who and What God is and that He [God] Will, I say again, WILL be all that David [and the rest of us] need at all times—the way I see this Psalm, in large part, is that it's an example for us! The whole of The History of The Bible can be an example for us to observe.

> "David does not seem to suggest he is in the position that many of the illustrations I've highlighted indicate—Hard Times." [*IBID*]

There are a few troubling thoughts in verses 19-22. Though David acknowledges God as being in Full Control overall, he seems to think God doesn't realize the gravity of the evil of humankind. These four verses remind me of Peter in the Garden of Gethsemane, where Jesus prayed before He Laid It All Down on the cross. Peter thought he needed to help Jesus fight the intentions of the henchmen coming to arrest Jesus and march Him onward to Pilate's Judgement Hall—by cutting off the ear of the High Priest. Jesus needed no help here, nor did God in Psalm 139. I guess David, in pure innocence, just wanted to let God know he was on His side.

> Surely Thou wilt slay the wicked, O God: depart from me, therefore, ye bloody men. They speak against Thee wickedly, and Thine enemies take Thy name in vain. Do not I hate them, O LORD, that hate Thee? And am not I grieved with those that rise against Thee? I hate them with perfect hatred: I count them mine enemies.
> (Psalm 139: 19-22)

Whither shall I go from Thy spirit? or whither shall I flee from Thy presence? (Psalm 139:7)

This verse is a powerful declaration. David once was the *meek and mind Shepherd Boy* of The 23rd Psalm. Psalm 23 is an impactive verse of The Bible in so many ways. For example, it talks about leadership (Sovereign Leadership) that can sustain us in every possible manner, and it allows us to have a visual of Hope forever.

David *was* The Shepherd Boy, King, Runaway King, Adulterer, Killer, Husband, Father—and after all this and more, God calls David a man after His own HEART! Go Figure!

When David wrote Psalm 139:7, I see how all the issues of his life brought him again to where he realized Who God is and that God has always been there for him in the Good Times and The Bad Times. When David messed up, he was quick to call on this Source of Life for forgiveness—and then David seemed to move in the direction that Repentance is supposed to take us—but *Sometimes David Messed Up Again—Sound Familiar?*

As we continue from Psalm 139:8, let's take some of the complex expressions of David apart piece by piece. Suppose we have open eyes, an open heart, and a Psalm 51:10-13 attitude. In that case, we'll take away something from the rest of the Chapter—some things which will carry the day for us when we face similar trials and otherwise different trials David may not have encountered. Maybe, when *we run out of the Desert* for a spell, into The Oasis, we'll experience the same Refreshing David suggests in The 23rd Psalm and the one in the 139th Psalm.

If I ascend into heaven, You are there: if I make my bed in hell, behold, You are there. If I take the wings of the morning and dwell in the uttermost parts of the sea; even there shall Thy hand lead me, and Thy right hand shall hold me. If I say, Surely the darkness shall cover me, even the night shall be light about me. Yea, the darkness hideth not from Thee, but the night shineth as the day: the darkness and the light are similar to Thee. (Verses 8-13)

I sense a bit of a *No-Man's-Land* here on David's part—not on God's Part. As I look again at verse seven, "Whither shall I go from Thy spirit? or whither shall I flee from Thy presence?" David seems to sense there is an indefinite area of thought here as he writes this Psalm, while at the same time *he knows, that he knows, that he knows God is All In All*! We The People often say Yes LORD, we agree wholeheartedly with Who You Are and What You Will Do—BUT? What about this issue LORD?

No-man's-land looks like an unusual, confusing, or indefinite area, especially of operation, application, or authority—the no-man's-land between art and science.

It's a little hard for us mere humans to come to grips with the complete picture of what Someone Who is From Everlasting To Everlasting pans out like—After all, 'I'm Only Human!' God does not observe life and things with human eyes as we do. I see this in, "Yea, the darkness hideth not from Thee; but the night shineth as the day: the darkness and the light are both alike to Thee." (Verse 13) Dark and Light the same—HMMM? Probably this is just me—all the rest of you folks *'always get the picture clearly.'* Might we think the problems we face are the other person's fault?

Walk With Me Please as we look into some of what is often a Quandary of Sorts. Please don't get me wrong, thinking I'm putting words in David's mouth by making some alliterations, allusions or inferences about "No-Man's Land," which may not sound as if that's what he meant when he wrote the words of Psalm 139 and elsewhere. I'm simply trying to look at both sides of things like someone playing devil's advocate may do. A devil's advocate is a person who campaigns for a less recognized cause for the sake of argument.

Verse One of the 139th Psalm starts us off by saying— "O LORD, Thou hast searched me, and known me." If I read between the lines even just a little, I can *Know* that even if David was a bit unsure on some things, God *Knows* where his Heart and Motive are in any process that may seem to be questioning somewhat about what he [David] was writing.

As a writer, I glean comfort because I'm floating in a stream of sorts while writing my stuff. If I sometimes write with a bit of reservation about certain things, but my heart and motive are in it to express as best I can what I feel God is saying, I know God will direct me to the right place to make the point be right and not just look or seem right!

Now, this said, let's walk along together through a valley of sorts, definitely not "the Valley of The Shallow of Death." Let's think of a valley that has God prepared on both sides of the hills and mountains, creating a protective boundary from which we can come to grips with the issue of the Sovereignty of God.

If I ascend into heaven, Thou art there—*if* I make my bed in hell, behold Thou art there. *If* I take the wings of the morning and dwell in the uttermost parts of the sea; even there shall Thy hand lead me, and Thy right hand shall hold me. *If* I say, Surely the darkness shall cover me, even the night shall be light about me. Yea, the darkness hideth not from Thee, but the night shineth as the day: the darkness and the light are identical to Thee. (Verses 8-13)

I see the word 'IF,' and I think question mark (?). As I look back to verses one and four, I kind of dodge in and out of where I am in the moment to include a place where I've never been yet—Someday, I will be there—Heaven.

"O LORD, YOU have explored [hunted and sought hard] every possible avenue of life in the past, the present, and the tomorrow which is not yet on the horizon concerning me, and YOU know what I will be saying next!" (JBI—Jacob Bergen Insight)

If this is true, and it is, then why am I even mentioning these thoughts. David has long ago found out that even *if* God knows everything about us, everything we'll say, question wise or insight wise, He [God] wants us to converse with Him. God, in turn, intends to input to us through The Holy Spirit the things which will help us glean a greater understanding than we may presently have as to WHO HE IS!

When Moses asked God what he should say when people asked who God is, God said, tell them I AM That I AM! HMMM—if that doesn't settle it, nothing will—right? The non-believer may not be any farther ahead from this statement, but those who have a relationship with The Almighty will know and understand that God is, as Psalm 139 clarifies—ENOUGH; Everything For Every Situation about which we may be in a Quandary!

The Psalmist David begins verse 8 by presenting two diversely mighty opposites [inverses]; contrary, inverted, flipsides of two places on the map of eternity—Heaven and Hell! David says, You LORD are everywhere *I might conceivably run to* if I had a mind to do so—I don't have 'any intention' to run from YOU—Why would I, everything I need is right here with YOU LORD!

God is in Heaven, but why would He want to be in Hell? Sorry to disappoint you here, but all I will say is that God is God all the time, and He does what He needs to do all the time—Jesus had a proper reason for going to Hell after He was dead and buried. When God has a job to do, He gets it done!

If I take the wings of the morning and dwell in the uttermost parts of the sea; even there shall Thy hand lead me, and Thy right hand shall hold me, [hover over me]. (Verse 9)

God's presence is *Unstoppable*—the speed of light is 186,000 miles per second; this is about as instantaneous as we could imagine—one second, we're safe on land where we live, and the next moment might be a million miles away!

Even if God moved us from one place to another this quickly without any say-so from us, we needn't be distraught—if God did this, it would be because, for one, He knew we could handle it; *if* God did this, it would be for a purpose He understands—we might have reservations. However, by Faith, we need to allow God to do just that if this were to be the plan, He had for any one of us.

David seems confident that even there, God's hand would lead him. These days would pan out in the ways he should travel for a purpose. God's right hand would hold him firmly in place no matter how many tornadoes, hurricanes, tsunamis—spiritually speaking [or physically speaking] he would need to contend with—this is God at work. I *KNOW* that if this were my destination in God's will, I would have a few tremors, no matter how much Faith I thought I had. Throughout the process—If I absorbed my Selah Moments at The Oasis—reflecting on God's Goodness, my strength and restoration would be there when I needed to manage the storms.

Most of us will likely never see such drastic changes in *Spiritual Weather*, or for that matter, in the Physical Weather Patterns. For most people, life takes somewhat of a typical trek within which we also live by Faith, doing the Will of God in the Season of Life we're in and at the place and pace God has for us in that place. God is present everywhere—believe it or not! There's colossal comfort in *Knowing* the following verse can be a refuge for us no matter what!

"Lord, I think of myself at this early morning moment as if having wings of flight into Your presence. Whether seemingly lost at sea—wherever I Am, Your Hand, Your Eye, Your Presence itself is guiding me!" (Verse 9)

Just as a million miles in God's perspective is like walking across the street [in terms we would liken this thought to] for Him, night and day fall into the same category. Genesis begins the dialogue of our journey by saying—

> In the beginning, God created heaven and the earth. And the earth was without form and void, and darkness was upon the face of the deep. And the Spirit of God moved upon the face of the waters. And God said, let there be light: and there was light. And God saw the light, that it was good: and God divided the light from the darkness.

And God called the light Day, and the darkness He called Night. And the evening and the morning were the first day. (Genesis 1:1-5)

If everything God did was for a planned purpose in His World of Creation, we ought to be satisfied—but we're not! We've looked at verse eight, *"the wings of the morning and the uttermost parts of the sea—"* a million or more miles—were always the same as walking to our neighbour next door. Then *if* the difficulty [as we see it] of God using the Dark times of our lives for His advantage and purpose to be fruitful, as though they were not a problem because He saw them only as stepping stones to another goal in His Light; these scriptures make sense for me! Please read the following verses carefully—introspectively (in a self-analyzing way).

If I say, Surely the darkness shall cover me, even the night shall be light about me. Yea, the darkness hideth not from Thee, but the night shineth as the day: the darkness and the light are equal to Thee. (Verses 11&12)

Why should I 'Check In' my personal feelings at the door and walk into the room with Ultimate Faith [not carelessly in a ka sera sera way]? Because of the following verses—.

Thou hast possessed my reins: Thou hast covered me in my mother's womb. (Verse 13)

This verse is The Kicker of the first thirteen verses of the 139th Psalm—it puts me in the mindset of God having everything in place concerning My Moment [My Life] from before I was 'physically compacted' in the little bundle of joy I was at birth. I feel a sense of God placing me into The Oasis [Psalm 23] along with my parents to allow for us to indulge in a Selah Moment of gratitude for God's every provision.

Bless the LORD, O my soul: and all that is within me, bless His holy name. Bless the LORD, O my soul, and forget not all His benefits: Who forgiveth all thine iniquities; Who healeth all thy diseases; Who redeemeth thy life from destruction; Who crowneth thee with lovingkindness and tender mercies; Who satisfieth thy mouth with good things; so that thy youth experience renewal like the eagles. (Psalm 103: 1-5)

"My thoughts are as if You are holding the reins of my heart—gently keeping me on track—as protected as I was in my mother's womb!" (Verse 13)

These words present a positivity (willingness), a constant knowing for me to reflect on God's care for US! If we look at synonyms for positivity—the picture of our existence does undoubtedly not appear bleak. *If* in this life someone cared this much for me in physical reality, I would think I was already in Heaven—I would have positivity, eagerness, zeal, enthusiasm, positiveness, readiness, confidence, willingness, consent, and inclination—to do God's will no matter come what may.

When we break down these words again, we develop another mega perspective of there being so much more God has for us that we could never exhaust His resources. Then if we break those words up again into more synonym selections, it seems there is no end to the terms we can use to express The Heart of God! God Is Certainly, without reservation on my part—ENOUGH! We often sit back in our easy chairs, musing over what we don't have rather than what we do have. I guess we're still human—Too Bad!

Just peek back at verse eight again for a moment—

"If I ascend into heaven, You're there: if I make my bed in hell, there You are again!" When we realize that Heaven and Hell are two opposites, God's Love perspective and context are even more than AWESOME—if that is possible!

We come to expect Night to Be Night—and then it turns out that we cannot depend on that when we look at God. We may look at a situation and see no Hope—but then God comes around and says, "Wait Just A Minute!" You are missing the point—there are no hopeless situations in 'MyWill!' [We are The Benificieries!]

And we know that all things work together for good to them that love God. To those folks called according to His purpose—hope is at the ready. (Romans 8:28)

So when we're 'set back on our heels' and think, "It's Over," the story has only just begun from God's point of view. To be 'set back on our heels' pictures out as a look of surprise, unease, bemusement, perplexity, puzzlement, confusion—in a fashion where it affects our ability to function and or perform adequately.

When I observe verse eight longingly, I see the depth of God's love and concern without angst, for every ditto mark repeatedly expressing why He made me [and you]. While I was still unborn (making abortion a hard pill to swallow), God already had a grip on the reins that would guide me here and there in life. The sad part is that by our choices, as we grow towards maturity, we often choose not to let God manage The Reins. God covered us in the womb and protected us from the onslaught of life that would demand we choose and decide one way or the other about this issue and that—To Obey God Or Not To Obey His Leading. Once outside the womb, the Course of Life lay open before us—often making the 'Not To Obey God' option more desirable because it's attractive to the eyes.

"What's better than being led by The Master's Touch? We can train a horse to turn by pulling on the reins left or right—or we can neck rein them by laying the reins on the horse's neck on the right or left side." (Psalm 139:13)

Sound Familiar— "And the LORD God took the man and put him into the garden of Eden to dress it and to keep it. And the LORD God commanded the man, saying, of every tree of the garden thou mayest freely eat but of the tree of the knowledge of good and evil, thou shalt not eat of it: for in the day that thou eatest thereof thou shalt surely die. And the LORD God said, It is not good that the man should be alone; I will make a helpmate (a woman) for him. (Genesis 2: 15-18)

There's a considerable distance (gap) between Heaven and Hell, a vast spread between right and wrong; there is a significant span between obedience and disobedience.

The songwriter wrote, "Jesus knows all about my struggles [troubles]." There are many variations of these thoughts, and each of them presents a picture of something way more than a DEAD Jesus! The songwriters suggest that Jesus is alive and well today— ministering in HOPE and administering HOPE Moment by Moment Every Moment of The Day—Another Snapshot of Psalm 23.

Before and after Searching for Me, Jesus Knew All He Needed to Know To Get The Job Done!

◊ THE VISTA VIEW—THE OASIS ◊

WHEN WE STRUGGLE TO MAKE SENSE OF LIFE

Where can we run when we struggle to know which way is up? Do we run away from God, or do we run to God? When we search The Scriptures, we have many illustrations or examples of people who tried it both ways. Adam and Eve were the first to hear from God—they met with God at a particular time in The Garden of Eden every day.

I find no record of Adam and Eve's meetings with God in The Garden of Eden before they disobeyed God. Obviously, they met with God in The Garden because this is where God explained the format their lives were supposed to take. God instructed these folks in the Rights and Wrongs—but I believe there were also times where they had the intimacy of God's presence—in The Cool of The Day before they sinned.

Before the Great Exodus from The Garden of Eden, before Adam and Eve disobeyed God, there were No Struggles mentioned in The Bible. So, we can assume that life was Good—because God Is Good! Being in God's presence in the right relationship is always Good! We are in the same position—we can stay in God's Presence or run from God's Presence, hiding, because of the Guilt Sin always brings.

David, in Psalms 139, talks about God so clearly we should have no problem understanding Who God Is—He is Everything We'll Ever Need—this is the story of Psalm 139. I've quoted from this Psalm extensively—but I've not yet tired of what it held 'back in the day' and what it still holds for us today.

"Is it possible to try to escape from God when He has His rein on us? David seems to think so because he wonders how and where he might run from God if this was his goal. He thinks of the heavens, hell, the farthest reaches of the sea—David realizes there's no escape—If we choose to do so, we'll suffer the consequences."

If I say, Surely the darkness shall cover me; even the night shall be light about me. Yea, the darkness hideth not from thee, but the night shineth as the day: the darkness and the light are similar to thee. Thou hast possessed my reins: thou hast covered me in my mother's womb. (Verses 7-13)

Repetition can be tedious [uninteresting]—but it doesn't need to be boring! Timothy in the New Testament suggests—"Study to show yourself in the proper light in The Presence of God so that your life will exemplify or illustrate that you are indeed a Child of God!" These are my paraphrased thoughts for the following

"Study to show thyself approved unto God, a workman that needeth not to be ashamed, rightly dividing the word of truth." (2 Timothy 2:15)

In Chapter Eighteen, Part Three of *The Sermon*, we've looked at some of what is often a struggle as we Walk With God. Looking back allows us to garner a fuller relationship with our Creator. Please don't get me wrong, thinking I'm putting words in David's mouth by making some alliterations, allusions or inferences about "No-Man's Land," which may not sound as if that's what he meant when he wrote what he wrote in line with what he said in Psalm 139 and elsewhere. I'm simply trying to look at both sides of things like someone playing devil's advocate may do.

As we move forward through Psalm 139, The Sermon, Part Four, let's move slowly and carefully for fear of missing The Point of God's Faithfulness. There are reasons to observe God's Faithfulness so that we can be a part of the Solution and not a part of The Problem. Please Grasp Those Reasons!

If someone fails in their relationship with God, we who are spiritual need to help restore that person in the spirit of meekness. Consider the case that we failed, tempted beyond what we can handle—then what? Help carry another person's burdens, thereby fulfilling the law of Christ. If we think we are something when we are nothing, we have a problem. Let everyone prove their work—then they can rejoice in themselves alone and not in another. For every person shall bear their own burden. Let those who have learned the word communicate what they have learned—in Word and Deed! (JBI Re Galatians 6)

HEART SENSE

Faithfulness—What A Boon (Benefit)!

———————————◊———————————

IT'S OF THE LORD'S MERCIES that we're not consumed because His compassions fail not. They are new every morning: great is Thy faithfulness. (Lamentations 3: 22-23)

"I am unworthy of all the kindness and faithfulness You've shown me. When I crossed this Jordan, I had only my staff, but now I have become two camps." (Genesis 32:10)

Chapter Eighteen The Sermon Part Four Scriptures
Matthew 22:34-40
Psalm 139; Psalm 51; Psalm 23; Genesis 3:8
Psalm 139:14; Psalm 9:1-2; Psalm 139:17
Psalm 139:18; Psalm 23; Psalm 139:19-22
1 John 3:16; Psalm 139:19-22; Genesis 6:5
John 21:15; Ecclesiastes 3:1-8
Isaiah 55:1-12; Psalm 139:19-22
Psalm 139:23-24; Matthew 21:1-5
Psalm 139:7; Psalm 23
The Vista View—The Oasis
Psalm 139; Luke 22:40-44; Hebrews 12
Hebrews 12:1-4; Hebrews 4:15-16
Ephesians 6: 13-18
Heart Sense

Chapter Eighteen

The Sermon—Part Four

◊

Psalm One Hundred & Thirty-Nine

(Dedicated To Biblical Truth-Sayers—Not Nay-Sayers)

FAITHFULNESS—FAITHFULNESS IS A KEY INGREDIENT, a Key Instrument for forming a Relationship, which opens up Fellowship. The central tenet or principle tied up in and cinched exactly right [as if cinching the saddle on a horse] is, Who is at the head position of Life—created with people in mind.

The Faithfulness of God becomes an example for us—If we never had an example of Faithfulness, we could never be Faithfull to God and or other people! Faithfulness detaches us from ourselves as being Numero-Uno. (Matthew 22: 34-40). This passage is one of my go-to sections for describing a relationship with God and other people [our neighbours].

"But when the Pharisees had heard that He had put the Sadducees to silence, they were gathered together. Then, a lawyer asked Him a question, tempting Him, saying, Master, which is the great commandment in the law? Jesus said unto him, Thou shalt love the Lord thy God with all thy heart, and with all thy soul, and with all thy mind. This is the first and great commandment. And the second is like it; Thou shalt love thy neighbour as thyself. On these two commandments hang all the law and the prophets." (Matthew 22: 34-40)

I'm plotting a course for *The Sermon, Part Four*—Beginning at Psalm 139:14. I'll fail if I don't have a Plan and a Purpose. Beginnings—We can't have an End without a Beginning. It matters not whether it pertains to Life itself or any other issue or project. This book would not have happened if I had no plan or purpose.

During the writing of *Searching For A Heart of Gold; Not A Pot of Gold—* [*Searching For The Heart of God*], I Hope and Pray [as I have done every time I've approached my computer screen and keyboard] that I've put God at the Head of my thoughts. Offering Him praise in a spirit of thanksgiving for every word He allows me to access and use to spread His Word in relational ways—for someone out there to get a good look at the Faithfulness of Jesus.

"I will praise You; because I'm fearfully and wonderfully made; marvellous are Your works; my soul knows this right well." (Psalm 139: 14)

The 139th Psalm is all about the 'Always Present God; The All-Knowing God; The All-Seeing God'—. We often use "Omnipotence, Omniscience, and Omnipresence" to say the same thing. Over time I've added other words— Omni-Relational, Omni-Personal [All-Personal; All-Relational]. Any Message I Hope to convey here must include Psalms 51 as an Overture to this message of Realizing The Sovereign God Is The Beginning and The End!

In this my early morning start, the first song which came into my spirit was "The Goodness of God!" (by Songwriters: Jason David Ingram, Brian Johnson, Benjamin David Fielding, Jenn Johnson, Edward Martin Cash)

The Goodness of God is a Prayer, talking about Loving God—Heart To Heart Stuff; as far as I'm concerned. It talks about The Mercy of God; about Him holding us in hands; it pictures us from our earliest wake-up call and onward till we go back to sleep— The Whole Story being God! As the song says, it speaks to *The Goodness of God*. The theme continues with words and chords relating to The Faithfulness of God. What a beautiful rendition of expression to God. We need to listen to it in a Quiet Moment—Like the 23rd Psalm plays out for us when we take a "My Moment!" A Selah Moment!

Early this morning, in one of my "My Moments," a thought came alive—I thought about The Garden of Eden; how it '*Must Have Been*' the First Psalm 23 Moment in History. The inference of Genesis 3:8 suggests that God met with Adam and Eve in the cool of the day even before they ate from the wrong fruit tree. "The Garden Of Eden" Must Have Been A Vivid Picture for David, The Author.

Within the song's framework is *The Goodness of God*; I open this Chapter with The scripture from Psalm 139:14; —.

"I will praise thee; for I am fearfully and wonderfully made; marvellous are thy works; and that my soul knoweth right well." [IBID]

To do this right in writing this Chapter and everything I write, I need to step back a step or two to reflect on the times when it seemed 'Darkness' would overwhelm me— (VS. 11); God was coming to me as a Messenger of Light. Jesus said, "*I Am The Light of the world!*" Then in verse thirteen, we see a picture of God being in total control of my existence from before the creation of the universe to the very moment I'm in today! So, let me never forget the Faithfulness of God! See— (Psalm 9: 1-2)

"I will praise Thee, O Lord, with my whole heart; I will show forth all Thy marvellous works. I will be glad and rejoice in Thee: I will sing praise to Thy name, O Thou most High."

Verses fifteen and sixteen continue the theme of God's Faithfulness—we could go on endlessly on a rant of sorts and stretch it out like an elastic band that will not snap back and strike us down, but by the hand of God, we'll experience the extension of a Love we cannot fathom!

How precious <u>are Thy thoughts</u> to me, O God! How significant is the sum of them! (VS 17)

If we've come this far by faith, we've experienced our Father in Heaven at work in our lives many times. Jesus shows us this picture in The New Testament as He lived in a physical body by the sufficient example only God can provide. God <u>ALSO</u> 'allows us to become what God always wanted us to be—' To Be Like Jesus!

God didn't create a Chasm separating us from Himself. The temporal 'clay people' we are today, so many years forward from when Jesus walked this earth, leaves us with equal access to God. We can have physical access to Jesus today, as those Jesus walked with back then, doing Good and Healing all manner of sickness, disease, and broken hearts—. There's a Great Gulf between Sin and God's Goodness! We cannot meld the two together to look the same. But Jesus died to Bridge The Gap through Forgiveness.

Phil Wickham wrote *Living Hope*, a beautiful song; he expresses thoughts about a Chasm separating God and us; how Jesus was and is The Living Hope—providing Mercy and Grace Enough to close the Gap as we confess our sin, repent, and turn to God. Phil says Hallelujah and begins praising God—Being The One Who set us free.

The Psalmist realizes in verse seventeen how precious and real it is to know God has thoughts about us—Good Thoughts, and they are never-ending. We are not just a blip on the radar screen for God to see us swiftly passing through time and thinking— 'Oh, What was that?'

> If I should count them, they are more in number than the sand: I'm still with You when I awake. (Verse 18)

I've never tried counting sand pebbles—have you? I'd wonder if I did—I may wonder about you if I saw you counting grains of sand. After not too long a period of doing so, we would soon come to grips with this verse in a Realty Sense. We'd quickly understand the meaning of futility and God's provision as much Greater than our mathematical counting skills. Even if we were to count a million grains of sand, we wouldn't have a hope of measuring as much as God's knack for doing so. God's math is different than ours—He counts in the number system of Infinity— this is much different than even our high-tech means of counting.

Here's The Kicker—when I wake from the dream I have of counting sand granules and wake up frustrated, God presents me with the gift of Hope— 'when I awake, I'm still with thee.' (Verse 18). My frustration has not separated me from God—He's Still There With Me, as close as the mention of His Name.

After the first eighteen verses, we have a break in the theme. David has a Mood Change from his observation of God's Goodness and overall care for us who have a relationship with Him. David seems to have ducked out of The Oasis [Psalm 23] and gone back into the world of the Desert.

Now David sees all the evil people, as he thinks of them as— all who don't respect God and acknowledge Him for Who He is. David's in a mode where he feels God may hold His tongue and not 'rip the sinners apart'—David thinks God should; David expends four verses of the 139th Psalm [19-22] berating evildoers.

Didn't Jesus say in John 3:16, "God <u>so</u> [hugely] loved the world that He gave His only begotten Son, that whoever believes in Him would have eternal life? Who was David to pass judgment on these folks? Until God finally reviews the Hearts of all People and says, "I gave you all of your earthy time on Planet Earth to notice me, and you didn't; now it's time to pay The Piper—" who are we to judge? God will judge at The White Throne Judgement.

> Surely Thou wilt slay the wicked, O God—depart from me, therefore, ye bloody people. They speak against Thee wickedly, and Thine enemies take Thy name in vain. Do not I hate them, O LORD, who hate Thee? Am not I grieved with those that rise against Thee? I hate them with perfect hatred—I count them mine enemies. (Psalm 139: 19-22)

I realize my tenuous, shaky, weak— presentation of David's words in this passage may be out of context, as I refer to them in the way I do above, until I see these four verses from the perspective of verses twenty-three & Twenty-four. In verses twenty-three & twenty-four, I see David looking at his own heart and surmising he may be or has been off track himself in his relationship with God betimes. Now, a tender heart of repentance may be in order— we are all as guilty as those David so badly berated in verses 19-22.

The Bible does tell us not to judge because we may face judgment by the same standards as we measure others. So, David has looked at the world and realized that it's not a pretty place with wolves of sinful intentions.

> And God saw that the wickedness of man was great in the earth and that every imagination of the thoughts of his heart was only evil continually. (Genesis 6:5)

Might we say that we have no hope of survival in a world bent on going it alone without God? The Garden of Eden was The Garden of God. Should we even think that the problem lay with God if this was The Garden of God, and everything for earthly existence went wrong? I don't think so! God gave us a choice to serve Him because we loved Him more than the delicious fruit. Might it be God asked Adam and Eve to decide about a 'calling to serve?' Was the Opening line of human existence meant for us to Love One Another? Loving each other in our skin isn't always easy!

Jesus was asking Peter about some stuff in John 21:15. He could also have directed the whole conversation at all the disciples, "Lovest thou me more than these? These—what did Jesus mean by '*these?*' There were boats, fish, other disciples, the cares of life, family, the necessities of life—? All *these* things were necessities of life; even the cares of life were necessary ingredients of the melting pot we all fit.

Rightly or wrongly, I believe that Jesus was saying there is a time and a place for everything under the sun. I think Jesus may have been suggesting there are Seasons of The Year for a reason—and there are Seasons of change in which we need to be ready to go where we may not want to go because Our Master needs us there.

A TIME FOR EVERYTHING

There is a time for everything and a season for every activity under the heavens: a time to be born and a time to die, a time to plant and a time to uproot, a time to kill and a time to heal, a time to tear down and a time to build, a time to weep and a time to laugh, a time to mourn and a time to dance, a time to scatter stones and a time to gather them, a time to embrace and a time to refrain from embracing, a time to search and a time to give up, a time to keep and a time to throw away, a time to tear and a time to mend, a time to be silent and a time to speak, a time to love and a time to hate, a time for war and a time for peace. (Ecclesiastes 3: 1-8)

I have a challenging motif when I write, but the thoughts are directly from the Bible to find the context and perspective by looking at what came before and after said verses. Often, I present things in a JBI [Jacob Bergen Insight] fashion to play in The Devil's Advocate Arena to help us think everywhere—somewhat outside the box—this may or may not be the best course from which to write, but this is where I feel '*called*' "to Meddle!" Maybe there's a better word than "Meddle," Maybe Intervene or Intercede is better!

Does God need my help to work as I do in this manner of writing—NO! He can and does what He knows is best—He Is God! However, whether we understand it or not, 'God works in mysterious ways His wonders to perform' [this is not scripture; however, there are scriptures which bear this out].

Ho, every one that thirsteth, come ye to the waters, and he that hath no money; come ye, buy, and eat; yea, come, buy wine and milk without money and price. Wherefore do ye spend money for that which is not bread—and your labour for that which satisfieth not? Hearken diligently unto Me, eat ye that which is good, and let your soul delight in fatness. Incline your ear, and come unto Me: hear, and your soul shall live; and I will make an everlasting covenant with you, even the sure mercies of David.

Behold, I have given him a witness to the people, a leader and commander to the people. Behold, thou shalt call a nation that thou knowest not, and nations that knew not thee shall run unto thee because of the Lord thy God, and for the Holy One of Israel; for He hath glorified thee. Seek ye the Lord *while you can find Him*, call ye upon Him while he is near: Let the wicked forsake his way, and the unrighteous person their thoughts: and let them return unto the Lord; He will have mercy upon them; and to our God, for He will abundantly pardon.

My thoughts are not your thoughts, neither are your ways my ways, saith the Lord. As the heavens are higher than the earth, so are My ways higher than your ways, and My thoughts than your thoughts. For as the rain cometh down, and the snow from heaven, and returneth not thither, but watereth the earth, and maketh it bring forth and bud, that it may give seed to the sower, and bread to the eater: So shall My word be that goeth forth out of My mouth: it shall not return unto Me void, but it shall accomplish that which I please. It shall prosper in the thing whereto I sent it. (Isaiah 55: 1-11)

Does God need us each individually? Yes, and No! God can do everything to bring eternity into play by Himself. God also makes choices—not from a human perspective or in a human context, but because He knows the outcome of all things. God chooses us and calls us out from the crowd of people like David talks about in Psalm 139: 19-22 to be a part of the earthly time to come to the place beyond earthly time as we know it. God chose us in Him from before any earthly time. He knew who would come to Him, and in this scenario, God calls each of us to a specific season, time and place to work with Him for eternity's sake.

Please look at the following for how God may work with what we see as frail human entities. Jesus needed an earthly process to bring a prophecy to fulfillment—He set the example by human means.

And when they drew nigh unto Jerusalem and were come to Bethphage, unto the mount of Olives, then sent Jesus two disciples, saying unto them, go into the village over against you, and straightway ye shall find an ass tied, and a colt with her—loose them, and bring them unto Me. And if anyone says anything to you, ye shall say, The Lord hath need of them; and straightway he will send them. *God did all this to fulfill* that which *the prophet spoke*, saying, tell ye the daughter of Sion, Behold, thy King cometh unto thee, meek, and sitting upon an ass, and a colt the foal of an ass.
(Matthew 21: 1-5)

LORD, Search my Heart in these regards.

Search me, O God, and know my heart: try me, and know my thoughts: and see if there be any wicked way in me and lead me in the way everlasting. (Psalm 139: 23-24)

A Call to commitment—As I see it, David has seen all the Wonders of Who and What God is—He has seen the result of doing things God's way, and in this light, I see David saying—Do it Your Way LORD. LORD, if You had to do a do-over—Do It Again LORD just As You Have Done In The Past—You Have Things Under Control!

Life finds us feeling a little peaked at times from beginning to end. We may feel *a little poorly* because the twists, turns or detours life presents are not always to our liking. If we think this is only true today, we need to think again! Indeed we face a host of issues to get through life.

We are just trying to get through life instead of honouring the One Who can not only get us through but desires more than we can imagine to get us to where we can appreciate Life itself because of The Life-Giver. We may 'feel' these issues more than we 'know' them—Knowing is better than just having a feeling about what we're searching out. (IBID)

POOR ME!

Whither shall I go from Thy spirit? or whither shall I flee from Thy presence? (Psalm 139:7)

Singing The Blues [Re. *I Never Felt More Like Running Away*], released in 1956, is a Melvin Endsley song. As I continued here with My Sermon on Psalm 139:7, this song had me backtracking to thoughts that speak well to this verse's words.

Many of us had *Heartaches By The Number* while growing up—so Ray Price seemed to think when he sang *Heartaches By The Number* (Written by Harlan Howard and released in 1959) about his woman problems. Woman or man problems are only one of the issues of life which have us feeling like we want to run away from it all. Many a parent has felt like this as they watched helplessly as their children strayed to experience the pitfalls on the Road to Their Perceived Happiness.

If I have just one more thing to say here at the end of this Chapter, it's this, and it's a Direct Message—!

The LORD is my Shepherd; I shall not want. He maketh me to lie down in green pastures: He leadeth me beside the still waters. He restoreth my soul: He leadeth me in the paths of righteousness for His name's sake. Yea, though I walk through the valley of the shadow of death, I will fear no evil: Thou art with me; Thy rod and Thy staff comfort me. Thou preparest a table before me in the presence of mine enemies: Thou anointest my head with oil; my cup runneth over. Surely goodness and mercy shall follow me all the days of my life: and I will dwell in the house of the LORD forever.

The 23rd Psalm.

Sometimes, we need to get out of this world for a season and have an Oasis Moment. Times come upon us when we need to soak in the Presence of God—Today was one of those days for me. For much of today, my wife and I enjoyed "*I Sing Praises To Your Name;*" for a while, I felt like I'd died and gone to heaven.

TAKE A REST
RESPITE

WHEN GOD CONCOCTS SOMETHING IN A MELTING POT—
BLENDING EVERYTHING TO BE ONE ENTITY—SUCH AS SOUP, HE
CAN ONCE AGAIN SEPARATE THE ITEMS TO BE AS AN AS YOU
WERE SOLDIER SCENARIO—WE CAN'T EVER SEPARATE SOUP TO
BE AS IT WAS BEFORE WE GROUND UP AND BOILED ALL THE
INGREDIENTS.

◊ THE VISTA VIEW—THE OASIS ◊

—This Vista View Is Not Just For Chapter Eighteen—

—But The Whole Book—

LET'S PRAY

LORD—We've come a long way from Page One to where we are right now—Including Front Matter and Empty Pages. I've amassed (stockpiled) over 154,000 words—over 723,000 characters, over 870,000 characters with spaces, more than 3,600 paragraphs, and more than 17,500 lines so far in *Searching For A Heart of Gold; Not A Pot of Gold.* I cannot even imagine how many days, hours, minutes, and seconds— I've spent at my computer—except to say that I've been at it for about 18 months.

I'm getting tired LORD—but not discouraged—You know All About This—Psalm 139. Every second I've used to write this book has been worth it because every time I've sat down to write, I have prayed to start each session and praying that if I can affect at least one person to begin or continue to keep on keeping on, it's been time well spent. If not one other person ever has a life change, apart from me, I will say— "Thank You LORD for being here with me and showing me how to get from Page 1 to Page 470 [The End]".

Being in Your Presence is worth every drop of Sweat. Luke 22:44 says You sweat Great Drops of Blood to pay for my sins. If I stopped here, the picture looks grim, and I may have reason to conclude obtaining my salvation was a chore for You! However, Hebrews 12 tells me it wasn't a chore, but rather A Joy! Amen!"

And when He was at the place, He said unto them, Pray that ye enter not into temptation. And He was withdrawn from them about a stone's cast, kneeled, and prayed, saying, Father, if thou be willing, remove this cup from Me: nevertheless not My will, but Thine, be done. And there appeared an angel unto Him from heaven, strengthening Him. And being in agony, He prayed more earnestly—His sweat was great drops of blood falling to the ground. (Luke 22: 40-44)

Wherefore seeing we also are compassed about with so great a cloud of witnesses, let us lay aside every weight, and the sin which doth so easily beset us, and let us run with patience the race that is set before us, looking unto Jesus the author and finisher of our faith; Who for the joy that was set before Him endured the cross, despising the shame and is set down at the right hand of the throne of God. Consider Him that endured such contradiction of sinners against Himself, lest ye be wearied and faint in your minds. Ye have not yet resisted unto blood, striving against sin. (Hebrews 12: 1-4)

So, let's cancel any idea that Jesus regretted Paying The Price To Get The Job Done. Yes, Jesus Prayed to The Father and said, "If it's Possible, Let This Cup Pass From Me!" In the position of being *The Son of Man* [Human For A Season], Jesus felt every emotion that we have ever felt—in this way, The feelings of our infirmities could touch him.

For we have not a High Priest Who cannot be touched with the feeling of our infirmities; but was in all points tempted like as we are, yet without sin. Let us, therefore, come boldly unto the throne of grace, that we may obtain mercy and find grace to help in time of need. (Hebrews 4:15-16)

While not giving up His position as The Son of God, Jesus [God in The Flesh as Immanuel] was able to see the whole process as a Joyful Experience rather than a chore or task because He was Laying It All Down For Us! As far as Jesus was concerned, everything He is, always was, and ever will be and do was for 'US'—He Is The GREAT 'I AM!' God so loved The World that He Gave!

LORD, here I am again—I just want to Thank You Big Time for Your anointing, which apportioned or doled out strength to stay the course when I was weak. On my own, I couldn't conjure up or summon up One Word that would make any difference in changing one person's life—that includes me!

We live in a world—especially today, tomorrow, and the tomorrow farther afield, where my neighbour and family may not have the same feelings about things that I feel opposite to them— this is their right! Let's Practise respect!—God Is Still In Control!

So, what's my part to play as I search out how I can have the Heart of God as I walk this life with others—also created in the Image of God! Just pray t to be like Jesus and the example He set on the darkest night of His earthly life—in The Garden of Gethsemane. Peter wanted to fight physically to fix the problem—Jesus said (not His actual words), Peter, this is not a physical battle—it's a Spiritual Battle! Peter, put down your sword and use the Sword of The Spirit—which is the Word of God!

> Wherefore take unto you the whole armour of God, that ye may be able to withstand in the evil day, and having done all, to stand. Stand therefore, having your loins girt about with truth, and having on the breastplate of righteousness; and your feet shod with the preparation of the gospel of peace; above all, taking the shield of faith, wherewith ye shall be able to quench all the fiery darts of the wicked. And take the helmet of salvation, and the sword of the Spirit, which is the word of God: Praying always with all prayer and supplication in the Spirit and watching thereunto with all perseverance and supplication for all saints. (Ephesians 6: 13-18)

Let's give Thanks with Grateful Hearts that Jesus fought the battle on The cross—and He didn't form an army to win the fight against Sin. If Jesus had assembled an army, we'd of had no Hope for an Eternity of Peace.

THANK YOU—THANK YOU—THANK YOU!

Amen!

So Be It!

SO
IS IT REALLY ALL ABOUT WHAT'S IN OUR HEARTS THAT COUNTS?

◊◊◊

Scriptures in Chapter Nineteen; RSVP;
Epilogue and About The Author

Hebrews 3:15-17' Hebrews 9:27-28; Revelation 3:20

———

Acts 16:30-31; Romans 3:23; John 3: 1-9; Romans 6: 20-23
Romans 5:6-8; Romans 10:9-13; Romans 5:1; Romans 8:1
Psalm 119:165; Romans 8:38-39;2 Timothy 2:15

———

Matthew 22:32-40; Psalm 139; Jeremiah 29:11-13
Matthew 6:28-34; Psalm 139:23-24; Psalm 23

———

Jeremiah 17:9

Chapter Nineteen

Searching For The Heart Of God!

———————————◊———————————

HEART SENSE

Gardens—what do we think of when we think of Gardens? When the subject of Gardens comes to mind, some of what I think of is *Beauty*! When I think of Flower Gardens like The Gardens of Versailles in France.

The Garden of Versailles is near the Palace of Versailles—in France. *The Lay of The Land* (Chapter One of SFAHOG—This book) of The Garden of Versailles spreads out considerably. This Garden displays 300 hectares of forest—hundreds of acres of flower plots—35 km of canals—373 statutes—600 fountains—Dating back to Louis XIV. It's hard to resist this kind of Beauty.

Might there be more to it than Beauty—an interesting Question? I can think of a few things off-hand—growth, maturity, boundaries. Thesarus.com has a few synonyms worth noting— back yard, bed, field, greenhouse, nursery, patio, terrace, conservatory, enclosure, hothouse, patch, plot, cold frame—OASIS! Many areas of life are worth noting for the differing Seasons they represent.

In addition, Thesarus.com has segments of related words that are like the relatives who visit us from time to time—Eden, paradise, Arcadia, Garden of Eden, Promised Land, Shangri-la, heaven, heaven on earth, utopia—and there are hundreds of more words that give us available connections we can use when we reference Gardens.

Life is genuinely picturesque (charming)— 'Is It not?' Oh, "Lest I forget Gethsemane—." It's tough to find any descriptive synonyms for "Gethsemane." I found two somewhat related—Knat and Gath—it's hard to offer expressions for knat; however, gath leads me down the Garden Path with a few suggestions—*choke, deep, throat, neck*—.

The way I see it, The Garden of Gethsemane does not rate too high in this world. I'm *shocked* (dumbfounded) when I try to find the significance Gethsemane holds out there in our world today. What do you think when someone uses the following words— *choke, deep, throat, neck*? My first thought is— "SUFFERING!"

If we can imagine the *Garden of Versailles* by the description I laid out above, and we supply the 'ADD-IN' *Gath*, "suffering, [my definition]," how much enjoyment might we experience at Versailles.

Now, let's take a gander at The Garden of Eden— Promised Land, bliss, dreamland, fairyland, heaven, dreamworld, milk and honey, never-never land, paradise, perfection, pie in the sky, seventh heaven, wonderland—. As I see it, there's a lot of Selfie Stuff in these definitions—not much of JESUS in our sights [The Vista Views—The Oasis].

So, we can begin to understand that there's much more involved in our Oasis Moments (respite and thinking times) than just cruising The Green Pastures (Psalm 23) when we think of Gardens. Yes, The Garden of Eden allows us to imagine (*I Can Only Imagine*—by Bart Millard—Mercy Me)—Please look at something I mentioned earlier in this book—

> Amongst these songs of desperation by some very talented and famous singers, I cannot resist mentioning another gifted and admired singer, who has his perspective of 'Imagination.' Bart Millard wrote and sang *I Can Only Imagine*. The difference spirals into another avenue of Heart Stuff— gripping me with the love of a differing kind than what we all experience while doing life every day. Bart sings these words; *I can only imagine* the feeling of walking with Jesus (The Answer Man), [and what my heart will feel]. I wonder about many things I don't fully understand. Many folks have their questions about the difficulties The Bible asks us to accept by faith. Heaven is the 'Vista' and or reality of God—not the 'imagination' of what 'a heaven' will be. [IBID]

Here in Chapter Nineteen, we are nearing the End of *Searching For A Heart of Gold; Not A Pot of Gold*. I'm now zeroing in on *Searching For The Heart of God*—this has been my target all along.

If we zero in a little deeper into what the message of The Garden of Gethsemane suggests—and might I say, Booms Loudly as if in Times Square New York—I'M HERE FOR YOU! —signed JESUS!

The Garden of Eden had us in a Two-Fold Scenario—One signpost read, "No Trouble or Sorrows Here;" The other read, "This Way To The Trouble Tree! [my paraphrase]" As we look at the scenario of The Garden of Eden, there are many stories we can come up with as we dig deep enough.

The Trouble Tree
(Author Unknown)

The carpenter I hired to help me restore an old farmhouse had just finished a rough first day. A flat tire made him lose an hour of work, his electric saw quit, and now his ancient pickup truck refused to start. While I drove him home, he sat in stony silence.

On arriving, he invited me in to meet his family. As we walked toward the front door, he paused briefly at a small tree, touching the tips of the branches with both hands. When opening the door, he underwent an amazing transformation. His tanned face was wreathed in smiles, and he hugged his two small children and kissed his wife.

Afterward, he walked me to the car. We passed the tree, and my curiosity got the better of me. I asked him about what I had seen him do earlier.

"Oh, that's my trouble tree," he replied. "I know I can't help having troubles on the job, but for sure, troubles don't belong in the house with my wife and the children. So I just hang them on the tree every night when I come home. Then in the morning, I pick them up again."

He paused. "Funny thing is," he smiled, "when I come out in the morning to pick 'em up, there ain't nearly as many as I remember hanging up the night before."

We had a good offer in The Garden of Eden— "Hear What I Say, and You Won't Have Any Troubles To Hang On The Trouble Tree!" If you think you have a better offer, That's Your Choice To Accept!" Fast forward many years———and we see Jesus in The Garden of Gethsemane saying—I'm Here For You—Just Ask!

Searching For The Heart of God may come with a few caveats, provisos, or conditions. Just like in The Garden of Eden, It Was God's Way Or The Highway—Jesus said— "I Am The Way, The Truth and The Life—No One Can Circumvent [or sidestep] the route to Eternal Life, Heaven—Relationship With The Father, Jesus is pretty much saying you need to Do It My Way! The Via Dolorosa, The Way of The Cross, is the path I chose to give you Hope."

One of The Preparatory Parts of this Journey was undergoing the Darkest Night of Jesus's Physicality as The Son of Man—In The Garden of Gethsemane.

So, The Garden of Eden went awry (askew, wrong) for us because Adam and Eve made a Big Mistake—They Listened to The Wrong Voice. From here on and ever after in this life on Planet Earth, we would be trying to work our way Home—Back To The Garden of Eden [In A Sense].

Searching For The Heart of God is Two-Fold for sure! It's a matter of Right and Wrong—Black and White (Nothing to do with the colour of our skin)—This Way or That Way—On God's side, the Way He talked about in The Garden of Eden or Not—! Basically, this is the only Caveat. The way to facilitate this will be outlined in R.S.V.P. a bit farther along in *SFAHOG*.

The things I've talked about many times in this book may have had a Hypothetical Slant to them. However, I've never proposed them to be Hypothetical [imaginary]. The way I see it, I do this to talk about things as if they were somewhat like The Parables—Easier to be understood this way.

Our choices always fall into Two Camps—Physical and Spiritual. We begin life in The Physical and either End Life in The Spiritual, or we don't. Consequences (penalties) or Rewards are the End Points. As it was in The Garden of Eden—the choice was ours then, and it remains for the duration of time as we know it now on Planet Earth.

The Road Not Taken
(BY ROBERT FROST)
Two roads diverged in a yellow wood,
And sorry I could not travel both
And be one traveller, long I stood
And looked down one as far as I could
To where it bent in the undergrowth.

Then took the other, as just as fair,
And having perhaps the better claim,
Because it was grassy and wanted wear;
Though as for that, the passing there
Had worn them really about the same,

And both that morning equally lay
In leaves no step had trodden black.
Oh, I kept the first for another day!
Yet knowing how way leads on to way,
I doubted if I should ever come back.

I shall be telling this with a sigh
Somewhere ages and ages hence:
Two roads diverged in a wood, and I—
I took the one less travelled by,
And that has made all the difference.

I've said it many times, and it bears repeating, "There are Two Columns, Two Roads, for each of us from which to choose our Journeys Destination.

THE VISTA VIEW—THE OASIS

—Choose you this day Whom you will serve.

—While it is said, Today if ye will hear His voice, harden not your hearts, as in the provocation. For some, when they had heard, did provoke—howbeit not all that came out of Egypt by Moses. But with whom was he grieved forty years? Was it not with them that had sinned, whose carcasses fell in the wilderness? (Hebrews 3:15-17)

—Behold, I stand at the door, and knock: if any man hear My voice, and open the door, I will come in to him, and will sup with him, and he with Me. (Revelation 3:20)

Each chapter ends with The Vista View—The Oasis throughout this book. It's with good reason that I've laid things out in this way. The intention is always to allow us to reflect on where we've been, so we can have a stronger hope of getting there because we've always Taken The Second Look—or Two—or Three! Repetition can be tedious—but it can be helpful!

In Chapter Nineteen, I included The Heart Sense and The Vista View—The Oasis within The Chapter Boundary because this is the Final Chapter, and it just seemed fitting to try for a comprehensive look at this point in The Game.

As I've written this book, it's a given that there are realities in life that demand action. Life transpired as it has in the course of Sin, becoming more cancerous every day—God will never wave a magic wand to cure the ills of humanity. People say, "Why Doesn't God Do Something?" I fully believe that God could wave as if it were a magic wand to fix the world's problems. But He stands true to His Word that Sin, when it's finished brings the death that sin always brings—shown to us in the works of The Flesh. The results will be as God spoke in The Garden of Eden.

Genesis 2 and 3 tell the story of the coming to life of Adam and Eve. The degeneration of life because sin became the choice of Adam and Eve—even when they were fully abreast (*well-informed*) of the consequences and the process of the degenerative— the death of humankind took its toll throughout history, and it's worsening today.

From the very beginning, God knew the twists and turns sin would take, and He knew what would be necessary to keep humanity from dying off—this necessitated Salvation. Jesus came, died to save us, and promised that eternity would once again offer everything lost in The Garden of God. The story is all-encompassing, and I would need to rewrite The Bible to tell the whole story. God could End The World At Any Time if He chose to do so. However, by predetermination, He knew the cancerous sin would destroy the world. Now, those who decided to go God's way have a place to go to escape The Fire of Hell.

Beauty like that of The Garden of Versailles, and even more significant, existed in Eden. Adam and Eve didn't cherish God's best—enjoy all of what God is, and God was then and still is today— Enough! Christ Followers have always had an open eye for the future God Promised. We wait for The Return of Jesus.

> And as it is appointed unto men once to die, but after this the judgment: So Christ was once offered to bear the sins of many, and unto them that look for him shall he appear the second time without sin unto salvation. (Hebrews 9:27-28)

Though The God Story is a Never-Ending Story— I Must End My Telling of The Story Here—Because *Searching For A Heart of Gold; Not A Pot of Gold*, must end here as I've reached the extent to which I set out to Tell The Story—The number of Chapters and Pages must stop now!

God Has Searched For Us—

Now It's Time For Us To

Search For The Heart of God!

—Stay Tuned For R.S.V.P.—

—The Invitation—

—Epilogue—

—About The Author—

—Other Books by *Jacob Bergen*—

—The End—

RSVP—THE INVITATION

<u>Everybody Is A Somebody: in The Eyes of God</u>

GOD HAS A WILL, A PLAN, AND A PURPOSE

GOD ALWAYS HAD A WILL, A PLAN, AND A PURPOSE

GOD ALWAYS WILL, HAVE A PLAN, AND A PURPOSE

FOR EVERYONE

UNTIL HIS PLAN FOR EARTH AND ALL THAT IT IS NOW,

IS COMPLETE.

UNTIL THAT TIME, WE CAN CHOOSE TO GET ON BOARD WITH HIM:
ONCE THAT DOOR CLOSES, OUR CHOICE TO GET ON BOARD WITH HIM IS OVER.

HERE IS YOUR

R.S.V.P

YOUR INVITATION

"THE INVITATION"

GOD IS WAITING FOR YOUR REPLY!

R.S.V.P

WHO GOD IS

WHAT MUST I DO
TO BECOME A CHRIST-FOLLOWER?

What must I do to be saved? And they said, Believe on the Lord Jesus Christ, and thou shalt be saved, and thy house. (Acts 16: 30-31)

—Who Needs Salvation—?

Everyone has sinned; we were born sinners; we've all avoided living out God's plan. (Romans 3:23)

There was a man of the Pharisees named Nicodemus, a ruler of the Jews: he came to Jesus by night and said, Rabbi, we know You are a teacher come from God: because nobody can do the miracles You do except God be with him. Jesus answered and said to him, Verily, verily, I say to you, except a person be born again, he cannot see the kingdom of God. Nicodemus said to Him, how can someone be born when they're old? Can they enter their mother's womb again and be born? Jesus answered, Verily, verily, I say to you, except a person is born of water and of the Spirit, they cannot enter into the kingdom of God. That which is born of the flesh is flesh, and that which is born of the Spirit is spirit. Marvel, not that I said to you, you must be born again. The wind blows here and there, and you hear it, but you can't say where it comes from or where it will end up—so, everyone born of the Spirit is like that. Nicodemus answered and said to Him, "How can these things be?" (John 3:1-9)

—Why Do We Need Salvation—?

When we live without following Christ Jesus, we don't live out God's righteousness (morality)! What fruit did you have then in those things of which you are now ashamed? For the end of those things is death. But now being made free from sin, and become servants to God, you have your fruit unto holiness—in the end, everlasting life. For the wages (fruit) of sin is death—but the gift of God is eternal life through Jesus Christ our Lord. (Romans 6:20-23)

We need Salvation to spend life after death in God's Heaven—Many folks believe we automatically go there—Not So!

—How does God provide salvation?

When we were yet without strength, Christ died for the ungodly at just the right time. God didn't wait for us to make all the right moves—it's a good thing because He'd still be waiting! In our sinfulness, we had no clue of how to obtain Salvation. We can rationalize laying it down for someone who respects life and lives within those boundaries—it's easy to appreciate that gracious people can motivate others to give it up for worthy people. But God so loved the whole world, giving the Life of His Son—while we were still in a wasted state of morality—useless for His Plan to Come to Completion! (Romans 5: 6-8)

—HOW DO WE RECEIVE SALVATION? —

If you confess the reality of The Lord Jesus with your mouth—believe in your heart that God raised Him from the dead, you will obtain Salvation. Salvation is a 'Heart Thing—' this is where we believe in God, believing Jesus has already done everything needed for us to have eternal life; the mouth is what we use to declare our faith in God! The Bible says whoever believes in Jesus like this has no reason to be ashamed. Our nationality has nothing to do with God's wish to treat everybody the same—we just need to call out to Him! For whosoever shall call upon the name of the Lord shall be saved. (Romans 10:9-13)

—What are the results of salvation?

We have received the justice of God when we believed what He said about Salvation—now we have peace with God through our LORD Jesus Christ! (Romans 5:1)

Now, if we are in Christ Jesus, we are not condemned no matter what anybody else says—if we don't follow after the things of the world that deny God, but we live according to how The Bible says we ought to live, hearing the voice of The Spirit of God, we are indeed free from Spiritual Death. (Romans 8:1)

Great peace have they that love God's law: and nothing shall offend them. (Psalm 119:165)

I'm convinced that death, life, angels, principalities, powers, things present, things yet to come, height, depth, or any creature will separate me from God's love, which is in Christ Jesus! (Romans 8:38-39)

If you believe Romans Road leads to the path of truth, you can respond by receiving God's wonderful gift of salvation today. Here's how to take your personal journey down Romans Road:

—Admit you are a sinner.

—Understand that as a sinner, you deserve death.

—Believe Jesus Christ died on the cross to save you from sin and death.

—Repent by turning from your old life of sin to a new life in Christ.

Through faith in Jesus Christ, Receive God's free gift of salvation.

After you realize the truth of the Scriptures we've looked at; a simple prayer will do—

"God Be Merciful To Me A Sinner. Forgive me of my sin of rejecting You—Thank You for Saving Me!"

That's it—You Are A Christ Follower—

To know how to grow in this New Life, Find a Bible Believing Church, Read The Bible Regularly, Mix With People Who Believe Like You Now Do, Share Your New Found Faith In Christ and—

Study to show yourself approved unto God, a workman that needeth not to be ashamed, rightly dividing the word of truth. (2 Timothy 2:15)

Epilogue

EACH OF US HAS A STORY—lecturing others with our personal beliefs puts pressure on them to do their story our way does not usually work. To hesitate to share thoughts and information about what may be good and morally truthful can imply we are not true to ourselves or the God in Whom we believe. The resources of the Bible can be enough to make it all work. Many people think of The Bible as outdated and irrelevant to life's situations. Looking at the stories in The Bible, and placing them alongside the concerns of life today, may prove more relevant to real-life than we know. Let's never forget that it takes all of us to make life work: God and People!

Many folks don't grasp what the Bible says and may never get it, but we have a chance to change this through our lives of openness with them. Sometimes the grasp of understanding slips past us because of the many views people have about The Bible; the Bible is trustworthy. The representative picture is clearer once we accept God by faith. We just need to believe what He says He is for us in our day-to-day issues. We can be safe in His care because of what faith presents as the dawn of existence.

Why did I write *Twin Towers of The Heart* [three books ago]? Each of us is on one side or the other of the different topics of living life to the full. Divided hearts keep us aloof from total usefulness globally because of the absence of concern for others, which may be evident in how we think about and care for ourselves. We might have a strong mandate for self-survival; external survival owns part of this book's message. We need to articulate the long and the short answer; the short answer comes first. The short answer embraces our remembrance of 9/11.

Nine/Eleven still beckons us to remember some of the past so we can live in the present to display our lives in all God wants from us to benefit other people who are of equal value to the rest of the world. How we live on and why we all have a legitimate place in life, makes the whole story come alive. These feelings are like a merry-go-round in our heart of hearts. These images are flaming arrows to show us how to evaluate our position to make some right choices in living our book of life—this is challenging.

Each of us is but a small measure of the reality of the book of life. Some of us might just be a word in the book of life; others may be a note; others will be full-scale novels in the living book. However, each has the capacity to be a sentence, paragraph, or chapter, but none of us is the whole book; we do this together. Like it or not, we accomplish life with each other and our Creator; this is an evolution for some folks.

As part of a book, we illustrate ourselves as words, entire line sentences, paragraphs, pages, and chapters—fifteen, twenty, or thirty chapters or more in length. It will be colossal when our final chapter shines as brightly as a spotlight of importance and becomes a major lesson of life and learning. If this light is a massive laser beam in front of the world to point out what made this hour and final nanosecond of our lives available, then our value level increases with everyone else. Accepting that God is all we need sounds unreal (surreal); might this be a valid choice? I may as well believe in fairy tales if I believe that everyone on this planet—in this universe—will think as I think.

Fantastic, if we could say this is possible for everybody. Life often offers too many options for our lives. It is hard to find one truth in the whole melting pot of humanity that will serve adequately enough for everyone. We'd all like to understand how and why the universe is as we see it before us—is this possible with so many offerings of personal conscience and the desires built up over the many years of our tenancy on earth?

Whether we accept God as true or choose evolution, we hold to a belief system. We need to hear what is shouting at us from all corners of the ring. Our determinations become pains of survival (WYSIWYG). However, faith becomes the tool we use to get where we think we are going.

Either way, we need faith because faith is believing in the unseen or unknown. Choosing God is an option, and we'll all decide which option we will follow. It takes less faith to understand Someone, not something, always takes credit and responsibility for all the beauty we see in people or things—in living and in dying. When we trust Someone with this kind of power, and He shows it to us through love, the rest of the story develops understandingly. People wrote about God as long ago as written records exist; this is history: HIS STORY.

Only a glimpse of the total magnitude of God appears before us as it nestles inside this visual picture of the short answer. The image of the heart inside the heart of God, or the heart of hearts, pleads for development. This story comes to focus in the long answer. Every idea tends towards good or evil and becomes part of our story. The whole scenario plays a significant role in highlighting our journey's best and worst segments. Hope allows the best to win out through the yesterday's within our today, as the tomorrows of life live out in us. Getting up in the morning seems a little easier when life has great importance. An energetic reason for living each day offers belief and expectancy.

The long answer begins with an insatiable propensity for the written word as the starting point. People who read avidly gain knowledge. The Good Book tells us we are chapters of thought that come alive in and through other people. Those who make time to observe life and other people see our journey as a gift. We are live video presentations to all who watch us. Those of us who are words come to life are cinemas presenting full-length screen productions to an audience of the world; other folks learn from us. As we evaluate our inadequacy to make a difference, we often reflect too much on our past failures.

The long answer continues as long answers always do continuously or near endless. Because of an insatiable craving for journaling about nearly everything seen and read, brevity becomes an enemy. Sometimes I think the biggest mistake anyone ever made was to invent the pencil or pen. It might even go back to as far as when our ancestors used lead, coal, or a flintstone as writing tools to etch out their feelings, to move thoughts from their minds into the mind of others in this old-fashioned way. Maybe it was the cave person's idea, or perhaps it was God's idea; dare we say it?

Trusting in the facts so far as they go can clearly show us God is and has always been in charge of every situation—this is something everyone must decide individually. A thorough search of the universe may imply mere chance may not be the best option. It is tough to explain the how's, especially the why's of life's situations, so everyone is fully satisfied; another story could come alive here. The pioneer of all creation, the Builder of all time, promises to be ready for us; we also need to be willingly prepared for Him—the danger is not an enemy when we trust Him.

Searching for a Heart Of Gold; Not A Pot Of Gold—opens the door to many adventures. We take the tour of thoughts and concepts that might suggest we abandon any attempt to make the best of life to get ahead—wealth-wise. I hope I've not meant we should all become hermits, paupers and the like and only ever just go to work for eight hours a day, come home and read The Bible for the rest of the evening, and go to bed and do it all over again the next day—.

I hope and pray that we put God first [and I'm speaking to myself as well] in our passage of Earthtime—yes. As everyone who has and is living out the reality of life knows, there are many avenues we need to travel in life to get from birth to death and beyond into Eternal Life. Life has much, if not everything, to do with setting priorities. The Bible clarifies that if we set God at the top of our list of all the entities on our to-do calendar, we will achieve the success that God has in His Plans for each of our end-around runs.

An end-around run, play, or scheme has us skirting the issue or problem we face by circumventing integrity to get what we want when God wants something different and better for us—actually, He wants to show us His Very Best Plan. I realize there are many examples of this scenario, and it's not always a *once size fits all scenario.* The explanation of an *end-around-run* is— "a solution to a problem that avoids the problem rather than dealing with it directly."

An example we might look at is when the builder thinks the job lacks success in the set timeline with the Union Workers in a building project, like a Union Run Building Project. Hence, they bring in other workers in the off hours to do work that belongs to the Union Workers. I once fit this scenario years ago when my employer sent me to a Union Job Site to do some work, and the workers asked me not to come to work there because they were striking. So I left, and my boss sent me back after hours to do the job—I see this as an End-Around Play.

Many examples of the 'End-Around-Play Scenario exist. Football exhibits the art of deception play to get the job done. The opposing defence thinks the receiver will come straight ahead from his left flank—through their defence; he turns right—takes the handoff from the QB, and goes "End-Around" to gain yardage. Quarterbacks have much power in their hands.

Throughout *Searching For A Heart of Gold; Not A Pot of Gold*, this is the primary route we must take if we are going to be fully in line with The Plan of God—His command to us for how we will be in His perfect will. I (we) fail often, and this is when I'm *SOOOOO* glad that God employs or facilitates a Grace and Mercy Program so we (*I*) can make it through life intact to the end of the journey.

Matthew 22:32-40 often surfaces throughout our time in this book because it tells the Whole Story of "The How-To" of not only *Searching For A Heart of Gold; Not A Pot of Gold* indirectly. By physically fighting for our rights to do *what we think God is telling us to do*, sometimes, in the process, we may have lost out on the DIRECT COMMAND of God to hear what The Bible shows us about the given situations we all need to deal with in doing LIFE! The Direct Route looks like the following—.

I am the God of Abraham, Isaac, and the God Jacob? God is not the God of the dead but the living. And when the multitude heard this, they were astonished at His doctrine. But when the Pharisees had heard that He had put the Sadducees to silence, they gathered together. Then one of them, which was a lawyer, asked Him a question, tempting Him, and saying,

"Master, which is the great commandment in the law?"

Jesus said unto him; you shall love the Lord Your God with all thy heart, and with all thy soul, and with all thy mind. This is the first and great commandment. And the second is like it; you shall love thy neighbour as yourself.

On these two commandments hang all the law and the prophets. (Matthew 22:32-40)

Put God First In All You Anticipate Doing

Your Neighbor Next

Then you (us)!

Yes, I know there are many details to overcome while doing life. The Realities of doing Life are not EASY BY ANY STRETCH! There's no 'Quick Fix' for doing life—but the process outlined in the above Scripture shows us the Target At Which To Aim!

The DIRECT ROUTE LOOKS LIKE THIS—

> Praying always with all prayer and supplication in the Spirit, and watching thereunto with all perseverance and supplication for all saints; (Ephesians 6:18)

It's another Whole Story to try to figure out PRAYER— However, it's simply talking to God—this is not always on our knees; we need to work on the other realities of life. So while we do that, let's Keep Looking Up in our spirit [in our mind]. Hey, Please don't think I said to take Your Eyes Off The Road—or off the ball in doing life.

TRUSTING THAT GOD KNOWS WHAT HE IS DOING—This is another Biggee! If we've learned anything from the many times I've mentioned Psalm 139, we should've realized that God Is Always In Charge—He Knows Everything. My wife and I watch the TV Series *Blue Bloods*, and sometimes his compadres ask Police Commissioner how he already knows what they are about to tell him—His Reply is, "I'm The PC; I Know Everything." He doesn't know everything, but God Does! There's a vast difference between earthly leaders and God, The Greatest Leader Of All Time!

> I know the thoughts that I think toward you, saith the Lord, thoughts of peace, and not of evil, to give you an expected end. Then ye shall call upon Me, go and pray unto Me, and I will hearken unto you. And ye shall seek Me and find Me when ye shall search for Me with all your heart. (Jeremiah 29:11-13)

> Seek ye first the kingdom of God, and all these things shall be added unto you. And why take ye thought for raiment? Consider the lilies of the field and how they grow; they toil not, and neither do they spin. And yet I say unto you, That even Solomon in all his glory was not arrayed like one of these. Wherefore, if God so clothe the grass of the field, which today is, and tomorrow is cast into the oven, shall He not much more clothe you, O ye of little faith?

> Therefore, take no thought, saying, What shall we eat? What shall we drink? or, Wherewithal shall we be clothed? (For after all these things do the Gentiles seek:) for your heavenly Father knoweth that ye require all these things.

> But seek ye first the kingdom of God, and His righteousness; all these things shall be added unto you. Take therefore no thought for the morrow: for the morrow shall take thought for the things of itself. Sufficient unto the day is the evil thereof. (Matthew 6:28-34)

If and when we come from a Christian and or a Christ Follower Perspective, we may deal with life differently than those who don't hold our view or set of beliefs. Sometimes we think everybody should grasp Life and Eternity precisely the way we do—this is not happening. Just because I see something one way doesn't mean everyone will see it my way and follow my fully intended loving intentions to help them find the Truth, which will one day become fully evident—at least, this is how I see it!

Life, as it is in our world, will never change to be how it once played out. We think we have the Golden Rule thoroughly handled in our lives, and we may have, but we may just have left out an entity that might just knock us down—The Truth of The Someone Who got life going in the first place—I Call Him God! I call Him Jesus!

> Search me, O God, and know my heart: try me, and know my thoughts—And see if there be any wicked way in me, and lead me in the way everlasting. (Psalm 139:23-24)

> The Lord is my shepherd; I shall not want. He makes me lie down in green pastures—He leads me beside the still waters. He restores my soul—He leads me in the paths of righteousness for His name's sake. Yea, though I walk through the valley of the shadow of death, I will fear no evil—for You art with me; Your rod and staff comfort me. You prepare a table before me in the presence of mine enemies—You anoint my head with oil; my cup runs over. Surely goodness and mercy shall follow me all the days of my life—and I will dwell in the house of the Lord forever. (Psalm 23)

For now, I will conclude the bulk of this book with the words of
this *Epilogue*
By Saying—Stay Tuned!

ABOUT THE AUTHOR

I'm a Christian from the Judeo-Christian Perspective. I believe in what The Bible says—there is one God Who has and shows Himself active in Three Persons of equal authority. These Persons are The Father, The Son Jesus, and The Holy Spirit.

I'm a writer—That's What I Am! If I could do life over again, this is what I would do from my earliest formative, productive years. However, a retraction to this declaration is in order. Why or how can I say this without causing an enigma or muddling the waters?

I believe that everything in our lives, as we have lived them and live them, are placements in time to learn from and become better people at what we do and how we involve others in our lives.

I believe that everything in my life had a purpose—a time of preparation for something else that happened in and through me—throughout my journey. Therefore, I may have been unprepared for today and unready to face tomorrow if I had been a writer earlier.

I'm married, have four sons, twenty grandchildren, two great-grandchildren [*2 boys*], and another Great-Grandson has a planned arrival date of June/22. All our grandchildren Are Great.

I've lived in Steinbach, Manitoba; Winnipeg, Manitoba; Belleville, Ontario; Vancouver, BC; Saskatoon, Saskatchewan; Prince Albert, Saskatchewan; Calgary, Alberta; I now live in Invermere, BC, Canada. I was born in Steinbach, Manitoba, Canada, on September 12, 1946.

My family was nominally Christian. By that, I mean that my parents believed in God but did not always serve Him in the strictest sense of the word 'Christian.' By the time I was twelve, my folks had become Christ Followers—they accepted Jesus Christ as their day-to-day companion and friend. My conversion was at age twelve, although some interruptions were on this course until I was thirty-five years old.

How did I become a Writer? From as far back as when I was about fifteen or sixteen, I wrote little notes explaining what I believed and how I felt about what I believed. At one time, I wrote awful little notes and put them in places for people to read because I thought this was funny.

At another time in my life, I wrote nice and invitational notes for people, trying to share my faith differently. One way was to write notes and go out after midnight when most people were sleeping and put them in their mailboxes; I was fearful, and an arrest for prowling might have been my fate, but not thinking things through, I did it this way.

I was young, and sometimes I displayed that youth in the wrong ways; however, I had a writer's heart and had to get it out. Since then, I have written articles and books. I have a writer's heart—anyone with a writer's heart knows this is hard to contain.

Along with the present book, I have self-published six books—It's Jacob! My Name Is Jacob! What's Yours? (2002); The Mandate (2006); Twin Towers of The Heart (2016); Bridging The Gap (2018) and Everybody; Everybody Is A Somebody (2020)—and now Searching For A Heart of Gold; Not A Pot of Gold (2022)—Paper Back (ALL), Hard Cover (2), and E-Book (All). If you Google Jacob Bergen Books, these should appear on Amazon and other places.

Well, there's much more than meets the eye in the life of Jacob Bergen. Yes, my physical, historical makeup is mud, the same stuff as anyone else's makeup, and that by the Hands of God—with the dirt he created. I hope that *All Of My Books* capture some of your heart.

We cannot trust our hearts; take that to the bank. The heart can turn on us in a moment, and often the heart is hard to pin down. (Jeremiah 17:9)

CAN THIS BE?
GO FIGURE

Previously Published Books—

—It's Jacob; My Name Is Jacob; What's Yours? (2002)—
—Amazon (World Wide) and Other Places Online—
(Ebook, Paper Back)

—The Mandate (2006)—
—Amazon (World Wide) and Other Places Online—
(Ebook, Paper Back and Hard Copy)

—Twin Towers Of The Heart (2016)—
—Amazon (World Wide) and Other Places Online—
(Ebook, Paper Back and Hard Copy-To Come)

—Bridging The Gap (2018)—
—Amazon (World Wide) and Other Places Online—
(Ebook, Paper Back and Hard Copy-To Come)

—Everybody; Everybody Is A Somebody (2020)—
—Amazon (World Wide) and Other Places Online—
(Ebook, Paper Back and Hard Copy-To Come)

Now
—Searching For A Heart Of Gold; Not A Pot Of Gold (2022)—
—Amazon (World Wide) and Other Places Online—
(Ebook, Paper Back and Hard Copy)

—Next Book—
—2024—

—THE VAULT—

<<<>>>THE END<<<>>>
IT HAS BEEN MY PLEASURE
GOD HAS BEEN MY HELPER
HE IS MY STRENGTH
MOMENT BY MOMENT!

Manufactured by Amazon.ca
Bolton, ON